The Changes of Cain

The Changes of Cain

VIOLENCE AND THE
LOST BROTHER IN CAIN AND
ABEL LITERATURE

Ricardo J. Quinones

PRINCETON UNIVERSITY PRESS

PRINCETON, NEW JERSEY

809.93
Q7c

Library of Congress Cataloging-in-Publication Data

Quinones, Ricardo J.
The changes of Cain : violence and the lost brother in Cain
and Abel literature / Ricardo J. Quinones.
p. cm.
Includes index.
ISBN 0-691-06883-6 — ISBN 0-691-01502-3 (pbk.)
1. Brothers in literature. 2. Cain (Biblical figure), in fiction,
drama, poetry, etc. 3. Abel (Biblical figure), in fiction, drama,
poetry, etc. 4. Violence in literature. 5. Human sacrifice in literature.
6. Bible. OT. Genesis IV, 1–15—Criticism, interpretation, etc.
I. Title.
PN56.5.B74Q56 1991
809'.93352045—dc20   90-23971

This book has been composed in Adobe Galliard

CONTENTS

PART FOUR: *Tomorrow's Cain*

ACKNOWLEDGMENTS

IN COMPLETING this book, I was assisted notably by numerous financial grants and other help from my home institution, Claremont McKenna College. I am grateful to President Jack Stark and to the Dean of Faculty, Ralph Rossum, for their generous encouragement. I am especially thankful to Shirley Gould for her generous gift in support of the Family of Benjamin Z. Gould Center for Humanistic Studies, and to the Chair of its Board of Governors, Edward Gould, CMC '65. My colleagues at CMC, Stanton P. Welsh, Vice President for College Relations, and Donald A. Henriksen, Vice President for Research, have been constant in their support. My administrative aide, Richard Drake, was very helpful in the final stages of preparing this manuscript.

It is delightful to recall the winter and spring of 1981, when I was a senior fellow at that most pleasant and resourceful of scholarly centers, the Villa i Tatti. I would like to thank then Director Craig Hugh Smyth and the current Director Walter Kaiser for their support.

Portions of this book in various stages and forms have been read at Indiana University; Harvard University; SUNY-Stony Brook; SUNY-Binghamton; Cornell University; the University of Virginia; The Graduate Center, CUNY; Baruch College, CUNY; Rutgers University.

Several intrepid colleagues consented to read portions of the manuscript—and some even its entirety. I am grateful to Myron Simon, Harvey Gross, Wendy Furman, Ralph Ross, and Nicholas Warner for their efforts. Their comments were taken to heart and even occasionally made their way into the text. I was amazed at the number of references to Cain and Abel I received from my colleagues Nicholas Warner and Roberta Johnson (now at the University of Kansas). A constant help throughout the writing of this book was Johanne Hall, Vice President of Development, Scripps College, whose companionship was dearer to me than I am able to say.

This book I would like to dedicate to my four sons.

* * *

Excerpts from *Cain's Book* by Alexander Trocchi are reprinted by permission of Grove Press, copyright 1979.

Excerpts from *East of Eden* by John Steinbeck are reprinted by permission of the publisher, Viking Penguin, a division of Penguin Books USA Inc. Copyright 1952 by John Steinbeck, renewed copyright © 1980 by Elaine Steinbeck, John Steinbeck IV and Thom Steinbeck.

Excerpts from *Demian* by Hermann Hesse, translated by Michael Roloff and Michael Lebeck, are reprinted by permission of Harper Collins Publishers Inc. Copyright 1925 by S. Fisher Verlag, © 1965 by Harper & Row, Publishers, Inc.

Excerpts from *The Caine Mutiny* by Herman Wouk are reprinted by permission of Doubleday, Inc., copyright 1951.

The Changes of Cain

INTRODUCTION

OUT OF THE vast repertoire of Western myth, one myth stands apart for the extraordinary longevity and variousness of its appeal. This is the Cain-Abel story, which has been present to the Western consciousness since the biblical era as one of the defining myths of our culture. The dramatic elements of the story are powerful enough—the first murder, banishment, the first city—but as we probe the inner resources of the story, we find many other qualities that account for the proliferating and enduring strength of the theme. Very early the theme entered into alliance with the foundation sacrifice, and very late it joined league with the concept of the double. These two associations suggest that at its heart Cain-Abel reveals an encounter with the lost brother, the sacrificed other, who must be gone but who can never be gone. But the story represents not one but actually two contending responses to this fact of existence. Thus it is ready to represent radically different moments in our cultural history.[1]

A phrase that has come down to us from the French Revolution can instantly bring to mind the fuller and more complex dimensions of the Cain-Abel story. I refer not to the triadic slogan, *liberté, egalité, et fraternité*, but rather to that residue of the Terror, *fraternité ou la mort*.[2] It was Chamfort who brought this sinister coupling within the embraces of Cain and Abel when he remarked of the apostles of fraternity, "la fraternité de ces gens là est celle de Cain et Abel" ("the fraternity of these people is like that of Cain and Abel"). Their homicidal philanthropy he rendered as meaning: "sois mon frère ou je te tue" ("be my brother or I'll kill you"). If we consider the very elementary definition of *fraternal* as "that which is proper or belonging to brothers," then we can see how the recourse to Cain and Abel opens the issue to far-reaching and fundamental dispute. Originally the Cain-Abel story was not about brotherhood but about brothers, yet the same contradictions that overtook *fraternité* were ever-present in the meaning of Cain and Abel. It too bears in its background the dream of the human family, the pastoralism of the heart, a vision of unity and concord and cooperation so basic that it can only be summarized in the unconscious innocence of siblings. And yet cutting across this unity it brings difference, discord, and division; the Cain-Abel story represents a shattering reminder of the fragility of the human compact. In fact, the great purpose of the Cain-Abel story has always been—whatever its guise—to address a breach in existence, a fracture at the heart of things.

But perhaps there are other reasons to associate Cain-Abel, as Chamfort has done, with the bitter consequences of *fraternité*. To be sure, such a vision of human concord does not go well with the Terror. And indeed, a scrupulously detailed study by Marcel David has restored the dire alternative to its larger context, where, but for rare exceptions, *fraternité* did not stand alone with *la mort*, but was joined by the other two phrases of the triad, as well as with the unity and indivisibility of the Republic. Thus, its fuller meaning was that all of these were so important that in the balance a true defender of the Republic would be willing to risk his life to preserve them. In this restored sense, then, the collective memory is mistaken, perhaps misled by the closeness of the last-named word, *fraternité*, with the alternative, *la mort*. Nevertheless, such psychological dislocations themselves may be quite revealing and are usually worth some lingering attention. In this sense, the public misremembrance might be an accurate symptom of some complicity between the two apparently contradictory phrases and might suggest that, as in Cain-Abel, there is an interlocking relationship between brothers and death, which the phrase rightly recollects.

Before the eighteenth century, brotherhood and blood were habitually conjoined. One drank blood from a cup with a sworn brother, and this practice summarizes the more fundamental enterprise in which comrades are engaged—that of risking and shedding blood. The second use of brotherhood, only apparently opposed to this other, is that of spiritual adventurers, religious pilgrims who have adopted a life of wayfaring (morally but also perhaps physically) and who have committed their lives to a brotherhood of the spirit, thus desiring to reconstitute the social fabric that has disintegrated around them. This purpose of *homo viator* is itself based on blood, the blood-beginnings of the society such wanderers are abandoning and the redemptive sacrifice of Christ. In following the pattern of Christ they have entered into the discipleship of the blood. Hence it is that Dante, in that paramount book of pilgrimage and brotherhood, the *Purgatorio*, should have blood in such strong presence: the blood that is spilled by the violence of human nature and the blood that is offered, as it were, in voluntary imitation. When the men of the Enlightenment came to describe *fraternité* in their dictionaries and encyclopedias, these two antecedent meanings were so preponderant (and barbaric) that they resorted to other phrases in order to indicate the developing ideas of the universal brotherhood of humankind.

But these older and restrictive ideas of brotherhood are not the only limitations of the phrase. The structural tandem of *fraternité* and *la mort* is in some way interlocking so that indeed *fraternité*, more than being the violated ideal, might be a "purveyor of the Terror." The concept of brotherhood developed in the time of the Revolution does itself depend upon an act of violence; it requires the absence or the removal of the father. In this sense, brotherhood presents an image of a truncated family, and is consequently itself incomplete. And, as the masculine-dominated language of brotherhood would indicate, it is hard for brotherhood not to be exclusive, not only of sisters but of others as well. The so-called fraternal orders became enclaves of exclusivity whose separatism was reinforced by a jargon and a ritual of secrecy. Fraternity implied a priesthood, wherein the professed interests of a common humanity were at odds with special associations. Thomas Mann in *Der Zauberberg* brings this paradox to light in an uncomfortable way for the liberal reformer, Settembrini. It is for these reasons that *fraternité* may have found it difficult to shake off its own blood beginnings. It is perhaps appropriate to recall that after the great early days of 1790–91, and the enormous and heady revival after long silence in 1848, the last great movement of *fraternité* was among the combatants in the trenches of World War I.[3]

But there is an even greater complicity between this residual phrase from the French Revolution and Cain-Abel. As the biblical story and its long and productive history remind us, the opposite of brotherhood is death—and this is why the coupling is so deceptively persuasive. In our system of polar correspondences, the break in the ideal of the former (brotherhood) calls forth and can only be called forth by the latter (death). The loss of the ideal of the former means the triumph of the latter, and this would suggest that *fraternité* and *la mort* are as interlocking and coterminous as are Cain and Abel.

But the Cain-Abel story would not have had the great history it demonstrably has had if it stood merely ready to provide arguments for those who harangue darkly about the ironies of existence and the liabilities of human idealism. To be sure, the spiritual century that began with the dreams of the French Revolution ended with the horrible exposure in *Heart of Darkness*, a work that could be called the Bible of early modernism. But we must recall that another central expression of modernism was *The Secret Sharer*, where Cain and Abel are crucially present, and where Cain is now supportive of another order of being. The remarkable quality of the story this book will tell is that Cain, so potently and insistently subversive of the ideals of unity and community, will himself become a figure of regeneration. In this latter incarnation he will not be a speaker on behalf of a dangerous or insecure idealism, but will live in response to the breaks in existence, the divisions in nature and in human society, to which he will attempt to bring some unity. The presence of this Cain serves in defense of modern culture. Whether as a violator of order or as an active agent of reintegration and a dynamic partner, it is his changes that we follow.

•   •   •

In their very natures Cain and Abel and Ulysses are poles apart, as far apart as the Hebraism and Hellenism of Matthew Arnold, and as different as the Greek and Judaic methods of representation shown in Erich Auerbach's classic essay, "Odysseus' Scar."[4] But there is also intriguing intercrossing between the two, intercrossing that suggests comparison in the first place. Both Cain and Ulysses are wanderers, and curiously in no early or authoritative text is there record of the death of either (of course, apocryphal or later imaginative literature would rush in to fill this evident lacuna). But even this latter resemblance suggests difference. One reason Cain does not die is because in lieu of Adam and Eve he becomes the true progenitor and patron of evil in the world: in fact, he becomes the serious Christian exemplum of the continuity and enduringness of evil. For Ulysses, on the other hand, it is his very adherence to the light of life (the value urged on him by his mother in book 11) that seems too valuable to die.

But there are other more serious differences. The story of Cain-Abel is beset by guilt and moral concern; its arena of debate addresses the rightness of actions and finally the legitimation of the self. In the happy resolutions of Ulysses' character, such concerns, or rather the inner turmoil and deep debate that such concerns prompt, are not pertinent. To be sure, there is a moral quality to Ulysses, and he undergoes many trials—some due to his own foolhardiness, as when he barks out his name to the injured Cyclops. But, particularly in the end, this happy and resourceful man experiences no inner and dire division as to the rightness of his conduct. Typically, although modern readers may recoil at the God-sent rightness and personal blitheness with which Ulysses dispatches his enemies (and their consorts) at the epic's close, he himself experiences the bloody end as the natural and moral consequence of his exemplary life's purpose.

The Cain theme is centripetal, marked by inwardness, emotional tension, and secret conflict, by moral struggle and the closing off of possibility. It looks forward to the continuity of evil, even to its aggravation, and to the grim consequences of action. The Ulysses theme (whose rich and enduring history has been so ably expounded by W. B. Stanford) in Hellenic fashion deals with centrifugality, with movement out into the world, with resourcefulness, rationality, and freedom, and finally, completing the loop, with a return to the reintegrated family.[5] A good example of these differences also comes from Conrad's *The Secret Sharer*. The narrator describes the boat's passage as it leaves the Meinam River and is about to enter the Gulf of Siam. The ship will sail down the Malay archipelago, cut across the Indian Ocean, complete the circuit of Africa, and sail up the

Atlantic Ocean to home. But that is not what the story is about. It is not an adventure story but rather a morality play (a phrase that will also be used to characterize *Billy Budd*) that involves the deepest issues of the human community, but does not take place within human society. Its stage is far from all human eyes (and here Conrad is perhaps repeating a vacancy in the Genesis text itself, where Cain kills Abel when they are alone in the field). Having all the makings of an adventure story, *The Secret Sharer* declines the gambit and instead confines itself to a cabin, where a psychic and moral drama of intense and complex interiority will be fought out.[6]

As we probe further into the core of the contrasts even more important differences are revealed. Joyce chose episodes from *The Odyssey* to overlay his modern epic precisely because of the multifaceted nature of Odysseus' personality and the many relations into which he enters. For Joyce, he is father, husband, son, lover, adventurer, and returned traveler, the first gentleman of Europe and the inventor of the tank. But the one relationship that the polymorphous Odysseus does not seem to have is that of brother. There is a reason for this. The Cain-Abel story labors under an historical shadow; the antagonists stand at the head of lines of descent. To have a brother is to have a history. It still surprises me whenever I read in some accounts that Christ may have had three brothers. We do not want great heroes to have brothers; brothers are not for the sons of destiny. They are like faded photographs, distorted variants of the true form that they nevertheless resemble, unwanted shadowy duplications, where what the spirit really craves is uniqueness. Brothers suggest the possibility of failed prospects (what I call the shadowy other) that remind us of what was left behind, of the loss intimately connected with any success, of the deaths required by existence. The hero may travel with an entourage, even disciples, but he should have no brother. Achilles, Orestes, and Hamlet may have friends or confidants, but no brothers.

But even this contrast is not sufficient. Cain and Abel are active in a fuller human context both in their own structured binary relationship and in history itself. For this reason we can see why Cain-Abel is unlike Faust, Don Juan, Prometheus, Satan, the Wandering Jew, and even Frankenstein. The theme does not present us with a single-minded hero, driven through a string of successive episodes toward some far-off goal. Not fame, nor glory, not knowledge, nor love—none of these by itself determines the character of Cain-Abel. The theme is concerned with a genuine complex of issues and relationships. In fact, its moral force is derived from this essential encounter with another, which means that its fuller expression is dualistic. (This fact may provide us with bases for identifying maladaptions of the theme when, rather than being dualistic, the theme becomes monovocal; that is, it emulates the singularly driven voice of the other themes from which it differs. Perversions of its nature occur when Cain at times becomes the "other" to the medieval imagination: the Jew, the black. The same may occur in modern literature—and here high modernist Hesse's *Demian* comes closest to offending—when Abel becomes the anonymous representative of some herd mentality.) In some ways this explains why the Cain-Abel story is actually a *thème de situation* and not a *thème de heros.*[7]

.   .   .

The Cain-Abel theme has had an extraordinarily rich and diverse career. The appeal of the theme—its durability and its variety—is perplexing when we acknowledge, as we must, that Cain-Abel is in its appearances, and even in its inner core, a stark and unlovely theme, prompting one writer to call it "gloomy."[8] It is marked by murder, bringing with it, as Claudius realizes in *Hamlet*, "the primal eldest curse," that of fratricide. Its motivating emotion, envy, is loathsome and practically inadmissible. Indeed one of the theme's constant functions has been to provide figures and events responsible for the growth of an evil that is reprobate and unregenerate.

The long duration and appeal of the Cain-Abel story may in large part be explained by the potency of its nuclear account, by the power of the words and the graphic actions that strike us undeniably. The language itself is memorable and has echoed resonantly throughout Western literature. "Am I my brother's keeper?" "The voice of thy brother's blood crieth to me from the ground." "A fugitive and a vagabond . . ." "My punishment is greater than I can bear." Whether intact or altered, these lines in the classical languages or in their modern renditions (as the sixteenth-century English above) have the power to arrest attention and to direct it to a new kind of significance. The story of Cain-Abel has generated its own power of allusion.

The actions themselves, murder and banishment, are highly dramatic and the issues they provoke are compelling. One of the greatest bequests of Judaism (as well as of Platonism) to the West is a sense of justice, not justice negotiated but justice inviolate. God hears the cry of Abel's blood. There is something in the principle of divinity itself that insists that the victim's voice be heard and that justice be done. A crucial characteristic of the Cain-Abel theme is that it never relinquishes this constitutive part. A murder has been committed, a death has occurred. As Arturo Graf, the great Italian thematologist insisted at the beginning of this century, "Sia che si vuole, tu, Caino, hai ucciso il tuo fratello" ("No matter what you say, you Cain have killed your brother").[9] The fact that someone is responsible cannot be swept under the rug. If justice must be served this means that the theme cannot avoid making a judgment.

This also means that the theme unavoidably contains extensive social ramifications. When God places the mark on Cain, its purpose in protecting him from retaliations is, in the mind of more than one expert, to ensure the end of blood vengeance. The first murder carries in its wake the explosive potential for accelerating reciprocal violence, the vendetta, the feud, the civil war, and as such it will draw the attention of Augustine, the *Beowulf* poet, Dante, Machiavelli, and Shakespeare—obviously one of the theme's more formidable lines of development. The cry is an ancient one, uttered again by the angel in Byron's *Cain*, "Who shall heal murder?"

But the story is based upon other forms of experience that are psychically even more penetrating and enduring. Intrinsically the theme is devoted to presenting the stark and basic fact of *division*, division that is so unyielding as to become part of the essential matter of existence itself. Although this is the fundamental datum that determines many of the component parts of the theme, it itself experiences some refinement. The fraternal context of the Cain-Abel story means that division becomes more emotionally vibrant as the *tragedy of differentiation*. Such differentiation is painfully realized at the moment of the *offering*, when one of the brothers has his essential nature endorsed over that of the other brother. The *arbitrariness of preference* thus compounds the tragedy of differentiation and brings home the fact of division in a way that is particular to the Cain-Abel theme.[10] Furthermore, the divisions of the brothers within the Cain-Abel rubric show a great capacity to assume the nature of rival principles and thus enter into great dualistic schemes.

Division, the tragedy of differentiation, the offering, and the arbitrariness of preference have become distinguishing features of the Cain-Abel theme. But there are three other residual forces in the theme that are equally determining and that also deserve to be signaled in these introductory remarks. They are *violence, envy,* and *mystery*. While serving to set off the Cain-Abel story from allied themes, their abiding presences, in conjunction with the other great issues just indicated, help explain why it is that Cain-Abel has superseded other stories of "rival brothers" within or without the Bible and has become such a predominant part of the Western imagination.

Cain-Abel is based upon facts of sheer division. Unity of whatever sort—familial, tribal, even personal—the virtual starting point of the theme, proves to be elusive and even illusory. However much we may wish them to be so, no two things can ever be equal. "All things being equal," is a phrase born to be contradicted. If two people do the same thing, according to the Latin dictum, those two things can never be the same. Difference is apparent in the very conditions of existence, in the very relationships of couples. That relationship itself promotes asymmetry has been shown by René Zazzo's book on twins (one that incidentally exerted strong influence on Michel Tournier). Even in the minds of identical twins, one of the pair is regarded as dominant.[11] What story is more indicative of this principle, tests it more fully, than the story of brothers? This also shows why it is that in postromantic literature Cain and Abel must eventually merge with doubles and twins. These latter two acquire the essential characteristics of the Cain-Abel theme. Difference is also essential to our understanding of time and space. Time is made up by distinguishing one moment from another. In fact, a serious contemporary writer, Jacques Derrida, regards temporality itself, finitude, as an outright product of violence. Even if space is regarded as mythic—we can come back again to the same place—no two objects can occupy the same space. This shows, as Tournier reasons in *Les météores*, that because they cannot occupy the same space, even twins must by necessity have different perspectives. As we shall see, Tournier's two major novels may be fully located amid the issues being discussed here.

More particularly, the durability of the Cain-Abel story is derived from its capacity to confront dire division at the most elementary, even primitive level, that of the falling-out of brothers. The fraternal context of the theme is all-important; brothers serve to intensify, epitomize, and generalize all sorts of discord and division in a particular way. The appeal of the theme is not simply division, but division within a context of extraordinary unity. Where the expectations of communion, innocent, unself-conscious unity, have been so great, then the facts of difference are all the more startling. This is why we are drawn to use the phrase "the tragedy of differentiation" to describe the intrusions of difference and of destiny into such a unity. Where we had all the more reason to expect harmony, the varying pulls of individual destinies are all the more painful. Here in this context of fraternal communion and division, the Cain-Abel story does more than express the falling-out of brothers; by means of the brothers it finds occasion to offer powerfully compact tellings about ruptures in life itself. The Cain-Abel theme thus becomes a master story for addressing fundamental divisions in existence and, perhaps even more important, varying ways of response to those differences.

One of the many associations into which the Cain-Abel theme enters in the course of its long career is the foundation sacrifice. But this is more than a casual encounter; it is a meeting that is derived from the core of the theme itself. Augustine was the first to make much of the similarities between the biblical brothers and Romulus and Remus. Despite the differences between them—distinctions he was careful to make—Augustine saw them as archetypally related: each locates the foundation of the city in the blood sacrifice of the brother. In *Les météores* Tournier adds to the pairs of brothers involved. Referring to Esau and Jacob, Romulus and Remus,

Amphion and Zethos, and Eteocles and Polyneices, Tournier's interlocutor, Father Seelos, speaking to his diminished and beleaguered congregation in the divided and recently walled-in sector of East Berlin, reminds them that these brothers have mysteriously one thing in common: "That thing is a city. A symbolic city that seems every time to demand the fratricidal sacrifice."[12] Tournier's account is indicative because it is clear—as his own works make plain—that over these other pairs, Cain and Abel seem to preside, almost as if their story were the master story, covering in the fullness of its own materials matters that are treated incompletely or less suggestively in the other stories.

That Cain-Abel figures prominently in foundation sacrifice has recently been argued by Hyam Maccoby in his *The Sacred Executioner: Human Sacrifice and the Legacy of Guilt.*[13] To summarize, Maccoby readily allows that the Cain of the Israelite redaction of Genesis is a murderer without any ritualistic or communal associations. However, by capitalizing on textual duplications, resonances, and anomalies, and indicating the various cultural levels and accretions in the text, he proceeds to construct a Kenite saga in which Cain, and not Adam, is the first ancestor. Cain performs a ritual foundation sacrifice, not of his brother but rather of his own son—Abel. Although Maccoby's arguments are plausible, one wonders why Cain and Abel need to be transformed—and at such great lengths—into a father and son since as brothers they seem to have done so well. If this is not clear from the biblical narration itself, it is certainly clear from the ways that history has regarded the story.

The brother sacrifice, over which Cain-Abel presides, contains a powerful range of emotional elements—perhaps even more powerful than those of the father and son. In any event, the component parts and energies are different. Brothers are true intimates, coevals and cohorts into whose elementary unity a terrible division and separation must intrude. The sacrificed brother has thus greater possibilities for indicating a lost portion of the self, a self that is abandoned, sundered, the twin, the double, the shadowy other, the sacrificed other that must be gone and yet can never be gone. The sacrificed brother is thus better able to express all the dimensions of some lost portion of life that the foundation sacrifice in its fullest meaning acknowledges.

The primary situation of an original equalness indicates that, better than father and son, the brothers are suited to represent not only individuals in contention but individuals with basically different attitudes toward the very conditions of existence. For instance, when confronted with the facts of existence that blood sacrifice seems to typify, Abel and his followers and heirs separate themselves and seek out purification in atonement. This is prototypically Christian. In a later, but less edifying transformation, Abel will be equally devoted to unity, but to a unity based upon disregard and unawareness. In their selfishness, Cain and his progeny may create discord, but correspondingly in a later epoch, their very quest for selfhood can lead to a reintegration of the forces that had been so sorely divided. The accrued value of the Cain-Abel story seems to show itself in the larger confrontations and transformations that it prompts.

It is from this elementary pattern of brotherly loss as expressive of the conditions of existence itself that other elements of the Cain-Abel theme—elements that distinguish it from other themes involving brothers—are derived. Although other versions of the brother sacrifice confront the tragedy of differentiation, the Cain-Abel story seems to engage the human family more fully—from early unity to later division—and in more of its relationships. Brotherhood, as we can imagine, is a potent cultural force that the theme presents (in its many variations). But so is fatherhood. In fact, as we shall see, there is a prevailing psychological and social relationship between the presence of the father and altered evaluations of the respective sons. But the father figure plays an even more central and dramatic role, and it is this role that helps distinguish Cain-Abel from the other themes. Difference between brothers is rendered more grievous by what I call the arbitrariness of preference, the fact that some arbiter, divine or paternal, but always fatherly—and hence authoritative and decisive—is rendering judgment vis-à-vis the difference. The tragedy of differentiation is aggravated by the arbitrariness of preference, the pathos of which is increased by the sense of earlier unity and unsuspecting innocence.

The tragedy of differentiation and the arbitrariness of preference are powerful presences that are unleashed from within the confines of the story and that reverberate throughout the psyche, as they do throughout history itself. A poignant and powerful emotional center of the story and of the theme is of course the offering by as yet untested, undefined young people. Generations of readers have reflected in pained anguish upon the mystery of the offering itself, the careless indifference of it or the heart-rending innocent pathos, and then upon the terror of rejection, what it means to have one's being invalidated. Of our authors it is perhaps Steinbeck who captures the pathos of this moment best. But for many of them the offering is at the center of life—all life is an offering where one is being judged. The Cain-Abel story is potent because it presents the first offering, the first venture out of the self, out of an undifferentiated and unconscious communion, and into an objective world. Brotherhood, where young innocence and communion are epitomized, will increase the pain of difference. The offering quite naturally then forms the first definition of character; it is a fundamental presentation of the self. How vulnerable the offerer is and how massively crushing can rejection be. This might explain the special appropriateness of the Cain-Abel story within a setting of artists. The ventures of art are distinctive presentations of the self, where the totality of one's being is defined and placed on the line.

All of the brother stories reflect basic facts of division, but only in the Cain-Abel story does division rise to the level of great dualistic principles in contention. Very early, Cain-Abel lent itself to presentations of large, opposed principles. An extraordinary part of the theme's appeal rests precisely upon its dualistic nature, and hence upon a contest of values. When one brother rises, as Abel does in the predominantly Christian era, the other falls; but in the romantic and postromantic era, it is Cain who attempts to rise and Abel who most certainly falls. The reason for the emergence of Cain-Abel as a ruling theme may be found in this dualistic scheme; it is at its best when it presents rival principles in opposition.

The Cain-Abel story thrives not only because it is dualistic but because the dualisms to which it lends itself are expressive of the dominant energies in various epochs—here we refer chiefly to two, the Christian and the romantic. A substantial polarity is thus established, where each term of the dichotomy represents a powerful and representative amalgamation of forces that are so large and compelling as to be a summary of an epoch. In the classical Christian era, the Cain-Abel story represented the formidable conflict between the conservative, skeptical, and urbane (even urban) pagan intelligence—Cain—and the militant, aspirant, religious personality—Abel. When we come to the nineteenth and twentieth centuries, we again see that Cain and Abel are opposing one another across an essential polarity, one that is expressive of the dominant and rival energies of the time. Now, however, it is Cain who becomes "idealistic" and Abel who becomes "realistic"—in the temperamental and typical sense in which Schiller intended the terms. The essential drama that the Cain-Abel theme represents in the modern world is that between a questioning, dissatisfied, probing critical intelligence, keenly aware of division and somehow in search of a better order, and a non-aspirant Abel, who by virtue of some personal accommodation or by simple resignation is more accepting of the contradictions of life. In the case of Abel we witness a figure who had been representative of a revolutionary religious spirit, coming to stand for the consolidation of the religious spirit with the social structure of the day. If Cain and Abel can come to represent large, rival principles, then in the course of time, large opposing principles can find their figures in Cain and Abel.

Violence is crucial to the Cain-Abel story in all of its aspects and throughout its history. At its origins, Cain-Abel does not only show difference, it shows division: its dualisms are conflict-ridden. The adversarial nature of the subject suggests opposition, and its confrontations are inevitably violent. At the center of the theme is a vortex of emotional fury that is compelling because it is so graphic (as indeed the theme's appeal to visual artists has demonstrated), but also because its consequences are so irreversible. At the same time they may be continuous: that is, the extremity of violent behavior prompts its own duplication. "Who shall heal murder?" is the cry heard again and again because violence breeds its own repetition. Violence calls forth violence and immediately, as we have already seen, locates the subject within the profoundest issues of social justice, even those concerning revolution and the changes of regimes. More primitively, instances of proliferating as well as escalating violence within the theme's tightly drawn nexus of relationship produce for Cain progeny that are monstrous.

Violence may thus serve as the basis of larger consequences for the Cain-Abel theme. One such consequence is the theme's tendency to replace Adam and Eve where the concern is the continuity of evil. The proliferating nature of violence, its capacity to breed a response in its own likeness, may be the basis of something that is irreparable in the theme. For this reason the children, Cain and Abel, may become more acceptable surrogates than might the first parents.[14] Moreover, as the great male and female polarities, Adam and Eve are needed to reconstitute the race. Not marked by violence, their lapse—and it becomes only that—betokens reparability. As a sexual fall (and ignoring the theological sense of disobedience), it may be regarded as more human and even more humanistic; that is, it has nothing of the monstrous in it. Interesting later consequences may also follow from these curious distinctions: when the "affective sensibility" of the Enlightenment will place Cain and Abel in decidedly domestic circumstances, that is, will remove Cain from his isolation and provide him with a sister-wife, then the character of Cain himself seems more inclined to regeneration.

Violence is terminal but it is also decisive. And although moral courage is probably superior to physical courage, there is nonetheless something crucial in acts requiring physical courage. In the development of Cain, such characters as Shane or Will Kane in *High Noon* become "point men," individuals who take on the gravest responsibility at the moment of greatest risk. The key to the presence of violence in the Cain-Abel theme might be precisely its involvement in such critical moments. Cain-Abel persists in showing the dramas of people brought to a crossroads, where some kind of radical action is required involving either the community or the self. The theme will invoke the trauma of violence to bring to birth a new moment of being, even a new dimension of the self that leads to a revivification of the community. But all of these instances will require some form of violence. Hence even the double and the twin, when conjoined with the Cain-Abel story, will be compelled to undergo some violent sundering. The theme will find it hard to relinquish its primal rooting in the brother sacrifice.

Along with its other designations, those of *homo ludens, homo faber*, and *homo necans*, humankind is also envious: *homo invidiosus*.[15] Envy is universal (even chimpanzees evidence sibling rivalry); it is logical (no two things can ever be equal); and it is constitutive (Melanie Klein insists that we take it in with our mother's milk).[16] But the fact that it is endemic to human nature has not kept it from being considered the most repellent of emotions. Francis Bacon has called it a "vile and loathsome affection." In fact, it is so repugnant that it dare not reveal itself. In *Billy Budd*, Melville considers envy to be the one inadmissible fault: ". . . though many an arraigned mortal has in hopes of mitigated penalty pleaded guilty to horrible actions, did ever anybody seriously confess to envy?"[17] One of its qualities is a skulking interiority. Most vices are forward-moving and fairly outstanding; only envy is recessive, betraying a sulking neediness. For this reason, Aristotle can define envy as a defect for which there is no mean: to be half-envious is not a moderate virtue. It broods over feelings of wantingness, of lack; it shows the devastation that is the disease of the shriveled heart. This is all contained in the language. Consequently, the French can say "J'ai envie de," which we translate as "I desire," but in truth what is meant when we say it in English is, "I want that." Envy betrays a wantingness, a great need.[18]

As always, a crucial witness is Dante, and although he will reveal in his *Commedia* this perverse and inadmissible quality of envy, he will show something else: the large extensiveness of envy as a theological and social problem. In some way, when Aristotle denies envy a mean, he is also demoting its importance. In any theocentric worldview, however, envy assumes extraordinary proportions. The definition of God in Dante's great poem is that such divine goodness is utterly without envy—"La divina bontà che da se sperne ogni livore." The fact that such an avoidance of envy is most appropriate to divinity might indicate that envy is more suitable for humans; nevertheless in the *Purgatorio*, that most confessional of poems, the one sin that Dante will only partially own up to is envy (he will quite acceptably spend much more time on the lower terrace where pride is purged).[19] But this compliance with the general reluctance to admit envy is concidental with another view, that of envy's theological and hence social pervasiveness. We might understand this better by comparing envy with jealousy. Jealousy is immediate, catastrophic yet circumscribed—Othello is jealous. Envy is subtle but more extensive and pernicious—Iago is envious.[20] In this sense then, envy was Lucifer's sin, and Wisdom tells us that "by envy of the devil, death entered the world." Lucifer's pride, according to Augustine, made him envious and this drove him to turn from God and then to destroy God's creation, by which he felt himself to be replaced. The menacing she-wolf that so intimidates Dante at the beginning of his aborted ascent has been freed from hell by envy. This particular conjunction of envy with the she-wolf exhibits the social extensiveness of what is primarily a theological vice. In the central cantos of the *Purgatorio*, envy slips its narrow mooring within the series of the seven deadly sins and, with the aid of Augustine's discussion in the fifteenth book of *The City of God* (where, incidentally, the large and typical roles of Cain and Abel are described), becomes a major social force, a frustrated expression of that large theology of desire that returns humankind to its divine origins.

Nevertheless these two aspects of envy—its inadmissibility and its theological and social extensiveness—may be brought together and comprehended when we realize that the Cain-Abel story is not only dualistic but is usually triadic. The anger of the sibling is a displaced anger that is really directed against God, against the figure that bestows favor so arbitrarily. What this means is that envy exists in protest against God's grace, against God's favor. At its heart then envy is repellent because it lives in opposition to the conditions of existence. The quarrel of envy is ultimately a quarrel with God—its arena, or its façade, is a hatred of those whom God favors. When this animosity is directed toward a sibling or a cohort we are in the midst of a Cain-Abel story. That the enmity is actually directed against God explains why envy is so reluctant to show its face. When it does, it does so against the secondary object, the naturally unsuspecting Abel—who, after all, committed no wrong and, in Melville's language, does not reciprocate malice. This explains all the more fully why Cain is so ulterior and divided and why Abel is so innocent. The reason for the offense is beyond his comprehension as well as beyond his help. This also explains why, although the larger motif of *frères ennemis* enjoys universal recurrence, the theme of Cain-Abel can only enjoy a long and revealing history in a theocentric culture, which means a Judaeo-Christian culture.[21]

Through all of its historical alterations, an inherent suitability persists between the Cain-Abel theme and envy. This has to do with closeness of relationship as well as enclosed space. Envy is a directed emotion that involves comparison among approximates. From Hesiod on we have been instructed that the potter only envies another potter.[22] It would be crazy to envy the flight of the eagle or the dolphin's plunge. As Unamuno, that remarkable clinician of the soul, informs us, "envidia es una forma di parentesco." Envy requires a relationship. Consequently, brothers may be called upon to represent the prototypical situation of envy. One is naturally drawn to make invidious comparisons between brothers.

The situation of envy also requires a constant physical presence. Envy might be allowed to dissipate itself if some kind of spatial relief were possible. One does not envy someone in the next village (again Unamuno). Envy requires physical proximity, and brotherhood can provide the closest of physical relationships. This is why the Cain-Abel theme finds such ready shelter aboard ship (think only of *The Secret Sharer, Billy Budd*, and *The Caine Mutiny*). As Melville tells us in *Billy Budd*, " . . . there can exist no irritating juxtaposition of dissimilar personalities comparable to that which is possible aboard a great warship fully manned and at sea. . . . Wholly there to avoid the sight of an aggravating object one must needs give it a Jonah's toss or jump overboard himself." But there is a larger significance to this importance of physical closeness. As it serves to aggravate antipathy it also tends to make inevitable the imminent clash. Consequently, the lonely isolation of the brothers, the fact that they go out to the field alone, is a structural and physical component of the theme that is morally required. The tight closeness of brotherhood in the spiritual and physical sense lends to the theme its aura of unavoidability, in fact, of necessity.

The Cain-Abel story, from the first, was enveloped in mystery. This might be seen on the level of story itself; from the original spare telling to the most prolix and elaborate *Finnegans Wake*, there is reticence, if not confusion, not only as to the question of *why* it has happened but even as to *what* has happened. We must also acknowledge that at the heart of the theme is radical differentiation at so fundamental a level, that of siblings, as to defy further explanation. The story is mysterious because it confronts such essential irreducibility. In these circumstances one looks to some kind of ultimate causation. Kent, compelled to acknowledge the difference between Lear's daughters, can only return causation to the stars, and the basic inclinations of temperament derived therefrom (in this attribution Shakespeare was like many of his age, including Francis Bacon):

> It is the stars,
> The stars above us, govern our conditions;
> Else one self mate and [make] could not beget
> Such different issues.

$$(4.3.34-37)$$

In the Cain-Abel story (the sisters in *King Lear* may provide female counterparts to the brothers), these considerations are aggravated when the differences are profoundly moral. The tragedy of differentiation leads to the larger reflection on the mystery of iniquity. "Is there any cause in nature that makes these hard hearts?" (3.6.81–82). The point of such apocalyptic questions is that they are unanswerable, that they lead to the blank wall of the unresolvable. But we must look at the kinds of conditions that provoke such questions. And the Cain-Abel story, for reasons mentioned and to be demonstrated, presents such conditions.

But beyond that of a tragic and irreducible division in human experience itself, mystery has another and not unrelated meaning—one from which we derive our sense of "mystical." The Cain-Abel theme is part of a *mysterium*, an arcanum of knowledge that some could penetrate and understand should they possess the proper key or clues. The Greek *musterion* indicates a secret thing or ceremony, one that can only be entered by the *mustes*. In terms of action, of course, Abel is the passive partner, but in terms of understanding he may be the exalted one, the one who is searching for the higher meaning in the earthly drama. Abel then becomes the type for Christ, who will finally and for all time provide the key to the *mysterium*: his revelation is the crucial piece that makes sense of the otherwise undecipherable puzzle. (It is curious that this meaning of mystery is not different from the modern version of what we call a mystery novel, which requires the final clue or the last deciphering for everything that is present to become clear and fall into its rightful place.) But such a grand design requires a remarkable designer. We come to see that the vindication of Abel rests upon the eternal fatherhood, and indeed traditionally, throughout the course of the theme, this tight link between Abel and the overarching control of the father will be critical. Envious Cain's war is in actuality directed against the father, and in the remarkable transformation that the theme undergoes in the epoch of romanticism (and later), the vindication of Cain will be strongly dependent upon the demotion of Abel, to be sure, but even more clearly upon the absence of the father.

· · ·

Myth, as it were, is a cover letter whose purpose is to disclose inner reserves and energies not immediately apparent in the literal account of the story itself. It contains in order to release; it formalizes in order to set loose. As we shall see, there are large historical relevancies of the Cain-Abel theme, but on the more intimate as well as universal level of myth, what the retold and revised story releases are those pressures showing the interactions of unity and disruption, of communion and the processes of individuation. The Cain-Abel story has lent itself to many versions of the varying pulls of unity and of division. In a creational, monistic view of the world, one dominated by the ideal of unity, Cain can stand forth as the malefactor who not only abhors but actually destroys unity. Division is a tragic product of Cain's actions, and he, unlike Abel, is content to live in its midst. But there is another version of the story, one that would regard the sense of unity as illusory, as belonging to myths of the early age of the race and of the individual, where we were integral and at peace. Such a unity never existed; instead the individual is confronted with the facts of difference, with individual consciousness, and with the needs of selfhood. Where in the first case, division threatened community, here in the second, individuation must transcend undifferentiation. This act of separation, consciously and unconsciously pursued, calls to mind an act of violence, even murder. And this must be the other inner psychological need to which the Cain-Abel story responds and feeds. The violence of Cain against his brother comes to represent necessary physical and psychical facts of individuation, the flight from an undifferentiated communion that is either stagnant or does in fact only serve to conceal a real disruption. The physical slaying of the brother assures the coming into being of the self. If the urge toward unity and the necessary relegation of Cain to the role of malefactor is typical of the classical Christian era, then this possible regeneration of Cain is typical of the Byronic and post-Byronic epochs.

The reason why the coin may be turned over and the reverse employed where the obverse had stood is that a compact of issues radiates from the center of the Cain-Abel story: disruption and community, union and separation, individuation and undifferentiation. These are the powerful forces that the theme contains and discloses. The particular value of the theme as a cultural indicator is derived from the fact that at its core these forces are so highly dynamic and ready to lend themselves to such startling transformations.

In its structural components and, more important, in its secret reserves and hidden resources, the Cain-Abel story is admirably suited to reflect the complexities and shifts of a revolutionary age. In the post-Byronic age, which was responsive to the waves set in motion by the French Revolution, Cain has become the quester, the metaphysical rebel, the force in search of new ideas and new modes of being. As in Augustine's *City of God*, this is still a story *contra paganos*, but now the daring one is Cain, and the subservient, even stagnant one—shall we say, the citizen—is Abel. Abel becomes conservative, as the ethical imperatives that he has come to represent have been conventionalized. This conventionalization of the ethical that leads to the progressive pejoration of the qualities of Abel is one of the most stunning cultural facts of the modern world, and is central to any discussion of the post-Enlightenment versions of the Cain-Abel story. But the demotion of Abel does not automatically mean the elevation of Cain. It has the effect of removing a stable moral center and guide from the endeavors of the theme. This gives us some clue as to the purposes of Cain. Through his character, his thoughts and responses, the author will struggle to assert—and this with evident difficulty—a new moral and ethical code. This is why the Cain-Abel story is such a powerful one in the literatures of the nineteenth and twentieth centuries. It is perfectly poised to acknowledge any dissatisfaction experienced with the more traditional religious and moral values (hence the demotion of Abel), and to dramatize the struggle on the part of a character, offended by the conventional moral code, to create a new moral center that has a basis that is violent, dire, and problematic, as paradoxical and contradictory as the character of Cain himself. The Cain-Abel theme provides a perfect locus for the fuller ramifications of this moral ambiguity in the modern world, and those works that treat most fully both aspects of the dialectic—that of liberating possibility as well as the presence of guilt, the role of the ethical and the role of destiny—seem to be the works that receive our respect and are ranked among the great works of the modern epoch.

Involved in violence, burdened by guilt, Cain seems to be a greater figure than the boisterously enterprising Ulysses (as adapted by Tennyson), or the largely passive and suffering Ulysses of Joyce. He does act and his actions are based upon a laudable quest for freedom, for dignity, for some form of human worth; but these very actions seem implicated in violence and call forth the shouldering of some harsh destiny and necessity. An element of dire intractability will never be absent from the theme, but this also means that the theme issues a call for an encounter with reality, with history and its consequences. This is no Promethean theme, no projection of an absolute will, but rather one that shows the will meeting reality, and this dire and dual confrontation will be true from beginning to end.

In its broadest sense, and we shall raise this argument again and again, the Cain-Abel story involves an encounter with history—oppressive, inevitable history, or history transcended and transformed, but never ignored. In fact, perhaps the greatest contribution of the theme will be the program it provides for scrutiny of the ambiguities of human action, understood in the full complexities of historical change.

PART ONE

The Three Traditions

Chapter One

CITIZEN CAIN

FROM THE outset it must be recognized that the greatest revolution—certainly the longest-lasting—in the history of the Cain-Abel theme was the first, when the biblical brothers were transformed by Philo and later by Augustine into universal, rival, and contending principles. This was the critical moment of emergence for Cain-Abel as a theme of significance and extensiveness. Despite our own time's justifiable suspicion of dualistic thinking, it must be acknowledged that the reason for the theme's assumption of such appeal and force was precisely its dualistic properties—the very same properties that would account for its continued effectiveness in the world after Byron. Cain and Abel represent the possibilities of grand dualisms. As such, in the classical Christian era, they served to express the tensions of a genuine polarity between the reigning secular mind and the nascent strength of the religious mind.

At the beginning of his great commentary, "On the Birth of Abel and the Sacrifices Offered by Him and by His Brother Cain," Philo shows the powers of the dualistic conception of Cain and Abel (as well as his own powers of formulation):

> It is a fact that there are two opposite and contending views of life, one which ascribes all things to the mind as our master, whether we are using our reason or our senses, in motion or at rest, the other which follows God, whose handiwork it believes itself to be. The first of these views is figured by Cain who is called *possession*, because he thinks he possesses all things, the other by Abel, whose name means "one who refers all things to God."[1]

Four major expositions, the one indicated, the precedent commentary, "On the Cherubim, the Flaming Sword, and Cain, the First Man Created out of Man," as well as two following, "That the Worst is Wont to Attack the Better" and "On the Posterity of Cain and His Exile," are based upon this fundamental division. The expositions themselves, in the midrashic haggadic fashion, are tied to the conclusion of Genesis 3 and to Genesis 4, and raise from the texts a remarkable philosophical interpretive frame.

The superiority of the Cain-Abel polarity is evidenced in the ways that it has superseded the highly relevant struggles between Esau and Jacob. In Cain-Abel there is a legitimate polarity, with each pole representing a significant force and figure—however much Philo might demote the secular intellect, he is far from dismissing it. Esau, however, is merely abject. Despite this supersession, the later story provides retrospective illumination and even foundation support for the Cain-Abel story. In fact, it plays a crucial role not only in Philo's interpretation but, directly by way of Philo, in Ambrose's as well. It provides support for Philo's conviction that in the strife between brothers we are indeed witnessing a contest between not only rival personalities but also rival principles and that, moreover, the opposition between them is unbridgeable and irreconcilable. This confluence of Cain and Abel and Esau and Jacob will invariably have dire implications, extending even to our own time where it will be broadly invoked by Joyce in *Finnegans Wake* and Tournier in *Les météores*.[2]

After Isaac's entreaty (Gen. 25.21), Rebecca is made fertile. The twins toss and turn within her. When she asks what this might signify, the Lord answers, "Two nations are in thy womb, and two manner of people shall be separated from thy bowels. . . ." Philo fixes upon these words in order to support his contention that Cain and Abel do represent opposing principles. In another less elaborate exposition, *Questions and Answers on Genesis*, Philo calls these references to "nations" and "peoples" "a most useful distinction of opposed concepts, since one of them (one of the twins, one of the nations) desires wickedness, and the other virtue."[3] Such interpretation invokes a necessary corollary: elevated to the level of essential principles, the differences between the brothers become much more intractable. "For one of them is heavenly and worthy of the divine light, and the other is earthly and corruptible and like darkness" (*Questions and Answers*, p. 441). Thus, if Philo passed on the metaphor of the two ways to the Church fathers, he also introduced a difference between them that was well-nigh insuperable when translated to the level of basic, opposing principles. One belongs to the powers of light, the other to the powers of darkness.[4]

Philo places all of these speculations within a larger philosophical frame, one beginning with Adam and Eve. If his philosophy is Platonic, it is also Jewish. The goal of his elaborate allegorical interpretations is to introduce philosophy to Genesis, but it is also to impress upon philosophical minds the wisdom of Genesis. Going beyond the literal meaning of the passage to the allegorical, Philo regards the union of Adam and Eve as that of Mind and Sense. "For there was a time when Mind had neither sense-perception, nor held converse with it, but a great gulf divided it from associated interdependent beings. Rather was it then like solitary ungregarious animals" (2.43–45). The mind was a deep-water box, a true womb of sensory deprivation, until it was united with Eve, the glittering, fluttering world of light and motion. This conjunction amounted to something of a fall, a fall into sense, not because sense is failed, but because of the attitudes of mind that followed its introduction to sense. The fall is not, as in the Platonic sense, a physical one, but is, in the biblical sense, a moral one.

Far from being defective, the sense impressions were too attractive, too potent. The mind became enamored with the impressions it received and began to think that they were of its own making. The first offspring of this union of Mind and Sense (Adam and Eve) was Cain, whose name, for Philo, is etymologically related to the word for "possession": "For the Mind thought that all these were his own possessions, all that he saw or heard or smelt or tasted or touched—all his own invention and handiwork" (p. 43). This attitude, flushed with new excitement, leads to a kind of heedlessness, arrogance, and irreverence—the attitude of Cain.

Several figures bring this new attitude from philosophy into history: they are Alexander, Pharaoh, and Laban. Of these, Alexander is the most important because in using him as a negative example Philo is confronting the basis of his own culture (in fact, confronting the *political* identity of humankind as enunciated by Alexander's teacher, Aristotle), and finds it wanting. The encounter is more pressing, since Philo lived in Alexandria. Early Hellenism, with a political basis of culture, is being measured against later Hellenism, with a religious basis of culture. Philo finds Alexander's statement that he is the master of all that he sees to be foolish (of course, Aristotle would have thought the same but for different reasons): "The words showed the lightness of an immature and childish soul, the soul of a common man and in truth not of a king" (p. 47). The confrontation is far-reaching. From the background of Wisdom literature—David and Solomon are indeed the kings with whom Alexander is being compared— Alexander is found deficient. His soul is common and not kingly because it lacks a religious philosophy. It believes what it sees. But, in another sense, as a true Hellene, Philo is judging Alexander from the basis of Greek tragedy itself. He is like Tiresias confronting Oedipus and telling the ruler that he is the blind one. The true philosopher, true mind, is blind to sense, whereas unenlightened Oedipus (or Alexander) only believes what he sees.

We are reminded even more specifically of Greek tragedy when Philo, quoting Pharaoh's words from Exodus (15.9)—"I will destroy with my sword; my hand shall have the mastery"—responds, "Fool is it hidden from you that every created being, who thinks he pursues is actually pursued?" (p. 55). The remarkable irony of a tracking tragic fate haunts the presumed master of that fate. Oedipus is caught in his own castings. Philo, that genius of first-century syncretism, that master of seeking out meanings, the philosopher of the Midrash, gives expression to universal tragedy. To Laban's declaration, "the daughters are my daughters, the sons are my sons, the cattle are my cattle and all that thou seest are mine and my daughters" (Gen. 31.43), Philo responds passionately (one of the characteristics of his style is precisely this direct address, where through the centuries he confronts individuals, button-holing them, as it were, and rebukes their deluded folly): "The daughters, tell me. Do you say they are *your* daughters? How yours?" (p. 49). And we can imagine him like Leopold Bloom, another Hellenized Jew, in his Lear-like state of mind, concluding, "Nobody owns anything."

Philo's tragic apprehension is based upon a philosophical skepticism, perhaps in the way, which we know to be so, that Montaigne's *Apologie de Raimond Sebond* is so prevalent in Shakespeare's *Hamlet* and *King Lear*. How can we be said to own anything if our tenure is so fleeting, if not only objects but the very categories of our minds, our powers of reasoning and our sense impressions, are so fragile and fleeting? "Is my mind my own possession?" Philo asks rhetorically, before hastening to devastate that stronghold with a list of its failings. "That parent of false conjectures, that purveyor of delusion, the delirious, the fatuous, and in frenzy or melancholy or senility proved to be the very negation of mind" (p. 77). Earlier, in an allegorical interpretation of Laban's possessions, Philo draws up a catalog of human error and debility. We can have no mastery, not even over the fundamental testimony of our senses. Rather than being master the mind must follow the senses slavishly. Philo's expositions, as do Montaigne's, become brilliant essays whose central purpose is to attack human pretension: "In us the mortal is the chief ingredient. We cannot get outside of ourselves in forming our ideas; we cannot escape our inborn infirmities . . ." The very identity that possession requires betokens essential limitation. The religious mind does not find this limitation acceptable, but the secular Cainite mind can live within the limits of such liability.

Such skepticism can never be thorough-going; it must always serve as the means to another purpose, which in Philo's case is to attack the presumptuous attitude that humankind, Cainite man, possesses or owns the qualities he most familiarly assumes to be his own: his arts, his reasoning powers, and his sense impressions. On the more immediate moral front, this can all be translated into the attitude: "I did it all by myself." This attitude is familiar in the contemporary notion that one is "self-made" or even "self-taught," as if we invent rather than acquire the forms of intelligence.

Philo is concerned to promote a religious basis to culture, one that is God-centered. Only God is, only God has being, only God can be said to belong. He has no need of anything external to himself. "Himself is His own light. For the eye of the Absolutely Existent needs no other light to effect perception . . ." (67). Except for the fervor and power of Philo's expression, this concept is not unfamiliar in classical and Christian Platonic thought. What is of particular relevancy for us is the way Philo describes God's fullness of being and humankind's dependency. Philo here introduces the notion of citizenship, which, with its varieties of nuances, becomes an essential part of this theme—Citizen Cain. Cain, who aspires to possession, to rights, to identity, is the founder of the first city. Abel then becomes the figure of the right-thinking man who knows he is a stranger and a sojourner among earthly things. The core of Augustine's thought—with two critical differences—is present here in Philo:

> In relation to each other all created beings rank as men of longest descent and highest birth; all enjoy equal honor and equal rights. But to God they are aliens and sojourners. For each of us has come into this world as into a foreign city, in which before our birth we had no part, and in this city he does but sojourn, until he has exhausted his appointed span of life. . . . God alone is in the true sense a citizen, and all created being is a sojourner and alien, and those whom we call citizens are only so called by a license of language. But to the wise it is a sufficient bounty, if when ranged beside God, the only citizen, they are counted as aliens and sojourners, since the fool can in no wise hold such a rank in the city of God (*en te tou Theou polei*), but we see him as an outcast from it and nothing more. (pp. 79–81)

If Philo has demoted Alexander from king to common man, he has also discounted the value of political identity, or citizenship, so dear to Alexander's teacher. Only God is a *polites*. The wise man does not pretend to citizenship; that is left to those who follow Cain. The wise man knows that we are all *braceros*, sojourners; in fact, the notion is precisely that of pilgrims. Philo does more than introduce two ways; he actually introduces three (and this will be a fundamental bequest to Augustine): that of true citizenship (God), that of false citizenship (Cain), and that of earthly alienation (Abel, who by understanding his derivative status, or better his lack of status, is thus in a better position to acquire full citizenship).

THE RACE OF CAIN

The story of Odysseus-Ulysses is a self-contained one, extending little beyond the hero and namesake of Homer's book. The book does not entertain the historical perspective; it does not engage the future. Revealing its origins in Genesis, Cain-Abel is in every way historical, announcing the beginning of history. Cain's story is not self-contained; more than an individual of a particular time, he initiates a race that will be used to account for the continuing presence of evil itself. Throughout this book, Cain and Abel will be treated as figures of historical bearing, as types for continuing processes and contrasts. In particular, despite the presence of Abel, the aim of the Cain-Abel story in many instances is to account for the origins of evil but also for its continuing career. Each of the two, but more so Cain, comes with a retinue and a repertoire.

Cain's followers are kings and philosophers. We have already seen Philo's condemnation of kings who are guilty of false appropriation. In his

"The Posterity and Exile of Cain," Philo discusses the philosophers. "That the human mind is the measure of all things, an opinion held they tell us by an ancient sophist named Protagoras, an offspring of Cain's madness" (p. 349). Cain is the progenitor of sophistical reasoning, and as such he has a direct connection with the foundation of cities (centers of sophistication) and with those supreme figures of humankind's overweeningness, Nimrod and the Tower of Babel.

Since, according to a literal understanding of the biblical text, it may have been impossible for Cain to have built a city, Philo then supplies an allegorical reading of the text. What is really meant by the city are "demonstrative arguments." Philo has an antipathy to formal philosophy, to philosophy that has no moral or religious base, to philosophy that lacks *sophia*. Merely rational exercise of argumentation, or even critical analysis, brandishing the weapons of logic and syllogistic procedure, he regards as part of the arsenal of Cain. "With these, as though fighting from a city wall, [Cain] repels the assaults of his adversaries, by forging plausible inventions contrary to truth. His inhabitants are the wise in their own conceit, devotees of impiety, godlessness, self-love, arrogance, false opinion, men ignorant of real wisdom, who have reduced to an organized system of ignorance lack of learning and culture, and other pestilential things akin to these" (p. 357). Philo is a religious humanist who has a sense of "right reason" (*ho orthos logos*) and true wisdom, which are opposed to purely formal philosophy (organized systems that have no basis in religion). The natural consequence of this city founded by Cain is the Tower of Babel, with which God becomes disgusted, bringing down "upon their sophistic devices a great and complete confusion." Philo explains more specifically his allegorical point: "By a tower is meant a discourse working up each (immoral) doctrine which they introduce." In "On the Confusion of Tongues," Philo is even more elaborate about the tower and its specific descent from Cain. "But all these [the impious people who devised the tower of Babel] are descended from the depravity which is ever dying and never dead, whose name is Cain." Unlike Abel, who since he offered the firstlings of his flock gave testimony to his reliance on a First Cause, "the impious man thinks . . . that the mind has sovereign power over what it plans, and sense over what it perceives."[5] It is this self-love that Cain's children raise to the heavens. The city is the place of "vice," the tower the place of "godlessness."

Cain, we must recall, was not only sire to a progeny, he also initiated a process of deterioration and moral decline. Essentially suspicious of the urban attitude, Philo does not regard favorably the so-called advances in material civilization. Consequently, he regards the development of metallurgy and the arts of weapon making as the contributions of subsequent generations to the decline initiated by Cain. Philo half-allegorizes, half-

moralizes the sons of Lamech: Jabal, Jubal, and Tubal-Cain. Their arts
and crafts merely provide the technological basis for waging war.

The fundamental division between the two brothers is carried on
throughout history, and this is because the division is philosophical. Abel
represents an ideal of right conduct and true being that can never die;
Cain represents that depravity that is ever dying and never dead. This is
not understood, Philo tells us, by those who are devoid of *paideia* and do
not understand the differences between "wholes and parts and between
classes and species." Cain's murder of Abel must always be suicidal since
he is always willing to destroy the best part of himself:

> Wherefore let every lover of self, surnamed "Cain" be taught that he has slain
> that which shares Abel's name, the specimen, the part, the impression
> stamped to resemble him, not the original, not the class, not the pattern,
> though he fancies that these, which are imperishable, have perished together
> with the living beings.

In perpetrating his deed, Cain only proves himself to be Cain. Echoing
God's own expression in Genesis 4, the same said to Adam earlier and
later used in Lamentations, "Hekhah," Philo exclaims, "What have you
done? . . . You have proved to be your own murderer, having slain by
guile that which alone had power to enable you to live a guiltless life"
(p. 255).

Philo's understanding is a profound one. Cain's guilt is irremediable
because in killing Abel he has killed off his own better possibilities, his
own access to his ideal nature. But, in its way, this action, like Abel's ideal
category, is also deathless. And this is Philo's intriguing and ingenious
interpretation of the sign that was placed on Cain, "namely that on no
occasion did he meet his death. For nowhere in the Book of Law has his
death been mentioned. This shows in a figure that, like the Scylla of fable,
folly is a deathless evil, never experiencing the end that consists in having
died, but subject to all eternity to that which consists in never dying" (p.
319). This is the most vivid and compelling reading of the sign presented
in the time of late antiquity. Not bothering whether it is a horn, the
shakes, or charred skin, Philo regards the sign as a mark of the perdurabil-
ity of evil, the never-endingness of the human capacity and willingness to
do the stupid thing, to mess up. Such hard realism is part of the properties
of the Cain-Abel theme and will rarely leave it.

·   ·   ·

After Philo's, the next important uses of the Cain-Abel theme are those
found among the second generation of New Testament writings: the first
epistle of John, the general epistle of Jude, and Hebrews. These texts certainly aided Philo's assimilation in the West, and the last, might be carry-

ing on the direct influence of Philo, particularly in its assignation to Abel of the role of stranger and pilgrim in the earthly city. When these texts are historicized, it is also clear that they are engaged in an anti-Gnostic polemic, one in which Cain is a major figure.[6]

If the first three centuries before Christ could be described as representing the Hellenization of the East, the first three centuries of our era could be regarded as the Orientalization of the West. Coming from the East, a remarkable phalanx of religious movements, sects, and speculation advanced on the West. Among these many religions, cults, and sects was Gnosticism.[7] Actually, under a single rubric, Gnosticism covers a wide variety of individual works and beliefs. Geographically, it reached from Iran, to Syria-Palestine, to Egypt. It was attacked by such pagan writers as Plotinus, as well as by such Christian heresiologists as Irenaeus, Clement, Origen, and Tertullian (in fact, for a long time much of the testimony concerning Gnosticism emanated from the works of these prosecuting attorneys).

Gnosticism shared in the three major trends deriving from the East: Jewish monotheism, Babylonian astrology, and Iranian dualism.[8] More specifically, its various forms and configurations seemed to center on three principles: evil, alienation, and gnosis.[9] Frequently using commentaries on Genesis, Gnostic texts attempted to account for the origin of evil by distancing the creator from the creation. Other powers had intruded, and these intermediate powers are often identifiable with Mosaic conceptions of the world. They are hostile authorities, or archons, who delight in oppression, the hard rule of law, and blood sacrifice. Through no fault of the supreme deity, these inferior powers come into being, often through the ill-advised work of Sophia, who, neglecting to consult with her consort, the All-father, was responsible for the births of these crude powers, variously called Ialdaboath or Sammael. These later creations are actually ignorant in their strength; each thinks in his folly that "he is God and there is no other God." This unknowing creation proceeds to create an entire hierarchy of other subdeities (from 7 to 365 in various tracts), who then comprise the system from which those who still manage to retain some remnant of the divine light struggle to escape. For the Gnostics, life presents the constant need to escape from these "authorities of matter." Consequently, when Adam and Eve eat from the tree bearing knowledge of good and evil, they are not actually defying the supreme deity, they are in fact defying the minor authorities—identifiable with the Mosaic code of ethics and ritual. In fact, a simplistic way of putting it might be that Gnosticism is concerned with overturning the Mosaic rule. Certainly this is true in relation to Cain, where the banished Cain of Genesis, in the new dispensations, is turned into an heroic rebel against "the authorities of matter." It is curious that, although Byron dismisses any suggestion of Manicheanism in his *Cain*, several of the crucial premises of Gnosticism are current in the work.

Perhaps explaining the extraordinary modern interest in Gnosticism is the notion that humankind's position in regard to the world that exists is one of alienation. We are obliged to separate ourselves from it and from all its lures and attractions. To take the lure of the world is to submit oneself to the dread reign of necessity. The only means of liberation is gnosis, or knowledge (in a more modern sense, "consciousness"). This knowledge is primarily knowledge of the transcendent God from whom all the earthly demands and obligations seem to bar one. Once a person possesses this knowledge he always possesses it. Mainly Christian (although there are pre-Christian Jewish versions of Gnosticism as well as pagan ones), Gnostics believe that Christ is the revealer, not the redeemer. He saves from ignorance, not from evil.

Gnosticism manifested itself in extreme asceticism, or, as its opponents charged, in extreme libertinism. Its aim was purification (as was the aim of its later descendants, the Cathars and Puritans). Limiting its longevity, its asceticism extended to the denial of marriage and procreation. An extreme rejection of the world is found in the ascetic doctrines of Marcion, who was denounced by Prudentius for "abhorring unity." Marcion chooses to frustrate the powers that be by observing "perpetual abstinence." His God is not the Old Testament deity who encouraged humankind to wax and multiply—that is merely the injunction of the lesser powers, ignorant of higher laws, for whom "the reproductive scheme is an ingenious archontic device for the indefinite retention of souls in the world" (Jonas, p. 145).[10] As Bacon would later declare, "He that hath wife and children hath given hostages to fortune."

The idea however that once we possess gnosis we always possess it leads, on the other hand, to a sense of impunity, a kind of spiritual pride in inviolability. By the end of this book, particularly in the later chapters, one might be astonished by the works that could be called Gnosticism modernized, and that suffer from the same disdain that consciousness directs at the "authorities of matter." Since they are golden—the children of light—Gnostics believed they could do anything they pleased, without tarnishing their true gnosis. Irenaeus concludes, "the most perfect among them freely practice everything that is forbidden." Normal Christians receive grace "on loan"—it may be taken from them. "But [Gnostics] have grace as their own possession . . . and for this reason it will be increased for them" (Jonas, p. 139; Foerster, p. 363). Evidently it is within a much larger ethical and social structure that Christianity will establish itself, and perhaps also in a more tragic encounter with time and history.

It is within this briefly summarized historical context that we are bound to understand the presence of Cain and his lineage in the New Testament.

The first Epistle of John refers to a controversy taking place among the Johannine followers. One of the points of difference this anti-Gnostic tract wishes to establish is that between Gnosticism's evident disdain for "works" and the importance of good deeds within the Christian community: "Little children, let no man deceive you: he who doeth righteousness is righteous. . . . And he that committeth sin (*amartia*) is of the devil" (1 John 3.7–8). The persistent indication of this righteousness is brotherly love. In this context it is not surprising that Cain should reemerge: "Not as Cain who was of that wicked one, and slew his brother. And wherefore slew he him? Because his own words were evil, and his brother's righteous." Cain is used as a cautionary example to underline the early Christian insistence that it is impossible to separate goodness from virtue and virtue from good works. Cain was of the devil's party from the beginning, when his sacrifice (his own evil works) was done poorly, thus indicating a poor attitude. This in turn resulted in a more heinous act, the murder of his brother. Here, the figure of Cain is not seen to be a worthy one at all, but is regarded as being in the line of Satan.

That there is a "way of Cain" is even clearer in the general epistle of Jude. Cain is part of a line, and has his own progeny. An urgent warning is delivered by Jude against "ungodly men, turning the grace of God into lasciviousness." This line of men includes Cain, and here he is linked with other figures who habitually appear with him in Gnostic texts. "Woe unto them! for they have gone in the way of Cain, and ran greedily after the error of Balaam for reward, and perished in the gain-saying of Core" (11). Korah (Core) and his clan and his allies (Dathan and Abiram, also mentioned in some Gnostic tests) were swallowed up by the earth because of their opposition to the newly assumed priesthoods of Moses and Aaron (Num. 16). Balaam is not such an extreme case of perversity since he later, to the surprise of Balak, did follow the Lord's behest and blessed the tribes of Jacob and Israel (Num. 22–24). But the other affiliation is clear—the fallen angels, Cain, Esau, the Sodomites, Core, and others—all names found in some Gnostic texts as worthy rebels and dissidents and hence comrades of Cain.

The fullest use of the Cain-Abel theme in the New Testament occurs in Hebrews, where Abel now stands at the head of a long and noble line of the faithful. This is the famous chapter 11 on faith: "By faith Abel offered unto God a more excellent sacrifice than Cain, by which he obtained witness that he was righteous, God testifying of his gifts. . . ." The witnesses of Abel's faith are the signs (undisclosed) by which God indicates his preferences for Abel's sacrifice over that of Cain, and the "miracle" of Abel speaking after his death (certainly by means of his blood that cried out). The other heirs of faith, Enoch and Noah, Abraham and Isaac, and Jacob and Sarah, form a mighty line that lives on the promise of faith, indicating

that they are "strangers and pilgrims on the earth" (13). These same figures form the mighty contingent liberated by Christ when he harrowed
Hell, and are celebrated in painting as well as in Dante's *Commedia*. That
they are pilgrims and strangers indicates that they are seeking a new country, otherwise they would have been content in the old countries they left
behind (Heb. 11.15). "But now they desire a better country, that is, an
heavenly: wherefore God is not ashamed to be called their God: for he
hath prepared for them a city" (Heb. 11.16). When Augustine came to
write the *De civitate Dei*, the structure of thought, the affiliations and
principled divisions, and the terms of the discourse were all prepared for
him, present potently in the full expositions of Philo and here in the extraordinary chapter of Hebrews.

· · ·

In the 1920s, Viktor Aptowitzer wrote that the idealization of Abel was
no Christian invention, but rather a borrowing from Philo: "Die Kirche
hat sie aus Philo entlehnt."[11] One of the heaviest borrowers was Ambrose,
whose liftings from Philo are blatant and copious—entire sections at a
time. Siegfried's is a good list of some of them. This dependence was of
course well known; in fact, as the saying went, if Philo was another Plato,
then Ambrose was a Christian Philo.[12]

Ambrose's *Cain and Abel* is closely related to another of his homilies,
Paradise, which it follows and upon which it directly depends. For Ambrose, the Cain-Abel story is one of continuity, diffusion, and even inten-
sification of the original sin. But the notion of the two ways, gleaned from
Philo, becomes the basis of the larger, dualistic pattern of Cain-Abel.

> Cain means "getting" because he got everything for himself. Abel, on the
> other hand, did not, like his brother before him, refer everything to himself.
> Devotedly and piously, he attributed everything to God. . . . There are two
> schools of thought, therefore, totally in opposition one to the other, implied
> in the story of the two brothers. One of these schools attributes to the mind
> itself the original creative source of all our thoughts, sensations and emo-
> tions. In a word it ascribes all our productions to man's own mind. The other
> school is that which recognizes God to be the Artificer and Creator of all
> things. . . . Cain is the pattern for the first school and Abel for the second.[13]

Although he follows Philo closely, Ambrose gives a cruel interpretive
twist to Philo's thought. As we can expect, he uses Esau and Jacob to gloss
Cain and Abel. The two nations and two peoples in Rebecca's womb now
become "two classes of peoples." Ambrose turns the notion of the two
ways derived from Philo Judaeus against the Jews; the two classes of peoples that the theme describes now become the old ways of the Jews and
the new ways of the Christians.

These two brothers, Cain and Abel have furnished us with the prototype of
the Synagogue and the Church. In Cain we perceive the parricidal people of
the Jews, who were stained with the blood of their Lord, their Creator, and,
as a result of the child-bearing of the Virgin Mary, their Brother also. By Abel
we understand the Christian who cleaves to God. (pp. 361–62)

Not only does Ambrose note division; he must also insist upon an opposition of values so basic that it can know no reconciliation. "Those who
are by nature contraries cannot abide for long in one and the same habita-
tion." From the Old Testament itself Ambrose takes his verbal justification. "On the day in which I shall slay every first-born in the land of
Egypt, I shall sanctify to myself whatsoever is first-born in Israel" (Num.
3.13). Ambrose's gloss proceeds: "This does not refer to one occasion or
to one crisis, but to all time. Once wickedness is renounced, virtue finds
immediate entrance. The departure of evil brings about the introduction
of virtue and the same effort that banished crime leads to an adherence to
innocence. . . . There is no harmony between Christ and Belial. . . ." (p.
417). The world is a moral seesaw, where the superiority of one involves
necessarily the debasement of the other, and vice versa. Particularly is this
so when there is such intense moral engagement. It should also be remarked that this same spirit of division and exclusivity finds intellectual
justification in the Pentateuch itself.

The order of birth of the two brothers—that Cain is the elder—also
assists Ambrose's interpretation. If the Jews were the first to receive the
message of God, then they enjoy some parallel with Cain who was first-
born. But the later historical phenomenon (Christianity-Abel) is the more
favored. Hence Cain precedes Abel at their first mention in Genesis; but
when reference is to their activities, then Abel is mentioned first. Much is
made of these different orders of birth and work throughout Christian
commentary. There is another corollary to the order of mention. Since
wickedness was mentioned first, this means that moral perfection is not
behind us—not in childhood—but rather in front of us, in the later ages
of humankind as of the individual. "No one is without sin, not even an
infant one day old, although he never committed a sin" (p. 366).

In Ambrose's account, Abel is idealized. He does not bring accusation
against his brother. Rather it is the very presence of blood that denounces
Cain. Abel maintains his brotherly devotion, but Cain's own deeds accuse
him. This same pattern of charity encountering obduracy extends to the
mark of Cain. Ambrose regards it as an indication of divine mercy, "He
wanted the wanderer to have time for reflection and by such kindness inspire him to change his ways." But this is not the way it turned out, because Cain did not seek repentance but merely further life. That is, like
Jerome, Ambrose sees in Cain the stubbornness of the carnal mind for

whom a few additional years would be preferable to death. In this Cain was mistaken: the added years only increased the penalty, "inasmuch as he lived in the midst of fears and spent his extended period of time in fruitless labors" (p. 436).[14] Cain was banished. "He passed from a life of human kindness to one which was more akin to the rude existence of a wild beast" (p. 437). Rather than the founder of a city, Cain is here well on his way to becoming sire to the "abhorred other" and the monsters and other such creatures as Grendel and Grendel's dam depicted in the following chapter.

· · ·

The commanding figure of the Western Latin Church was Augustine. He absorbed and summarized so much of the past and determined so much of the future. J. M. Evans has argued that what Augustine made of the Genesis narrative was "to dominate the Church's thinking on the subject for the next thirteen centuries and longer."[15] In Augustine's masterpiece, *De civitate Dei*, Cain and Abel occupy the universalized and rival positions that we have seen them on their way to assuming since Philo. Cain becomes the representative of the earthly city and Abel of the heavenly city. But Augustine does something else: he involves Cain and Abel in the practical foundations of the city. By historicizing the brothers he engages them and what they represent in the profoundest meanings of earthly life, its origins, its principles, and its goals.

Augustine's first sustained treatment of the Cain-Abel theme appears in *Contra Faustum Manichaeum* (c. 398). Continuing the basic line of Ambrose, he describes Cain and Abel as representatives of the old ways of the Jews and the new ways of the Christians, respectively. For Augustine the parallels are compelling. "Abel, the younger brother, is killed by the elder people of the Jews. Abel dies in the field; Christ dies on Calvary." Similar to Cain in denying his crime, the Jews show obduracy in denying Christ. As Cain is condemned to till the ground fruitlessly, indicating his carnal intelligence, so the Jews are condemned to work over the sterile field of the Law. Finally, Cain's greatest punishment is in being separated from God. He asks for continued life but is not repentant. "For his mind is carnal; for he thinks little of being hid from the face of God. . . . This is the carnal mind that tills the ground, but does not obtain its strength. . . ."[16]

When we come to the masterpiece, and particularly the famous fifteenth chapter, Augustine does not forsake this view. Indeed, at one point (15.7) he refers the reader to his earlier work. But there is no question that in the *City of God*, Cain and Abel as representatives of the two cities have gained preeminence. After describing Cain's actions as "the founder of the earthly city," Augustine adds, "He was also a figure of the

Jews. . . ."[17] Although not absent, the thought has been transcended by a grander concept. If Cain is typical of the earthly city, he could be Christian or pagan as well as a Jew. Peter Brown has written well of the change in Augustine's conception. Formerly, "it was the symbolic outline of the event that had then preoccupied him. Now Augustine will draw from it patterns of archetypal motives that sway real men, in all ages and in all countries: it is like coming from the unearthly, symbolic figures of Type and Antitype that face each other in the stained glass windows along the walls of Gothic cathedrals, to the charged humanity of a religious painting by Rembrandt. . . ."[18]

Augustine's contribution to the theme is enormous. He finds it extraordinary that the two greatest cultures of which he is heir, Roman and Judaeo-Christian, should coincidentally mark the foundation of the earthly city, or history itself, with the murder of a brother. Romulus and Remus are regarded as cultural parallels to Cain and Abel. As a story that echoes through the centuries involving other pairs of brothers, including Amphion and Zethos and Polyneices and Eteocles, it joins brothers (even twins), murder, and the foundation of the city (see Introduction).[19] Augustine opens the fifth chapter of book 15 with the powerful sentence, "Primus itaque fuit terrenae civitatis conditor fratricida. . . ." The founder of the earthly city was a fratricide. But the role of such fratricidal sacrifice is not only limited to the origins of the earthly city, it extends throughout history and raises a fundamental question about the blood origins of life itself. Cain-Abel is such a potent theme because it provides opposed responses to that question.

Although Augustine brings together Cain and Abel with Romulus and Remus in a broad cultural comparison, he is also careful to distinguish between them. The distinction is crucial. There is no difference between them he asserts, "unless it be that Romulus and Remus were both citizens of the earthly city." The quarrel between them shows how the earthly city is intrinsically divided against itself. The quarrel between Cain and Abel is largely one-sided. Although it shows the enmity that might exist between the two cities, that of God and that of man, in fact, it is different because Abel has no interest, unlike Remus, in the goods of the earthly city. The distinction is important because it tells us much about the Cain-Abel theme. Augustine in effect distinguishes between theme and motif, between the Cain-Abel theme and the larger motif of brother-strife into which it may generally fit.[20] Romulus and Remus are *frères ennemis*; they exist in enmity because they both desire the same thing, the goods of the earthly city. In effect, they come to resemble each other. Cain-Abel does not rely on undifferentiation but rather on radical difference: the brothers do not resemble each other (and even in mural paintings efforts are made to distinguish between the brothers). At its heart, then, the Cain-Abel story shows radical difference, perhaps later even the arbitrariness of preference; it will be much later before it comes to acknowledge interchangeability.

The extraordinary appeal of the Cain-Abel theme lies precisely here: the duality represented by Cain and Abel is a genuine polarity. The brothers have come to stand for the two most dominant aspects of this early epoch of critical change: the pagan secular point of view attached to the values of the earthly city and the religious spirit that denies such stable location and personal identity and instead embraces the values of pilgrimage, even of dispossession.[21] By an extraordinary transposition, of the kind that will occur several times in the course of this study, when Cain becomes a city-dweller, Citizen Cain, then Abel becomes the vagabond, the wanderer, and, in this case, the bearer of new values. But the fact remains that although demoted, the values of the earthly city—no less than in Augustine—are not debased, and far from being outside the pale are altogether commanding, even prepossessing, and are able to constitute one significant voice of an invaluable dialogue. All this is to say that there exists in the great formulation a genuine persistence of contending values. The pull of the secular values of the earthly city are clear and powerful to the senses, and the possibilities of their true transcendence are as difficult as they are rare. It is Abel who must fly in the face of fact, who moves toward voluntary exile, or alienation, and who accepts disconnection for the sake of a higher connection.

Abel, in a genuine revolutionary change, becomes the wanderer, prototype of the most basic image of the Middle Ages, *homo viator*, humankind as pilgrim. Cain, for his part, becomes something of a stay-at-home. The subtitle of Augustine's great work is *contra paganos*. Pagans are precisely non-combatants, those who are fixed, etymologically, to the soil—they have put down their stakes, and hence their modern development as *peasants, paisanos, paysans*. They conservatively hold to received belief, while Abel as representative Christian is a militant, one who refuses to settle down. He is, in fact, a pilgrim: sure of his destination, he makes only a passing commitment to the scenes along life's way.

The solidity of Cain, who had been a fugitive and a vagabond, depends upon the values of the earthly city—and these are a sense of place and of identity in regard to place. The polis—the city-state—and the nation become organizing centers of identification and of affiliation. When in times of social breakdown or conquest, or of internal disruption, the solidity of the organizing center disintegrates; or when the true values of the earthly center are seen to be inferior, if not defective, and humankind possesses a better vision or hears the music of a better harmony, then Abel comes to the foreground as a spiritual pilgrim who is part of a restored brotherhood and a better community. Summary illustration of the importance of this concept for Christian thought can be gained from Dante's *Purgatorio*, the

site of active and voluntary renunication, where the dimensions of the
earthly city, the walls of any native city, are becoming increasingly unreal.
Uprooted by exile, Dante comes to abide within the order of pilgrimage.
In canto 13, where significantly envy is purged and where, later, on the
same terrace, a distraught and terrified Cain bursts upon the scene, Dante,
still functioning within the residual expectations of the earthly city, asks
a new group of souls if any among them is Italian ("s' anima è qui tra
voi che sia latina"). The phrasing is inappropriate and Dante is mildly
corrected:

> "O frate mio, ciascuna è cittadina
> d' una vera città, ma tu vuo' dire
> che vivesse in Italia peregrina.

(O my brother, everyone is a citizen of a true city; What you meant to
say was "who lived in Italy as a pilgrim.")

(ll. 94–96)

One should notice here that the fundamental values of citizenship and
of the city are still embraced even while their location is transferred. One
suffers displacement for the sake of a better placement, but the final location is still the city and one's true status is still that of citizenship. This
shows why the culture of the Mediterranean, a culture of cities, was a powerful antagonist in a vital polarity.

But the alienation of Abel is a product of spiritual vision as well as of
social breakdown. His purpose is not only to redeem the time, but, as
T. S. Eliot expressed it in *Ash Wednesday*, to "redeem / The unread vision
of the higher dream." Cain's understanding is too time- and history-
bound, in the grip of the authorities of the world. In contrast, Abel aspires
to understand his role in the higher drama, one that is addressed in the
unfolding of Christian eschatology. The earthly drama of tragic sacrifice,
as of Christ, whom Abel prefigures, is actually part of a larger process of
redemption. Abel then is an initiate in an unfolding mystery, where a key
discovery needs to be made, that of Christ, in order for the entire puzzle
to become clear.

This mode of thought has two important implications for this study.
First, eschatology requres a final postponement of judgment; in fact, a
postponement until the final judgment when all will be revealed. Not only
is this deferment to a higher vision a part of better wisdom, it is part of the
better nature of Christianity. Such a vision can only have positive social
benefits: one is less willing to brand someone as a social outcast, as "the
other"—one is more inclined to let his actions do that—when social life
itself is fragile and temporary, and one's own being is that of a pilgrim.

But Abel is a pilgrim for another reason, one more deeply implicated in the central event of the theme, which will bother Augustine as much as it did Dante: the death of the brother. Like the Florentine poet, Augustine was not ignorant of the pagan foundation sacrifice, nor of its true meaning. He simply deplored it. The spiritual condition of pilgrimage that Abel adopts comes to stand for a vision of existence that is opposed to all the values of such sacrifice. The legend of the fratricidal foundation of the state, or of a people, becomes a parable. It comes to stand for the inevitable sacrifices and losses that are part of the conditions of life. From the depths of his own personal experience Dante rejects this version of life and of existence. Augustine does so, as well. The sacrifice of the brother means the sacrifice of the "other," that which a nation, or a people, or even a self, must give up by virtue of becoming itself. With good reason then, the religious mind demotes the identity gained by the self as much as it does the stability of the polis, because each is based upon the foreclosure of otherness, which is represented by the original sacrifice of the brother. The meaning of the foundation sacrifice—here we are alluding to Romulus and Remus whom Augustine is so careful to distinguish from Cain and Abel—is that nationhood, like selfhood, not only involves but actually requires victimization and guilt. What is left behind is the lost brother. This means that the sacrificed brother becomes the shadowy other—or the double—when the self struggles to assert its autonomy, its authenticity. It is interesting that the emergence of the double in modern (Byronic and post-Byronic) versions of the theme is intimately associated with the quest for authenticity, with a need to reclaim the other. Also significant, when this more authentic self is achieved, the double, as the lost brother, must in turn be sacrificed as one of the requirements of the Cain-Abel theme.

The religious mind is too much aware of the blood costs, the guilt, and consequently identifies the earthly city (and all that it entails as far as selfhood) with its blood beginnings, which are not only located at the origin, but which make their constant demands throughout existence. The goal of the religious pilgrim is therefore not selfhood but rather atonement, or "at-onement," a reconstitution of the original brotherhood, whose severance was required by the conditions of existence. The earthly city cannot offer such at-onement because its existence depends prototypically upon the sacrifice of the other. Its identity and that of selfhood do not include brotherhood, because the brother has been destroyed, or left behind. Only in the spiritual community of pilgrimage does one achieve true brotherhood—thus the instinctive form of address in Dante's *Purgatorio* is "O frate mio." And it is in the condition of pilgrimage that one atones for the inevitable losses of existence.

Earthly nationhood and earthly selfhood are not real entities then, since they are forever involved with the necessary sacrifices that sheer living requires. Oddly enough, earthly identity is actually a duality—hence the persistence of the double in later thought—involving the reluctant but necessary sacrifice of the other, the shadowy brother who can never be gone. Every nation or every self is based upon such imperfection, the original sin, the fitting prototype for which accordingly is not Adam and Eve, but rather Cain and Abel—and this is another reason for the gallant supersession of the falling-out of the brothers over the lapse of the parents: its component parts are simply more powerful. Religious writers, in their need for perfection, in their need to restore an original unity, consider these sacrifices an unbearable cost. In their need for atonement, they do not possess the capacity to live with guilt; they are not willing to live with the cracked mirror of history, and must transcend history in mystery and eschatology. They are haunted by the presence of the brother who has been left behind and with whom they seek to restore the original union, and this is the true meaning of the foundation myths at the origins of the earthly city.

This powerful appeal represented by both parts of the polarity speak from the inner resources of the Cain-Abel theme—those energies that it awakens and that account for its long-standing hold on the human imagination. Although Augustine and the other thinkers, whose own works and ideas reach their culmination in Augustine's masterful historical projection, brought about a genuine revolution and transformation in the theme, which would continue to hold its place and appeal for such imaginations as Dante and Milton, in the end, it was superseded by another vision, that shown by Machiavelli and, with all his true dramatic complexity, by Shakespeare. This was the vision of the Sacred Executioner; in its turn it would provide the paradigm for the many versions of a regenerate Cain in the modern world, but all of these in their quest for authenticity, for a reintegration of the self, show the force of their original material by acknowledging the costs and the guilt at the sacrifice of the brother.

Chapter Two

MONSTROUS CAIN

BORN IN THE religious nomadic cultures of the East, the Cain-Abel theme soon ceased being a localized theme, and acquired mobility, even universality. Although it was taken over and developed by religious thinkers in the large urban centers, such metropolises as Alexandria, Milan, Rome, and the African coastal cities, it was used to express an anti-urban and, almost coincidentally, an antisecular sentiment. Very early, Josephus, in his *Antiquities of the Jews*, found the city to have been the product of a curse on Cain. Associated with sophistication, city life required a complexity of involvement and interchange that seemed by itself to banish simplicity. Cain "put an end to the simplicity in which men lived before the invention of weights and measures."[1] Life declined badly, and the crafts that were developed by Cain's descendants only resulted in craftiness. Weights and measures, and the regulations they required, seemed to promote not only restrictions but also devious ways of outwitting the regulators. In a larger sense, urbanity itself is an indication of a secular mind. There is this connection between Philo's attack on sophistry and his identification of Cain with irreverence. Because sophistry is reason without reverence, intelligence without genuine *sophia*, it is easily deemed the natural recourse of the city-dweller, over whose mode of thought Cain presides. In addition, the city is a place of violence. It cannot seem to escape its blood-beginnings. Those pagan rituals of blood sacrifice that seemed so propitiatory were to Augustine accurate metaphors of an inescapable reality: the city, founded in blood, continues to live by blood.[2]

The version of the story, where Abel becomes the pilgrim and spiritual wanderer between two worlds, and Cain becomes the citizen, the wellspring of all the vices associated with city life, bears some implications for the second major tradition. In it, Cain becomes not only a wanderer but an accursed outcast and criminal, one for whom no recuperation is possible. Although both lines of understanding and presentation would continue throughout the Middle Ages, it is the second, that of Cain the monster opposed to all values of civility, that this chapter will describe. What the two traditions share is the inheritance of intractable, binary opposition. The world is divided drastically, and never the twain shall meet. As this binary opposition continues, what we notice when we turn to the tradition of the monstrous Cain representing the abhorred other, is that all polarity is removed from the theme. Extraordinary and competing values were represented both by Cain as citizen and by Abel as pilgrim and representative figure of the mystery of Christian eschatology; the theme prevailed because it gave expression to the fundamental duality of the early Christian era, where significant values were in conflict. This same capacity for polarized thinking, for creating a genuine duality, does not exist when Cain becomes the other, whether this other be literal monster, Jew, black, heretic, schismatic, *homo profanus*, or cannibal. Predominantly Christian medieval culture resorted to Cain (the absence of Abel will be meaningful in more ways than one) in order to set apart its adversaries. Here the branded man becomes the brand, the marked man, the marker. Cain not only represents the difference of what is alien, he actually serves to reinforce that difference. Cain is used to mark off and isolate that which has been unincorporated; in fact, the mark of Cain insures that no such assimilation can take place. Thus Cain can enter into no polarity, or a highly unstable one at best—and this is the major difference between the two traditions. The aetiology of difference is used to erect a wall of noncomprehension. The mark of Cain is used as part of the epistemology of the other; its design is to prevent discovery, to close off understanding. But the danger is greater: such stamps of otherness used to insure unassimilability mean that the other can never become similar. The fuller meaning of this is that the dominant agency of culture risks losing the energies, values, and positive contributions that the vagrant and the fugitive can make to the structures of authority.

BEOWULF

The Cain-Abel story has traveled well. We can point to its inherent nuclear strengths, to its vacancies and anomalies, to its resiliency (its ability to enter into and share forces with other stories—as we shall see, that of Ham, the parable of the cockles from Matthew, the Wandering Jew), but I doubt if we can ever fully account for its extraordinary appeal. With the spread of Christian apologetics, the Cain-Abel story found extensive shelter in the Teutonic North, where it suited an entirely different culture, that of an heroic warrior caste.[3] An older and basic journal article, Oliver F. Emerson's "Legends of Cain, especially in Old and Middle English," has shown the extent of the appropriation of the Cain story.[4] In fact, there is no secondary bibliography richer than that devoted to the literatures of Old and Middle English. In none of these works has the story been put to such intricate and substantial use as in *Beowulf*. The author of *Beowulf* knew what he was doing when he adapted the Old Testament account of Cain and Abel to the needs of a Teutonic warrior society. What is remarkable is the way that the materials of the Cain story (here the excision of Abel will become noteworthy) are not simply *appli-*

qués but take on the appurtenances of the northern culture and enter most fully into the moral circumstances of the poem. This appropriation is evident in the designation of the murder weapon. It was not with a rock, nor with a stick, and certainly not with the jawbone of an ass that Cain slew his brother, but with the kind of action most common to combat, *ecg-banan*, or sword-fury.[5] As if to intensify the familial violation involved, the poet underlines the fact that Cain slew his *angan brether*, his only brother, thus depriving the family of any male heirs. In fact, the relationship is fit even more tightly into the network of kinship, when Cain is accused of killing his father's child, his *faederen-maege*, perhaps even his "father's youth." The language makes clear, beyond simple genealogical descent, the entire network of familial relationships, what the coming of Cain's descendants and all that they represent mean for the society of *Beowulf.*

The fit between the Cain story and the values of the tribe is further clarified in the account of Cain's punishment. Marked by murder, Cain is compelled to flee the pleasures of human society, *man-dream fleon*. But his fate is not simply that of a wanderer; he is restricted to the wastelands, *westen warode*.[6] To be banished forever from the human community is almost beyond thought; it is to be made one with the powers that haunt the outlands and to suffer from such murky associations, indeed from monstrosity.

The monstrous progeny of Cain thus stand at the opposite pole from the values exhibited by "Citizen Cain." In the culture of *Beowulf*, the simple material values of civilization are not demoted, as they are in the former pattern where Abel expressed a spiritual need for atonement. Here a material culture is trying to secure itself from primitive horrors. The simple, plain offerings of civilization, such as secure sleep, untainted meals, conviviality, and even communion, are highly desirable goods. In fact, the practices of accommodation, those that secure peaceful resolutions, are highly valued. Cain's kin are notable in their violation of the ways that society tries to make peace. Significantly, Grendel and his dam refuse wergild, the epitome of compromise and accommodation. What is even more horrible, they are cannibals, thus denying the final consummation of the flames. (Again and again, we will be brought to remark on the intriguing appropriateness of cannibalism for the Cain-Abel story.) If, within the patterns of the Citizen Cain, the "dematerialized" values of Abel seek atonement for the necessary blood-origins of existence, in the midst of the monstrous progeny of Cain, a material culture lives in dread of the outcast, the banished other who returns to avenge his deprivations. The threat comes not from any sophisticated urbanity, adept at resolving ruptures in existence, but rather from the irrational forces that threaten civilization itself.

The concern of *Beowulf* is with a material culture struggling to preserve the peaceful bases of civilization, and with the precariousness of such attainments. This is the consistent pattern of events in which Cain and his offspring play their parts, and which indicates the fuller meaning of the monsters' assaults. The pattern, with many overlapping parts and phrases, seems to begin with a positive act of civilization or creation, the stability and even hopefulness of which is subsequently threatened if not undone by a destructive act born out of emotions of envy and resentment. If such menace is always present, then we can understand how, by having a progeny, Cain has come to provide the mythical basis for the continuity of evil.

The first surge culminates in the construction of Heorot, the splended meadhall where Hrothgar and his retainers can gather in peace and conviviality. No sooner does the poet celebrate its triumph than, proleptically, he forsees its destruction by biting fire *(lathan liges)*. This fire may be the result of another destructive event that the poet also anticipates, the eruption of swordhate *(ecg-hete)* between son-in-law and father-in-law. This animosity has its origins in *wael-nithe*, envy of weal (75–85).

The next lines describe Grendel's own hostility to the songs coming from the meadhall—his own envy of weal. But the sound he hears, more particularly, is that of the Scop relating nothing less than the biblical account of Creation. The creation-lay establishes a forceful parallel with the construction of Heorot in the preceding episode. And just as Heorot is destroyed, so the Creation itself is marred. But, crucial for the culture of the poem, it is not Adam and Eve's sins that frustrate the powers of Creation, but rather the actions of Cain. Actually, the Scop does not allude to any First Fall; rather, he omits the lapse of the first parents and proceeds to the falling-out of their kin. Just as the meadhall is destroyed in anticipation, so here the poet leaps beyond the Creation to the coming of Grendel and his ancestry in Cain. Along with other monsters and giants, Grendel has held to the moors, the outlands, from the time God proscribed them as kin of Cain *(in Caines cynne)*. God punishes Cain for slaying Abel; the poet laconically adds that Cain derives no pleasure from that feud, *faehthe* (86–114). As the destruction of Heorot is brought about by the feud based upon envy, so here the ruin of Creation is made manifest in the feud, it too derived from envy. The entire grouping of events is a major example of cultural appropriation, in which dominant parts of the Cain-Abel story are brought into compliance with the needs of another society.

Just as there is an evident connection between Cain and the feud, so there is a connection between each of them and the monsters. In a crucial essay, "Differentiation and Reciprocity in Lévi-Strauss and Contemporary Theory," René Girard helps us make those connections.[7] He argues that monsters are expressions of social reversals that provoke the crisis of culture known as undifferentiation. In this conflict, antagonists meet with such reciprocal violence that they themselves begin to resemble one another, in effect, becoming indistinguishable. We will witness this same crisis in Dante's *Inferno* as the outgrowth of civil war (itself a more massive version of the feud). There it will not yield monsters but rather monstrousness (including, again, cannibalism) and will take place under the sign of Cain (the *Caina* section of Cocytus). The reason that the Cain-Abel theme is appropriate to such crises of reciprocal violence is that it epitomizes "internal" as opposed to "external" conflict, where, in the former, the possibility of resemblance is greater. Furthermore, as brothers, Cain and Abel better suggest conflict that is symmetrical. (We must recall that the use of Cain here differs from the Philonic and Augustinian meaning of Cain and Abel, where the brothers are sharply differentiated.) Following Girard's argument, we could say that the structure of such symmetrical conflict calls forth undifferentiation. Because relationships are clearly demarcated and defined, the very closeness of the relationship and the clarity of the boundaries serve to aggravate the consequences of conflict. This would mean that when such relationships are violated, and the fraternal relationship is rendered antagonistic, the consequence is not mere slippage but even greater inundation, as if a dam that were operating under great pressure should suddenly collapse. Indeed, systems of relationships are pressure-laden because they operate as barriers against such chaos. The crucial nature of the boundary makes the disaster all the greater, as if all civilization and society were returned to their primordial conditions. What is demolished in the eruption of the feud, and as a consequence of brother-strife, is the possibility of all demarcation, and this means the powers of symbolism itself. In the mess of undifferentiation monsters are revived, and it is their coming that announces the crisis. It is for this reason then that the horrors that Grendel visits upon Heorot are associated with the hostilities between father-in-law and son-in-law, and that the defeat of the powers of Creation is brought about not by the lapse of Adam and Eve but by the same monster and his derivation from Cain. The monster, the feud, and the particular nexus of relationships suggested by the Cain-Abel theme exist in the context where Creation is undone, and where the horrors that are unleashed are those coming from undifferentiation.

This nexus of association helps explain the conspicuous absence of Adam and Eve from the account of the Fall. A heroic warrior caste is not too troubled by the falling-out of men and women; the real problem could not be discord between the sexes, but rather the falling-out of kin, the conversion of the reciprocal bonds of generosity and loyalty into their deadly opposite, the feud. The feud is the inversion of reciprocity, just as cannibalism is the inversion of brotherhood. Hence the more suitable figure to represent this deformation of values is Cain, the antagonist of the first quarrel and the progenitor of the host of evil spirits who continue to bedevil the human struggle to achieve social harmony. The outbreak of the feud, and its accelerating reciprocal violence, to which there seems to be no end, is indeed monstrous and the worst horror that the society of *Beowulf* can imagine because it is the exact inverse of its values. The Adam and Eve story does not lend itself to this account; in this sense its values are more humanistic than monstrous. Cain in his banishment and mark could more readily yield a monstrous progeny, while Adam and Eve, as is stressed in the Introduction, are needed to reconstitute the race. They are not to be associated with monsters, nor with the continuity of unregenerate evil. Their message is one of eventual reincorporation, where the original powers of the Creation are vindicated, where all obstructors are frustrated. The banished Cain stands perpetually for the other. In fact, in the recuperation of Adam and Eve, Christianity still has need of a fall guy. The supersession of Adam and Eve by Cain and Abel in the stories of the continuity and extension of evil is given further effective witness in *Beowulf*.[8]

But of even greater importance for the poem is the role, or rather nonrole, of Abel. The predominance of feud would indicate that hostilities are undifferentiated and consequently Abel could have no role in such circumstances. But there are other reasons. In the classical patristic version a dialectic actually exists between the values of the earthly city and those of the heavenly city. No such rival principles exist in *Beowulf*. The opposite of civilization is not a value but a monstrosity, not a positive polar opposite but rather a negation, a nonentity. Envy itself is marked by absence, by want. In this, of course, *Beowulf* shows forth the positive strength of its values, because in its code community is a positive good, having no need of evil in order to exist. In this sense, the use of the monstrous progeny of Cain in order to designate its antimyth differs from the application of Cain to Jews or blacks. One can sense that such application in these latter instances indicates a want in the defining culture, and thus could be interpreted as complying with the criticism frequently heard in the 1960s that the other is a contrivance employed by an orthodoxy in need of reassurance: in order to feel saved, we must damn.[9] While the faults of this line of reasoning are patent—it ends up by asserting that only that which is negative is real—nevertheless, one can see that it has had some historical validity. In the case of *Beowulf*, however, it loses all effectivness. To be banished far from mankind is not only sufficient punishment, it is its own punishment and not to be construed as part of a dialectic of opposing values.

The ethic of *Beowulf* thus reveals the virtues of a positive, heroic, and material culture, one to which the values of Abel are simply not germane. Not yet become spiritualized, or dematerialized, the culture of *Beowulf* exhibits little interest in transcendence. The poem does not refer to the virtues of the Sermon on the Mount, nor does it indulge in feelings born of contempt for the world—a later medieval attitude that is too often taken to be synonymous with Christianity. Human attainments might be fleeting—and although located in materiality, the poem does rise to such reflection—but they are not unworthy. If the major object of the human endeavor is the establishment of an enduring material culture, then the virtues of Abel are simply not present to consciousness. This is another way of saying that in the civilization of *Beowulf*, there is no discrepancy in morality between what is human and what is divine: the envy of the gods is not directed against those who act dutifully, loyally, and virtuously. There is no evidence that Beowulf's enemies are anything other than God's enemies, or, put another way, there is every evidence that Beowulf is God's hero in his struggle against Grendel and Grendel's dam.

If we call to mind the two forms of brotherhood, that of blood brotherhood and that of the discipleship of the blood, we see that the absence of Abel is part of the predominance of the former. There is no need to atone for the sundered brother, the outcast or fugitive other. And it is this that accounts for the absence of Abel—his absence is directly connected with the devaluation, even outright dismissal of the other and of any claim he might have on life itself, let alone on its value. Perhaps because it senses itself to be so endangered, the society of *Beowulf* is one of extraordinarily good conscience.

But there are other, more intriguing ways by which *Beowulf* enters into the pattern elicited by Cain and Abel. It is a foundation poem, one where an order of being and of conduct is redeemed from the monsters, from ultimate undifferentiation, and its hero is a Sacred Executioner. Beowulf himself differs from the Sacred Executioner because in no sense is his conduct anything but exemplary and heroic, with little ambiguity, nor any intricate connection between ambivalent actions and positive outcomes. But, like later Sacred Executioners, he enters into dangerous points of action and assumes great risks—physical, to be sure, but also moral. The risk encountered is that his violent actions will not be redemptive but will only replicate what he was first called to redress. This legacy of original violence, and a kind of retributive curse that attends it, associates *Beowulf* with the fuller ramifications of the Cain-Abel theme.

But in Beowulf's case, as in those of the Sacred Executioner, the pattern that we must allow is one where condemnation is risked but finally avoided, where temptation is presented but overcome. This is the importance then of the cautionary example described by Hrothgar himself, of Heremod who succumbs to avarice and is thus guilty of severing the ties of reciprocity between lord and thane (898–915). After his first victory, this antitype is presented as a warning to Beowulf. There are those who believe that Beowulf's death following the struggle with the last dragon is in some way an indication of a relapse or defect as had affected Here-mod.[10] But the value of this counterexample is that Beowulf avoids this failure. After defeating the monsters, he rules peacefully and honorably for fifty years, and it is Wiglaf's anticipation (another prolepsis) that only in Beowulf's absence—that is, as a consequence of his death and not of his misdeeds—will the Geats become vulnerable to the encroaching disasters of feud and foreign invasion. Any condemnation the poem musters is di-rected against his thanes who deserted him in his time of need.

The bad case of Heremod does emphasize the pattern of the Sacred Executioner and its relevancy for the poem, that is, it shows the dangers to which violent actions are necessarily exposed. The danger is that the Sacred Executioner does not introduce a new order, but only adds an-other link to the chain of repeated crimes. This is yet another reason why Cain and violence are so inextricably united—each produces a progeny bred in its own likeness, and each is thus involved in the historical conti-nuity of its kind. Such replication amounts to an astonishing curse; rather than breaking the rounds of repeated crime, the failed leader only adds to them. Moreover, such failure returns the realm to the undifferentiation that the actions of Heremod (whose avarice dissolves the differences between lord and retainer) or the monsters create. Clearly Beowulf func-tions within the pattern of the Sacred Executioner. By not repeating the misadventures of Heremod, his own actions—violent though they may be and hence dangerous—elude fatal replication and are even legitimized. From a pre-Christian era we can discern the lineaments of a post-Christian solution.

•   •   •

When the Jew and the black are associated with Cain, the apparent oth-erness of religion and color is made inveterate and unredeemable.[11] In this sense, the two groups may be coupled as "taboo" peoples. Nevertheless, Christian attitudes toward Jews and blacks were complicated by differ-ences in the origin, nature, and history of the two groups. Christians and Jews shared a common theology and geography. The Jew may be an alien, but his culture is inseparably implicated with Christian culture, with its theology, literature, and typology. The relations of blacks and Christians were not encumbered by such intricate confraternity of theology or even by physical closeness. Blackness itself occupies a dim portion of the mind, while blacks were pushed to the limits of the known world. "The black dishonored was the black unknown" (Devisse, p. 46). The Jew is in our midst, while the black inhabits a distant world—one for that very reason exotic and barbaric. A crucial passage from Dante's *Paradiso* (5.81) sum-marizes the point. Dante pleads earnestly with Christians not to behave foolishly, to take their vows seriously, and not to undertake preposterous ones. "Sí che'l Giudeo di voi tra voi non rida!" ("So that the Jew in your midst does not deride you"). The phrase speaks volumes. One could not imagine at the time the same caution applied to blacks. For one, they would not be "in your midst," and second, the Christian would have no fear of the black's derision. But they would fear that the Jews, who were not only more familiar with the original biblical texts (and as a consequence, Christians were from time to time forbidden to enter into biblical dispute with them), but demonstrated a sobriety and restraint in their manner of living that could only stand in rebuke of frivolousness. Moreover, the Jews adhered to a social and ethical theology that, although ritualized, was clear to the senses. Christianity, on the other hand, adopted beliefs that were enveloped in mystery and far from clear to the senses: a virgin birth, the death of a God in the most ignominious manner, ingestion of its God's body and blood, and an otherworldly ethic. In this sense, we can see that the Jew "in your midst" is really the Jew within the Christian, that is, the secular, worldly mind that has trouble accepting and adhering to a theology that challenges reason and material intelligence.

Christians could turn with such venom on Jews partially because they might be uttering truths to which the Christian sensible mind consented but dared not admit. A different kind of relationship exists between Christians and blacks. Blacks suffered from horrific associations with blackness, with processes of denigration. Sinners were consigned to outer darkness. Virtue was light. Sin itself was black. And like sin, blackness could be repulsive and alluring at the same time. One could speak, as Hawthorne did, of the power of blackness.

Given these fundamental differences, it is not surprising that Jews and blacks, however much their fates might be intertwined, would exist on a seesaw in their relations with Christianity. The movements within the Church that created animosity toward Jews were the same ones that led to openness to the other people of the world, including blacks. Historically, the argument of supersession of the Jews by the Christians was the very one that led to the missionary attitude toward the Gentiles. It was by such universalism that the Christian Church justified this supersession. Consequently, the exclusion of the Jews not only made possible, but actually insisted upon a mission to the blacks (or the Ethiopians, as they were called). In fact, in that very period of ecclesiastical expansion, when after centuries of isolation Western Christendom began to renew its interest in Africa and the East, the growth of the Church between the times of Gregory VII and Innocent III had dire consequences for the Jews. Anti-Judaism and anti-Jewish policies were pseudoarguments by which the Church could express and extend its authority. The very period—the thir-

teenth century—that marked the beginnings of the systematic expulsion
of the Jews from the West coincided with the Church's expansion of its
interests in Africa and Asia (Devisse, pp. 141–42).

In his meticulous account, *The Church and the Jews in the XIIIth Century*, Solomon Grayzel reaches the dismal conclusion that "by the middle
of the Thirteenth Century the Jews were well on their way to the complete exclusion from Christian society which eventually overtook them"
(p. 83). Anti-Judaism, which had been an integral part of Christian theology, had since the First Crusade begun to be transformed into concrete
political action (Mellinkoff 1, p. 18). Popular pogroms in the wake of the
Crusades and a systematic policy of social degradation had violated a kind
of equilibrium that permitted Christians and Jews to coexist, and this was
actually countenanced by Christian thought. To be sure, the Jews were
the physical victims of the wave of destructive resentment, but the Christians themselves were morally and spiritually victimized by such hate-filled
vilification. In permitting and even encouraging the anti-Jewish actions
and policy, the Christian churches lost touch with their own ideal purpose, their own better vision. The Jew may have been superseded and expelled, but so was the image of Abel, the pilgrim-harbinger of a spiritualized Christianity. Such exclusion inflicted damage on the very essence of
Christianity. If Judaism is a religion of the excluded brother (think of
Cain, Esau, Ham, and others), in developing the pattern of Abel, Christianity attempted to transcend the need for such exclusion by virtue of a
larger pattern of incorporation. Judaism is more of a national religion,
with a special identity; consequently, it may be willing to incur the guilt of
victimage. Christianity was more of an universal religion, and should have
thus been unwilling to sacrifice the excluded brother.

To be sure, in fourth-century sarcophagi and in the thought of Ambrose, Cain was aligned with the Synagogue and Abel with the *ecclesia*
(there is also some indication that these associations did have political
consequences; Seiferth, p. 48). But there was a largeness of vision in the
entire eschatology into which Church and Synagogue fit that tended to
deprive anti-Judaism of its animosity. For one, the development of Christian sacred history included the prophets of the Old Testament as forefathers, and the relationship between the two dispensations was one of
anticipation and fulfillment, rather than of differentiation. The relationship of the New Testament to the Old is one of Concord: *Concordia Veteris et Novi Testamenti*. This tradition was as living and as appealing as
was that of *adversus Judaeos*. In this larger and frankly more inspired
philosophical vision, the relationship of the Church to the Synagogue, of
Christian to Jew, is enrolled in the mystery of the divine will that will be
revealed at the end of time. The Synagogue may be pictured as being

blindfolded, not blinded. In the fullness of time, the veil will be lifted for all. The division that exists is not between two historical entities but rather between the divine plan and the human vision. Wolfgang Seiferth's remarkable book, *Synagogue and Church in the Middle Ages*, is most valuable for showing the presence of this higher vision—as well as for indicating the causes of its demise—and for advancing the notion of "equilibrium," to which I alluded earlier. This notion implies that there are certain relationships and problems that defy exact theoretical formulation (as, for instance, the relations of Church and State, Empire and Papacy, Jews and Christians). These relationships elude resolution, depending instead upon a kind of human maturity and good will, a vision and a confidence exhibited by blessed human leaders and happy times.

Clearly, the problem with equilibrium is its elusiveness, its very precariousness. In the wake of the Crusades, in the period of proclaimed papal supremacy, from the time of Gregory VII through the early fourteenth century, and under the added pressures brought about by fears of the Black Death, this fragile equilibrium was strained beyond repair. A theological conception became popularized and debased; sublime statuary art was translated into popularized and contemporized stage figures; and the religious, philosophical, and aesthetic qualities of the beautiful but earthly Synagogue were translated into Jew-baiting. The concord between Judaism and Christianity became historical difference, and eschatology was reduced to stark dualism. But it was a dualism without polarity; in this transformation the Jew became the other, and this otherness was underlined by his assimilation to Cain.

In this opposition, the Jews took on the characteristics of Cain, and together with the Christians entered into a relationship with all the animosity of a sibling rivalry. One of several contributions of Rosemary Ruether's *Faith and Fratricide* lies in the second term of its title. Not only did the Jewish-Christian struggle take on the outward attributes of the Cain-Abel struggle, it also inherited the internal dynamics of a family quarrel, provoked by the closeness of the Cain-Abel story for the long history of Christians and Jews. Although Caligula initiated the first pogrom against the Jews of Alexandria in 38 C.E., still the superior skepticism of the Roman mentality could well afford to wash its hands of sectarian Semitic squabbles (a gesture that itself drips with scorn at vulgarity). Only the shared yet differentiated heritage of Christians and Jews could provoke such rancor.

The involuntary "Jew-badge" decreed by the Fourth Lateran Council of 1215 indicates a long association between the mark of Cain and the Jews. The Jew was marked by circumcision; the Jew was a wanderer. "Circumcision was given by God to the Jews, not as a sign of divine favor, but as a mark of their future reprobation." From the very beginning in the ritual of circumcision the Jews were marked with "otherness," and otherness was reinforced by their association with Cain. A verse commentary on Genesis by Peter Riga emphasizes this association:

> Divine wrath gives Cain a sign so that he will not be killed.
> The Hebrew has a sign so that he cannot be killed.
> In truth, that he lives on earth in the midst of his enemies
>   is rather amazing.
> No king, no duke, no powerful person kills him.
> His skin has been cut as a sign to everyone.
>
>   (Mellinkoff, 1.17–18)

The notions of Jerome and Ambrose that the mark of Cain was imposed upon him in order to keep him from felicity, to preserve his odious existence and thus inflict greater punishment, thus finds latter application in unhappy circumstances. Like Cain, Peter Riga continues, "the Hebrew, a wanderer, roams the earth; / Movement possesses him and wandering drives him on." In fact, in 1146, Peter the Venerable will use the legend of a wandering Cain to justify expropriation of Jewish property in order to finance the Second Crusade (Mellinkoff 1.8).

As early as 1204, Innocent III expressed his desire to mark the Jews. In a letter of 1208 he contends that the princes have offered protection to the Jews, and have even made use of them as financial agents in the collection of usury. Innocent argues against this protection by linking the Jews with their mythical ancestor, Cain. Like Cain, they are marked with "shaking of the head" (*tremorem capitis*) in order that they might be spared, but spared for the sake of an eternal servitude. This eternal servitude is punishment for the slaying of Christ, whose blood, like that of Abel's against Cain, cries out against them. Their actions, instead of receiving such secular protection and reward, "calls down His blood upon themselves and upon their children." The Jew-badge of 1215 was a direct result of the conflation of Cain and the Jews in unhappy political circumstances. The papal decree, implemented in France and in England and then throughout Europe, was only annulled in 1781 by emperor Joseph II of Austria, but then disastrously restored by Hitler.[12]

There is some dispute as to if the classical pagan world entertained any special antipathy toward blackness.[13] This was not the case with the Christian fathers. As we have already indicated, in the allegorical, spiritualized sense of the world, that which is evil is low and black, and that which is good is high and light. The binary bind expressed by the Children of Light and the Children of Darkness took possession of the Christian imagination, and was brought by its Puritan representatives to the New World. One did not need to know blacks in order to abhor blackness.

From its origins, then, the Christian association with blacks was fraught with imagined peril. The devil was black (but not possessed of conventionalized negroid features). But when the devil was no longer the fallen Lucifer, but rather a more humanized temptor, urging the wavering soul into evil, then it was possible to represent him as a black person. In this sense, the black, like the Jew, was diabolized. But where the Jews as a race were held responsible for the death of Christ, blacks, who were pictured as more athletic, enter into Christian iconography as actual executioners of Christ, of John the Baptist, of St. Stephen. Blacks were also depicted as captives, in short, enslaved.[14]

Cain is not used as a parallel figure to explain the mentality of the blacks, or even to assure a condition of otherness. The blacks were already other, even when domesticated and familiar. To the Christian mind, the association of blackness with Cain, or even of blacks with Cain, is not one for which we must search. Very early, it was clear that Cain was tinged with blackness, either because he was charred by the unavailing sacrificial fire or from the smoke thereof. If, as some legends assert, Abel was born of the coupling of Adam with Eve, Cain was derived from the union of Eve and the devil, and his offspring were black. But the most important source of the conflation of Cain with black people came from orthographic error and legendary confusion. Just as Cain would later be fused with the Wandering Jew, so in earlier legends was he associated with Ham, who snickered at his father's nakedness. There is a similarity in the stories inasmuch as each of the wayward sons is cursed as well as banished. The land of Ham's banishment was thought to be the area of the Nile, and Ham traditionally came to be associated with the continent of Africa, and hence with blacks. In the Middle Ages, Ham's name was spelled Cham. This was easily confused with Cain. In the medieval mystery plays, Cain's name is also Chaym. In fact, in *Beowulf*, a lapse inserts the name of Ham where context requires Cain (Friedman, pp. 99–107).

·   ·   ·

The Cain-Abel story received vivid depiction in one of the longest-lasting and most extensive expressions of popular art, the medieval mystery cycle or—deriving its name from the religious commemoration with which it was first associated—the plays of Corpus Christi.[15] Sometime after 1311, when the feast of Corpus Christi was decreed by Clement V, and before the first recorded mention of such dramas in 1376, a remarkable series of plays were made part of the communal celebration. Lasting four or five days, perhaps even longer, cycles of dramatic presentations showing major events of Christian salvation history were played out on carts in such communities as Newcastle-upon-Tyne, Kendal, Preston, York, Beverley, Wakefield, Chester, Lincoln, Norwich, Ipswich, Worcester, and Coventry.

From these, four have survived: the texts from York, Chester, Wakefield, and the so-called N-town. In the first three of these, the Cain-Abel story, as it did in the great mural programs emanating from Rome, occupies a forceful position.

The Cain-Abel story is such an integral part of the mystery cycles because it prefigures the central event of the Christian drama, the passion of Christ. Unlike what occurs in *Beowulf*, in the Corpus Christi plays the qualities and attributes of Abel are extremely important. As he does in the mural programs, Abel prefigures Christ and his death is seen as part of a line of sacrifices, including the story of Abraham and Isaac and the massacre of the Innocents, that lead up to and in fact are "explained" by the death of Christ.

If Abel, in his obedience and mildness, provides the moral centering of the presentations, Cain provides the dramatic centering. This is not to say that Abel is painfully prissy or sanctimonious, simply that Cain in his changeful mobility and manic ferocity is the source of dramatic action. If in *Beowulf* Cain is the progenitor of monsters and, by application, of the monstrousness of the feud, in the medieval mystery plays he is all too common. But this recognizability does not spare him from degeneracy. In this presentation of the non-tither, there is no need for exotic horrors. From within its own midst, the city (or manor) has spawned a delinquent for whom the fitting pattern is Cain. The ordinary man on the street is subnormal, profane, a loutish cur whom we have produced by our own specialized means. Although it is possible to regard this Cain as a perennial who was cut from the street corners of existence—a kind of citified smartass, a tough-talking, shrewd dealer—it is clear that he has nothing of urbanity about him, nothing of the sophistication that Philo deplored. This "Citizen" Cain is actually part of another lineage, a monster without monstrosity, a wretch bred out of the hardships of life and the unregeneracy of our own natures. This creature is as threatening to social values as was Grendel—in fact, we see the same symptoms of social distintegration and undifferentiation—and in his obduracy threatening to religious values as well. For this monster, this other that is so clearly part of human nature—part of us—and so intractable, Cain is the suitable patron.

The changes of Cain present an open account of cultural assimilation: Cain has managed to merge with Synagogue and with the Wandering Jew, as well as with Ham and negritude.[16] He found ready work in the culture of *Beowulf*. In a valuable journal article, Pearl F. Braude has shown the equal appropriateness of the parable of the cockle (Matt. 13.24–42) for the Cain-Abel story.[17] In its account of tares in the good wheat, the parable had already been used for characterizing Jews and heretics. Somewhere in the twelfth century, the parable came to infiltrate the Cain-Abel story and became, in addition, an account of the hazards of false tithing.

This is clear from the fact that at times even Abel was depicted as offering a bundle (rather than the sacrificed animal)—bundles for Heaven from Abel and for Hell from Cain. Their respective sacrifices came to be made before an altar. The tithe, or tenth, was defended as making up for the tenth-part of the angels whom Lucifer took with him to Hell. Cain, proverbially "the first-born of the Devil," joined that party in refusing to tithe properly. By the twelfth century, the tithe—*decimas, dîme, zehende, tiends*—was collected throughout Europe, and the word *decimas* occurs for the first time in a commentary on Cain and Abel. There is even a further connection between the tithe and Jews and Cain. In fact, the anti-Jewish policies of the twelfth and thirteenth centuries were in part related to the Church's growing need for revenues. A prosperous Jewry that was acquiring Christian properties but that was exempt from the tithe not only enjoyed some social advantage but also cost the Church important income. A broad coming-together of interests and forces thus insisted that Cain, also associated with Jews and heretics, the first fall guy as well as the mark, could be useful in warning the delinquent.

If this seems to be heavy theological baggage to place on the head of a mere tax dodger, we must also appreciate the social dimensions of the mystery plays—the communal rapport of which Cain seriously threatens. We do not have to accept his full argument to see that the late John Gardner, who understood the nature of *Beowulf*, and was thus attuned to the social interdependence that is being subverted by Cain, was insightful when he wrote, "The poet establishes in dramatic form the relationship between man's feudal commitment to God, the mutual commitments of lords and vassals within the human community (both ecclesiastical and temporal), and man's commitment as lord of nature. The pageant is thus not only religious but also social."[18]

Cain as the profane other, the other that is not only in our midst but within us as well, the *homo profanus*, overzealous in the pursuit of vulgarity, shows all the aggressiveness of the new *homo economicus*. The fourteenth century was a century on the move, with new forces in society threatening to break out of the ecclesiastical and social containment. Chaucer's roster of characters in the General Prologue to the *Canterbury Tales* provides evidence of these new pressures working on social and religious constraint, and Dante had already responded in his great *Commedia* to the mobility and centrifugalism that was contributing to the disintegration of his society. With these new forces a new ethic is presented, one justifying a new aggressiveness in relation to life. Cain might be regarded as a figure for these forces.

Even in the most dignified of the pageants presenting the Cain-Abel story, the *pagina secunda* of the Chester cycle, Cain is still a sharp dealer. He has no intention of offering "clean corn." What he offers is presumably what has already fallen to the ground. His purpose in offering is personal gain, the kind of investment calculated to bring him more "worldly bliss," and if it does not, then God is his debtor. At the sacrifice, the Chester Cain, claiming the rights of the elder brother, aggressively pushes ahead of Abel, and, after the visible signs of God's favorable response to Abel's sacrifice, blames his brother for trying to "pass [him] in renowne."[19]

Cain is uniformly presented as a hard man who is ever ready for retaliation and who prides himself on being able to give as good as he gets. The deleterious social effect of these attitudes is shown in the rebellious sidekick servant, who mirrors his master's methods. Such replication leads to proliferating animosity and its own measure of undifferentiation. As much as in *Beowulf,* or in the *Inferno*, master and man represent a microscopic picture of a society at war. In the lamentably incomplete version of the York series, the text resumes when Brewbarret, or Strifebrewer, Cain's servant, seems to be mocking Cain for the obviously unfavorable reception that his poor offering has merited. When the drunken Cain invites him to come within arms reach that he may be more properly repaid for his jesting, Brewbarret pretends that he has broken his toe.[20]

In the much more famous *Mactatio Abel* of the Townley cycle, part of the group of plays written by the so-called Wakefield master, a servant, named Pikeharness (or harness-thief) both mimics and returns his master's curses, vulgarity, and blows.[21] Cayn the master is hard pressed to drive his team of horses, and receives little help from his man. In fact, they exchange mutual vilification and ultimately blows. Pikeharness summarizes the aggressive philosophy that unites master and man: "Yai, with the same mesure and weght / That I boro will I qwite" (ll. 51–52).

The York Cain was adept in curses; this Cain is equally suited to scatology. His servant (serving the practical purpose of bringing a high-spirited audience to attention) invites those who persist in making noise to come blow on his anus ("black hole") until their teeth bleed. Unrelieved anality is the frame of reference for this Cain and his likeness. Karl P. Wentersdorf is probably not being overly serious when he writes that such excremental fixation "expressed for the medieval world the repulsiveness of thoughts and acts which were believed to constitute a serious defiance of divine law."[22] He reminds us that although a kind of scatological reference could be useful in scaring off the devil, literally voiding sin (fighting fire with fire), still the invitations to ass kissing were more scurrilous than not, and in fact were an indication of a *monde renversé* and of the reversal of social values that Cain and his man represent. This scatology is a further extension of undifferentiation. To jump ahead, when in Part Three, "Dramas of Envy" we come to Peter Shaffer's *Amadeus*, we witness a transvaluation of these values when a sign of Mozart's divine direction is precisely his vulgarity and his own readiness to discharge the divine afflatus.

In its presentation of the sacrifice, the *Mactatio Abel* provides an example of the arguments the man in the field employed to dismiss tithing. As we saw in the Chester and York versions, the arguments are rough and rationalistic, activated by a grumbling avarice and lack of generosity, but also by a harshness of spirit bred by the hardness of life. Cain argues, what has God given to me, that I should be so generous to him? Abel responds that tithing acknowledges the gift of life. In mock seriousness, Cain raises his hand and swears that he never borrowed a penny from God, and what he gave the last time is still in the hands of the priests. He protests that there is no reason for him to offer gifts to God since his own life is worse off than that of others. Far from being a friend, God has been a foe to Cain and his fortunes. Evidence is that Cain is impoverished and never seems to thrive. In fact, Cain's arguments smack of a rugged individualism—he will take care of himself. Far from being unsocialized, Cain is all too recognizable. He betrays a self-interest that Philo identified as the mark of his breed. Yet, this new social force that Cain represents has little of skeptical urbanity about it; rather, in the vivid and far-reaching medieval imagination, it becomes, in itself and more importantly in its consequences, monstrous.

It is, of course, possible to be too solemn in discussion of this play. There is, after all, something extraordinarily engaging in this dramatic process whereby a figure from the past is so totally contemporized. At times, the upstart comic audacity of Cain is dramatically brilliant, as when he is willing to swear on a stack of Bibles that he does not recall ever borrowing a penny from God, so how could he possibly be owing anything; or when he proffers his grain to the tune of the child's rhyme (the medieval antecedent of our "one, two, buckle my shoe . . ."), and manages to shortchange God in his offering; and the last brilliant stroke when he takes special audacious refuge in the king's pardon (a residual analogue to God's protective mark), while inevitably Pikeharness persists in undercutting such claims. To be sure, this is vibrant comedy and there is something in comedy that resists crystallization, particularly of the tendentious sort. The irrepressible dramatic urge delights in bringing home an ancient story, particularly in scandalizing a hightone ancient legend with homespun vulgarity. Although such recognition is delightful, nevertheless, we have to concede that aesthetically, the drama falls short because its transaction is unidirectional: it contemporizes but fails to mythologize. It shows Cain in our daily lives; but it does not lift our daily lives to any higher level of insight and thought. This will require less "municipal" and "local" springs of art.

Moreover there is some value to Eleanor Prosser's objection that these "obscenities are comic solely by means of their obscenity" (p. 80).[23] One begins to weary of the relentlessness of the vulgarity and begins to see that it does possess some purpose other than the simply comic. If seriousness can be self-defeating, than comedy itself is capable of springing its own trap. There is such a thing as laughing oneself to death. Laughter is indeed turned against the audience when it identifies so fully with the ugliness of Cain. That this particular other becomes oneself is far from flattering. The other is not outside of us, but is a recognizable part of our daily behavior and speech. There is some point to Baudelaire's contention that comedy itself is satanic and bespeaks a fallen world.[24]

· · ·

The question suggested by Peter Thorslev, one of the more perceptive students of romanticism, is still a pressing one: how can we understand the transformation of the loutish Cain of the medieval mystery cycle into the splendid intellectual rebel of Byron's creation?[25] The question, grandly historical, nevertheless conceals a disruption. Byron's Cain is not homologous with his medieval namesake. The medieval Cain is grotesque in his bald and broad humor, reeking of the earth and of unremitting profanity and scatology. He promises no scintilla of regeneration. In Byron's Cain there is nothing in the least tending toward profanity, no comic trivialization to take the sting from the seriousness of his venture, his guilt, and its consequences. To trace his ancestry adequately one must look back to Hamlet. This becomes clearer when we see that the homologue to the medieval Cain is not Byron's Cain but rather Shakespeare's Caliban. This final figure helps complete the development of the medieval Cain as the abhorred other, the other that is shown to be more and more within human nature. On the other hand, Caliban's role and presence in *The Tempest* receive clarification when they are considered in this line of descent, amid the issues raised by the monstrous progeny of Cain and the abhorred other.

Large, shaping significance is given to the subject by recourse to a splendid sentence from G. K. Chesterton: "There is no value in a version of the brotherhood of man that does not cover troglodytes and cannibals."[26] The sentence reaches back to *Beowulf* and forward to *The Tempest* and beyond, posing a particular challenge in the epoch of the French Revolution when the ideal of *fraternité* would become so widespread, and the reality of troglodytes so far from consciousness. As it happens, Caliban is both a troglodyte and a cannibal: he is confined to a cave and his name is an anagram for cannibal. And although he has no brother, he nevertheless figures prominently in Shakespeare's last great brother drama, *The Tem-*

pest, where his function, like Cain's, is once again to disturb visions of community and harmony.

Following in the line of the hard-bitten Cain of the medieval mystery, Caliban is proficient in the habits of harsh response.[27] Prospero describes him as one "who never yields us kind answer." So limited is Caliban's nature that the art of language only results in curses: "You taught me language, and my profit on't / Is, I know how to curse." Indeed, his first words are curses. Although there is no need to insist on a direct connection, nevertheless it is clear that Prospero is invoking some association with Cain when he declares that Caliban was "got by the Devil himself / Upon thy wicked dam" (1.2.321–22). When he is first uncovered by Trinculo, Caliban is thought to be stinking flesh; the two of them together are in turn thought to be a monster and then a devil by the drunken Stephano. Confronted by such unredeemable distortion, Prospero can only call him: "A devil, a born devil on whose nature / Nurture can never stick. . . ." Such a degenerative nature seems linked with the inevitable processes of bodily decay: "And as with age his body uglier grows / So his mind cankers" (4.1.188–90).

Caliban elicits none of the horrific associations of Grendel and his dam; like the Cain of the medieval mystery, he is a contained and confined force. In the pageants, Cain is restrained by the larger controlling processes of sacred history; we can endure him because we know his part in the overall scheme is minor and brief. Caliban is restrained not by the unfolding of history (although he does seem to pick up the most stupid habits of his European "betters") but rather by a higher force and a better nature—that of Prospero himself. He is thus primarily a figure for parody and for trivialized comedy. Yet, despite his subordinate role within the hierarchy of human faculties, the very presence of Caliban is enough to call into question the better vision of human community and its possibilities. Just as Gonzalo's vision of an innocent Golden Age is undercut by the wise-cracking cynicism of Sebastian and Antonio, so the marriage masque that Prospero creates for his daughter's wedding (a Renaissance "Prayer for My Daughter") is interrupted by the sudden recrudescence of the all-but-forgotten "beast Caliban and his confederates." The element of earth momentarily intrudes, and the reapers who had joined together with the nymphs in a graceful dance now "heavily vanish." Prospero himself is thrown into a cosmic funk as he is forced to contemplate the silliness of humanity's spiritual aspiration in the face of an infinite universe. The other, Caliban, induces the vision of a far more desolate otherness, that of an alien universe.

Thinking back to *Beowulf* and the larger significance of the rampaging descendants of Cain and the disruption they and the feud bring to the *comitatus*-ideal, the brotherhood of the Teutonic warrior caste, we can ponder the further connections between Caliban's inveterate baseness and the larger theme of brother-dispossession in *The Tempest*. Miranda hears at great length and presumably often how Antonio supplanted the unsuspecting Prospero; in the course of the play, this earlier deposition is replicated when Antonio in his turn urges Sebastian to kill his sleeping brother, the king, Alonso. The presence of Caliban is integral—as abhorred other, as unredeemable darkness, as troglodyte, and as cannibal—to this subversion of the ideal of community implicit in the notions of brotherhood and cosmic harmony. We must understand the larger vision of brotherhood implied in the creation of the other. Usurpation and dispossession for Shakespeare are corollaries to the feud and civil war, and to suggest the threat implied by each he resorts readily to images of conflict and intractability, qualities that Caliban shares with Cain. Furthermore, as the quotation from Chesteron indicates, although the farthest relationship possible may exist between brotherhood and cannibalism, still they do share a relationship. It is no accident that the story of Cain-Abel, showing the loss of the brother, must find its ultimate representation of disorder in cannibalism.

But a strong misgiving sensed in Shakespeare's most visionary work, like a shadow over the mind that is present but not quite acknowledged and rendered conscious and explicit, lifts it to an even greater height. This is the sense his character type, Prospero, conveys that, as *magus*, he oversees a world on the brink of enormous change. *The Tempest* is a "new world" drama in more than one way. To be sure, the idea of a world order is threatened by an unformed upstart, a derelict, an outcast, who resumes his assault and readies his approaches. The greatest works of the English Renaissance, *King Lear*, Spenser's *Mutabilitie Cantos*, and John Donne's *Anniversarie Poems* all capture this sense of impending change. But the cataclysm is so great in imagination because of the larger yet hovering thought that the change is warranted, or, at least, not without its justifiable motives. In a sense, we can say that all brotherhoods are restrictive and endangered, but endangered because they are restrictive. Their restrictiveness, although a sign of their specialness, of their differentiation, is also an indication of their ephemerality. Their fence of distinction becomes like a line drawn in the sand, not so much warding off as inviting oblivion. And this finally must be the retrospective light that the figure of Caliban casts back on the hulking mass of Grendel, and that Shakespeare, with his greater sensitivity to the historical moment, permits us to see and to pursue. Cain as outsider is a perpetual reminder of the continuity of evil, of the ever-present threat to the forces and the forms of civilization. But he is also a sign of the outsider knocking on the gates, looking to get into the warmth, desiring a piece of the action. The issues of Cain and

Abel, and the character of Cain as Sacred Executioner are so compelling because they call attention to the great tensions of order and disorder, including an order that is restrictive and declined and a disorder that may be regenerative. That this theme, so involved with history, should summon us to such judgment is only an indication that this is a calling history imposes upon us daily and ever so more forcefully.

Chapter Three

CAIN AS SACRED EXECUTIONER

CITIZEN CAIN and monstrous Cain constitute two well-known traditions of the Cain-Abel story. Each comes surrounded by a repertoire of common qualities and familiar patterns that will continue to have a part—large and small—in later versions of the theme. But there is another tradition, an unexpected and powerful one, that will have an even more active part in the changes of Cain in the modern world, one that more fully reflects its complexities and problems. This is Cain as Sacred Executioner. The phrase, already utilized in the preceding chapter, is borrowed from Hyam Maccoby's *The Sacred Executioner: Human Sacrifice and the Legacy of Guilt* (for which, see Introduction).[1] The Cain we have in Genesis 4 is perhaps only implicitly a Sacred Executioner, but the Cain that we have come to possess, the one that history and the theme's own potent resources have created for us earns such a designation in a much fuller sense.

That complex and lengthy cultural period that we call the Renaissance was responsible for many new attitudes that were crucial in the formation of the modern West. One such fundamental concept undergoing change was that of time. Even historians of science and economic historians today acknowledge that the concept of time emerged in the Renaissance and was instrumental in shaping a new set of attitudes, attitudes that could be called "proto-industrial." What the Renaissance promoted, and here Rosenberg and Birdzell are right, was a change in attitudes that permitted a "growth-system" conducive to innovation.[2] Essentially what the Renaissance introduced was a changed attitude toward change itself.

The Cain-Abel story seems to fit into and benefit from these new attitudes toward historical change. Although, in its essential elements, expressive as they are of violence and disruption, the Cain-Abel story is not a conservative myth, traditionally, it had lent itself to accounts of degeneration, and this is as true of Citizen Cain as it is of the monster-spawning Cain. But of course in a different epoch, there is no reason why Cain and Abel could not come to stand equally for regeneration. What we will come to witness is a new Citizen Cain, this time not viewed from the perspective of religious "atonement" but rather one willing to live within the contradictions of history, for whom history can only be a cracked mirror, but whose motives and actions are directed toward peace and social order. We are of course alluding to Machiavelli's New Prince, who has the courage to enter into historical change and out of this dynamic and difficult moment to create viable and enduring institutions. It is not so much that the Cain-Abel story is utilized in these accounts, but that its own internal dynamics are in accord with this new historical moment, and themselves undergo reflective alteration because of the changes brought about in other modes of thought. It should be emphasized, however, that such alteration does not occur simply within a generalized frame of thought; it is expressed in such critically pertinent stories as Romulus and Remus, and in Shakespeare's great brother-dramas, where, indeed, the Cain-Abel story is present by name in important instances.[3] The changes in Renaissance thinking not only comply with but actually foster the possibilities for change and innovation contained in the Cain-Abel story.

We must remember that this is not a Faustian or a Promethean theme; in its basic components, the questions it provokes, Cain and Abel is social and, as a consequence, its ways are modulated. If Romulus or Cain is vindicated, it is because each is able to guarantee a rule of law, or place a limit on personal willfulness, in the same way that ritual might be utilized to dispel the envy of the gods against required acts of human violence. The way to historical innovation is validated because these actions, we come to realize, are not dominated by heedlessness but by a serious attempt to satisfy the powers that be. These twin motivations, endemic but submerged in the Cain-Abel story, of violent disruption and yet the assumption of guilt, of action and yet of conscience, are responsible for the appeal of the theme in the Renaissance and, especially, beyond.

THE DEGENERATION OF THE SACRED EXECUTIONER: DANTE AND CIVIL WAR

To invoke Dante at this moment might appear to be something of a regression, since in essence his response to Cain and Abel follows the larger pattern laid down by Augustine. Such reversion might be even more surprising, particularly after the discussion of *Beowulf*, which indeed in an ethos not yet Christian (despite its author's clearly Christian status) anticipates the solutions as well as the difficulties of the pattern of the Sacred Executioner. Nevertheless, there are strong reasons for introducing Dante at this point. Although it is a cliché of Italian and modern cultural criticism to juxtapose Dante and Machiavelli, if Cassirer's work is any indication, such a conjunction can prove to be enormously effective and revealing.[4] For as much as Dante may be looking backward, and indeed his *mythos* is conservative, he was responding precociously to developments that would only gain force in the modern world. For instance, his Ulysses is a potent presentation because, in that figure, Dante anticipated the energetic expansionism of Western man—indeed the occidental expansion. And if his superior creation has created problems for later criticism, it is

only because Dante's own evaluation of his character was superseded by
the events that he anticipated. And as Ulysses' cohort in Hell is Guido da
Montefeltro, who by his own admission was more of the fox than the lion,
we can see that some of the code words of the Machiavellian Prince were
not unknown to Dante—indeed they are Ciceronian and classical.

But there are other, more important reasons for linking the two. Max
Weber is certainly correct in his argument, made in "Politics as a Vocation," that both politics and religion preside over and represent two methods of response to the same event: a "dark event," the foundation sacrifice. Dante and Machiavelli, two Florentines of the early and High
Renaissance, are among the purest instances of the religious and the
political.

Like Augustine, Dante was not unaware of the meaning of foundation
sacrifice; as we have said, he simply came to deplore it. The consequences
of civil war were such that Dante came to realize that society required for
its peaceful functioning not a foundation myth based upon blood sacrifice
but rather a divinely ordered myth based on justice and charity. If the
Sacred Executioner was to put an end to accelerating violence and to undifferentiation, Dante found that, contrary to expectations, those were the
very products of civil war, and that civil war has its own foundations in a
modern ritual sacrifice. The Buondelmonte murder, the origin of then
contemporary Florentine history, is purposefully described by Dante as
such a sacrifice, an act of propitiation to the God of War, which instead of
being regenerative turned out to have the opposite effect. Civil war, its
causes and its consequences, is the basic reality that Dante must encounter, and in so doing he explores the deepest recesses and specific realities of Citizen Cain, and even of his later reformed version, the Sacred
Executioner.

Dante, although depending upon Augustine in many ways, and particularly, as we shall see, on the Fifteenth Book of the *City of God*, carries no
built-in opposition to the city. Even in the *Paradiso*, in the celebrated
encounter with Charles Martel, Dante takes as a basic assumption, one not
requiring proof, that life would be worse if humankind did not live in
cities (8.115–17). And even in the Earthly Paradise, Dante is promised he
will only be a "silvano" (or "forester") for a short period of time: his true
destination is to arrive at that city and be a citizen in that city where
"Christ is a Roman" (*Purgatorio*, 32.100–102). Accordingly, we should
not be surprised that Dante's Cain is not a Citizen Cain, but rather a monstrous one who is the more monstrous because he is so real. History itself
has bred its own flavor of monstrosity. Like *Beowulf*, Dante's *Commedia*
is a poem of civilization: the danger is the feud not the sophisticate (although some deleterious aspects of urbanity certainly infect Dante's bad
counselors). The feud that leads to civil war has a way of unleashing mon-
strosities that are more horrible than are all the monsters. The accelerating

reciprocal violence, the undifferentiation and replication all mean that it is impossible to distinguish rights and wrongs. Where all are guilty, as in Shakespeare's first historical tetralogy, justice itself is the primary casualty. Rather than serving to limit undifferentiation and reciprocal violence, the foundation sacrifice is its sanctioned progenitor, its original cause. For this reason, then, Dante must take current actions back to their sources, the foundation sacrifice, and in the debilities of the source, any conception of a Sacred Executioner must also suffer.

The Cain that we first encounter in *Purgatorio* 14 is a Cain different from others we have known. Although bursting upon the scene in the terraces of envy, he does not fit the conventional epitomes of envy. Rather, as an admonitory example, he enters crying out line 14 from Genesis 4, "Everyone that findeth me shall slay me" ("Anciderrami qualunque m'apprende"; l.133). Although he arrives as a lightning bolt and departs amid a detonating report of thunder, he is an awful, a terrible, but not a monstrous Cain—such as we will witness in the lower Inferno. In fact, Cain makes his appearance there not simply as the prototype of the first murderer, the killer of his brother, but as the representation of the fuller social consequences of that and of similar actions in history. That is, he is so terrible because he must continue to live as the first victim of the personal terror brought about by the atmosphere of reciprocal violence, the vendetta, that he helped introduce. His context is decidedly historical, since he comes following Guido del Duca's heartrending account of the degradation of his native Romagna. A cursed land is followed by the first cursed criminal, who is the titular head of the deterioriation that the Romagna has come to know. Hence Cain is presented not as the epitome of envy, but rather as the initiator of violence who turns out to be its natural and retributive victim, living in dread of retaliation. This is a picture of Cain the terrorized, not Cain the terrible. And this is his legacy—and that of envy in its larger social implications—to the ravaged Romagna.

In the Caina, the first section of the Cocytus, we encounter a fuller picture of the consequences of civil war, and its terrible, unrelenting divisions. Another disastrous effect of civil war is undifferentiation, whereby antagonists—victors and victims—come to resemble one another. This results in another significant alteration in the Cain-Abel story. Within the experience of civil war, or its more primitive antecedent, the feud, the Cain-Abel theme loses its polarities. Everyone comes to be contaminated by the spreading guilt of reciprocal violence. The more pernicious effect, of course, is that no one can speak for justice (which is why one of Dante's persistent questions concerns the presence of any just people amid the ruins of the divided city). So it is then that in the Caina, that initiatory and determining stage in the downward and degenerative processes of Cocytus, the true gateway to Hell, the brothers are victim-culprits, so bound together by mutual animosity as to be practically indistinguishable. The brothers are so constricted because, like Cain and Abel, they are from the same womb, "d'un corpo usciro." But there is more than poignancy at brotherly division here in the lower Inferno. The Alberti brothers are actually locked together in a ferocity that mimics their earlier and pacific unity as innocent children. The very structure of brotherhood makes up a situation of doubleness and hence of reciprocity. In the cruel intensity of Cocytus' infernal punishment, they are perversely compacted. The very links that should have bound them together in an ideal of brotherhood are here reinforced with a terrible vengeance, that of undifferentiation. If the feud is the opposite of reciprocity, then undifferentiation is the travesty of communion. The brothers reflect the political divisions of the time: one, Napoleone, was a Ghibelline and the other, Alessandro, was a Guelph. The division was exacerbated by the arbitrariness of parental preference: to Napoleone, their father left only the *decimas,* or tenth of the patrimony. The brothers literally killed each other, and the feud continued when Alberto, the son of Alessandro, killed Orso, the son of Napoleone.

Ever since my essay, "Ulysses' Brother: The Cain-Abel Theme in Dante's *Commedia,*" I have belabored the significance of the changes that Dante brings to the Cain-Abel story. What the feud and civil war, or, rather, Dante's explorations of their consequences, have done is to convert the differentiated Cain-Abel into the larger motif of *frères ennemis.* By means of the processes of civil war, there is little possiblility of differentiating one brother from the other. But, Dante feels, this is the inevitable logic of Citizen Cain. In a startling transformation, Cain, rather than representing the limited but genuine values of the earthly city, now becomes a monster; Citizen Cain has been transformed into his own monstrous progeny. Indeed, as we shall have occasion to reiterate, when history becomes a nightmare, then Cain is a monster, both presiding over and reflecting the consequence of undifferentiation. When the antagonists of Cain have become his counterparts and not his opposites, this means that the values of Abel have been lost to the city. Different from *Beowulf,* however, this does not mean that the values of Abel have been lost completely, that Abel is not germane. Rather, his agents have become those rare instances of single just men and women—dear to Milton as well as to Dante—who stand in isolation against the overwhelming and preponderant deterioration of their times. Historically, the values of Abel have been banished from the city, and the only alternative left to any Abelite figure is separation, the time-honored condition of pilgrimage. From the depths of his own personal experience, Dante transforms exile into the purposive and positive religious experience of pilgrimage. This means of course that (as we have already witnessed in Philo's thought and in Hebrews) earthly citizenship is no longer viable; it becomes the debased alternative to genuine belonging in the City of God, the intermediary stage to which is real viability, or pilgrimage.

Through his spokesman, Marco Lombardo, in *Purgatorio* 16 Dante argues that the disintegration of moral polarities—the very possibility of justice itself—is the direct product of the larger confusion of Church and Empire. The encroachment of the one upon the legitimate powers of the other has meant for each a loss of its purpose, the larger undifferentiation. Although this means ideally that disaster, historically caused, is not necessary, realistically the patterns of events indicate that it has become typical and preponderant. If disaster does make historians of us all, this reality drives Dante back to seek out the origins of his own and his city's debacle. When Dante turns to the original event of modern Florentine history, he finds a murder—the Buondelmonte murder of 1215—that he deliberately casts as a blood sacrifice. Although Dante had clear conceptions of the real and theoretical possibilities of a just society, the tenure of such a society is all too brief. It stands exposed not only to historical change and human malfeasance, but also to its own blood beginnings, which await their moments of opportunity to spring and reassert their primitive sway. This means that the city does not do, cannot do, what it was intended to do. Founded to preserve humankind from the brutalities of existence, it does exactly the opposite, unleashing them on an unsuspecting and vulnerable society in a more horrid and monstrous way. If the ultimate contest of the story of Cain is with blood origins, with the capacity to overcome those origins, violent though they may be, and thus elude the closing grip of history, then Dante sees little possibility for regeneration. Rather, like Augustine, he sees the city trapped in the divisions of its origins, and such original sin always manages to reassert itself.

Cacciaguida's historical chronicle of the happier more primitive days of the Florentine commune leads up to the former grandeur of the Amidei family, one of whose daughters was jilted by Buondelmonte and who then retaliated by murdering the young man as he rode in a carriage to church. The civil war that follows destroyed the Amidei family. And for the Buondelmonti, who were latecomers to the city, it would have been better had they been thrown into the Ema river, rather than be actors in such fateful events. The *but* or *ma* of the concluding tercet is forceful, like a vast historical sigh at what was not to be:

> Ma conveníesi a quella pietra scema
> che guarda il ponte che Fiorenza fesse
> vittima nella sua pace postrema.

(But it was needful that to the wasted stone which guards the bridge
Florence should offer a victim in her last days of peace.)
(*Paradiso*, 16.145–47)[5]

The wasted stone was the statue of Mars that stood at the entrance of the Ponte Vecchio. Here, Buondelmonte's carriage was assaulted on Easter

Sunday. The feast of the Resurrection following the sacrifice of Christ stands in ironic contrast to the consequences of the Buondelmonte murder. What Dante has done in this tercet is to call attention to two different versions of blood sacrifice, the one of the earthly, the other of the heavenly city.

It is for this reason that I wish to concentrate on Dante's description of the original event, the origin of Florence's troubles: the murder of Buondelmonte and the origins of the civil war that can be traced to the division of the feuding families. The tercet in which Dante describes this event is in itself among the most powerful in the entire *Commedia*—this by virtue of its compact poetic density and its radiating scope of reference; the murder of Buondelmonte on Easter Sunday 1215 is described in terms of a foundation sacrifice that yielded far from beneficent effects. This description brings Dante to other, far more profounder interpretations of the divided city.

René Girard has written compellingly in *La Violence et le sacré* of the sacrifical murder as a kind of self-regulating device whereby society stabilizes and maintains itself. The scapegoat absorbs the blows of society, bundles them up and carries them away with him. The net effect of this process of "unanimous victimage" is the prevention of precisely that kind of process of accelerating reciprocal violence and undifferentiation that the feud and its heir, the civil war, seem to engender. Hence the importance of this primitive "dark event" at the origin of what was for Dante modern Florentine history. It was to put a halt to the wheeling exchange of violence that foundation sacrifice was established. This may have been in Mosca dei Lamberti's mind when he uttered the pernicious advice that became so notorious, "Capo ha cosa fatta" (What's done is done), and thus persuaded the Amidei not merely to hurt the offending Buondelmonte but to kill him (*Inferno*, 28.107). Mosca is rightly punished in Hell for this bad counsel. His advice was nefarious because it did not put an end to hostilities, but rather initiated the extraordinary long and bloody cycle of hostilities, of attack and counterattack, that came to typify proceedings of Guelphs and Ghibellines and subsequently the replication of these procedures in the antagonisms of White and Black Guelphs. This advice was the "mal seme," the bad seed for the Tuscan people: its tendency was to proliferate and reproduce its own repeated chain of likenesses. The advice brought its own power of retributive replication, as Dante was inspired to remind Mosca: "la morte di tua schiatta," the death of his own line. What is produced is a kind of retaliatory ferocity, of the same kind with which Farinata is able to respond to Dante, reminding him of how difficult he will find it to return to Florence. The end result of this original sacrificial act is the kind of accelerating reciprocal violence, marked by indistinguishability and undifferentiation, as aggressors become victims and are obliged to undergo the pain to which they had put their erstwhile opponents. The replicative mirror effect of these actions is indeed maddening, and their greatest victim, particularly of the self-justifying mutual recriminations, is justice.

In the same way that the strife between Whites and Blacks is not the beginning, so it is not the end. There is a worse horror, a more infernal product of the processes of undifferentiation: degradation, a downward cycle of pejoration resulting finally in a terrible reversal. Here I would like to refer to Walter Burkert's *Homo necans*, man the hunter.[6]

In Burkert's theory, the practices surrounding the hunt—hunting, killing, distributing, pleading, propitiating, cleansing—all were related to and in some way the dim ancestor of the foundation sacrifice. Both Girard and Burkert—whose respective works appeared coincidentally in 1972—recognize at the heart of society a "dark event" that is violent, and each recognizes this dark event as somehow necessary to existence and even social life.[7] Each acknowledges, consequently, a tragic basis to existence.

Dante turns things around. The foundation sacrifice does not result in the organized prevention of cycles of recurrent violence. This is not to be seen as a violation of Girard's theory, only the recognition that his schema of ritual origins undergoes elaboration in history, as he himself argues.[8] Similarly, the rites of *Homo necans* do not precede ritual sacrifice, rather, in Dante's experience of history, they follow it. The end product of the sacrificial victimization of Buondelmonte was Fulcier da' Calboli, the hunter of the remaining White Guelphs in Florence.

This description occurs in the canto of the *Purgatorio* (14) parallel to that of Cacciaguida in the *Paradiso*. Another father figure of an earlier generation laments the mutability and decline that have afflicted his region, in this case, the Romagna. Guido del Duca, like Cacciaguida, rehearses the litany of names that were once great and are now obscured; he too bemoans the process of bastardization that has taken place. Most families are better off who do not seek to reproduce themselves in such degenerate times.

Dante begins this encounter by having Guido del Duca describe the flow of the Arno to the sea as a process of bestial deformation: the inhabitants along the river's course in turn pejorate from pigs, to dogs, to wolves, to foxes (ll. 29–57). The foxes are, as we shall see, the Pisans, and the wolves are the Florentines. In this capacity, they are of course far from innocent, and that is one of the consequences of the long-lasting civil war: a general distribution of guilt. But even Dante must express his horror when the triumphant Blacks in effect hire a professional soldier, Fulcier da' Calboli, to be their willing instrument of extirpation. Guido forsees the arrival of Fulcier, the "cacciator di quei lupi. . . ." ("the hunter of those wolves"; ll. 58–66). In 1303, Fulcier assumed the post of *podesta* of

Florence—a post he was to reassume in other towns of central Italy in the course of his rather long and evidently prosperous career. He hunted down the families of the Whites and brutally killed them (Dante, in fact, regards him as a hireling, a bounty hunter who is reimbursed for his activities by being extraordinarily reappointed to a second semester as *podesta* beyond the usual single term of six months). The entire episode reeks of the slaughterhouse, as indeed the victims are described as "antica belva," old cattle ready for market. Calboli as hunter emerges covered with blood. "Sanguinoso esce dalla trista selva" ("Bloody he comes out of the wretched wood"). Dante rightly casts the Buondelmonte murder as the mythic reenactment of an ancient rite, an immolated victim is offered to the mutilated statue of the God of War. But this did not turn out to be a propitiatory rite, rather one that led to more carnage, in fact, the very undifferentiation that the scapegoat sacrifice was intended to avoid. In this process of reversal, monsters are bred. The hunter as butcher emerges from the carnage. *Homo necans* is the result of the original murder. The blood beginnings of existence are not atoned but rather are made all too patent. But there is an even more important reversal. The *città partita* has become the *trista selva*. The city itself has regressed to the savage place that its very foundation was intended to transcend. Its mean streets have become the savage wood, and man has reverted in his nature to being a hunter. Far from representing a refuge from savagery, the city, in its blood sacrifices and carnage, seems dedicated to reproducing the *selva oscura* that Dante first intended to elude. This is why his false start at the poem's beginning must be corrected by another commencement. His regeneration requires that he be brought right up against the thigh of the beast.

Rather than resolving these antagonisms, the closed confines of the city seem to aggravate them. The wall of preservation has become a mechanism for entrapment. The citizens, like rats, gnaw at one another within its confines. Consequently, the ultimate statement of this process of undifferentiation and degradation, the ultimate act of reversal whereby the *città partita* becomes the *trista selva* must be cannibalism. Charles Singleton has urged us to dismiss anthropophagal speculations in *Inferno* 33 as unworthy.[9] But why should they be unworthy? From all that we have learned there is nothing unknown to human conduct in that practice. Even the chimpanzees do it. To acknowledge the anthropophagal implications of the Ugolino epsiode is not to infer that Dante condones such practice, but merely to underscore the extreme processes of undifferentiation, degradation, and reversal that the political vehemence of the time seems to have unleashed.

This Massacre of the Innocents is the nadir of the hopelessness that Hell must finally promote. As in Shakespeare's *Richard III*, nearly a century of civil war has given birth to undifferentiation. No one can speak for justice in the terrible tangle of charge and counteraccusation (as the Ugo-lino-Ruggiero struggle would illustrate). The massacre of the children is an indication of the closing of the future, as a final source of innocence is removed. In his condemnation Dante has recourse to a classical city: Pisa is a "novella Tebe," a new Thebes, which itself was divided by several brother-murders, and, as a consequence, worthy of invocation as a nega-tive ideal by means of which Pisa's own transgressions may be mea-sured. In some ways there is a connection between Thebes—the brother-murder, the divided city—and cannibalism. If we see why the foundation myth of the brother murder is at the origin of the divided city and, for Dante as well as for Augustine, results in the terrible process of undifferen-tiation, we also see it is not only implied but intellectually necessary that this same process should involve cannibalism. The divided city—and this explains Dante's vituperative invocation of Thebes—results not only in undifferentiation but also in reversal, the products of life itself are turned against their roots. Cannibalism is the end of this process, and the true inverse of fraternity, both of which prospects are contained within the Cain-Abel story.

. . .

When Cain makes his distraught appearance in *Purgatorio* 14, he is at-tended by a group of familiars. His entrance takes place on the terrace where envy is purged. Moreover, the central moral question of these can-tos derives its answer *verbatim* from Augustine's Fifteenth Book and from the very section where Cain is introduced to carry the rubric of the earthly city. In this canto, so marked by a sense of civic decline—and fit thus to be correspondent to the central cantos of the other two canticles—Guido del Duca laments his own sin of envy, but then turns to humankind to bemoan a common affliction: "O human kind" he cries out, "why do you set your hearts where needs must be exclusion of partnership?" ("O gente umana, perché poni 'l core là'v'è mestier di consorte divieto?"). In the subsequent canto this question is resumed by Dante and answered (in Au-gustinian language) by Virgil:

> Perché s'appuntano i vostri disiri
>   dove per compagnia parte si scema,
>   invidia move il mantaco à'sospiri.
> Ma se l'amor della spera suprema
>   torcesse in suso il disidiro vostro,
>   non vi sarebbe al petto quella tema;
> ché, per quanti si dice piú lí "nostro"
>   tanto possiede piú di ben ciascuno,
>   e piú di caritade arde in quel chiostro.

(It is because your desires are fixed where the part is lessened by sharing
that envy blows the bellows to your sighs; but if the love of the highest
sphere bent upward your longing, that fear would not be in your breast.
For there, the more they are who say *ours*, the more of good does each
possess and the more of charity burns in that cloister.)

(15.48–57)

The two points for discussion here—the provenance of the passage
from the Fifteenth Book of *The City of God* and the extraordinarily large
social role of envy—are actually connected. In chapter 5 of book 15 Augustine makes the distinctions to which we have already alluded in Chapter 1: unlike Romulus and Remus, Cain and Abel are not motivated by the
same desires, "for Abel was not solicitous to rule in the city which his
brother built."[10] This means, on the other side, that Cain did not kill his
brother out of fear for his own safety or in defense of his own provisions,
but rather "he was moved by the diabolical, envious hatred with which the
evil regard the good, for no other reason than because they are good while
themselves are evil." This is a theological scheme, whereby evil is radical
and by its nature irreducible to further explanation. The passage that follows is the one upon which Dante relies:

> For the possession of goodness is by no means diminished by being shared
> with a partner ("consorte") either permanent or temporarily assigned; on the
> contrary the possession of goodness is increased to the concord and charity
> of each of those who share it. In short, he who is unwilling to share this
> possession cannot have it; and he who is most willing to admit others to a
> share of it will have the greatest abundance to himself. (p. 482)

The fact that Dante has clearly used this remarkable passage from Augustine is less important than is the total context of Cain-Abel, the earthly
city, social discord, and envy that are at the heart of the larger vision that
inclines Dante toward Augustine, and which he finds corroborated by his
personal and public experiences. The earthly city is defined by the actions
of Cain, and his motivation is envy, which is here translated into a problem with enormous social repercussions.

We anticipate here a large change in the meaning and associations of
envy. Harry Stack Sullivan suggests that envy may be "the active realization that one is not good enough."[11] Even though the concept has been
internalized and made dependent upon the subject's sense of his own
worth, it does not conceal the explosive social ingredients of envy: how
precisely does one live with the realization that one is not good enough?
How does society, and the informing mythos of any social structure,
assuage or sublimate such realization? Immediately we sense the larger

social significance not only of envy but of its placement in the Cain-Abel story. Dante's conception of envy goes beyond Sullivan's in that he specifically locates it in a moral philosophy with strong social and ethical connections.

As Marco Lombardo explains in canto 16, it is because the Church and the Empire have lost respect for each other's separate but coordinated function that the vision of any higher ideal has been lost. If the Church, in its institutional being and in its leading representatives, is seen to be striving for the same things as ordinary natural man, then the particular vision of which the Church is guardian will itself be discredited. Moreover, if the Church intervenes and thwarts the power of the Empire, then the secular power devoted to maintaining social order will find itself thwarted. The Church and the Empire have become tangled up, as undifferentiated in their actions and goals as have the political parties of the day, the religious orders, and the individuals, such as the Alberti, who are so ferociously interlocked in the Caina.

Envy exists, Dante means, because the vision of any higher purpose and goal has been discredited. But the particular vehemence with which people strive for the unworthy goals and the particular horrors perpetrated are explained by Dante's sense of humankind possessing an innate, powerful, and undeniable urge to return to God. When this desire is frustrated, the mimetic energy still remains active but misdirected, and the violent reversals of which the lower Inferno bears witness are the result. This is an extraordinarily condensed version of the theology of desire that motivates Dante's thinking. It does explain, however abridged, why envy can be so massively destructive as a social force. In the course of this book only one other thinker will have the same consciousness of the large social potency of envy, and that is Unamuno.

The *Inferno* is meant to depict the Hell that the city can become (in our own day, the power of the American cinema has brought this realization home). In Dante's poem, the Cain-Abel theme, rather than being different from Romulus and Remus, actually enters into the same association with foundation sacrifice that Augustine first suggested. This means that the qualities of Abel are exempted from the *Inferno* and that brothers become as undifferentiated in their new violent attachments as were Romulus and Remus: they become subsumed under the rubric of *frères ennemis* and indeed, in this new format, Cain becomes monstrous. Foundation sacrifice is not only the foundation myth, it becomes the prevailing myth of the earthly city, the primitive act from which the city can never seem to shake free. Committed then to processes of devolution, Citizen Cain can only terminate in cannibalism.

In order to realize his qualities, Abel must escape the confines of the earthly city and find his true nature by means of pilgrimage, by which he hopes to atone for the lost brotherhood of the foundation sacrifice and reconstitute the true brotherhood of the heavenly city. For this reason, brotherhood, so disfigured in the *Inferno*, is recaptured in the *Purgatorio*, the canticle whose dominant mode is fellowship on the way of pilgrimage. But the brotherhood is that of a spiritual brotherhood, a new confraternity that joins together those who have set loose from their native confines. For instance, the sublime meeting with Forese Donati in cantos 23 and 24 (along with canto 8, the most representative cantos of the *Purgatorio*), is informed by the sense of spiritual recognition in the face of physical disfigurement. In fact, the separate locations of the Donati family, forming one of the crucial triptychs of the poem, is an expression of the disintegration of the social world that the *Purgatorio* so poignantly records. Personal destinies divide families and while Piccarda will be a touchstone for Paradise, and Forese will make his way in Purgatory, the wayward and headstrong Corso is hell-bent for destruction, where intimations of his death suggest his own disfigurement, when he will be left "vilmente disfatto." Earthly life is a process of undoing, for which then the brother sacrifice is a fitting metaphor. Amid the damage and the terror, a new calling is issued to a better brotherhood. This means of course that the *Purgatorio* is itself steeped in blood, the blood that is shed and the blood that is generously offered, that is, the discipleship of the blood.

In canto 5, for instance, two violent deaths recall vividly the bloodshed at the death agony. Jacopo del Cassero, wounded in desperate flight, watches his life blood leave him: "e lí vid' io / delle mie vene farsi in terra lago" ("and there I saw a pool growing on the ground from my veins"; 11.83–84). Buonconte da Montefeltro, wounded through the throat, describes his own death flight, "fuggendo a piede e'nsanguinando il piano" ("flying on foot, and bloodying the plain"; 1.99). But this same violent shedding of blood finds its counterpart in the Christian sacrifice. At the gates of Purgatory, the third step of recovery was colored porphyry, "sí fiammeggiante, / come sangue che fuor di vena spiccia" ("so flaming red as blood that spurts from a vein"; 9.102–3). And we can comprehend some of the moral trauma in this process when Provenzan Salvani frees himself from pride and liberates a friend, when begging for ransom money in the square at Siena, he brought himself to tremble in every vein ("si condusse a tremar per ogni vena"; 11.138). The warrant of this blood discipleship is indicated by Forese when he explains to Dante why it is that the souls flock to the tree of abstinence; it is the same desire that led "Cristo lieto" to call out to the Father, "quando ne liberò con la sua vena" ("when he made us free with his blood"; 23.73–75). The *Purgatorio* thus counters the myth of foundation sacrifice so dominant in the *Inferno* with its prevailing mythos of a renewed brotherhood of the spirit joined in pilgrimage and based upon the blood sacrifice of Christ.

As a member of a genuine community, however, Dante never relinquished his hopes for eventual reconstitution of the earthly city itself, and not only any earthly city, but the Florence that he knew and loved as a child and that nurtured and fed his talents and development as a young man. We should bear this in mind when we say that we do not demote the remarkable presentations of brotherhood and fellowship that prevail in the *Purgatorio* by stating that Dante's highest quest is for fatherhood. In fact, brotherhood as such (*fratellanza*) is a phrase only employed once in all of Dante's works, indicating a kind of alliance of arms, and as a consequence an inheritance from the system of loyalties and obligations of the feudal nobility.[12] To be sure, Roman thought gives little expression to brotherhood and this is as it should be if the city itself was founded on fratricide.[13] Virgil indicates as much when he portrays Aeneas, whose association is familial and genealogical, as carrying father and leading son, and when he confirms that the foundation of the line that led to Rome's greatness was dependent upon exclusion, the death of Turnus. Christianity also preserved brotherhood for the monastic orders, and its own controlling myths were genealogical: Father, Son, and Holy Ghost. Christ could have no brother and nowhere does Dante mention his own.

The overarching quest of Dante's poem is for fatherhood, because Dante's heroic energies are directed at reconstituting the fallen and sundered human community. In this enterprise the sustaining figure is the father, primarily because he has the encompassing vision that is able to contain the terrible, rival energies of life and that converts rivals by intellectual justice into complementary forces; that is, he makes brothers into sons. The great plague of Dante's time was that component parts had become adversarial: Church *versus* State, love *versus* knowledge, Franciscan *versus* Dominican, and Guelph *versus* Ghibelline. Opposites had become exclusive rather than mutually defining. Only the father, and not the brother, has the capacity to rise to the level of the higher vision and restore mutuality. In fact, for Dante, and this is essential for our story, brotherhood depends upon fatherhood and would be lost without it. This explains why the central encounter in each of the canticles is with a large father figure, Brunetto Latini (*Inferno*, 15), Guido del Duca-Marco Lombardo (*Purgatorio*, 14–16), and Cacciaguida (*Paradiso*, 15–17).

It would of course be inappropriate here to manufacture another dualism, one of brotherhood *versus* fatherhood. But, subdued though it may be, a kind of tension exists between the two ideals. They are not, after all, twin ideals. It is only in the modern world that brotherhood comes to the front with a conceptual and ideological force quite different from the prior two traditions, that of the blood brotherhood and that of the discipleship of the blood. These two forces themselves actually required the presence of Lord or Savior. The third historical emergence of brotherhood only occurs at the cost of the real or symbolic death of the father.

THE NEW PRINCE AS SACRED EXECUTIONER

In the greatest mutations along the way of the Cain-Abel story, Machiavelli's role is truly revolutionary, despite the fact that he only refers to Cain and Abel in a very minor poem.[14] Machiavelli is so momentous because he turned Augustine's—and Dante's—views upside down, and effected a return to the prior pagan conception, where Romulus—who enjoyed archetypal associations with Cain in Augustine's account—becomes a Sacred Executioner from whose actions many good things accrued to Rome. Machiavelli's horizons are unmistakably historical and political. Where Augustine builds upon two cities, a procedure that almost necessarily demotes the earthly city, Machiavelli limits the horizons of his perspective to humankind in history, to one city. In this sense, his contributions may be said to re-paganize the theme, to de-theologize it. If, in *Beowulf*, Abel is not present to consciousness, in Machiavelli's advice to the prince, the fate of the innocent is all too evident: the unarmed prophet perishes.

If in Machiavelli's thought the foundation crime may in certain circumstances be overcome, that is, if history itself can be transcended, this can only be done within history and not without pain and difficulty. Machiavelli's supreme myths have to deal with necessary conflict and decision. Since he, like almost everyone else before him, accepts as a political fact that only one person can rule or found a state, it is almost necessary that mythical and real brothers are pitted one against the other in the dire dilemma of political power. His vision of power is exclusive, requiring that the brother be discarded—precisely the exigency that Augustine and Dante wished to transcend in their vision of the inclusiveness of charity, where indeed all the losses of life are restored.

Nevertheless, despite these grim, although acceptably harsh conditions, Machiavelli still embraces the Renaissance vision of possibility: some founding figures have emerged and can emerge who have the capacity to enter into historical change and out of its ambiguities and necessities restore human order. The quandary with which Machiavelli confronts the New Prince is far more difficult than that facing Plato's philosopher-king. Machiavelli has brought the traditional dilemma into history, into crucial moments of choice and power. By the very means of actions that are morally ambiguous, if not evil, Machiavelli's Prince must produce institutions that are viable and that contribute to the order and the welfare of the state. We can see why these changes brought about by the most important political philosopher of the modern world not only contribute to future arguments upon which Cain-Abel, as a theme, depends, but also appeal to the deepest energies and resources of the theme. This is primarily so because Machiavelli gives impetus to a closer scrutiny of historical change, to the intricate complexities of human life, and to a realistic assessment of the role of violence in effecting change or development of any sort. One should not imagine that because it is based upon a vision of the world that assumes division and violence, such scrutiny is immoral. Rather, what it seeks to establish are sound bases for evaluating genuine and long-lasting principles of change—change that is regenerative rather than degenerative.

Machiavelli effects this possible rehabilitation of an original act of violence by creating "space" around the event, or a larger forum for discussion and evaluation. Here *space* of course means greater breadth of judgment, but it also implies greater intricateness, even a kind of inextricability between event and consequence. Because means and ends are placed on the same continuum, it is erroneous to state that this is arguing that the end justifies the means. What Machiavelli does is enlarge the domain of what we call the "event." Rather than separating intention, act, and consequence into discrete units, he sees them as part of a larger duration, where indeed they are part of a single unrolling phenomenon. Judgment, then, is not confined to act but must include intention, which, however, might only be retrospectively revealed by later actions. Machiavelli does not look to one act or event but rather to a series that includes intention, event, and further acts. At decisive moments in history, new individuals are called to acts that might be ambiguous, but the meanings of these acts are revealed by later acts that themselves help to reveal intentions, or persistent purposes. The fundamental question that Machiavelli asks is, was the New Prince violent in order to destroy or violent in order to mend? Was he dominated by private ambition or by the common good? In Romulus' case—and this makes Romulus the realistic yet heroic model for the New Prince—it becomes clear that the Roman founder had acted for the common good and not out of private ambition.[15] This is demonstrated by the fact that he immediately organized a Senate, reserving to himself only wartime powers as commander-in-chief of the army and the power to convoke the Senate. He submitted his individual will to the rule of law and the general good, actions that are vindicated by the fact that the institutions that he established continued to exist even in the time of the Republic. Where Augustine would present us with an earthly city that was irretrievably marred in its very foundation, Machiavelli shows us a revolutionary foundation act that may be legitimized.

With this important emphasis on intention; with the creation of space around the event; in fact, with the enlargement of what constitutes the

event to a larger complex of interrelated forces, which are difficult to separate; with the possibility that a "murderer" might even be a hero—a Sacred Executioner who endures evil in order to save the state—we can see
what a contribution Machiavelli has made not only to the political account
of Romulus and Remus, but to its archetypally joined parallel story, that
of Cain and Abel. We can anticipate Conrad's *The Secret Sharer*, where
Leggatt's act—the so-called murder of the surly mate, the act that brands
him as Cain—is inextricably connected to his saving the ship, and where,
moreover, the young captain's appropriation of the vagrant otherness of
Leggatt is instrumental in his own revitalization of the sagging structures
of authority. The pattern of political legitimation provided by the Sacred
Executioner has bold implications for the regeneration of Cain, and points
to a new and potent revolution in attitudes toward change. We further see
what contributions Machiavelli made to the legitimation of new regimes
in the early modern period. Rather than justifying any kind of takeover or
conduct on the part of the New Prince, Machiavelli's main contribution
was in the program of greater scrutiny that he advanced to judge the complex bases of action. If he wrote that the unarmed prophet perishes, he did
not write that the armed butcher triumphs, but that the armed prophet
may be victorious. The problem, as always, seems to be one of distinguishing which is which.

   These political and thematic lessons were not lost on Shakespeare. In
his second tetralogy of English history, Henry Bolingbroke is himself seen
to be Machiavelli's early modern prince, the founder of a new house at a
decisive moment of historical change, a Sacred Executioner who enters
into evil and not only overthrows his monarch but is ultimately responsible for his death. Shakespeare makes clear reference to the blood beginnings at the foundation of a new state when, at the end of *Richard II*, the
already weary usurper, confronted with the corpse of his predecessor, protests that he is full of woe "that blood should sprinkle me to make me
grow."[16] Accusatory blood that blighted the earth it at first drenched is
actually a necessary condition for his growth. Later, in *2 Henry IV*, when
his efforts are redeemed in the good resolutions of his son (who shows his
own respect for law and the submission of individual ambition and caprice
to principles of good government), Henry IV then recognizes that he is
indeed a Sacred Executioner, as well as a *bouc émissaire*. With his death, all
the "soil of the achievement," the necessary and unavoidable acts that
went into the reestablishment of order, will go with him into the earth
(4.5.189–90). He is the original founding prince who enters into the dilemma of historical change, and with good purpose succeeds in renewing
the state. His revolutionary acts in the second tetralogy will be contrasted
with a similar revolution of the Yorkists in the first tetralogy, and by these
contrasts Shakespeare himself will add to the scrutiny of moral purpose
amid historical change.

This line of argument can help us place in sensible relationship the two grand historical tetralogies that occupied so much of Shakespeare's interests in the 1590s. Rather than a single cycle of eight plays, they are instead two interrelated attempts to deal with the same problem, the one that Machiavelli signaled as the most crucial of the early modern period. The essential problem is that of historical change, even revolution, and when and upon what principles original revolutionary acts may or may not be validated. This problem enters fully into the dynamics of the Cain-Abel theme, which will be concerned with scrutinizing with extraordinary care the limits and the possibilities of violence in effecting historical change.

The revolution of the Yorkists, which dominated the actions of the first tetralogy, failed when Richard III became a nemesis turning the principles of his house against his house. This denouement retrospectively exposed the original principles upon which the Yorkists framed their regime to be faulty. Instead of stability, cycles of repeated crime and reciprocal violence emerged. The question that is asked—and that is always being asked in the larger social dimensions of this study—is, who shall put an end to murder, and by what means? This is why the processes of curse, replication, and undifferentiation are so crucial: they indicate that the original actions may not be justified, but instead merely reproduce their own abhorrent likenesses—with a vengeance. The original actions of the House of York could not result in the establishment of any principles of justice. Indeed, there is a strong Marlovian strain in the Yorkist rulers, one that exposes an eagerness to possess the golden round of the kingship, but without any corresponding virtues or principles that would be conducive to good government. In short, their original acts of violence contained no principles—other than self-aggrandizement—for the sake of which such actions could be undertaken. In reality, then, no positive political ethic, nor even any principle of justice, can emerge from within the contents of the first tetralogy: the great deliverer, Henry of Richmond, the future Henry of Tudor or Henry VII, was whisked away from England when a youth, and thus was exempt from the evil that contaminated an entire society.

Providing as it does a program for scrutiny of the complex bases of action in history, the Sacred Executioner and, by extension, Cain-Abel provide devices of legitimation as well as of denunciation. Where the Yorkist actions fail to gain validation, the Lancastrian program arrives at legitimation. In fact, the contrast is intended and precise, thus showing that the two tetralogies are much closer in purpose than has been heretofore thought. The Lancastrian revolution itself begins with a violent disruption, the "dark event" of Richard's deposition, with proliferating revolution, and with the possibility that Prince Hal would become another Richard II, thus providing a mocking replicative curse on Henry's early actions. The curse, so active in the first tetralogy, is present potentially in the second. If Henry fails, then the hold of the historical past is irreversible, and humankind's capacity for resolute but difficult actions effecting change is denied. The primary dramatic question is will Henry and his son, unlike York and his sons, be able to surmount the original sin and evolve stable principles of government, and have they legitimized revolution and historical change?

There is no question that Henry's actions are ambiguous. Although it is true that Richard II misunderstood the bases of power, was emotionally manic in his responses, and was as guilty of abdication as Henry was of usurpation, nevertheless Henry, while submitting in principle to Richard, did return with a show of force that (although technically formed to restore his patrimony) struck at the very heart of Richard's authority. Of even greater ambiguity are Henry's ultimate goals for England. These must all be clarified in the course of his struggle to secure his rule and eventual peace.

In the issues they raise, these plays may be compared with the yet greater series, Aeschylus' *Oresteia*, itself dependent upon two revolutionary acts of violence: one condemned and the other eventually legitimized (in fact, resulting, as does *2 Henry IV*, in the triumph of law itself).[17] Each of the series is bound to explore principles of legitimation. Each addresses the question of replication and undifferentiation and the abiding question of how to act so as not to add to the series of crime and accusation. Clytemnestra's act of killing Agamemnon is not the act to end the previous cycles of reciprocal violence. Contrary to her expectations, she simply adds one more link to the chain of repeated crime, in fact, one that calls forth another act of violence. Her motives themselves are ambiguous: although she claims she is seeking justice for the murder of her daughter, she also needs to protect her relationship with Aegisthus. Subsequent actions do nothing to vindicate her original revolutionary act. She feels no guilt or sorrow, but rather brazenly challenges the compunctious chorus of elders; she dismisses her children; she cannot throw off her attendant bad dreams; and she presides over a land where fear reigns. Retrospectively there is nothing her regime can produce to justify her original intentions and to legitimize her actions. Rather than being separate, her later actions are revealed to be part and parcel of her general unworthiness for rule.

The second and comparable revolutionary act, that of Orestes, has a different motivation, a different psychology, and a different outcome. The urging of Apollo elevates Orestes' motivation. Nevertheless, the event itself is still terrible. But, unlike Clytemnestra, Orestes is overcome by guilt (which of course is different from her experience of fear). As Jacqueline de Romilly has so intelligently argued, the onset of Orestes' anguish marks the beginning of expiation.[18] The very fact of guilt indicates that his first act had not been in defiance of the gods, and that his intentions are still within the frame of a moral order that guilt itself acknowledges. Orestes' actions then are moved to the larger plane of contest between the forces of illumination, hope, and positive change (Apollonian) and the darker chthonic powers of unyielding moral principle. Necessarily by the closest of margins, the progressive forces are triumphant. In fact, their victory serves to establish the rule of law and not to abrogate it.

Henry IV's guilt is then of paramount importance in distinguishing his actions—his revolution—from that of the Yorkists. Unlike them, Bolingbroke does not exult in his triumph over his enemies, but is rather overcome with guilt and nearly spent by his own sense of the burdens and the responsibilities of rule. In addition, his concern for the kind of ruler his son will be shows his overriding solicitude for the fate of his land. This concern with later consequence—that his son be a just ruler—retrospectively clarifies and legitimizes his original intentions. In fact, it reveals the qualities of the original enterprise and shows them to be valid. Despite earlier comparisons with Richard II, Hal does manifest his worthiness—in fact, he is obliged to prove it twice, once by showing his sense of honor on the field of battle and the other by showing his respect for law. Each of these reformations derives from a significant encounter with his father, and in each Hal proves himself by revealing his own sense of the burdened responsibilities of rule. This, as it turns out, is a major point of contrast with the Yorkists.

Out of a revolutionary act, a regime of law has been reestablished. An original act of violence is not necessarily condemned to see its own image repeated in a chain of actions and reactions. In this way, if history itself may be transformed, the ultimate contest is over the possibility of regenerative change. During the Renaissance, Machiavelli and Shakespeare, unlike Augustine and Dante, sought to make their keenest contributions to the problems and needs of their times the formulation and the dramatization of the possibility that some original acts of violence might be legitimized. In this sense, the Sacred Executioner and a regenerate Cain share a mutual and interrelated interest. The Cain-Abel theme, in one of its predominant aspects in the modern world, fits in with a new mode of appraisal and judgment. The central motive is the validation of change itself in contest with the dark forces of history, but perhaps an even greater contribution and meeting point between the two allied interests is the program of scrutiny that they each provide, that is, the search for a realistic basis for analyzing and assessing actions in the extremely complex yet compelling arena of historical change.

The chapter in which Machiavelli justifies Romulus' action is entitled, "How a man must be alone to found a new republic or to reform completely its ancient institutions." The necessary sacrifice of the brother seems to be required by such dire exclusivity. But this sacrifice is a metaphor for the general loss of the other, the divisiveness and changes of life itself. In *1 Henry IV*, the emergence of Hal is actually dependent upon the defeat of Hotspur, his cohort-rival in the contest to determine what qualities are to be representative of the newly developed modern England.

> Two stars keep not their motion in one sphere.
> Nor can one England brook a double reign
> Of Harry Percy and the Prince of Wales.
>
> (5.4.65–67)

Clearly, Hotspur is not qualified to lead the new nation that England was becoming. His honor-bound code is anachronistic, recalling an outmoded chivalric society. He seems single-minded and, as such, incapable of coping, as Hal does, with the multiple and complex levels of new English society. In fact, what Shakespeare has presented in the character and conduct of Hal is not only a figure suited to be king, but, looking far into the future, a glimpse into the protoindustrial mind, one already conditioned to control the energies of existence, and by manifesting such control to master Nature and the conditions of life.

At the end of the nineteenth century, and even earlier, such a triumph had come to be too one-sided, and critics mistakenly came to regret the loss of the energies that Hotspur contributed. This lament is mistaken as far as the histories are concerned, but when it comes to the later tragedies, particularly *Antony and Cleopatra*, a new perspective is introduced. The sacrifice of the other in these historical bouts of dire exclusivity is regarded as too costly. Unlike the histories, the tragedies are not concerned with the virtues of the winners and the reasons for the defeat of the losers, but rather with the defects of the winners and with the qualities of the losers, whose absence detracts from the very achievement of the winners. It appears that the very virtues of the winners disqualify their victory, since they have no basis in fecundity, nor in any conditions for the sake of which actions are undertaken. In this sense, the means that are instrumental to success have become ends in themselves, and any deeper sources of conduct as well as grander goals seem to be avoided.

The conflict of Antony and Octavius must be regarded in the light of this readjusted vision. It would appear that in Shakespeare (and in this he is similar to Dante), the triumph of the Sacred Executioner has bred its own antitype. Lamenting the dire exclusivity to which the contest for rule has brought them, the victorious Caesar uses language similar to that employed by Hal in his conflict with Hotspur: "We could not stall together / In the whole world." The fatal development of the Roman Empire had room for only one ruler. Although recognizing this necessity, Caesar still regrets it:

> But yet let me lament
> That thou, my brother, my competitor

In top of all design, my mate in empire,
Friend and companion in the front of war,
The arm of mine own body, and the heart
Where mine his thoughts did kindle—that our stars,
Unreconciliable, should divide
Our equalness to this.

(5.1.40–48)

This striking repetition involves a revision. The facts of conflict and exclusivity remain the same, but their evaluations alter. We can recognize Octavius' true aptitudes for rule, and yet also be sharply cognizant of the deficiencies of these very qualities when they are obtained at the cost of the virtues that Antony possesses. The organization of world empire seems to have been gained not only at the cost of spontaneity, individual courage and heroism, generosity, and loyalty, but by the more serious loss of the fructifying powers of life that give meaning to conquest and to achievement. The larger question of "to what end?" has been set aside for the purposes of instrumentalism.

The ramifications of this revision for modern versions of the Cain-Abel story are enormous. In *Antony and Cleopatra*, division is still seen to be endemic and necessary, and the other, the mysterious brother, who here represents vital qualities and energies, must once again be sacrificed. But this is not a wholesome encounter; the virtues of the sacrificed brother are not incorporated into a new and rejuvenated calibre of being, which is the larger justification of such sacrifice (be it the Christian sacrifice of the Mass or any of the sacrifices that we shall witness in the accounts of regenerate Cain, where somehow the lost brother is brought back into a greater fullness of being). Such expansion does not occur here but rather a constriction of being. This new and painful division Schiller will address in the work in which he discusses the "idealist" and "realist" types that would come to dominate the nineteenth century. Such division would hold vital resonance for the Cain-Abel story, but with a startling shift. In the modern world, and particularly in the versions of a regenerate Cain and in some of the episodes presented in the chapter, "Cain of Future History," it is Cain who becomes the aspirant quester and Abel the contented domesticated personality—that is, the pagan—but who by virtue of his very acquiescence comes to manage and represent the powers of society. In this context of Abel's demotion and Cain's promotion, we are left to contemplate the casualties of another terrible division, particularly when Abel's social victories seem to be at the cost of the total loss of the essential powers now figured by the dispossessed and uprooted Cain.

PART TWO

Regenerate Cain

Chapter Four

BYRON'S *CAIN* AND ITS
ANTECEDENTS

> Western man has irrevocably been cast out—has cast
> himself out—of a childlike world of enchantment and
> undividedness. Since the days of his exile (or was it with-
> drawal?) he has been wandering the world. Wherever he
> goes he is readily recognized since he bears a burden for
> everyone to see—the burden of selfhood. The ego is at
> once his sign of Cain and his crown of glory.
> —Benjamin Nelson and Charles Trinkaus,
> Introduction to Jacob Burckhardt,
> *The Civilization of the*
> *Renaissance in Italy*

THE POSSIBILITIES for cultural confrontations between Augustine's version of the story and that of Byron are as abundant as they are startling.
The reversal of parts is nearly total. For Augustine, Abel was the quester,
the dissatisfied sojourner upon earth, the militant seeking to transcend the
civilized virtues of the tired pagan world, and the pilgrim longing for the
heavenly city. Cain only desires the goods of the earthly city; he envies
Abel simply because of Abel's spiritual innocence, and he is the prototype
for all those who are committed to violence and murder. His killing of
Abel coats the walls of the earthly city with blood, an original act of violence from which the city can never truly recover. Dante, as well as Augustine, provides vivid realization to this understanding. In Byron's version, Cain becomes the heroic quester, the dissatisfied sojourner. He is the
only character in the drama whose intelligence is probing, who seems to
be a character of consciousness as well as of conscience. If Abel becomes
the representative of a simple and contented domesticity—in effect he has
become paganized—then Cain resumes his former position as wanderer,
but without any monstrousness.

By this turn of the coin, the Cain-Abel theme is suited to serve as master metaphor for another profound and far-reaching cultural shift. Cain,
who had always been the dramatic center, has now become the moral center as well. Abel, who had been physically passive but morally whole and
complete, now is pictured as spiritually passive, succumbing to a kind of

stagnation or inertia, and coincidentally becoming the reigning figure for a civic stolidity that he had formerly avoided. This moral shift is of course in accord with other major cultural changes. In criticism, characters from literary classics who had clearly occupied the dramatic center of a work came to be regarded as occupying the moral center as well. Agonists from within Dante's *Inferno*, such characters from Shakespeare's plays as Richard III, Falstaff, and Shylock, and Milton's Satan are transformed from figures of moral inferiority but dramatic centrality into objects of compassionate understanding and moral significance.

But Byron has done more to his Cain. Clearly a divided, tormented, and questing object of our compassion, Byron's Cain has become a subject of moral significance and a center of value. More than simply making Cain sympathetic, Byron has endowed him with a questioning awareness. The mind endowed with a sense of division, with an awareness of difference, more seriously and more accurately seeks the reason of things. Byron has given the secular mind profundity. More than the domesticated religious mind represented by Abel—who earlier in his passivity had greater understanding than had his brother—Cain is now the character who needs to know "the mystery of [his] being." For this reason he courts Lucifer and comes away dissatisfied. Lucifer can help him no more than can Abel and his contentments. In this sense, however, the new secular mind becomes the more serious mind. If the primary experience of the human condition is that of difference and division, only Cain's awareness, if any, can lead to reintegration.

These forces help determine the pattern of the newly regenerate Cain, a pattern that Byron's verse drama initiates and that other works will follow. The patterns of *The Secret Sharer*, Hermann Hesse's *Demian*, *East of Eden*, and others that envision a regenerate Cain, will present a supremely conscious hero, one who is sharply aware of division and the need for separation, who, by means of violence, rupture, and symbolic slayings, will attempt to restore wholeness.

●   ●   ●

In observing the development of the character of Cain from the medieval mysteries to Byron's metaphysical rebel, we must recall that development is not always continuous.[1] The true heir of that *homo profanus*, the Caym, or Cain of the Corpus Christi plays is probably the subhuman Caliban of *The Tempest*. Better intermediation might be provided by a character like Richard III. Richard is, however, a villain-hero, who, by virtue of his personal skills and powers and the notable weaknesses of those around him, manages to rise to the top, if only briefly. He is not a buffoon and is not marked by coarseness. Although a hell-hound and offspring of Satan, he is not without his charm, which, in the decadent times caused by civil war, is a compound of wit and astonishing effrontery. In the character of Richard III we can say that the devil is given his due. But this also means that in later, grander characters the villain becomes less diabolized and more humanized, and we are offered some glimpses into the moral anguish of the wrong-doer in the type of drama that has come to be called "the tragedy of damnation."[2] Faustus, Claudius, and Macbeth, and also Milton's Satan, come even closer to the later Cain in that they are divided characters who perceive the right, yet seem incapable of willing it. In their dramas, there is little question as to the right course of conduct, yet, despite clear recognitions of their own delinquencies, they all march with eyes wide open toward destruction. Crucial as these characters might be in the aetiology of a regenerate Cain, an important difference, of course, is that in Byron's *Cain* the right itself is in question; what is being contested is the nature of the world. Byron's Cain is not driven to crimes of lust, power, ambition, or even destructive envy; he is rather motivated by just concerns (for instance, he finds the conventions of animal sacrifice repugnant). He addresses his concerns on behalf of a valid moral sensibility.

Shakespeare's last plays depict events that occur after a catastrophe. In an offhand fashion one could say that *The Tempest* begins where the last hopeful prospect of *King Lear* leaves off. In his final romances we witness a reduction in scope of the tremendous Christian drama: the human soul is not stretched to such a vast extent between Heaven and Hell. This reduction in the dynamic of extremes, in fact, the avoidance of radical solutions, exerted enormous influence on the fate and fortunes of Cain and Abel. This is another way of saying that in studying the emergence of the new Cain, the Cain of sensibility and questioning moral concern, attention must be paid to the role of the Enlightenment.

In many ways, as we shall see, the Cain-Abel story is not an Enlightenment theme, and yet it had a remarkable history and underwent significant changes in the epoch of the Enlightenment. In several crucial ways, the work that dominates that period as Byron's *Cain* did the nineteenth century was Salomon Gessner's *Der Tod Abels*.[3] Gessner's work, although theologically regular, is a prose-poem of civilization. In critical areas, it establishes major differences between its treatment of the theme and those works that preceded it (as well as many works that followed it). For one, evil is not radical. Cain, although tormented, is given to frequent experiences of reconciliation. There are other sympathetic qualities to Cain. Far from being a chiseler like the medieval Cain, he is genuinely distressed that his barren fields can yield no better material for an offering. He struggles against his own hostile feelings, and undergoes periodic recoveries. It is after one such recovery that the devil Anamalech intervenes to spoil Cain's life with an evil dream. But this source is external to Cain and not part of his nature. Consequently, there is no sense in this work that evil is radical, or that human nature is perverse. What overcomes Cain finally are passion and imagination—qualities that are alien to the true reasonable seriousness of his nature. Evil is not radical but rather a deviation and a disturbance.

If evil is not radical, then division is not permanent. In Gessner's remarkably influential, and, I believe, representative work, the family remains intact. Cain is never actually abandoned. If there is any meaning to the phrase "networking" then this prose-poem gives ample familial evidence of it. Fathers are wise, and sister-wives are loving. The family itself provides a supportive structure of insight and understanding for Cain, whom they know to be under great stress. Everybody is willing to blame themselves and exculpate Cain, or at least all effort is made to avoid exclusion. In fact, in this world where everyone seems to come together, and all dire solutions are avoided, the family itself is marked by unity.

The great contribution of Gessner to the theme is in this total domestication, but a domestication that is coherent and affectionate.[4] Abel has no premonitory, prefigurative attributes; there is no great mystery that he understands. In this he differs from the versions that preceded; but by virtue of the fact that he is not demoted either, he stands quite different from the versions that follow (Joyce, himself reflecting a romantic duality, will later refer to his Shaun-Abel as "dogmesticated"). If the Enlightenment has uprooted radical evil and has shunned division, it has also removed the great dualities from the theme. Every effort is made to bring Cain back into the fold. Thirza, the sister-wife of the dead Abel, cannot bring herself to curse Cain. Later, Cain will overhear her prayer for God's forgiveness for him. Finally, he is not allowed to wander off alone, as Mihala, his sister-wife, accompanies him in his wandering.

The human community makes every effort to avoid isolation, or even specialness. Because there is no willingness to register lasting blame, the mark that Cain receives is not indelible. Everything is recoverable, or at least forgiveable. This also means that in this work, so given to showing the virtues of a common unity, there can be no separate knowledge, no mystery, such as we saw historically in the concept of prefiguration, and such as we shall see revived in the sharp distinction made by romanticism between those who possess special knowledge and those who are subject to the common understanding. Gessner's poetic qualities do not escape the idyllic that he thought to leave behind him when he undertook a more tragic theme. As his recent commentator, John Hibberd, attests, "eighteenth-century sentiment transformed tragedy into a story of natural goodness and divine benevolence" (p. 107). The work strongly weaves together the worldly and the religious in a common sentiment of unity and of affectionate understanding.

In fact, no one seems to possess a higher awareness in *Der Tod Abels*, or it seems that everybody does at different times in regard to everyone else. Cain is, however, extraordinarily sensitive to the special favor that Abel naturally possesses: everything that he does seems to be graced—*Ihm lächelt die ganze Natur*. All Nature seems to smile upon him and return his own engaging smile. Such effortlessness and even openness are attributes of the Abelite character that will inspire later dramas of envy. The contrast between the brothers, although not elevated to the level of universal principle, is nevertheless real. Assisted by an angel, Abel concocts a special potion that saves his father's life, and for this is abundantly blessed. Cain is also blessed (in this world there is never only one blessing; thus it goes beyond the pathetic cry of the excluded Esau) but he has to ask for it. Nothing seems to come to him easily or in abundance. While Abel is *weibisch*, Cain is *rohe*. He cannot bring himself to show tenderness, but that does not mean he does not feel it. Accustomed to a stern world, he is thus stunned and moved when he overhears Tirza praying for his forgiveness. This roughness or sternness of Cain's character, an aspect of the dire consequentiality of the theme, will continue to show itself even in the versions of the regenerate Cain.

The devil Anamalech's vision of the future will provide the starting point for Chapter 11, where it will be discussed in fuller detail. The vision—fabricated and fanciful—shows Cain a future scene wherein his already depressed descendants are ambushed and enslaved by the children of Abel. Such a prospect enrages Cain and finally turns him pitilessly against his brother. But even in the midst of murder, Cain is presented as a person of strong principle. What arouses his fury is not any personal slight but rather the grave injustices perpetrated against his children. Although Gessner chooses to dismiss the prophetic warning that he himself has sounded, history would only confirm the rightness of his serious concerns. In fact, one could say that the great power of the work (and what distinguishes it from those of his contemporaries) emanates largely from this extraordinary vision, one that shows the origins of *l'inégalité qui est parmi nous*, and that takes the drama forever out of its pastoral setting and places it in the midst of the history that was emerging. It is as if Gessner foresaw from within the perspective of his social idyll the events that would put an end to the human family's unity, and cast all future generations into the conflicts of history. Testing the harmony and unity of mankind by its most essential and fundamental challenge, that of the Cain-Abel myth, Gessner finally resolves the story in favor of some ultimate restoration and reconstitution. But in this vision of the future, he has lifted the curtain on a new picture of brotherly division that had been overcome in the vision of harmony and affectionate understanding. Despite the best efforts of the idyllic imagination, the brothers will once again come to stand for polar opposites that, although based differently in society, culture, and temperament, will be as unbridgeable and as hostile as those we witnessed in the theological version of Cain and Abel. In this sense, we can see that the new drama of division and regeneration introduced by Byron and developed by his followers has many elements that differ as profoundly from the culture of the Enlightenment as they do from the theology of Augustine, and that the true backdrop to the theme's history in the course of the nineteenth century might not be the dire versions of the older Christian past but the more modern visions of the Enlightenment. This problem, a formidable one, will involve in some ways not only romanticism but the deepest meanings of modernism.

· · ·

As we note the changes in the character of Cain from the scapegrace of the medieval mysteries, we can see clearly that the eighteenth century—the mind and sensibility of the Enlightenment—specifically by the avoidance of drastic solutions, the unwillingness to radicalize evil, and the effort to keep the human family intact, made distinct contributions to the regeneration of Cain. Neverthless, between Gessner's version and that of Byron great changes occur. We notice that in Gessner's prose-poem Cain is still a subordinate figure, part of a larger process of social reconstitution, whose original lapse and final recovery do not in any major way depend upon him. The evilly inspired dream that throws him into a rage is externally derived, insinuated by the deceiving devil. But also externally derived are the wifely loyalty and the virtues Mihala shows that encourage him to carry on with hope and forbearance. Responsibility has been shifted to external agents. This is not a tragedy of damnation because, with the dissolution of responsibility, Hell itself has declined and tragedy is avoided.[5]

When we come to Byron's version and, following his, to many other postromantic versions in which Cain is a regenerate character, or on the way toward regeneration, if not sin then at least guilt reemerges and the active greatness of the Cain figure lies precisely in his acceptance of responsibility for what has happened.[6] The effect of this is to restore Cain to his true role as the more active, dynamic participant in the theme. Of course, in the dramas of envy, where Cain's anguish comes under scrutiny, there is little sense of regeneration, and in the revolutionary Cains of the future, there is little room for guilt. But in the fuller character that Byron established, Cain is no longer subordinate to a higher process. To be sure, he is the battlefield and the prize of great contending, dualistic forces—God and Lucifer—but his thoughts and his ethical and intellectual responses are the thoughts and responses through which the work has life. To a greater or lesser extent, this statement is true for the larger grouping of nineteenth- and twentieth-century Cains.

All of these versions share some characteristics that may commonly be distinguished from the pattern we establish by means of Gessner's *Der Tod Abels*. First, the Enlightenment looks for explanations that are inclusive, monistic, marked by personal geniality. It seeks to avoid radical separations or conclusions. Its essential model, emphasizing a common human nature and fellowship, is paradigmatic, asserting the importance of the present: peaceful resolution can occur without reference to long-standing historical grudges. In contrast, the period initiated by romanticism developed a broadly historical vision, wherein many of its explanations, as well as its solutions, were frankly associated with violence. Whether we look to the past or to the future, violence is a ready recourse. Baron Georges Cuvier's geological studies insisted that violent cataclysms accounted for changes in the surface of the globe; Darwin's own evolutionary formulae, although gradual, were not pacific; the French Revolution prescribed a violent solution to the problem of social inequality; and Karl Marx set into our language the notions of class conflict and violent revolution. In the twentieth century, despite some alterations, we are probably even more susceptible to explanations by violence. One has only to look at the titles of three works I cite frequently: *Violence and the Sacred*, *Homo Necans*, and *The Sacred Executioner*.

If the Enlightenment favors an integral inclusivity, nineteenth-century thought tends to be dualistic. These great dualities are inherently adversarial. Schiller expressed his admiration for the naive poetic sensibility, but really worked to validate the sentimental (conceptions that will loom large for the relations of Abel and Cain). In fact, if Philo's phrasing of the dualistic powers of the theme could serve as a summary of the classical Christian epoch, then Schiller's equally powerful formulation can serve with similar effectiveness to summarize the great dualities of the nineteenth century. Moving from the aesthetic dualism of the naive and the sentimental, he addresses a more fundamental duality of temperament, that of the "idealist" and the "realist." This shatters any possibility of the "unity of being" so admired in Gessner's work, and which Schiller himself assumes to be one of the major goals of civilization itself. "This brings me to a very remarkable psychological antagonism among men in a century that is civilizing itself; an antagonism that *because it is radical and based on inner mental disposition* [my emphasis] is the cause of an aggravated cleavage among men worse than any fortuitous clash of interests could ever provoke."[7]

Like Philo's, this language, establishing a fundamental duality in human experience, is powerful in its formulation. A deeply rooted temperamental division of character means that the dream of unity can never be achieved. The artist can never please universally, the philosopher can never convince universally, and the practical man can never see his actions approved. By this means is formed "an antithesis that is to blame that no work of the spirit and no action of the heart can decisively satisfy one class without for that very reason bringing upon itself the damning judgment of the other" (p. 176/357–58). The quotation is crucial because it shows the essentially dualistic nature of experience that the nineteenth century will take to be its most insistent purpose to transcend; it would be the basic experience it must always confront, as if division had now become, in contrast to the desires and goals of the sensibility of the Enlightenment, the essential "given" of experience.

These pages from Schiller's classic essay are crucial because they establish the essential axis along which Cain and Abel will come to be divided. It is not so much the actual terms *idealist* and *realist* that are useful, as are the characteristics belonging to each. What remains when you deduct the realist from the fuller aesthetic norm of the naive is "a resigned submission to the necessity (but not the blind necessity) of nature: an accession thus to what is and what must be." From the sentimental "nothing remains (theoretically) but a restless spirit of speculation that presses on to the unconditioned in all its knowledge, and (practically) a moral rigorism that insists upon the unconditioned in the acts of the will" (p. 177/358). To be sure, important presentations of Abel as well as of Cain, will elude these general characteristics, but in the course of the century, and beginning with Byron, it is clear that major developments of Cain and Abel will be along the lines established by Schiller. He communicated the sense of a new and radical division resulting in a startling and decisive typological contrast, with humankind divided between those who accept the limitations of existence (realists) and those who are aspirant and who bring to bear on normal experience the judgment of a moral standard that looks to the way things ought to be, the unconditioned (idealists). But what is frequently ignored in discussion of Schiller's thought is the sense, alluded to above, that this very division is inimical to the interests of a civilization committed to promoting unity in action and thought.

If Enlightenment culture could be blithely superficial, romantic culture assumed that there were hidden depths, profounder meanings, more fundamental concepts. The nineteenth century was divided not only horizontally but vertically between those who were content with surface explanations—positivism—and those who sought explanations that were less tangible. In this last alteration, reason had lost its gaiety and its strength, succumbing at length to self-protective professionalism and an undaring minimalism. The natural outcome of this process would be such unacceptable alternatives as Dr. Jekyll and Mr. Hyde.

All of these changes and conflicts—and each will receive particular exemplifications in the course of the following chapters—entered into and helped account for the new appreciation of the Cain-Abel story and the changed evaluations of the brothers. Historical understanding inclining toward violence; a sense of dominating dualities and divisions; and a discrepancy within mind itself between the special knowledge and the more common understanding—these are the factors that not only suggest the appropriateness of the Cain-Abel theme for a new age but also the changes that the theme itself will undergo.

Perhaps what is more important, looming behind these forces and reinforcing them are the ideals and experiences of an Age of Revolution. In the Christian presentation of the story, the authority of God the father and the justification of Abel went hand in hand. The role of each is integral: that of the sustaining father whose order will eventually make clear the mystery of the sacrifice of the son. The sensibility of the Enlightenment, as represented by Gessner's *Der Tod Abels*, altered many of the components of the drama, but retained the sense of familial integrity. The father maintained his sustaining role in the structure of the family, which was pervaded by a sense of affectionate understanding. The French Revolution, in killing the King, killed off the father, God the father as well as the earthly one.[8] *The Brothers Karamazov*, showing the fullest power of Dostoevsky's remarkable synthetic imagination, summarized this situation. In the absence of fatherhood, brotherhood emerges as an extraordinary ideal, and with brotherhood we witness the emergence of the Cain-Abel story as its dire and shadowy counterpart, one reminding us of other possibilities, such as *la fraternité ou la mort*.

If we return to the much-quoted sentence by Chesterton, (see above) we observe that the role of the Cain-Abel story will continue to present obstacles not only to the ideal of brotherhood but also to the other two parts of the mighty triad, to liberty and equality as well. In the dramas of envy, Salieri will exclaim that all the world is seeking liberty and that he is enslaved. In Wells's *The Time Machine*, equality seems to be a rare and precious achievement amid the extraordinarily vast processes of the universe. But it is mainly the ideal of fraternity with which the Cain-Abel story grows, that it invokes, and that it lives to put to the test. It is the very nature of the test that helps explain the new emergence of Cain as a probing and problematic hero. For the best of reasons he commits the worst of crimes. Violence itself seems to be strangely and paradoxically related to the ideal brotherhood. We can see that this paradox itself marks the special appropriateness of Cain for the poets and writers of an Age of Revolution. And the same problems that attend the outward acts of social regeneration also attend the inward acts of psychic development. They each seem to insist on the need for rebirth, but a rebirth that is traumatic and that cannot be achieved without a virtual or a symbolic slaying.

· · ·

Lord Byron may be credited with having introduced three major changes and having made one crucial addition to the Cain-Abel story, and they in turn have become determining features of the pattern of regenerate Cain.[9]

First, in regard to the death of the Abel figure, the event is presented as either ambiguous or surrounded by extenuating conditions in circumstance or motivation. Neither in Byron's work nor in later versions of the story does Cain deliberately set out to kill his brother. Here, of course, some of the space created by the overarching and influential pattern of the Sacred Executioner is apparent. Second, and this is of the farthest-reaching significance, Byron initiated the progressive demotion of the qualities and the virtues of Abel. At no time prior to this in the history of the story, with only minor exceptions, have the qualities of Abel been discounted. This progressive pejoration of Abel is a radical alteration. But in some sense it does not alter the dualistic structure of the theme (that will be left for the modernists to change). In fact, in the dualistic pattern of nineteenth-century thinking, any movement toward regeneration of Cain almost naturally required the decline of Abel. But there is an even larger change in the personal dynamics: the promotion of Cain and the demotion of Abel take place in the absence of the father. This not only points to a diminution in the role of the parental figure but also suggests a weakening in the very structure of authority itself. This refers us back with added corroboration to the earlier point that the vindication of Abel and the authority of the father are correlative.

Oddly enough, Abel's moral demotion has also saved his life. From being the sacrificial victim, he in turn becomes domesticated, and finally evolves into the self-protective survivor. From victim he is changed in astonishing fashion into the social and public victor; in short, Abel has become the citizen, the realist adequate to the accommodations that society requires, and Cain, in the see-saw biases of the story, becomes victim and quester. This first reversal leads to yet another. Abel's earlier spiritual simplicity, meaning a kind of integrity and an at-oneness, has been changed into simple-mindedness, or unawareness. The quality remains the same, but the evaluation is different, even undergoing a pejoration. This explains why even when Abel is a social survivor he is still demoted: his social promotion is based upon unawareness. If this is the case, then the divided Cain represents consciousness, even higher awareness. In an idyllic world, the conditions of the heart predominate; errors come from disturbances of the fantasy. In a divided world, conditions of the mind or consciousness predominate (what Schiller paradoxically enough called "the sentimental"), and failure comes from an inability to comprehend division and divergences. This is the third new element that Byron has introduced: a vertical division on top of the horizontal one. More and more, we shall witness a widening gap between the smug practical knowledge of the Abels—the realists—and the special, even more profound awareness of the Cains.

But even more important than these changes from within the structure of the theme is the double, the figure that Byron has added. In all of the works of regenerate Cain discussed within this larger section, the double is revealing and determining. It is his presence more than anything else, and all that it indicates, that sets off regenerate Cain from the Cains we encounter in the subsequent chapters, in "Dramas of Envy" and in "Cain of Future History." In the absence of the father, in the presence of the new ideal of brotherhood that must somehow make an accommodation with change, with violent change based upon the foundation sacrifice, the double, for a variety of reasons, emerges as a necessary companion for a regenerate Cain.

Regenerate Cain acts under the aegis of the Sacred Executioner. Consequently, just as Machiavelli conceptually introduced space to the moral issues of political revolution, so the double comes as a highly useful outside force that diffuses the tight and harmful energies of the compact nuclear family. The double may be a beneficent corespondent that introduces some needed space into the nexus of involvement. For this reason it is revealing that the double is necessarily absent in the closed dramas of envy. Although Byron introduced the double to the Cain-Abel story, his Lucifer does not play, as we shall see, a totally beneficent role. In fact, his message, while factual, will be regarded as pernicious. In the later versions of the regenerate Cain, with such examples as Leggatt in regard to the young captain, and Demian in regard to Emil Sinclair, we witness some of the services of the double. In Steinbeck's *East of Eden*, the full energies of the double do not inhere in the character of Lee, but he does play the role of the beneficent outside admonitor who struggles to break up the pattern of inherited guilt. But such differences aside, what the relationship between Lucifer and Byron's Cain does is establish the extraordinarily pertinent dimensions of the double for the Cain-Abel story in the nineteenth and twentieth centuries.

Generally, the double represents an intervention, one that is unwilled, momentous, and fatalistic; moreover, the double promotes a relationship that is self-defining and self-related; that is, it provokes a fundamental confrontation with the self, with one's fate and one's destiny. If the double issues a summons, he also comes in response. In some way, the sense of awe and dread, the impression of desperate fatality, of higher significance might come from the fact of doubleness itself. Ralph Tymms, in his *Doubles in Literary Psychology*, remarks on the "quite irrational and superstitious feeling of awe and mystery evoked by the confrontation of two identical persons."[10] But even when the intruder is not a physical likeness, feelings of awe or of mystery are still invoked. "Why do I quake? / Why should I fear him more than other spirits, / Whom I see daily wave their fiery swords . . . ?" (1.1.82–84). Cain wonders at the first sight of the approaching Lucifer. The reason is that, in Lucifer, Cain acknowledges a soul mate, one who is responsive to his own deepest needs and to the division that he already senses between himself and his family. Lucifer comes in response to a fateful separation that has already occurred. Lucifer is "another" who is "the same," and this kind of "psychic twinship," with all that it entails, promotes awe and mystery.

It is interesting that, although a residue, this sense of mystery undergoes revealing transformations. In the more traditional versions of the story, mystery is part of ultimate revelation, by virtue of which contingent events will be understood in their higher meaning. (Of course, mystery also inheres in the irreducible bases of division and difference.) In the modern versions of regenerate Cain, the force of mystery is contained in the energies of the emergent self, and for this reason the coming of the double is mysterious.

The double is a soul mate but he is also a co-conspirator. In this sense, it is of equal significance that the arrival of the double coincides with the demotion of both the father and Abel—a process that will only be accelerated in the course of the nineteenth century. The father represents an obstacle, a kind of roadblock to the serious validation of the unconscious motivations that are emerging, particularly when the self that is being called out represents a new order of being. He is the *diabolus* to the emergent *daimon*. Only with the assistance of a fellow conspirator can this new force of being come to expression. The double thus evokes this momentousness, bringing his corespondent to the edge of a new historical being. This explains the larger importance of the Sacred Executioner in the pattern of regenerate Cain; at a crucial moment of historical change, movement is being urged not only toward formation of a self but also toward a new order of being, one that differs from the past.

In this sense, of course, the double also replaces the brother. If Abel is to be reduced in value and stature, even to the extent of disappearing as a brother in later works, then the double fills the brotherly function. Curiously enough, he will also meet the same fate. This is why the modern versions of the regenerate Cain insist on *two* slayings: the first, a slaying of the conventional figure(s) (be they Abelites or father figures, and at times both), and the second, of the mysterious self, the other who is similar, but in reality not the same. Now that Abel is discounted, the double becomes the better other, the lost brother who returns to complement the self, but who must himself be sacrificed because the other is not the self. This of course shows that the coming of the double turns the direction of modern, regenerate Cain toward reintegration of the divided resources of the self. While it is clear that this does not happen with Byron's Lucifer—as it turns out, he is not truly a soul mate because he and Cain have discrepant interests—still Byron's work initiates the process of regeneration and, moreover, provides the necessary parts.

But there is an even larger suggestion. The coming of the double, rather, the appropiateness of the double as the brother who must himself be shed, is strong indication, in different circumstances, of the close relationship between Cain and Abel and the foundation sacrifice. In a more approving context, different from the serious historical reality understood and experienced by Dante, the double shows the function of the foundation sacrifice in its nobler sense, its better sense and, in all probability, its truer sense. At a turning point—hence the momentousness as well as the fatalism of the double's arrival—that which is old is mysteriously, strangely put aside, and that which is new is called out and ratified. Another meaning, another value, here in a more psychic sense, is placed upon change itself. The double serves the function of the slain brother, but in these cases (again Byron's Lucifer is not totally compliant) he is not an antagonist, but rather a helpful part of the self, in fact, the better brother, he who promises completeness. In this aspect of the double and a regenerate Cain, the myth of Cain and Abel acquires a new beauty that rivals the Christian paradigm of atonement, and is capable of incorporating into the origins of change and of civilization itself the myth of the lost brother— the essential meaning of the Cain-Abel story in its relation to the foundation sacrifice. In these new circumstances, the foundation sacrifice is a way of not only accepting dire facts of division and change, but also of corroborating and even celebrating change as a valued part of existence. The account of regenerate Cain emerges as a parable for existence, one in which the modern world, modernity itself, *die Neuzeit*, finds its most essential theme.

In Byron's *Cain*, the double arrives in an atmosphere of necessity and yet seems to offer the prospects of freedom. These paradoxical qualities are highly congenial with the dynamics of Cain-Abel. The encounter is secretive, conspiratorial, one in which special knowledge is communicated—knowledge not shared by all, and thus reinforcing the split already referred to between extraordinary knowledge and the common understanding. Cain does not wish to succumb to the stagnation of acquiescence in what is taken to be natural. He continues to possess some vestige of a paradisal need, some aspiration toward freedom and even immortality. Before the arrival of Lucifer, and indeed revealing himself to be a true adept for Lucifer's tutelage, Cain still remembers Eden and lingers around its gates, trying to catch a glimpse of the garden that was his "just inheritance" (1.1.85–87).[11] As Cain yearns for Paradise, so he yearns for immortality, or at least is repulsed by the prospects of mortality. This shows another relevancy of the double for the Cain-Abel story. It brings with it an atmosphere of destiny or mystery, of determinism and dire fatality, while also offering their opposites: freedom, vitality, even immortality itself. The double thus feeds the extraordinarily strong paradoxes of the theme. He, Cain, who abhorred animal sacrifice, was the first murderer; he, Cain, who thirsted for living freedom, added another link to the chain of repeated crime. And beyond that, he who yearned for unity, introduced the first breach to the human community, introduced the opposite of eternal youth and possibility, introduced the heavy weight of history and its consequences. The breach in domestic unity is perpetrated by the only character in the mystery who still possesses the instinct for eternity.

Byron's Lucifer is a double, but a damaging one; as a tutor he is far from beneficent. Yet he has come in response to some of the deepest instincts in Cain and to his situation. From its very start, the play presents a Cain who is divided from his family. In this sense, the division that events will starkly reveal, as well as aggravate, has already occurred. The starting point of the play is in fact disunion. Somewhat like Hamlet standing apart from the conventional familial observances, Cain does not participate in the prayerful devotions with which the play opens. Set apart, he breaks his silence only to utter pained, satirical reactions. But this dissidence is not the product of any debased instinct. If anything, exactly the reverse is true. While those around him have acquiesced to the inertial force of matter, have in effect descended into matter and into the stagnation of unquestioned rituals, Cain persists in asking questions born of serious religious and ethical concerns. Moreover, representing as he does the highest consciousness in the play, he is very mindful of his situation:

> My father is
> Tamed down; my mother has forgot the mind which
> Made her thirst for knowledge at the risk
> Of an eternal curse; my brother is
> A watching shepherd boy, who offers up
> The firstlings of the flock to him who bids
> The earth yield nothing to us without sweat . . .
> > . . . and my Adah—my
> Own and beloved—she, too, understands not
> The mind which overwhelms me . . .

> (1.1.179–89)

In a stunning, revolutionary change, Cain, the rebel-outlaw, the first murderer, has become the spokesman for new values, and this is particularly the case when acceptance of the normative smacks more of unquestioning acquiescence and resignation. Cain is the only person in the play who exhibits critical intelligence and who resists the blood demands of traditional sacrifice.

Lucifer's intervention breaks Cain out of his spiritual isolation and provides him with a soul mate, one who knows and shares his thought. Indeed, Cain's first questionings are rationalistic: Why should he, his siblings, and their descendants bear the consequences of their parents' fall? Why are sorrow and suffering necessary for good to emerge? These thoughts, loftier and more philosophical than those uttered by the medieval Cain, are nevertheless common. Lucifer comes in response to Cain's even higher aspirations; such thoughts, he informs Cain, reflect a more fundamental dissatisfaction. "They are the thoughts of all / Worthy of thought;—'tis your immortal part / Which speaks within you" (1.1.103–5). When Lucifer speaks deprecatingly of God's "tyrannical" isolation and mankind's community of suffering, these are compassionate thoughts that Cain has already entertained ("Thou speak'st to me of things which long have swum / In vision through my thoughts"; 1.1.167–68). The division is a sharp one between the spiritual response that Lucifer seems to offer to Cain's most fervent questionings, and the peaceful, yet unaspirant, domestication of Cain's family. Only with the coming of Lucifer does Cain discover a kindred spirit: ". . . never till / Now met I aught to sympathize with me. / 'Tis well—I rather would consort with spirits" (1.1.189–91). While the double provides communion, a rare experience for Cain, he is also divisive, as all doubles will be, consolidating the breach between Cain and the ordinary world that will forever be left behind him.

Not only are the doubles set apart in their special compact—only Cain will travel with Lucifer on this special ultramundane journey, a remarkable innovation that takes up the substance of Act 2—but the knowledge gained is special, not shared or even appreciated by the others. And although what first drew Lucifer to Cain was the latter's rationalistic questioning, which could be called typical of the *philosophes* of the Enlightenment, the knowledge that Lucifer imparts is the historical knowledge of the nineteenth century. In this fact we see a dimension of Byron's greatness—his acute responsiveness to the most critical happenings of his time. Maurice Mandelbaum, in his *History, Man and Reason*, argues that the paramount belief in the nineteenth century was "that an adequate understanding of the nature of any phenomenon and an adequate assessment of its values are to be gained through considering it in terms of the place which it occupied and the role which it played in a process of development."[12] And one of the first, as well as the greatest, of the newly emergent historical sciences was geology.

But here, of course, Byron's sense of change is far from evolutionary. Perfectly appropriate for the Cain theme, and showing his own sense of rupture and cleavage, Byron's presentation of historical change is violent and cataclysmic. In this he is following Baron Cuvier, whose work he cites in the 1821 Preface to *Cain*. A brief quotation from Cuvier will not only summarize his thesis but, more important, it will suggest the impact that his discovery had on Byron himself. Arguing against gradualism, Cuvier sees "sudden and violent causes" as explaining the changes on the surface of the earth:

> Life, therefore, has often been disturbed on this earth by terrible events. Numberless living beings have been the victims of these catastrophes; some, which inhabited the dry land, have been swallowed by inundations; others, which people the waters, have been laid dry, from the bottom of the sea having suddenly raised; their very races have been extinguished forever, and have left no memorial of their existence than some fragments, which the naturalists can scarcely recognize.[13]

One can discern the almost immediate impact of such lines on Byron: "their very races have been extinguished forever." And indeed, by way of explaining the complete disappearance of the splendid pre-Adamite creatures, Lucifer has recourse to the same sense of violent upheaval. The "intelligent, good, great, and glorious things" were obliterated

> By a most crushing and inexorable
> Destruction and disorder of the elements,
> Which struck a world into chaos, as a chaos
> Subsiding has struck out a world; such things
> Though rare in time, are frequent in eternity . . .
>
> (2.3.80–84)

Cain's journey takes him into "deep time," which was the particular discovery of the geologists of the eighteenth and nineteenth centuries. But this voyage under the guidance of Lucifer is not merely into deep time, it is, as I have indicated, into a particular kind of deep time, one marked by extinction and catastrophe. As it turns out, whether he knew it or not, Byron has taken sides in *Cain* on a particular quarrel in the geology of his day between the "gradualists" and the "catastrophists."[14] Not surprisingly, given his subject matter, his work endorses the views of the catastrophists. But the dimensions of the quarrel are of special interest because they serve to summarize the tensions between the Enlightenment vision of a particular unity to existence (and hence to the Cain theme) and Byron's new and significantly grimmer interpretation. This further shows that within the more modern and secular versions of the theme there exist stark oppositions of temperament.

The gradualists believed that changes in the earth's surfaces were caused by steady erosion, that no sudden, abrupt changes took place. This position rests upon a faith in "uniformitarianism" as to nature's proceedings. Nothing occurs in nature that does not reveal some adherence to regularly proceeding laws. This is fitting the "dignity of Nature and the wisdom of its Author." Nature worked by means of regular laws and cycles; it was in its final reckonings, restorative, with a system of balances that resulted in "timeless steadiness." This is a view that accepts without disquietude the activities of nature. In fact, and the analogy is not far-fetched, temperamentally, it shares the avoidance of dire conclusions that we have already witnessed in Gessner's work, and probably the conciliatory view toward the world that is represented by Cain's family.

As Stephen Jay Gould has argued, this gradualist view of change came to be identified with scientific method and consequently dominated the text-book view of history. But this view of things was based upon a false dichotomy, one that opposed the view of science with a creationist understanding of change. If the scientific method was represented by the gradualists, then all who opposed the gradualists must be opposed to this method, and consequently were suspected of being limited to the Bible and to creationist speculation. Since the catastrophists were opposed to the gradualists, they themselves came under this general dismissal. What this revision of the historical conflict failed to see was that there were some adherents to scientific method, that is, to systematic field observation, who believed that the data of observation supported the catastrophist view of deep time, in short, that one could be drastic and scientific. The catastrophists argued that "occasional paroxysm" had been the predominant mode of change (129). Cooling of the globe is the main explanation for cataclysms. "As the earth cools it contracts. The outer crust solidifies, but the molten interior continues to shrink and 'pull away' from the rigid surface. This contraction creates an instability that becomes more and more severe until the rigid crust cools and collapses upon the shrunken core. The earth's intermittent paroxysms are these geological movements of violent readjustment" (130). This means that abrupt changes have occurred and that these have been violent. Far from supporting a restorative view of the world, the history of the earth's surface indicates the extinction of whole groups of species.

Not confined to religious speculation, the catastrophist view of nature corresponded to the observable data, and, interestingly enough, is supported by later understanding. In order to account for the huge discrepancy of fossil remains between distinct geological levels (in this case the Eocene and Maastricht), Charles Lyell, whose *Principles of Geology* is most representative of the gradualist view, had recourse to the expedient of longer periods of time. If the gradualist view does not conform to the observable data, this is because longer periods of time have intervened between the levels than we suppose. Stephen Jay Gould comments: "Lyell's catastrophist opponents had long advocated an obvious alternative: no huge gap of time separates Maastricht and Eocene beds; rather, a cata-

strophic episode of mass extinction marked the end of secondary times—
and this great dying, rather than an immensity of interpolated time based
on no evidence, explains the discordance of faunas. We now know that the
catastrophists were right. . . . Again and again in the history of geology
after Lyell, we note reasonable hypotheses of catastrophic change rejected
out of hand by a false logic that brands them unscientific in principle" (pp.
175–76).

Byron is a visionary in several ways. He responded to the new geology
in the way that Edmund Spenser and Shakespeare in the Renaissance responded to the new politics and the new cosmology, in the way Dickens
reponded to the new industrialism, in the way H. G. Wells responded to
the new evolution, and in the way James Joyce responded to nuclear fis-
sion: he instantly, intuitively, and dramatically grasped its human meaning. The world is not a place of harmony and peace, of balance, compensa-
tion, and restoration, but rather a place of violence, degeneration, and
even extinction. History may not be a benign process of reason, of dignity,
and of wisdom, but rather one of arbitrariness, division, and conflict. In
dramatizing this view of the world in his *Cain*, Byron, profiting from a
new science, signaled the emergence of a new sensibility.

The catastrophist approach had an interesting corollary. In this view,
there is a direction in the evolution of the species toward more creatures
of greater complexity. "Since life adapts to environment, the harsher
worlds of our cooling environment have engendered more complex creatures better able to cope" (p. 130). If the data of experience lends cre-
dence to a sense of division, then on any evolutionary scale, Cain, who is
instinctively attuned to division, is the more complex character and hence
better able to cope. Byron not only signals a new sensibility, he has
evolved a new typology, a revolutionary one in the scheme of the Cain-
Abel story, and a potent one for the modern world. This sensibility is complex in its evolutionary form, but by virture of its complexity is the only
one capable of comprehending the need for unity. This is why Byron's
Cain stands at the head of, and establishes the pattern for, the later versions of regenerate Cains, be they in *The Secret Sharer*, in Hesse's *Demian*,
in Steinbeck's *East of Eden*, or in other works. In fact, the foil of Cain's
more complex awareness will not be innocence, but a kind of uncomprehending simplicity, an unawareness. The shift in axes is important; from
innocence and its opposite (the latter represented by Cain) to awareness
and its opposite (the latter represented by Abel).

Just as Byron recognized the human applicability of the catastrophist
views (and these views have in some large part met with later twentieth-
century corroboration), so too, he saw and signaled ahead of his time, the
contributions of the great modernist writers who encountered as the essential datum of their experience a world that was dualistic. This was their

starting point. Like them, Byron felt that only this presumption of division could lead to ultimate reintegration. Typically enough, only Cain in Byron's work entertains a vision of unity, since only he is aware of real division.

The second act of the play is a masterstroke, one that prepares us psychologically for the tragic ending. Far from being uplifting, Lucifer's tour of the universe is in fact depressing. "Alas, I seem nothing," is Cain's natural response to Lucifer's tutelage. And this, Lucifer answers, should be the "human sum of knowledge, to know mortal nature's nothingness" (2.2.417–24). Lucifer's contribution is literally alienating and in fact quite different in nature from the kind of wisdom that Cain was seeking. "I thirst for good," he at one point exclaims (2.2.238). And earlier, in pathetic and heartrending innocence he expresses his true need, "Let me but / Be taught the mystery of my being" (1.1.321–22). Throughout, Cain is seeking a more humane knowledge, but the science of his day has little comfort to offer.

For the romantic spirit, the end of the Enlightenment as a program of knowledge was despair at the consequences of knowledge. As Peter Thorslev has aptly phrased it in *Romantic Contraries*, "The Romantics . . . became all too painfully aware: they woke at the dawn of the new age to the realization that they had been robbed—of freedom, and of destiny as well."[15] But in Byron's extreme sensitivity there is something even more perspicacious. He reacted not only against science per se, but against the new science, that of vast historical and astronomical knowledge, and in so doing, established his kinship with Nietzsche, that other figure of remarkably sensitive and accurate premonition. While Wordsworth reacted against the disintegrative character of uniform intellectual analysis, Byron reacted to the terrible prospect of an infinity of worlds in an expanding universe, to the evidence of the catastrophic convulsions of the earth's surface. Byron's link to Nietzsche is a formidable one, and through Nietzsche to the modernist thinkers of the twentieth century. Rather than Wordsworth or Keats or Shelley, the romantic who anticipates modernism is Byron. Yet, oddly enough, he is the romantic most ignored by those who would make modernism into a kind of postromanticism, and who remain within the confines of English literature proper.

Pitched into despair by the prospect of future generations for whose propagation he is responsible and whose fates will be no less dismal, Cain is overwhelmed by the thought that it would be better to kill his infant son than to allow him to be the bearer of such an historical burden. The presence of his sister-wife Adah and the peaceful innocence of the sleeping Enoch prevent Cain from perpetrating a deed that was the product of only a passing fit. But the psychological preparation has been established. Retrospective reductivism and a keen sense of responsibility for future horrors throw Cain into a funk, which the rewarded pieties of Abel only exacerbate.

The fact of Cain's murder of Abel is not ambiguous, but the circumstances both before and after the event are evidence that this Cain is far from a despicable character, that he has mixed with sternness and anger attributes that are high-minded, ethically sound, and even noble. He is a very reluctant participant in the sacrificial offering, lending his presence only after the most persistent urging by his brother. He is offended by the stench of the burned flesh, but more importantly his pride is stung when the Deity prefers Abel's offering to Cain's own forthright and upstanding offer of a free and noble intellect. To be sure, Cain hardly displays what could be called a reverential bearing at the offering. He gives God what can only be called a take-it-or-leave-it proposition. That is, in his character he is such as God has made him, and if he is evil God should then destroy him. Clearly, the scientific determinism of Lucifer's grand tour has possessed his imagination. Nevertheless, his offer is a dignified one, that of a proud mind and spirit who refuses to kneel and who refuses to add to the blood sacrifices of the world. He is asking God to judge matters by the ethical standards of human reason. Rebuffed by God's rejection, Cain—in a brilliant reinterpretation of the biblical account—furiously strikes out at Abel when the latter attempts to block him bodily from desecrating the offending sacrificial altar.

After the event, the dignity and nobility of Cain's character are even more apparent. He is instantly aghast at what he has done. He is horrified that he who expressed outrage at the practice of blood-sacrifice has now himself become the first murderer. Despite the refinement of his sensibility, it is he who has introduced death to human life. Moreover, when the full round of curses is being delivered over him, it is not he who cries that his punishment is more than he can bear. That is the plea of the ever-caring Adah. Nor when he is told that he will receive a mark to spare him from blood-revenge is he content with simply contriving to carry on his existence. His mind is not carnal—in the theological sense; rather, he asks with a gallows determination, "No, let me die" (3.1.500). Like Hamlet's sorrow, Cain's internal grief is greater than any external manifestations could possibly indicate. Despite these indications of guilt and remorse, it would be false to Cain's character to assume that the play moves toward forgiveness. In fact, his character is shown by his refusal of forgiveness, his resolution in guilt.

One of the great legacies of Byron to the subsequent treatments of Cain is precisely in the sternness of his character (already witnessed in the "roughness" of Gessner's Cain). Henchard, in Hardy's *The Mayor of Casterbridge*, is a Cain figure who resolutely maintains that his punishment is not more than he can bear.[16] The novel is significantly subtitled, *A Story of a Man of Character.* And Leggatt, in Conrad's *The Secret Sharer*, swims off to accept a severer exile and penalty than that offered by a court of law. Curiously enough, in many modern instances where Cain is a regenerate character, a portion of his regeneration depends upon the sternness of his character, upon his own resolve in holding to his guilt as well as to his destiny. In fact, they are intertwined.

Cain has begun to think of himself not as a free moral agent, but as a character whose responses and nature are given: "That which I am, I am; I did not seek / For life, nor did I make myself . . ." God's Angel, who sets the mark on Cain's brow, seems to concur: "Stern hast thou been and stubborn from the womb." Cain seems responsive to this mode of thought, thinking that his rebellious nature derives from his early birth: "After the fall too soon was I begotten; / Ere yet my mother's mind subsided from / The Serpent . . ." (3.1.508–10). Byron's *Cain* fully exploits the inner resources of the Cain-Abel story as a tragedy of differentiation. But looking beyond the characters of Cain and Abel, we see that there are larger principles at war in Byron's universe. The differentiation of the brothers—their determinations of character and of response—has a cosmic source in the enmity between God and Lucifer: "the great double Mysteries! the two Principles!" (2.2.404).

And yet, in typical romantic fashion, and reflective of his own more civilized and even more amenable sensibility, Cain has a vision of unity. To Lucifer he expresses his wish, "would there were only one of ye! perchance / An unity of purpose might make union / In elements that seem now jarred in storms" (2.2.377–79). It is Cain who senses the higher divisions in the universe and who also, from his bitterest experience, knows the need for their reconciliation. Later, over the dead body of his brother, he regrets that Abel has died without an heir, an heir that in some future time might have united the two lines, and who, in the composite, might have produced a more temperate breed:

> I
> Have dried the fountain of a gentle race,
> Which might have graced his recent marriage couch,
> And might have tempered this stern blood of mine,
> Uniting with our children Abel's offspring.
>
> (3.1.556–60)

This vision of unity, the transcendence of differentiation, is the property of Cain alone (in this sense he anticipates the character of Japhet in *Heaven and Earth*, another "mystery"). This vision anticipates a new order that Cain can only adumbrate but not fulfill. In this sense, of course, the play is properly subtitled a mystery.[17] Allowance is made for future resolutions for which current evidence merely provides a fragment of the whole. It is, in fact, to such resolutions, to the more complex sheathings of vice and virtue, of tough-mindedness and sympathy, that twentieth-century modernists would aspire in their presentations of the Cain-Abel story.

But that is a greater future prospect. For the romantic Cain, no such atonement, literally *at-onement*, exists. In fact, that he cannot know true atonement is precisely the source of his expiation. That is, he more fully exemplifes and clarifies the nature of his namesake, and becomes a wanderer between two worlds. In fact, in full romantic fashion, his expiation might lie here in this stern adherence to a sense of division that is practically unalleviated.[18]

Chapter Five

THE SECRET SHARER

WHAT GESSNER'S *Der Tod Abels* was to the second half of the eighteenth century (and beyond), Byron's *Cain* was to the nineteenth century: each was a work of some originality, signaling a change in sensibility that in turn helped to spawn generations of followers. Conrad's *The Secret Sharer*, rather than initiating a period of reinterpretation, actually caps a near-century of development (and in this, of course, Conrad remains, pre-modernist).[1] Conrad carries on and develops the patterns and devices of regeneration that Byron introduced to the Cain-Abel story. These are (1) the continued elevation of Cain's character and motivation, and coordinately, and perhaps even more important, the further demotion of Abel; (2) the growing separation between those who adhere to the common level of understanding and the initiates in a special mystery, to which Conrad even adds the special cryptophasic language of twinship; allied to each of these, (3) Conrad's fascinating use of the double as co-conspirator and twin. All told, what Conrad has done is to expand the psychic and moral dimensions of the story, and in so doing he has added another page to the story of Cain as regenerate hero, Cain the Sacred Executioner, who, within the tight limitations of an intense moral drama, actually struggles to restore and revive a diminished social structure. Cain of *The Secret Sharer* continues to participate in a foundation sacrifice.

But in other ways Conrad's and Byron's versions of the story differ. For one, the disruptions in Conrad's story, although clearly matters of life and death, are not treated in as cosmically fundamental a style or design. Leggatt is not an intellectual rebel, a dissident and a disruptive character in a hopelessly divided world. He displays even less dark and savage grandeur than does Byron's Cain. Like Byron's Cain, he is an honorable person, but unlike Byron's Cain, his sternness of character does not show itself in hostility but rather in the severity by which he holds to his own destiny and is willing to accept his guilt. This temperamental roughness is the personal corollary to the essential facts of division and the hard choices that are part of the Cain-Abel story.

Where Byron introduced extenuations of motive, mitigating the act somewhat by its inadvertence, Conrad suggests even greater ambiguity around the event. It is never quite certain that Leggatt actually killed the surly mate (although the strong grip around his neck seems more than circumstantial). Moreover, in assertions that we are bound to accept as factual, his act of violence is actually responsible for saving the ship. That he is not a ruffian by nature is shown by his efforts to avoid further skirmishes. The Cain of *The Secret Sharer* is actually not divided but is a well-defined and integrated personality. Far from being subject to anguish and turmoil, he impresses the captain with his calm demeanor. If he is so well-contained and well-defined the importance of his coming obviously pertains to the young captain (whose name we never learn—an important indication that his personality is still in the process of formation).

Although the stories of regenerate Cain will create space around the event, that is, a moral space that makes room for greater complexities of judgment, the story itself requires a kind of physical closeness. Brothers themselves promote this kind of relationship, and suggest even further the nexus of involvement from which neither will ever be free. The physical setting of life on board a ship reinforces this requirement. Life at sea shows an isolated society, but one that in its very isolation seems to render more intense the gravest issues. Matters are stripped to moral fundamentals. Moreover, the very confinement suggests the unavoidability and even the fatal inexorability of the theme. Despite the moral expansion of the theme in Conrad's hands, the context itself suggests some of the grimmer aspects of the story. And indeed, while holding his ship at the head of the gulf of Siam, the young captain (also narrator) communicates some sense of the sheer momentousness of the journey involved: "In this breathless pause at the threshold of a long passage we seemed to be measuring our fitness for a long and arduous enterprise, the appointed tasks of both our existences to be carried out, far from all human eyes, with only sky and sea for spectators and for judges" (p. 92).[2]

The young captain seems to have had some premonition of the implications of the passage. "I wondered how far I should turn out faithful to that ideal conception of one's own personality every man sets up for himself secretly." That he should have entertained these concerns would have of itself indicated his own complexity. Nevertheless, what he seems to enjoy about life at sea is its absence of complexity, in fact, its very regularity and straightforwardness: "And suddenly I rejoiced in the great security of the sea as compared with the unrest of the land, in my choice of that untempted life presenting no disquieting problems, invested with an elementary moral beauty by the absolute straightforwardness of its appeal and by the singleness of its purpose" (p. 96). This is almost too much: with the coming of Leggatt he will encounter the opposite of every single virtue he thought the sea represented.

We know of course that the coming of the double is as much a response as it is a summons. The young man is called, but there is something in his nature that initiates the calling. If the double is divisive, he is coming in response to an already existent division. While valuing straightforwardness, singleness of purpose, the untempted life, the greater security of the sea, the young captain shows evidence, muted and subtle though it may be, of being not quite reconciled to the life of security that his choice of the sea seems to promise. Not only is he a "stranger to the ship" (including, of course, the crew by virtue of his recent appointment—they had been together for eighteen months), but, more important, he is a stranger to himself ("and if all the truth must be told, I was somewhat of a stranger to myself"; p. 93). That he assumes the anchor watch, where the fateful meeting occurs, is itself regarded as an irregular action for a captain. In short, the coming of Leggatt is not a gratuitous event, but rather in response to some maverick quality in the young captain. But it is more than maverick; it shows a higher responsiveness to the order of things.

From its origins in Genesis, where such fundamental divisions are described, to its role in the drama of Christian salvation history, the Cain-Abel story was invested with a sense of mystery. So, too, the double adds to the mysterious connections and resonances. The meeting takes place far from the scenes of domesticated society, in a kind of no-man's-land—the volume in which *The Secret Sharer* first appeared was called *'Twixt Land and Sea*. In the new, yet old, closed arena of the Cain-Abel story there is more than meets the eye. The evidence of the senses requires greater capacity for interpretation, for understanding. The slightly wayward, even fugitive, instincts of the young captain reveal his inner directions. This is why the double, the changed valuations of the Cain-Abel characters, with the greater emphasis on better awareness, and the sense of a momentous encounter, all come together in a sense of mystery.

The mystery is associated with Leggatt's coming and with the role he plays. The young captain is shocked enough at the apparition of a figure floating alongside his boat to let his cigar drop into the water. The captain's impression after a brief exchange was that Leggatt was about to swim away—"mysterious as he came." "A mysterious communication" establishes itself between the two. The phrase is used again and again. Leggatt later recollects the reassurance he felt in the captain's quiet voice—"as if you had expected me." When preparations are finally made for Leggatt to depart secretly, the young captain begins apologetically, "I won't be there to see you go." And then he resumes, only to cut himself short abruptly, an ellipsis that is rhetorically typical in the work, indicating an unexpressed but deeper understanding. "The rest. . . . I only hope I have understood, too." "You have," Leggatt reassures him, "From first to last" (p. 136).

From first to last. Although the young captain's understanding is not yet complete, his psychic life conveys him in the direction he wishes to go. His final understanding, with all that it implies of more fundamental division and separation, is that Leggatt has had imposed upon him the fate of

Cain. This is not Citizen Cain, nor the Abhorred Other with monstrous progeny, but rather Cain as Sacred Executioner, who performs a violent act that is responsible for the salvation of the state (here the ship of state), but one that brings a terrible sentence and judgment upon himself. Moreover, it is not a doom that he wishes to elude or deny. It is simply one that he does not wish to have pronounced by the common understanding.

In this sense the division between awarenesses is a part of the creation of space around the event, and this creation of space—one can call it ambiguity—is the reason for Leggatt's arrival in the presence of a young captain, who, although unsettled himself and not partner to the responses of "Bless my soul," has nevertheless committed himself to a life of singleness and straightforwardness. There is then a greater meaning to Leggatt's coming, one caught up in the inner reserves and secret resources of the Cain-Abel story. The untempted life of security at sea that the young captain has chosen is essentially a life of undifferentiation. Leggatt's intervention is fatalistic in the sense that he separates the young captain from that undifferentiated and secure life forever. From within an illusory community—in which division had already occurred—a call is issued to break with unity, to venture out into a fundamental confrontation with the self. The double, while offering a partnership of soul, compounds but does not initiate a break that may be unrecognized. Finally, the young captain must sacrifice his saving double. As Dante did to Virgil, he must slay his companion-guide if he is to achieve his true identity. The hard fact of experience is that "the other" although psychically similar, is not "the same," or the self. Momentarily their two lines intersect, but they are obliged to resume their divergent paths.

In this way, *The Secret Sharer* shows its even greater appropriateness for the Cain-Abel story. In Byron's *Cain*, Lucifer is not symbolically slain, even though his message is finally not endorsed. Perhaps because his message is not congenial, he does not become a true double. Although partial soul mate he does not become enough of the better other, the lost brother, to enter sufficiently into a relation of doubleness that would therefore require the second slaying. It is sufficient that his message is regarded as incomplete in the larger quest of Byron's *Cain*. But in *The Secret Sharer*, the dimensions of the foundation sacrifice are more amply fulfilled. A dreadful, even awesome and mysterious, sundering must occur. If the young captain is to achieve his own identity, Cain must assume his traditional role as wanderer, take up his own destiny.

It is categorically impossible to understand *The Secret Sharer* without reference to the Cain-Abel story. This is not only because of crucial explicit allusions to the language of Genesis 4, but because such realization is part of the young captain's own dawning consciousness, and because so many of the exchanges, actions, and emotions are dependent upon the realization. Moreover, the so-called inner reserves of the theme help to explain the movements of Conrad's masterpiece (when he finished it, he is reported to have said, "*The Secret Sharer* . . . is it!"),[3] the separation from the crew, and ultimately the separation from Leggatt, as well as many of the specific concerns of the story itself (for instance, that with language).

There is no question that Leggatt in his calm and resolute and unspectacular way is aware of the role he is meant to fulfill. When he relates to the young captain the events that led to his imprisonment, he indicates that the wife of the captain of the *Sephora*—her presence is an exception to the normal actions of Cain at sea—would have been only too happy to let him escape: "The 'brand of Cain' business, don't you see. That's all right. I was ready enough to go off wandering on the face of the earth—and that was price enough to pay for an Abel of that sort" (p. 107). Later, in the most crucial exchange between Leggatt and the young captain, the fugitive explains why it is necessary for him to leave and why he cannot allow himself to be returned to stand trial:

> "But you don't see me coming back to explain such things to an old fellow in a wig and twelve respectable tradesmen, do you? What can they know whether I am guilty or not—or of what I am guilty, either? That's my affair. What does the Bible say? 'Driven off the face of the earth.' Very well. I am off the face of the earth now. As I came at night so shall I go."
>
> "Impossible" I murmured. "You can't."
>
> "Can't? . . . Not naked like a soul on the Day of Judgment. . . . I shall freeze on to this sleeping-suit. The Last Day is not yet—and . . . you have understood thoroughly. Didn't you?" (pp. 132–33)

Intimations are necessarily obscure, as we shall see, in the allusive, cryptic style surrounding the mystery of Leggatt's nature. The captain recoils from accepting the harsh destiny that Leggatt must accept, but then chastises himself for succumbing to a "mere sham sentiment, a sort of cowardice." The Cain-Abel story enjoins such hard choices, and, particularly in the modern dramas of the regenerate Cain, inspires great resistance. A sentiment that Melville already expressed in *Billy Budd* is echoed in *The Secret Sharer*: there's nothing of a boy's adventure tale in this.

By a gradual process, Leggatt, the already-double, is assimilated into the captain's regimen. In fact, beginning with the moment when he puts on the captain's sleeping-suit, there are some ten references to this role as a double. What is of interest in this establishment of a spiritual twinship is the way it sets the cohorts off against the common understanding of the seamen whose lives adjoin but do not penetrate the closed circle, and the ways this relationship is sealed and insured by the secret language of twinship. After Leggatt recounts the harrowing details of the storm, the death of the first mate and his own imprisonment on that account, the link of communion between the two is tightened in obvious separation from the crew:

> We stood less than a foot from each other. It occurred to me that if old "Bless my soul—you don't say so" were to put his head up the companion and catch sight of us, he would think he was seeing double, or imagine himself come upon a scene of weird witchcraft: the strange captain having a quiet confabulation by the wheel with his own grey ghost . . . (p. 103)

In fact, in his self-imaginings he seems to relish the shock value this "discovery" would provide. "Anyone bold enough" to open his bedroom door "would have been treated to the uncanny sight of a double captain busy talking in whispers to his other self." When the search party from the *Sephora* comes on board, the young captain protects Leggatt, thus sealing their compact and sharing his crime. He senses that he, like Leggatt, would not measure up to the *Sephora*'s captain's requirements for a chief mate.

Beyond the young captain's imaginings of how he and his double would appear to the less knowing, the second point that stands out in this fact of doubleness is their secret communication. Their language is cryptic, punctuated by ellipses, particularly when, in the passage already cited, Leggatt seeks reassurance as to the captain's right understanding. In the perfect understanding and communion of cryptophasic twins, the one does not need to complete his thoughts because the other is so finely tuned that he can complete the interrupted thoughts in his own mind. Their conspiratorial whisper further seals them and their secret knowledge from the rest of the world. Leggatt is finally gratified that the young captain has understood.

> "As long as I know that you understand," he whispered. "But of course you do. It's a great satisfaction to have got somebody to understand. You seem to have been there on purpose." And in the same whisper, as if we two whenever we talked had to say things to each other which were not fit for the world to hear, he added, "it's very wonderful." (p. 132)

Their communication in interrupted sentences and whispers becomes the ultimate in the communion of twins, it becomes aphasic. Finally, no words need be exchanged. Immediately prior to Leggatt's departure, the young captain, in a gesture of protective sympathy—one that will return to save him and his boat—forces Leggatt to accept his hat. This action is inspired by another imagining of the young captain, a fraternal one, as he sees himself in Leggatt's position: "I saw myself wandering barefooted, bareheaded, the sun beating on my dark poll." He has put himself in the place of the outcast, the wanderer, the dark one—like Cain. When Leggatt no longer resists the offered cap, their communication ceases to be verbal: "Our hands met gropingly, lingered united in a steady, motionless clasp for a second. . . . No word was breathed by either of us when they parted" (p. 138). From interrupted speech marked by ellipses, to cryptophasia, and finally to aphasia, the communion of twinship between them is established.

Conrad's Cain is self-possessed, even remarkable for his calm sanity, the clarity with which he weighs alternatives and then accepts his fate. This elevation of Cain was begun by Byron (although some higher motivation was already present in Gessner's Cain). Conrad's Cain even goes beyond Byron's however; there is nothing of turmoil or turbulence in him. This means of course that Abel suffers a corresponding demotion. Rather than simply pious, Abel becomes more and more typified by unawareness, even stupidity. But this very stupidity has within it the seeds of further demotion. In its unawareness it can come to represent a "mindless tenacity," the sheer instinct for survival that typified the station managers in *Heart of Darkness*. As Cain becomes more heroic, Abel moves from simple piety, to unawareness, to a stupidity that is self-protective; but in fulfilling this last-named instinct, the simpler Abel becomes passively evil, in essence, requiring Cain as a scapegoat in order to protect himself. Evil in this sense is ingloriously petty, not radical. Perhaps continuing the de-theologized directions laid down by Gessner, the stories of a regenerate Cain do not partake of any "mystery of iniquity."

The great intellectual divisions of the nineteenth century had much to do with this reversal of roles and the demotion of Abel, a process I refer to as the "conventionalization of the ethical." In this process, Abel moves from simplicity to professionalism, or, as Joyce expressed it in *Finnegans Wake*, he moves from being charming to being chairmanly. Abel becomes associated with positions of authority, while Cain, completing the tandem, represents the figure of the outlaw. Nevertheless, Cain, although violating the ethical, or seeming to—and we must remember the crucial ambiguity here—actually bears witness to an older, more fundamental law and moral principle. He comes to represent the highest consciousness of the age, and this represents a fundamental revolution in the theme. Cain becomes the spiritual adventurer, trying to overcome conventional understanding, to transcend the ethical (as Kierkegaard has required) by means of a higher consciousness, moving toward the religious and the tragic in such a way as not to abrogate the ethical. This, as I have repeated (here in other terms), represents the great suitability of Cain for the modern world.

The philosopher who enunciated this important change in values and characterization was Schopenhauer, who, as Ian Watt informs us, exerted a primary influence on Conrad.[4] In a section called by his translator, "Ethical Reflections," Schopenhauer provides in expository form the specific bases for understanding this extraordinary change in values.[5] "Innocence is in its very nature stupid," he begins one reflection.

> A golden age of innocence, a fools' paradise, is a notion that is stupid and unmeaning, and for that very reason is in no way worthy of respect. The first criminal and murderer, Cain, who acquired a knowledge of guilt, and through guilt acquired a knowledge of virtue by repentance, and so came to understand the meaning of life, is a tragical figure more significant, and almost more respectable, than all the innocent fools in the world put together.

The division between those who understand (the conspiring cohorts) and those who do not, between the irregular and the conventional, but more important, between a divided, struggling consciousness and a kind of simple-mindedness becomes the main duality represented by Cain and Abel. The elevation of the Cain figure into a more significant figure was begun by Byron, but his elevation into a figure even more "respectable," that is, more meritorious and even virtuous, is a product of nineteenth-century German thought, of which our next author, Hesse, is an even more direct heir. This development of course requires greater elaboration than the simple equation of the conventionalized ethical with stupidity. The conventional becomes the domain of the unenterprising bureaucrat whose purpose is not only not to commit an error but not to be perceived as having committed one. This also means that the purview of the law has been altered (and this division within the law itself will obviously enjoy great play in the modern versions of Cain). In the passage quoted above from *The Secret Sharer*, it is clear that Leggatt is making a distinction between the law of the State, which is purely passive and negative, one might say, and the moral law, which requires a more positive (and hence more dangerous) action.

The essential division in the story is completed by the major contrast between the young captain and the older captain of the *Sephora*, who, I submit, embodies the qualities that have resulted in the degeneration of Abel. The conventional law as represented by the older captain is no longer moral or ethical, but is small-minded and mean-spirited as well. During the storm he actually defects. In words that we are obliged to take as record of fact, Leggatt assures the young captain that the older captain (whose correct name we never quite get) never gave the order to set the reefed foresail. Into this vacuum of authority Leggatt moves to take the burden upon himself, and in so doing saves the ship. It is important to note that Conrad specifically absents the structure of authority in this work, which is so devoted to the regeneration of Cain and the intervention of the double, and more important, which is so intent on using Cain to expand a limited moral code. The demotion of Abel in a work where the sustaining patriarchal structure is missing is also part of the pattern.

In *The Secret Sharer*, though, authority is worse than absent. It returns to reassert its preeminence, which means primarily to protect its record. The captain's aim is to deflect attention away from his own panicked ineptitude and to place it on Leggatt. Hence his unstinting emphasis on the event. His own nature cannot permit ambiguity or even recognition toward which the young captain wishes to direct him that Leggatt may indeed have saved the ship. "What do you think of such a thing happening on board your own ship? I've had the *Sephora* for these fifteen years. I am a well-known ship-master" (p. 117). The young captain reflects that this length of service and his "immaculate" command "seemed to have laid him under some pitiless obligation." The captain has created the scapegoat by means of an unconscious instinct for self-protection. He fails to recognize the provocation to which Leggatt responded, the possibility that Leggatt saved the ship and, more difficult to concede, the fact that these events took place as a consequence of his own defection.

What Schopenhauer and Conrad reflect is a genuine moral transvaluation that Byron helped initiate and that is perfectly legitimate. By any discerning higher law Leggatt (and following him the younger captain by contrast with the captain of the *Sephora*) is the more responsible and more virtuous soul. It is indeed a complicated matter, and that is the point of the regenerate Cain under the sign of the Sacred Executioner. Leggatt's role is that of a Sacred Executioner, whose virtue and whose crime—the saving action and the death of the first mate—are so intertwined that it is practically impossible to separate the one from the other. It is to this complicated interrelation that the young captain instinctively responds in his own receptivity to the double, finally now shown to be representative of ambiguity itself, and to which the unformed "Archbold" fails to respond. The more intricate weaving of destiny and circumstance is precisely the complication of understanding that Leggatt has brought with him, and it is the legacy he leaves.

All of this does not mean, of course, that Leggatt poses no risks for the young captain. The double is also divisive, separating the young captain from his ship, compounding the early sentiments of strangeness that he felt in regard to his first command. "Indeed," he confesses at one moment, "I felt more dual than ever." He realizes that "this sort of thing" could not go on for very long. The duality of his existence, the total identification with another self, the secret forms of communication, he sees literally as distractions pointing toward insanity. "I was constantly watching myself, my secret self, as dependent on my actions as my own personality. . . . It was very much like being mad, only it was worse because one was aware of it" (p. 114). The presence of the double, the intense self-consciousness that it provokes, separates the young captain not only from his ship and crew but also from himself, serving to block his instinctive life. And it is here that we approach the inner reserves and the critical ambiguities that make the Cain-Abel story so intriguing and appealing.

The intervention of the double represents a growth into self-consciousness, into awareness, and it is this awareness, prompted by the emergence of Leggatt, that separates the young captain from his shipmates as well as from the older captain of the *Sephora*. Yet, although necessary, this growth into self-consciousness can also jeopardize the fullest functioning of the self; its self-alienation can be an enemy to a reintegration of the divided resources of the personality. For this reason, Leggatt must depart if the captain is to be restored to himself. Alienation from the crew is harmful for a captain on his first command, but alienation from his most instinctive life is far more hazardous. This is the young captain's realization:

> But I was also more seriously affected. There are to a seaman certain words, gestures, that should in given conditions come as naturally as instinctively as the winking of a menaced eye. A certain order should spring on to his lips without thinking; a certain sign should get itself made, so to speak, without reflection. But all unconscious alertness had abandoned me. (p. 126)

We begin to see some of the real dimensions of the Cain-Abel story, the inner resources and psychic dimensions to which I referred at the beginning of this section. In post-Byronic literature the Cain-Abel story emphasizes the growth of awareness. Abel is demoted because in his innocence he lacks the possibility for such development. Part of this awareness is self-awareness. But to a certain extent, this consciousness of self represents a violation of primal innocence, of the sensed at-oneness of the individual with his environment. Hence the suitability of the violence, the sense of rupture, contained in the Cain-Abel story for the depiction of the psychic violence perpetrated when one splits up the primary self; a schism into consciousness has occurred, an act of estrangement from self and from other. This is why the character of Leggatt comes bearing identifications with Cain. As he is the force of social division, so he can also represent psychic division. In postromantic literature, in so far as this intervention of the double represents a growth in consciousness, Cain is a force for regeneration and expansion. But nevertheless, he still bears the marks of history and destiny. His calling is still a severe one. And just as he must accept his destiny, so the young captain must accept his identity. He can only do so by abandoning Leggatt-Cain.

Although the noted compliance of the double with the Cain-Abel theme serves to expand the dimensions of that theme, it is also clear that the alliance with the theme drastically alters the nature of the double. The double might come offering a kind of freedom, a noncommitment that suggests the postponement of choice; this prospect of a free-floating being could be confused with wholeness, with completion. Caught in the grips of the Cain-Abel theme, the double, although at first offering each of these possibilities, ends by being involved in a drama of choice, of identity, of history, and even perhaps, of fatality. If a wholeness is achieved, it is not achieved by immortality, but rather by the recognition of separate destinies and identities, in effect, by mortality itself. The import of the double in the Cain-Abel story is that there is a fate worse than death, and that is to be unformed, to be always other, to be a stranger to one's own life.[6] The danger, intellectual as well as personal, is that ultimate reality be attributed to the double, to that which is derivative, while the original source of the doubling is annulled.

Cain-Abel shows its roots in the foundation sacrifice—and in turn illuminates the meaning of that sacrifice—when it insists that the double himself must be abandoned, thus requiring not one but *two* slayings. This explains Cain-Leggatt's double function. In setting the reefed foresail he saves the *Sephora*, but in so doing he acquires a guilt that will always haunt him, and will always compel his destiny to be that of an eternal wanderer far from civilization. This is why he is a Sacred Executioner. His dutiful and heroic, risk-assuming act has made him a criminal. But then his role shifts. He is even more of a sacrifical figure within the personality of the young captain. The young captain experiences some of the pain of execution, when Leggatt becomes the sacrificed other, the lost brother who must be gone. He is the other half of the twinship, one that has brought illumination, consciousness, the sense of the higher complications of event and circumstance that in some ways have suited a deeper need of his personality—hence the coming of Leggatt. And yet, in order to save himself, to realize his own identity, intimately connected with his own instinctual life, the young captain must kill, as it were, be willing to shed the saving self. To refuse to do so would amount to a refusal of life itself. In this connection with the foundation sacrifice the Cain-Abel story becomes expressive of the conditions of existence. And just as the foundation sacrifice was required to secure the entity of the state, the rule of one, so the sacrifice of the double is needed to move from duality into identity.

This decision to accept separate destinies as well as identities—despite its ultimate acceptance of what the double may at first have come to deny, one's own death—is nevertheless a stirring resolution. Thinking back to the *Purgatorio*, one realizes that in abandoning Virgil, Dante experiences no diminishment of the self, but rather its fuller development. So it is that in *The Secret Sharer*, Leggatt, who needed to be abandoned so that the young captain could achieve his identity, had lowered himself into the water from whence he came, "a free man, a proud swimmer striking out for a new destiny." For his part, the young captain suffers no bereavement as he assumes now for the first time full command of his ship. "Already the ship was drawing ahead. And I was alone with her. Nothing! No one in the world should stand now between us, throwing a shadow on the way of silent knowledge and mute affection, the perfect communion of a seaman with his first command" (p. 143).

What Conrad has effected is a brilliant reinterpretation of the Cain-Abel story. While Byron provided the larger frame for regeneration, Conrad made some highly intriguing personal adjustments. This is seen in the use to which he puts two residual elements of the theme: the sentence placed on Cain and the much-discussed mark. The first murderer has not only become a revolutionary figure, but more importantly the upholder of a more significant moral law. Typical of the stern and complex regenerate Cain, he does not deny his guilt; he simply denies the competency of a court of law made up of twelve respectable townsmen to understand and hence to judge his fate. In so doing, he submits himself to a greater not a lesser moral law, to a greater not a lesser punishment. In fact, the fate he accepts falls under the interpretation of Ambrose: to prolong his life is to increase his punishment. And even more bravely, this modern Cain who assumes the burden of the old wanderer, does so with no special mark to ward off attack. The young captain, himself desperately engaged in trying to rescue his own ship, spares a thought for his erstwhile double: "his other self, now gone from the ship to be hidden forever from all friendly faces, to be a fugitive and a vagabond on the earth, with no brand of the curse on his sane forehead to stay a slaying hand"(p. 142). Cain, our true contemporary, bears no special mark, and this absence, or this unrecognizability, makes the acceptance of his portion all the more heroic. The pattern of the Sacred Executioner has a special relevancy for the Cain-Abel theme in the more modern versions intent on legitimizing Cain. But the difference between Conrad's version and the primitive ritual of blame and banishment is that society does not know that it has a redeemer in its midst. Society is ignorant, or rather, feels it in its interests to ignore the virtues of the executioner who is saving it. Leggatt makes a sacrifice that his society fails to recognize and he assumes a burden of which it is unaware. In the more modern versions of the Cain-Abel theme, and not only in those stories where Cain is a regenerate character, there exists a wide gap between the communal understanding and the agony undergone. The double contributes of course to the mystery of this discrepancy. With fuller understanding and with greater psychological realism than the useful but still schematic ideas of modern cultural anthropology, Conrad lays bare the true workings of the Sacred Executioner in human society.

This is not a story, as was *Heart of Darkness*, marked by an extreme split between unacceptable alternatives—a demonic energy and a depleted apathetic consciousness. By means of his double, the young captain enjoys a reintegration of forces that Byron had first anticipated in his *Cain.*[7] What one might say is that, by moving out and then returning, the young captain has brought the conquest of rebellious psychic energy to his command. Formerly, as we have argued, the Sacred Executioner was utilized for purposes of public legitimation: the state was changed and preserved only by means of the historical burden assumed by the New Prince. The more modern versions of the regenerate Cain seem to promise a kind of psychic renewal. But what *The Secret Sharer* does is bring psychic renewal to the structure of authority. In this sense, it continues to allow for the more public dimensions of the Sacred Executioner. If the ethical has been conventionalized, and the demotion of Abel is associated with the decline in the structure of authority (witness the defection of the captain of the *Sephora*), then the role of the sacrificial Cain would seem to inspire a renewed association of that which is conventional (in this case the captaincy of a ship) with the more enterprising psychic energies. *The Secret Sharer*, with all of its intensely internal aspects, is still a poem of civilization because it tests civilization's capacity to absorb elements that are discordant and complex. In this sense, the aim of the story is to return suppleness to authority. In this, of course, *The Secret Sharer* succeeds brilliantly. It will be left for two "parables" of American culture, *The Caine Mutiny*, with which this section concludes, and *Billy Budd*, a drama of envy described in the next section, to reverse this more fortunate conclusion.

Chapter Six

DEMIAN

IT IS USEFUL to bring together works that participate within a thematic relationship. This "bracketing" creates an inner space within which meaningful energies are exchanged. This motion is both prospective and, what is more interesting, retrospective. *Demian*, as we shall see, obviously fits into the pattern of the Sacred Executioner and benefits from association with Byron's *Cain*, as well as *The Secret Sharer*. But the vision within the bracketed inner space is also retrospective, as matters that have a submerged presence in a work like *The Secret Sharer* surface when confronted by the greater conceptual explicitness of a work like *Demian*.

In *Demian*, for instance, the double may be more explicitly associated with rebellious and fugitive psychic energies, and these energies are more clearly involved with the unconsciously directed quest for selfhood on the part of Emil Sinclair, that is, with his *daimon*. From this perspective, we can see that the coming of Leggatt is more than a casual matter. This is not a case of adding something from one text to another, but rather one of drawing out meanings that are present in *The Secret Sharer* and that simply need to be brought into relief.

Demian helps explain *why* and *when* the double itself must be sacrificed. Eva, Demian's mother (and much more), must mildly correct Emil's expressed satisfaction that in their presence he has finally come home, has finally arrived where he wishes to be. "One never reaches home," she tells him. And then, in a passage that I have already used to explain the need for Leggatt's departure, she has recourse to the imagery of intersecting lines. "But where paths that have affinity for each other intersect the whole world looks like home for a time."[1] The last three words explain that such intersection is temporary.

This leads to another correction, one that is not as mild. Demian, enduring by premonition his own death in World War I, undergoes a kind of catatonic experience. Emil, wishing to interrupt that moment and, as it were, halt that inevitable process, asks if he should go and see how Demian is. The extra significance to the exchange is indicated by the severity of Eva's reproof: "Don't be a little boy, Sinclair!" (p. 158/245) And immediately we return to the young captain's self-rebuke of sham sentiment and cowardice for refusing to allow Leggatt the dignity of his own destiny. We must also recall that even these stories of a secularized, regenerate Cain still carry with them something of the mystery of the necessary unfolding of events that was part of the sacred dramas of Cain in the Christian program of salvation.

We see the "why" of this second slaying explained—although the double is the true brother, he must be sacrificed because this other is not the same as the self. But *Demian* also explains the "when" of this symbolic slaying. It obviously occurs when Emil has fully incorporated his *daimon*, that is, when Demian has become himself. Demian departs when Emil no longer has need of him because he is his own *daimon*. The concluding lines of the story make this clear. At those moments when he is in communion with himself, Emil "need only bend over that dark mirror to behold [his] own image, now completely resembling him, my brother, my leader" (p. 171/257). The last words of course join the Cain-Abel story with the modern drama of psychic regeneration. The divisive double has been restored as brother, but also as master, that is, as the emergent psychic forces that he both marshalls and represents.

This perhaps brings us to the fuller meaning of the symbolic slaying in the drama of the Sacred Executioner, and that is the strong connection of Cain and Abel with foundation sacrifice: those who are slain are not only antagonists, obstructionists, *diaboli*, but are literally those who have paved the way, those who have been most helpful. One is obliged to shed, to discharge, as it were, not the grasping hands of a stultifying communion, those who would drink the blood from the real-life character, but those, like Dante's Virgil, who have been guides and leaders. This of course is in accord with the hard, even harsh, sense of division represented by the Cain-Abel story. At the same time, it reflects the more modern usages, where Cain is a regenerate character, still compelled to face dire realities, but a character of fulfillment and, as a consequence, capable of facing these divisions and sacrifices with resoluteness.

In *Demian*, Hesse places the drama of Cain most appropriately in the climate of full modernism. Its portrayal of the struggle of the young, of the displacement of the father, of the equal estrangement from cohorts, as well as from the past, of the beneficent action of guilt, as well as of the need to transcend guilt, of division as a given of experience, and of the capacity to overcome simple duality by the sensed multiplicity of characteristics complies with many of the characteristics of a young modernism eager to establish itself, not only by means of stylistic change but by a fundamental change in values.

Once again we have the opportunity to note the appropriateness of Stephen Spender's title, *The Struggle of the Modern*. Unquestionably, the modernist hero is a youthful hero, but one who is at considerable risk, indeed one who is entering very dangerous territory. Clavdia Chauchat's exhortation to the awakening modernist spirit of young Hans Castorp in the *Walpurgis Nacht* epsiode of *The Magic Mountain* emphasizes that

they must be "aventuriers dans le mal."[2] Demian, in a lengthy discourse to
Emil Sinclair, explains why, as Cain figures, they fit the coming change in
the mind of Europe: "That is why we are marked—as Cain was—to arouse
fear and hatred and drive men out of more confining idylls into more dangerous reaches" (p. 151/239). Cain as Sacred Executioner is involved in
difficulty and dilemma, exemplifying the hard choices of the political
leader who would introduce change. The regenerate Cain who participates in the pattern of the Sacred Executioner is accompanied by a similar
sense of danger, even direness. It is this very problematic quality that helps
make him a master figure for an age of revolution, where idealism mani-
fests itself in violence, a violence that it is difficult to absolve. This very
potency of the character of Cain also makes him a fitting modernist character, one who by means of separation is introducing a new order, not
necessarily a new political order, but one of consciousness and of values.

In the Cain-Abel story since romanticism, the figure of authority has
been notably absent. The king is dead, God himself is dethroned, and the
structure of authority is badly shaken: into this vacuum of authority Cain
enters as one who is not only searching for values but who is actively seeking to create new values. In *Demian*, the supersession of the father occurs
quite early.[3] In the need to satisfy some urge for notoriety in himself
(which can be explained by, as we shall see, the inherent doubleness that
has possessed his life), Emil fabricates a misdeed for the benefit of his confederates. He is then blackmailed by the loathsome Kromer. Sensing his
world shattered, he returns home and is scolded by his father for having
tracked mud into the house. "If you only knew" is the thought that enters
his head. "A strange new feeling overcame me at this point, a feeling that
stung pleasurably: I felt superior to my father!" The subsequent reflection
in *Demian* emphasizes the necessity of supersession as well as the pain at
the cost, the sensed withholding:

> This moment was the most significant and lasting of the whole experience. It
> was the first rent in the holy image of my father. It was the first fissure in the
> columns that had upheld my childhood, which every individual must destroy
> before he can become himself. . . . Such fissures and rents grow together
> again, heal and are forgotten, but in the most secret recesses they continue to
> live and bleed. (p. 18/115)

Just as in the advancement of Cain some form of violence seems to be
essential, so in Demian's progress, guilt is a curious aid. It first provides
that sense of estrangement and separation that seems crucial to the process
of individuation. Hesse outlines this theory of the essential nature of guilt
in his essay, "A Bit of Theology," where he explains his notion of the
stages of human growth within the broader polarities of two character
types. In this evolutionary schema, an essential step in the separation from

innocent at-oneness is the experience of guilt. "The way leads from innocence into guilt, out of guilt into despair, out of despair either to failure or to deliverance."[4]

At any point the development may be arrested, or the individual may even regress. And this of course is what occurs in *Demian*. The emergent psychic pressure that Demian represents, his inner double that is in truth his developing self, saves Emil from Kromer. But this intervention is external and premature. Rather than moving forward, Sinclair relapses into the world of his family, "back to the light, untroubled world of mother and father, my sisters, the smell of cleanliness and the pieties of Abel" (p. 44/ 140). The unified world of unbroken innocence is associated with Abel, again emphasizing one of the points of this book: that the essential fall is not that of Adam and Eve, perhaps not even that of Cain and Abel, but rather the sense of psychic division that the falling-out of brothers represents and that was inevitably present prior to the actual event. Following his salvation from the hands of Kromer, Emil does attempt to retreat to his former being: "I did not want to sacrifice Abel to glorify Cain, not just now when I had once more become Abel" (p. 45/114). One can immediately perceive that what daunted him was the inevitability of sacrifice if he was to become his own self.

The Cain-Abel story involves not only a duality but also a dialectic. On the psychic seesaw in which they are engaged, the powerfully conflictive brothers involve concepts in opposition. But of course, in order for there to be opposition there must be relationship. This is the broader meaning of Unamuno's formula that "envidia es una forma de parentesco." One can only contrast qualities that are on the same axis. If Abel represents innocence, then Cain, oppositionally, represents guilt. If Cain represents consciousness and selfhood, then Abel represents a kind of communal sentimentality. In fact, the Abelites in *Demian* are fittingly undifferentiated parts of a "herd mentality." This means of course that if Cain as the bearer of new values is separated from the past (and its structure of values), he is also separated from his contemporaries, who represent nothing new but simply the same values in a different age group. Modernism depicts the struggles of the young but it does not adhere to the values of a youth culture.[5] In fact, the youth culture exhibits the same Abelite qualities of the herd mentality, one that fears to be alone, and thus is antithetical to the lonely and dangerous road that Cain explores.

The indulgence of the youth culture is, as Stephen Dedalus discovered, an expression of the nostalgia of the old. Emil recoils from this folly: "I remembered civil servants in my home town, worthy old gentlemen who clung to the memories of their drunken university days as keepsakes from paradise and fashioned a cult of their 'vanished' student years as poets or other romantics fashion their childhood" (p. 142/229). The error and the wish seem to be the presumption of a stage of unity, whereas Emil Sinclair, from the beginning, knows only division. In the passage just quoted we find expressed the great appropriateness of the Cain-Abel story for modernism, whereby theme and movement conjoin to convey a sense of schism and separation from the emotional charges of fusion and communion. And Hesse makes quite explicit that this separation has cultural roots, as the Abelite mentality is associated with romanticizing poets themselves. The originating experience of modernism is division itself. This need for unity, in the dialectic of the Cain-Abel story, is associated with the youth culture that cannot sever itself from the herd mentality. Listening to the music coming from student bars, Emil hears the "methodically rehearsed gaiety of youth," and concludes, "False communion everywhere, everywhere shedding the responsibility of fate, flight to the herd for warmth" (p. 137/225). If the Cain-Abel story then represents dangerous summons—and this is what Lucifer, Leggatt, and Demian represent—it represents a call to disruption, in fact, to what is new. In so doing, it complies with the modernist rejection of "linearity," the methodically rehearsed. It is no accident then that Nietzsche, that prophet and prototype of modernism, is invoked as an heroic model, as "one man who had followed his destiny so relentlessly" (p. 137/225). Demian himself reflects on the herd mentality: "All this false communion—from the fraternities to the choral societies and the nations themselves—was an inevitable development, was a community born of fear and dread. . . ." Forcefully, he cinches the tight knot between the pastoral Abel and the need for communion: "The community spirit at present is only a manifestation of the herd instinct" (pp. 139–40/227–28).

The course of this book has moved between the alternative uses and defects of the obvious dualities presented by the Cain-Abel story. Dualistic thinking has to be one of the most fascinating "tricks" of the human mind. In our response to complementariness, the twentieth-century version of earlier attempts to overcome dualities, we have come to see that dualities are oppositional but not contradictory, that indeed, like Cain and Abel, they enjoy a nexus of involvement (both conceptually and historically). This simply means that dualities are not random choices, but participate on the same axis of meaning and, even more so, together comprise the defining horizons of a situation.

Hesse fully participated in the modernist motive to transcend dualities. In fact, the major essay where he makes clear his own sense of the multiplicity of beings that inhabit the human consciousness, "The Brothers Karamazov, or The Decline of Europe" (written in 1919, roughly the same time as *Demian*), figures more than marginally in *The Waste Land*.[6] There Hesse praises Dostoevsky's masterpiece as heralding the arrival of a new type of being, the "Russian man." "The Russian man is Karamazov,

he is Pavlovitch, he is Dmitri, he is Ivan, he is Alyosha. These four, however different they may appear, necessarily belong together, collectively
they are Karamazov, collectively they are the 'Russian man,' the coming
and already imminent man of the European crisis" (p. 73). As is evident,
this new type of human nature represents a complex mixture of discordant
elements. "And so," Hesse concludes,

> the "Russian man" (whom we have long since had in Germany too) is not to
> be adequately described either as a "hysteric" or as drunkard or criminal, or
> as poet and holy man, but only as the simultaneous combination of all these
> characteristics. The Russian man, the Karamazov, is at once murderer and
> judge, ruffian and sensitive soul, he is equally the complete egoist and a hero
> of total self-sacrifice. We cannot get at him from a fixed, moralistic, ethical,
> dogmatic—in a word, a European standpoint. In him good and evil, outer
> and inner, God and Satan are cheek and jowl. (p. 73)

The last sentence brings us into the midst of *Demian*, but the total context should remind us that when the god Abraxas is referred to in that
work as representing God and Satan fused, this is not to be read as a simple bringing together of dualities but rather as the complex register of a
multitude of forces all present and active in the new type of human being.

The double confirms division, he does not create it; his coming is in
response to an already existing breach. When Demian arrives, Emil is already witness to divided realms. One is the frankly idyllic world of his family (and here we can imagine him harkening back to the naive world of the
eighteenth-century pastoral, a world of unity such as was presented by
Salomon Gessner, in which prevailed

> mother and father, love and strictness, model behavior and school. It was a
> realm of brilliance, clarity and cleanliness, gentle conversations, washed
> hands, clean clothes, and good manners. . . . Straight lines and paths led to
> the future: there was duty and guilt, bad conscience and confession, forgive-
> ness and resolutions, love, reverence, wisdom and the words of the Bible. If
> one wanted an unsullied and orderly life, one made sure one was in league
> with this world. (p. 5/103)

Despite the false promises of security and order (just the sort of expectations that the young captain in part anticipated and that Leggatt contradicted), this is an edifying picture of naive sincerity.

The problem in its presentation of a matrix of unity is that it is a partial
picture. Another world impinges on Emil's familial idyll: ". . . it smelled
different, spoke a different language, promised and demanded different
things. . . . It was dominated by a loud mixture of horrendous, intriguing,
frightful mysterious things, including slaughterhouses and prisons, drunk-
ards and screeching fishwives, calving cows, horses sinking to their death,

tales of robberies, murders and suicides. All these wild and cruel, attractive and hideous things surrounded us, could be found in the next alley, the next house. . . . Everywhere this second vigorous world erupted and gave off its scent, everywhere, that is, except in our parents' room" (p. 6/103–4). One sees again why the double comes in some opposition to the structure of authority, even in its most genial and benevolent form. It is not merely authority that is being challenged but rather the entire system of benign unity that the father upholds. This harmonious world is idyllic (one can go back in thought beyond Gessner's vision of unity to Prospero's masque in *The Tempest* for earlier representations of this vision) and it is also associated, as we have seen, with Abel. This is another indication of the association of Abel with the sustaining figure of patriarchy, and the intervention of the double as a challenge to both.

By his false admission of a fabricated crime, Emil already indicates his need to ingratiate himself to the darker world, represented by Kromer. As an indication of this need, and as a respondent to the inherent division in his soul, Demian intervenes. This intervention is also evidence of the groping growth of Emil's own consciousness; his inept and unconscious gestures are in fact expressions of a shaping agency in his own life. This is the other important factor that will separate the regenerate Cain from the dramas of envy discussed in the next section. Cain is an active, growing, expressive force of new directions and new values. The coming of Demian thus creates exploratory space, in the manner of the Sacred Executioner, around the dilemma into which Emil was born and the necessary violence to which he is called.

The characteristic of Cain in much modern literature is consciousness, and this continues his long historical contrast with the simpler Abel. Not unexpectedly, he is also highly self-conscious, that is, aware of his own role and destiny. This is largely expressed in what has come to be called intertextuality, where the argument of another text is directly or indirectly taken up and confronted, as it were. Part of the secret, conspiratorial knowledge that Leggatt must impart is the nature of the role he has been called to fulfill as Cain. This is made clear by the work's texture of allusion. In *Demian*, in *East of Eden*, and what is most intriguing for our purposes, given its general location among the dramas of envy, in Unamuno's *Abel Sánchez*, the biblical text of Genesis 4 is itself explicitly confronted and interrogated; and in Unamuno's work, even Byron's play is confronted.

Addressing the mark of Cain, Demian argues that it is not so much a physical sign as a kind of presence, an aura that the authentic personality possesses. He turns around completely the order of the mark in Genesis. The mark does not follow the crime, rather the mark, as an integral part of his personality, precedes Cain. It was because Cain displayed this mark (that is, because he was exceptional in certain ways), that he was feared.

Because of the mark, he came to be regarded as strange, even sinister. The so-called sign indicating self-possession was converted into a mark of condemnation, a signal by which the "herd" could cope with the authentic power of Cain. It is interesting that Demian does not refer to this mark as inhering in Cain, so much as in his progeny: it is the children of Cain who inspire fear. Demian instinctively records a traditional element of the Cain story, and that is its historical nature, with Cain (and Abel) as progenitor of a line (pp. 29–30/125–26).

Cain also attempts to dissolve the tight dualistic nexus by creating space around traditional morality. Arriving in the full rage of Emil's puberty, he brings the consciousness of historical relativism. "What is forbidden is not something that is eternal; it can change." Demian then expresses in his own way the formula that was framed by Conrad (and suggested by Schopenhauer), one that has loomed as paramount in this chapter devoted to the extraordinary, changed evaluations of Cain and Abel: "It is possible for one never to transgress a single law and still be a bastard, and *vice versa*" (p. 64/158). *The Secret Sharer* would seem to lend validity to this complicated reversal. Indeed, the older captain ("Archbold") was guilty of serious crimes of defection and then of a need to protect his own reputation by overzealously blaming Leggatt; on the other side, Leggatt has apparently violated the public law and yet may be innocent in regard to the moral law. In contrast with Conrad's full dramatic depiction of a very complex case, the utterances of Demian do appear somewhat facile.[7] The question of whether one may clearly violate a public law, commit murder, for example, and still be regarded as innocent according to the moral law is never fully addressed. At one point, Emil does ask if the apparent moral impunity granted by the quest for authentic being, means that everything is permitted. Demian's response seems to skirt the central question: "Certainly you shouldn't go kill somebody or rape a girl." One could argue that paradoxically the moral adventurism advocated by Demian is made possible because of the legacy of Christian bourgeois morality that it has been Hesse's expressed purpose to attack. On the other hand, as we shall see, the kind of psychic fullness and personal reintegration that Demian represents would seemingly find such brutal acts abhorrent. The fullness that is sought within the dimensions of the Sacred Executioner is *never* tantamount to absolute freedom.

The personal evolution of Emil as Cain does require a slaying, although a symbolic one. In his search for his own nature he had rejected his father and his father's world. Like other of his young modernist cohorts (one can think of Stephen in Joyce's *Ulysses*), in the demotion of the biological father, he is in need of a spiritual father. But here we can perhaps see some difference between the Ulysses theme and that of Cain-Abel. Joyce's epic novel actually envisions a kind of rapprochement between Stephen and

Bloom, between *Geist* and *Natur*. There does seem to be offered, with all the ironic undercurrents, a blending of the ways, but the Cain-Abel story allows no such reunion. Emil is obliged to sunder himself even from his spiritual tutor. Pistorius and Emil come together over their mutual interest in the god Abraxas, who is the nominal equivalent of the kind of reconciliation between disparate qualities that Hesse had addressed in his concept of the new "Russian man." God and devil, good and evil are cheek and jowl, opposite sides of the same coin, and consequently joined by common matter. While Pistorius has knowledge of Abraxas, Emil is seeking to live its meaning. It begins to occur to Emil that Pistorius' ideas are devoid of personal reference; for instance, he seems singularly unconcerned with his own dream-life. His approach is ritualistic, schematic. In a fatal, unguarded moment Emil lashes out at his mentor, "What you are telling me there is all so—all so antiquarian." The accusation pierces Pistorius like a sword, because it coincides with Pistorius' own consciousness of his weakness. The antiquarian must be rejected, as Nietzsche instructed Hesse's generation, because it does not exercise critical intelligence, it does not bring historical knowledge into contact with contemporary experience. In the same way that the "herd" mentality is Abelite, so Pistorius' refuge in history seeks the security of Abel. In fact, he takes Emil's blow like a lamb. "When I had hit out" says Emil, "I had thought I would strike a tough, well-armed man—he turned out to be a quiet, passive, defenseless creature who surrendered without protest." The exchange functions strictly within the Cain-Abel duality. If Pistorius is Abel, then Emil in his aggressive act is Cain. Following this critical action, Emil walks for hours throughout the town: "During that walk I felt for the first time the mark of Cain on my forehead" (pp. 128–30/217–19).

The modernist quest for authenticity extends the domain of the Sacred Executioner to history itself. If the antagonist turns out to be an adherent of historical knowledge that requires no personal appropriation, then the mentor-scholar with his historical reliances may be as Abelite as the biological father with his harmoniously coherent world. The Sacred Executioner enters into change and out of the violence and hazards of change brings a new form of being. Historical change itself evokes the mystery and requires the violence that adhere to the pattern of the Sacred Executioner. Equally essential to this search is the double, who, as it turns out, is a guide to the mysteries. In fact, in the same way that the offering is the crucial means of differentiation in the Genesis text, so here an offering is determining. It is, however, an offering made to the new god of change, to the new god of history, and that is authenticity. Pistorius shies from the terrible new being to which Emil has been called by his own inner directions and his double. Where Emil moves forward, shedding father and mentor (that is, shedding the comforts and securities of established experience), Pistorius falters. In this sense, the offering of his own gift is deficient because it is insufficiently realized; the gift is a call he failed to answer, and in the severity and implacability of Cain and Abel's subservience to the new god of historical change, this new Abel must be sacrificed.

In the particular fondness of modernism for issues of authenticity and its extraordinary coincidence with many of the strongest features of the Cain-Abel story, particularly under the influence of the Sacred Executioner, we can remark here on another striking reversal of values. For Philo, the chief characteristic of Cain was that he referred everything to himself—in short, he was authentic. The phrase is derived from the Greek, *autos-hentes*, "one who works by himself."[8] But in Philo's religious view of the world, this is a debased quality, one inferior to the reverential attitude of Abel. Under the ascendancy of the Sacred Executioner, and its involvement with the foundation sacrifice as a parable of change in existence, Cain remains the prototype of authenticity, but as a bearer of new values, it is he who now enjoys the greater esteem. But even this picture of historical conversion is not entirely accurate. The modern Cain's search for authenticity is in some ways more congenial to the spiritual values of Philo, that is, it is a search for some wholeness and integrity of being—and it is in touch with such values that rape or murder would be abhorrent and unthinkable.

This very design of the Sacred Executioner, requiring attention to motivation and final realization, itself fits into the pattern of modernism, whereby one must not look to the initial modernist pronouncements, which frequently involve hostile and negative critiques of contemporary society, but rather to their development and final fulfillment. The early negative critiques are, as it were, apparent acts of preliminary violence, fitting within the pattern of the Sacred Executioner, and yet are required to create space around conventional thinking and are in need of development before fuller judgment may be rendered. In this sense, the code of the Sacred Executioner quite simply finds its fullest realization in the pattern, as well as in the program, of modernism.

Like skeptics who use intelligence to dishonor intellect, those who would demote the comforting continuities of historical knowledge make use of history in order to demote history (this, incidentally, is a very valid procedure that Nietzsche had already advocated).[9] Hesse, although adhering to the rigorous, even merciless demands of authentication, is actually an exponent of a native German tradition. The ideal seems to be the *Ding-an-sich*, the thing itself, without antecedent links, a solitariness in time. "Each man had only one genuine vocation—to find the way to himself. He might end up as poet or madman, as prophet or criminal—that was not his affair, ultimately it was of no concern." But it soon appears that his model is Jesus. "Someone who seeks nothing but his own fate no longer has any companions, he stands quite alone and has only cold universal space around him. That is Jesus in the Garden of Gethsemane" (p. 133/222). The problem is that when people try to imitate Jesus they falsify his conditions. The model that is provided is the futility of models. Authenticity requires a model-less universe, because authentication requires a different response to the absolutely startlingly new conditions of the moment. To seek security in the role of imitation is to seek to make a bargain with God, it is to render up a poor offering. In this sense, martyrs who seek martyrdom (as in Eliot's *Murder in the Cathedral*) are not actually being Jesus-like. ". . . they had models, they had ideals. But the man who only seeks his destiny has neither models nor ideals, has nothing dear and consoling" (p. 133/222).

The contention here is a deeply abiding one, represented almost five centuries ago by the controversy between Erasmus and Luther. From out of the depths of the German theological past, from the pages of Luther himself comes this quest for authentication without intermediaries, authentication that insists upon an orphanhood in time, radical, tragic discontinuity. And as Luther fought against the more benign and comforting Christian humanism of Erasmus, so modernists from Nietzsche onward set out against the ethical, historical culture of a reborn Christian humanism of the nineteenth century. The search for patternless being is not without pattern. In fact, as Hesse has indicated, the heralded Russian man has already made his appearance in Germany. Hesse's Cain has become a German Cain, and therewith a figure who attempts to define in modern times the essence of his country and of his countrymen's contributions to modern culture.

These larger associations will point to an apparent contradiction: the fate of Emil Sinclair is more than an individual one. As in other Cain-Abel stories, it is involved in a higher destiny, the formation of a new type of person from out of the convulsive changes of World War I. It is no accident that *Demian, East of Eden,* and even *Abel Sánchez,* each of which ranks among its author's fullest and most accomplished work, should have as their controlling myth the theme of Cain-Abel, and should be located in the time of World War I.[10] The growth of the individual Cainite figure has a coordinate in the pending massive landshift in the soul of Europe. Although not truly formative of the modernist style, the war is correctly regarded as a cultural watershed, a time of dislocation, disruption, and radical change brought about by means of convulsive violence. The two actions, the development of the modernist Cain and the background of the war, can truly merge. As the war announced a period of change in an atmosphere of violence, what better figure to represent the new order of psychic being—one based upon disruption—than Cain himself. The myth itself, as we have seen, is a foundation myth and the emergence of Emil Sinclair as Cain presents the character best suited to lead his time into a new order of being.

In this sense, of course, Hesse's Emil and Demian are indeed new princes in a time of radical historical change, who, by means of violence—in this case symbolic violence—are responding to the needs of a new time. Far from deploring the war—and this too seems to be an intriguing and morally dangerous modernist phenomenon—Hesse, through his characters, seems to welcome the war as a means of shedding an outworn culture. Oddly enough, the argument that began by disallowing the expectations of historical continuity, ends by accepting a kind of historical necessity. By a kind of psychohistorical interaction, the development of the Cainite Emil is in tune with the staggering alterations of the culture. Emil's individual development is deeply involved with the historical destiny of his age. He is consequently—and this is the traditional Cain-Abel component that we wish to emphasize—not actually free-standing. This is brought home, of course, when Demian (like Machiavelli, who invoked other rulers—Moses and Solon—to justify Romulus) invokes not only Buddha, Moses, Caesar, Napoleon, and Loyola, but also Bismarck, as men of destiny who emerged "*because* they were able to accept the inevitable." Within the Cain-Abel paradigm, as well as the modernist one, Demian gives final reference to history: "Always you must think of these things in evolutionary, in historical terms" (p. 152/239). But the historical terms in which he regards things borrows heavily from a kind of scientific determinism. Those species that survived in the predictably catastrophist range of Demian's speculations were those who were ready. "When the upheavals of the earth's surface flung the creatures of the sea onto the land and the land creatures into the sea, the specimens of the various orders that were ready to follow their destiny were the ones that accomplished the new and the unprecedented" (p. 152/239).

Curiously enough, the catastrophist theory already adopted by Byron in his *Cain* continues to play a role in this and (as we shall see) in other Cain-Abel versions. This is because the theory espouses violent historical disruption, a serious kind of historical limitation to the freedom of human maneuver, but more importantly, issues the call to a new figure who is capable of emerging and coping with the challenge within a drastically altered framework of events. Once again, we see that the story of Cain as Sacred Executioner involves change and disruption, but it also requires reintegration. From the divided world of his early childhood—and this division constitutes the essential datum of experience—the personal growth of the Cain character leads toward the possibility of psychic reintegration. But this personal regeneration, although not involving political legitimation, still has a broader social impact. Hesse's Cain brings with him a new order of being, and he is associated with the other new princes of the past who were able to do so.

Sadly, in reading German authors from Nietzsche onward, one must read with dual vision—one that fixes on the new type of man who was sought after, and the other that fixes on the far-from-new type of man who in fact emerged. We still cannot read German literature of this period without reference to national socialism. This is emphasized for us when we remember that of the two stirring words that close this small but resonant book, *brother* and *master*, the second is in its original German, *Führer*. Until such time as we ourselves are liberated from history, it would do well to reflect that, although in their temporary abrogation of the ethical—and any developmental approach to modernism must place emphasize on the temporary nature of their challenge—it is quite possible that writers like Hesse, and even Mann in some of his wartime reflections, could vaguely be associated with the rise of Hitler, it must be also asserted that, in their search for psychic wholeness and personal integration, they were as far as possible from the emotional *ressentiment* upon which fascism and nazism seemed to thrive. The Cain-Abel story, as presented here in Hesse's *Demian*, may contribute some light to that much larger and sadder cultural problem.

Chapter Seven

THE NEW AMERICAN CAIN:
EAST OF EDEN AND
OTHER WORKS OF
POST–WORLD WAR II
AMERICA

AMONG THE spate of American works all invoking the Cain-Abel story that appeared after World War II, John Steinbeck's *East of Eden* excels. In some ways, all of these works—and they include three films, *The Gunfighter*, *Shane*, and *High Noon* (only the second of which figures also as a prominent literary text), and two novels, Steinbeck's work, and Herman Wouk's *The Caine Mutiny*—are all concerned with defining the nature of the American experience, wherein the character of Cain becomes something of a national type.[1] Like *Demian*, these are all devoted to depicting a national Cain, one representative of the defining characteristics of a nation. In a journal note, to which we shall later return, Steinbeck declared the subject of his novel to be "my country for the last fifty years." Despite the fact that the subject matter of *East of Eden* covers American history from the death of Lincoln to America's participation in World War I, it is indeed about America's history in the twentieth century, in particular its emergence from World War II. Similar to the other works mentioned, Steinbeck's novel is about violence and guilt, about the justification of violence (hence its relation to World War II) and the transcendence of guilt. *East of Eden* abundantly shows, once again, how the elaboration of a national type is abundantly suited to aspects of the Cain-Abel story, and variations thereupon.[2]

In *Journal of a Novel*, the day-to-day account of Steinbeck's intentions, struggles, and changes while writing the novel, a series of entries shows the author's attempts to reconcile the two facets of the work—the local and the mythic—and to bring more clearly to the reader's attention the true dimensions of his work.[3] The fascinating account of Steinbeck's search for a title for his most ambitious work reveals his use of the mythic method as a needed framing device for his wide-ranging story and his understanding of the powerful and compelling human emotions contained within the theme itself.

In the entry for May 10, 1951, Steinbeck indicates his original title, and, humorously, why he changed it. Although it was to be called *Salinas Valley*, its focus was still national ("my country for the last fifty years"). He reported this to a "rich Texan" who was "far from literary." The Texan bluntly informed the novelist that the proposed title was all wrong: "nobody who doesn't live there is interested in the Salinas Valley. You had the title yourself. Everybody is interested in My Country. Call it that. Then they can connect it with their country."

The entry for May 15 indicates a change close to what the non-literary critic had urged, but one not to the liking of Pascal Covici, Steinbeck's editor at Viking Press, and to whom, as a kind of absent interlocutor, the journal entries as imaginary letters were addressed. "You don't like the title *My Valley*. I have never been a title man. I don't give a damn what it is called. I would call it Valley to the Sea which is a quotation from absolutely nothing but has two great words and a direction." Despite such disavowals, he continued to worry about the title and, in the entry of May 22, began to bring the title into closer relation with the foundation of the novel in Cain-Abel the story.

Cain Sign was the novel's third working title, yet despite its virtues and its reference to the "best known mark in the world," and Steinbeck's own interpretation of it as a protective rather than a punishing mark, it did not last. It simply did not contain enough reference to the local and historical nature of the book. *East of Eden* seemed to satisfy both needs. So, in the second of two entries for June 11, Steinbeck was able to record the more satisfying title. He had just finished writing what was to be section four of Chapter 22, where Samuel Hamilton reads aloud the first sixteen verses of Genesis 4. Since it is also the chapter where the still unnamed twins—Aron and Caleb—receive their names, in some ways it is a double naming:

> And now I set down in my own hand the 16 verses of Cain and Abel and the story changes with flashing lights when you write it down. And I think I have a title at least, a beautiful title, *East of Eden*. And read the sixteenth verse to find it. And the Salinas Valley is surely East of Eden. I could go on and write another page and perhaps it would be good, who knows. Or maybe not. What a strange story it is and how it haunts one. I have dreaded geting into this section because I knew what the complications were likely to be. And they weren't less but more because as I went into the story more deeply I began to realize that without this story—or rather a sense of it—psychiatrists would have nothing to do. In other words this one story is the basis of all human neurosis—and if you take the fall along with it, you have the total of psychic troubles that can happen to a human.

In fact, Steinbeck does come to appropriate both stories, the Fall and the Cain-Abel story, with the regeneration of the Cain character in the latter story dependent upon the recognition of the guilt of the father in the former.

In the same section of the novel, from which the title was finally derived, the council of elders, Hamilton, Adam Trask, and the Chinese house servant, Lee, speculate as to the lasting appeal of the Cain-Abel myth. Lee, whose function as a beneficent admonitor is to loosen the tight connections of the nuclear family, attributes the durability of the story to human guilt. "What a great burden of guilt men have! . . . We gather our arms full of guilt as though it were precious stuff." Although a Dutch uncle, Lee functions like a double by creating space around the event and thus working to loosen the hold of guilt. It is interesting that, as in Hesse's *Demian*, in *East of Eden*, Steinbeck seems to envision human development as passing *through*, but also *beyond*, guilt. Although guilt is a necessary step in separation and hence individuation, to fail to transcend guilt may be a formidable barrier to regeneration: Lee is the voice of freedom beyond the determinism of inherited guilt. At the moment, his voice is directed to Adam Trask in an attempt to stir him from his depression following his disastrous marriage to Cathy Ames. But the Cain-Abel story signals a prior fall, an antecedent division, that between brothers. Arguing that only those themes that are deeply personal and familiar can last, Sam Hamilton asks that the test of personal reference be applied. Adam, somewhat too quickly, responds, "I didn't kill my brother . . ." and once again, as we have seen in other versions, the thought is interrupted mid-passage, when the mythic level of experience suddenly breaks into consciousness. "Suddenly he stopped and his mind went reeling back in time" (pp. 268–70). Of course, he never killed his brother, but his brother Charles certainly tried to kill him.

Aside from the title and other such direct interrogations of the classical text—itself a consistent sign of some efforts at regeneration—Steinbeck makes use of other devices to clarify the story's frame. As the names of the sets of brothers would indicate, this is a *C* and *A* novel. The first father (the original tainted Adam, as it were), who emerges from the Civil War with a wooden leg and gonorrhea, and who fabricates a legendary heroic past while also embezzling funds from his office in Washington, is Cyrus. His first wife, the mother of Adam, commits suicide. He then remarries an Alice, and from this union Charles is produced. When Adam marries, he marries a Cathy Ames, and one might say that they produce Caleb and Aron, but in fact the twins are not identical twins, and may have been separately conceived by the legal husband Adam and by his brother Charles, into whose bed Cathy slipped after having drugged her husband. Of course, Abra, who acts as a countertype to Cathy, fits into this scheme.

These are practical and, unfortunately, somewhat mechanical devices for framing a story. They do indicate however one of the novel's main concerns, and that is the continuity of a pattern of guilt and division, a legacy of repeated falls as consistent as the first letters of the names that keep turning up. But the deeper reservoirs of the Cain-Abel story are also active in the novel. Steinbeck does tap the more enduring emotions, particularly the excruciating and infuriating agony of childhood rejection and the arbitrariness of parental preference. Whatever the book's failings—and they have not gone unnoticed—the emotional centers of the Cain-Abel theme that Steinbeck most compellingly presents bestow on the novel an essential and unforgettable seriousness. To be sure, Steinbeck utilizes the mythic method as a framing device, and like other modernists, in whose orbit his work definitely figures, he was also able to write from the heart of myth itself.

The tragedy of differentiation appears early in the novel, as the first set of brothers, Adam and Charles, are radically different. Adam "shrank from violence, from contention. . . . He contributed to the quiet he wished for by offering no violence, no contention, and to do this he had to retire into secretness, since there is some violence in everybody. He covered his life with a veil of vagueness, while behind his quiet eyes a full life went on . . ." (p. 20). Unlike the more faceless Abels that we meet in *The Secret Sharer* and in *Demian*, Steinbeck's Abel characters are simply less equipped for life rather than offensive. Charles, on the other hand, is more assertive, competitive, and aggressive, in some ways more lethal. There is apparently less conscious virtue in him, and consequently he too is ill-suited to bring about the later reintegration and regeneration that Caleb will effect. In fact, unlike Caleb, he is untouched by a sense of guilt. Despite this division within the family, it does not break out into conflict until the arbitrariness of parental preference is made evident. There was something in Adam that touched Cyrus—perhaps it was his vulnerability, his need for protection. When the father clearly looks with favor on Adam's offering of a foundling pup as opposed to Charles's costly pearl-handled pocketknife, Charles's protective attitude toward his weaker brother is converted into homicidal violence. Steinbeck clearly understands the personal importance of the ritual offering, that indeed in the offering, in its eager expectation of approval, an entire sense of self and of worth is involved. To have one's offering rejected is to have one's self denied, rendered worthless, obliterated. There is little wonder then that anger at this offense to the self should be displaced in anger toward the favored one. Steinbeck's *East of Eden*, consequently, begins as a drama of envy, that only in the second generation becomes a story of the regenerate Cain.

Much later, Adam's sons, Caleb and Aron, are similarly part of an innocent fraternal union that makes the essential differences all the more painful. But in this case, the arbitrariness of parental preference, although equally as pronounced and equally as hurtful, does not yield such damaging results. This is due to changes in the choreography of the surrounding characters and events, the presence of Lee and of Abra, and the contrast of Caleb and Aron along a familiar axis of character types provided by full modernism.

In another significant filial offering, Caleb wishes to express his love for his father by giving him a present of fifteen thousand dollars, money he made buying green beans at two cents above market price and then selling them to the British Army Purchasing Agent during the early years of World War I. The offering is that of Cain the entrepreneurial agricultural-ist, who accurately predicts the coming war. The scene is excruciating be-cause of the young boy's eager expectation of fatherly approval. Earlier he had debated with himself about how to sign the card: "To my father from Caleb" or the more man-to-man "To Adam Trask from Caleb Trask" (p. 540). The father, of course, rejects the offering, calling it war-profiteering. But again, Steinbeck dramatically portrays all that is involved in the offer-ing. The father prefers the more innocent Aron who is attending Stanford. He prefers the up-scale "idealism" of education to Caleb's capitalism. We may observe, however, in this parental preference some semblance of fear as well. Caleb's agricultural success is rejected because Adam's earlier ven-ture into transporting lettuce to Eastern markets had ended in dismal fail-ure. Adam will not allow that he undertook that project for profit, rather that he did it for the thrill of showing it could be done, for personal vic-tory. In both episodes, the earlier one with Cyrus and the later one with Adam, we find Steinbeck writing from within the most intense under-standing of the significance of the offering and the devastating implica-tions of its rejection. He also casts some light on the reason for fatherly preference: could it be that the father himself in some ways personally identifies with the needier one and fears the more capable sibling?[4]

The offering is even more significant because it shows a practical Cain, a Cain who becomes something of a national type at a crucial moment in his country's history. This offering is made from the profits of venture capital. In his *Cain*, Byron provides motivation for Cain out of his own high-mindedness and the bleak scientific picture of the world presented by Lucifer. Steinbeck is writing in an age that not only has accepted the scientific worldview, but is quite willing to benefit from its technology. The metaphysical malaise of Byron's hero in some sense has been quieted by the stunning possibilities of new technology, and America has become the center of that industrial power. In Steinbeck's national Cain it is no accident, then, that the newly regenerate Cain should show some aptitude for coping in the modern world.

Despite their differences, in the Cain figures of Byron and of Steinbeck we are not presented with motiveless malignity, with any mystery of iniq-uity. We are brought to appreciate more humanized Cains, a Cain of broad-ranging sympathies and high ethical standards in the one, and a Cain of perfectly understandable human emotions and ambitions in the other. But, as we have seen, there is another tradition, that of the monstrous Cain, and Steinbeck brings that tradition into the novel as well, as much to show the role of monstrous evil as to set off the reformation in the more humanly complicated emotions of Caleb. This malignant Cain is not a male, but a female—Cathy Ames—and we are reminded that Grendel's dam was a descendant of Cain. But in Steinbeck's scientific world we are not led to speculate about this malignant force in theological terms, but rather in genetic terms. And this brings together the two versions of the theme present in *East of Eden*. The one deals with a kind of genetic determinism, the mechanics of monstrousness, and the other with a need to overcome such genetic determinism, and in so doing to transcend the Cain myth itself. Cathy Ames, holding both *C* and *A*, and as the mother of Caleb and Adam, seems to be a generalized force that Caleb must come to understand and defeat as an inheritance if he is to survive. Aron, in his simpler Abelite understanding, cannot accept this presence in his past or in himself, and is destroyed by it.

Cathy Ames joins in her two names the *C* and *A* portions of the novel not to suggest any mixture of good and evil in her but rather to suggest the general permanence and overall presence of evil. Steinbeck introduces the section where he describes Cathy with the sentence, "I believe there are monsters born in the world to human parents" (pp. 72–75). Just as there are physical malformations, so can there be moral deformities. Cathy, although possessing some odd physical characteristics, is nevertheless quite pretty, even innocent-appearing, "as though nature concealed a trap." This reminiscence from *Billy Budd* is compounded when it is revealed that, like Melville's Claggart, she forges her iniquity with complete rationality. Since she is a monster, she can only regard people through a perspective that is monstrous, that is, by simplifying, isolating, and exploiting their (usually sexual) weaknesses. This single-mindedness allows her to achieve domination. After a grotesque trail of juvenile destruction she is able to visit her evil upon the hapless Adam, whom she finally wounds with a pistol, only after having born to him (and possibly his brother) the twin sons, Aron and Caleb. The final importance of Cathy is in the fact that both Aron and Caleb carry her blood. Can they overcome this deterministic inheritance? The previous generation had failed in their encounter with evil.[5] Adam was duped and the cleverer Charles made league with it. Aron is destroyed by the recognition of evil within him; it is only Caleb who absorbs this legacy of guilt but does not allow it to defeat him.

The Cain-Abel story has had a curious appeal to an age of science. Catastrophist scientific speculation encouraged a vision of alienation and violent division. If Cain abhors unity, then the Cainite character is better able to respond to the new conditions. But science has also introduced a new element, and that is determinism. One can see why this fusion of the Cain-Abel story with a scientific worldview presented dilemmas, problems, and opportunities for Steinbeck. As his biographer, Jackson Benson, writes, "Basic to his philosophy . . . are the beliefs that man is but a small part of a large whole that is nature and that this whole is only imperfectly understood by man and does not conform to his schemes or wishes. . . . In *East of Eden* Steinbeck adds a further element . . . ; in this materialistic, mechanistic universe, is there any chance for the individual to accept his own destiny?" Benson's response to his own question is a guarded "yes."[6]

Since the Enlightenment, the regenerate Cain is not an isolated character. He either finds a soul mate, a double, or a female companion. Caleb has an antidote to his mother's (and his putative father Charles's) characteristics in sage advice and in a loving relationship. In place of the secret sharer, or double, Caleb finds a confidant in the Asian Lee, who carefully oversees and tries to steer the fortunes of the troubled family. Although normally the force of domesticity works counter to the pull of the double, Abra works together with Lee in the regeneration of Caleb-Cain. The loving care of a woman is one of the great additions to the theme since the Enlightenment, as if somehow the woman had a greater connection with the more sympathetic (and less stern) forces of the universe, and her love introduces self-forgiveness and some sense of wholeness. There are other versions of the Cain story where the woman is absent, or even adds to the conflict, but Steinbeck's vision is kindlier, perhaps returning to the Germanic pastoral ideal within nature, one already presented by Gessner, where indeed some surrogate parents (Lee) are wise, and some women (Abra) are loving.

Steinbeck's *East of Eden* also shares in the changes that have come with modernism. This means of course that the axis along which the brothers figure, the terms of their interrelation, has altered. The traditional Cain, the original schismatic, has a divided consciousness. In modernism, this sense of division becomes a positive quality, indicative of superior alertness. It means not only complex awareness, but also a correlative respect for the conjunction of the many forces of life. Stylistically, the complex central consciousness, with a varied and complex emotional register, is the most distinctive attribute of modernism, both in fiction and in poetry.[7] This is part of the larger sensibility that seeks to expand the framework of consideration. The ideal seems to be a more fully integrated being, one bringing together the sexual, the morally sentient, and the conscious life. The Cain character, with his legacy of division and consciousness, seems a more suitable figure to bring about this fusion of qualities, while the Abel character, given his fundamental innocence, seems more likely to lapse into unawareness, or what is worse, and what seems to be the full opposite of the modernist Cain, single-mindedness.

Aron is the golden, more favored son, yet Steinbeck attributes to him qualities that are specifically demoted in modernism. "He had few facets and very little versatility." If Caleb is capable of more complex emotional shifts, Aron shows the very opposite of this trait. "Change of direction confused Aron, but that was the only thing that confused him. He set his path and followed it and he did not see nor was he interested in anything beside his path. His emotions were few and heavy"(p. 422). Aron cannot accommodate into the design of his being contradictory or fragmentary notions. It is for this reason that he is shattered by the revelation of his mother's life. His nature is not large enough to encompass irregularity. Although, to be sure, Steinbeck does not fully confront the serious involvement of Caleb in Aron's suicidal engagement in World War I, this is partially to be excused because the issue is the larger character faults of Aron. He is unable to perceive the twisted lines of life, and, what is more important, to live with them. He is more disposed to tear up the world that does not conform to his picture of it.

Not only is Aron a countermodernist type, literally an antitype, he is more specifically romantic, in the pejorative sense used by modernists. His vision is a projection of himself. He does not see the world but sees only what he wishes to see. In this sense, his unalienated vision, his unified sense of being, is dependent upon a denial of otherness. Abra discovers this in his so-called "love-letters." She later confesses this to Lee. "He doesn't think about me. He's made someone up, and it's like he put my skin on her. I'm not like that—not like the made-up one." Aron's love letters are not written to her, she thinks, "It's like they were written to—himself" (p. 500). In the modernist frame, romantic idealism is an indication of willful self-projection. Aron is an heir of Kurtz: "He was going to have it come out his way if he had to tear the world up by the roots" (p. 577).

In the complexity of his conscious awareness, Caleb still manages to maintain a hold upon existence. He is not Cathy Ames; his name, although showing an initial *C*, also contains the making of Abel—*aleb*. In this he shows how the new Cain so ideally fits the character typology established by modernists. But there is a third ingredient, which completes the triangle with Cain and modernism, and that is the American basis of the novel. Following World War II, American writers, for evident reasons, drew on the character of Cain to form the national type. This addition helps us resolve a moral dilemma, the relatively light and easy treatment of Caleb's guilt in relation to Aron's death. Aron is not so much killed as he is dismissed, that is, dismissed from the national stage. Steinbeck dismisses him because he is unworthy to be the national type, to be the representative, contemporary democratic American. We can think back to another foundation play, Shakespeare's *Henry IV*, and perceive the pattern in which Steinbeck's own work participates. Hotspur and Hal are rival cohorts, but rivals engaged in the struggle for kingship, and that means representativeness. When Hall kills Hotspur in actual combat, Hotspur has already been shown to be unworthy as the new type of the English being, the type ready to lead England into the modern world. Historical change calls for a new historical being, and this in turn calls for a foundation sacrifice, to mark and corroborate the new order. Similar to *Henry IV*, Steinbeck's book celebrates a kind of democratic love of variety over an anachronistic and somewhat romantic singleness of purpose. The Cain of modernism thus abundantly fills the needs of the new national type.

But there is another reason for Caleb's regeneration, also associated with the nature of the American experiment. Forced as he is to confront ruptures in experience, Caleb becomes representative of the American people, a nation of immigrants—what Oscar Handlin has appropriately characterized, under the title *The Uprooted*, as groups of people who have been called to leave behind the old ways and to endure the burden of change so that they can establish a new order. American is thus itself made from symbolic slayings, from sheddings of the past, from disruption, from all the sacrifices that accommodation to the new requires. In a masterstroke of moral elevation Caleb is made into the type of his country. Lee's attempt to lead Caleb beyond guilt comes by way of reconciling him to the violence in the American character and in the American past:

> "We're a violent people, Cal. Does it seem strange to you that I include myself? Maybe it's true that we are all descended from the restless, the nervous, the criminals, the brawlers, but also the brave and independent and generous. If our ancestors had not been that, they would have stayed in their home plots in the other world and starved over the squeezed out soil. . . . That's why I include myself. We all have that heritage, no matter what land our fathers left. All colors and blends of Americans have somewhat the same tendencies." (p. 570)

American experience is based upon a primary fact, upon the fact of groups of people willing to leave the "home plot"—and the phrase does leap out at us—and to endure the sacrifice and disruption that such a venture requires. The experience itself is admirably suited for representation by the regenerate Cain. In this sense, the inadequacy of Aron derives from his unworthiness to stand as a national type. In the larger sense, as the Civil War destroyed the agricultural and Edenic myth of an Adamic innocence, immigration and the emergence of America after World War II helped create the myth of a regenerate Cain. Steinbeck understood that the primary American myth had been transformed from the American Adam to the American Cain, and that World War II had represented the crucial experience by which a nation of immigrants had coalesced into a formidable entity.[8]

Ultimately, the Cain-Abel story relies upon a philosophy of change.

Unity and communion, truly founded or illusory, do not last forever, as new orders and new types of being emerge. Lee, Steinbeck's tireless mouthpiece, quotes from *The Meditations* of Marcus Aurelius, "Observe constantly that all things take place by change . . ." (565). But moving beyond philosophical change, Steinbeck's Cain enters into history. Caleb is another kind of Sacred Executioner involved in a foundation myth that requires a fraternal sacrifice.

．　．　．

Like the New Prince of Machiavelli, or Hesse's variant who responds to a new order of being (and who was first adumbrated in Byron's "mystery"), Caleb, the American type, is involved in violent change requiring sacrifice. It is interesting that the contemporaneous *Shane*, by Jack Schaefer, brilliantly invokes many of the same issues.[9] It is more directly a foundation work, wherein the Cain figure is more properly a Sacred Executioner, who assumes the burden of violence, and who sacrifices himself in order to establish a community. As a Western, *Shane* deals with outright violence, not symbolic or indirect slayings. Yet, like the others, it addresses the question of the role of violence as a necessary ingredient in civilization. Shane resorts to violence in order to remove it. One thinks back to *Beowulf* where a superior, even heroic violence is required to defeat the forces that threaten civilization.

But *Shane* is even different from *Beowulf*. This is because the main hero, as his very name suggests, is Cain.[10] In the modern tradition Cain himself is the Sacred Executioner; the action he undertakes by reasserting his former self is one of self-sacrifice. In this way it may be related to what is perhaps the greatest myth of the West, that of the gunfighter who is not permitted to reform, whose past catches up with him. Jimmy Ringo, in that starkly spare film, *The Gunfighter*, receives it as a blessing that he has been mortally wounded, and in some way a curse on the man who shot him to let it be falsely believed that he, Ringo, had actually drawn first. In the Ambrosian sense, to live on under the curse is a far greater punishment than is death itself.

Shane himself is not being pursued, but he is unable to avoid being a marked man. First, the role he assumes as Joe Starrett's hand makes him something of a point man. If Fletcher's people succeed in scaring him off, as they did the earlier hired man, that would be the key step in scattering the settlers. "Father was right. In some strange fashion the feeling was abroad that Shane was a marked man. Attention was on him as a sort of symbol" (p. 148). After the final shoot-out in Grafton's saloon, Shane, already wounded (much more seriously than the movie version would indicate, since it is a stomach wound and not a shoulder wound), expresses his own consciousness of his fate: "'A man is what he is, Bob, and there's no breaking the mold. I tried that and I've lost. . . . There's no going back from a killing. . . . Right or wrong the brand sticks and there's no going back'" (p. 263). Somewhat in the mold of Leggatt (and the other stern-natured Cains of destiny who existed even before Byron's creation), Shane has assumed the burdens of an heroic action, an action that is somehow necessary to the preservation of the "state," but one that nevertheless requires the sacrifice of the individual who commits the action. In a world where the gods themselves are envious, action itself is an extraordinarily volatile and ambiguous undertaking.

This is why when Shane enters the town, unlike the buckskin-clad Alan Ladd of the film version, he is dressed in black. It is not Stark Wilson, the hired killer, who represents dangerous violence but rather Shane himself.[11] His shirt and trousers are of a dark material, his belt and boots black, and his hat is black "with a wide curling brim swept down in front to shield his face." He is recognized to be a dangerous and mysterious force. When he determines to fight on the side of the settlers he reappears as the power of blackness. Young Bob, whose eager eyes are so imaginatively responsive to the drama of Shane, sees his ambivalence: "I remembered Ed Howells' saying that this was the most dangerous man he had ever seen. I remembered in the same rush that my father had said he was the safest man we ever had in our house. I realized that both were right and that this, at last, was Shane" (p. 242). When Shane rides off to the climactic confrontation, it is again through Bob's eyes that we sense something of the primitive terror in the explosive potential of violence itself:

> He was tall and terrible there in the road, looming up majestic in the mystic half-light. He was the man I saw that first day, a stranger, dark and forbidding, forging his lone way out of an unknown past in the utter loneliness of his own immovable and instinctive defiance. He was the symbol of all the dim, formless imaginings of danger and terror in the untested realm of human potentialities beyond my understanding. The impact of the menace that marked him was like a physical blow. (p. 249)

The explosive duality of this man of violence extends to those around him; like Leggatt, he comes issuing a challenge not only to his antagonists, but, even more dangerously, to those who adopt him (for example, Bob and Marion). The coming of Shane pertains to those whose lives and maturity he challenges and affects. They are the ones who psychologically come under his spell, that is, under the spell of the danger, the mystery, and the unknown that seems to tease them out of their settled lives of good sense and stability. This also explains the difference between Shane of the novel and Shane of the film. In the novel, Shane is the danger—he does not come simply to fulfill "the ancient dream of warrior righteousness," as does the cinematic Shane (and Beowulf, for that matter).[12] This explains why, yet one more time in this pattern of regeneration, Cain must be relinquished after his virtues are incorporated. The ancient brother sacrifice becomes the necessary symbolic slaying, the shedding of the disruptive other, whose own virtues have been here incorporated and tamed.

This is the work of the father, here not abandoned but only underestimated and finally shown to possess hidden virtues. In the psychic drama unleashed by Shane in which the family partakes, the father is Shane's true competitor and counterpart. As does the young captain in regard to the fugitive Leggatt in *The Secret Sharer*, he comes to Shane's aid physically. What is more important, he trusts him as a person of integrity. In this sense, his own regularity and stability have room to accommodate the stray and fugitive qualities of the Cainite Shane. By incorporating the qualities of Shane, the father brings back to himself his wife and son. In an act of violence, civilization is founded, but in the act of psychic violence—the complex process of sundering and incorporation involved with the second slaying—civilization is restored. Shane must leave because he is no longer needed. He becomes the shadowy self, the lost brother who has performed his function. He is the sacrificed one, called by his character and destiny to occupy the point of conflict, to be the person to whom things happen, not innocently, but inevitably bound up with his character.[13]

· · ·

It is fitting to conclude this chapter with another significant expression of the American character. Herman Wouk's *The Caine Mutiny* has been a remarkably successful novel, with close to 250,000 volumes in thirteen printings in the first eight months of its publication. But our interest does not lie in the book's success, but rather in its failure. Deeply flawed, *The Caine Mutiny* is of great interest precisely because of that flaw. The fault line that runs through the work amounts to a recantation of the dynamic of the Sacred Executioner, the pattern of which in many of its variations we have been following. What Wouk has done is to return the story to the same moral sluggishness, the same undifferentiation from which it emerged when Byron first put his hand to the Cain theme. But in so doing he has given us an accurate barometer of the morale of a decade, of a postwar mentality that, although understandable in its causes, denied civilization itself the powers of rejuvenation.

The Caine Mutiny betrays a high degree of literary self-consciousness (and this might explain its later drastic and vengeful turnabout). The character who provides the higher consciousness, the literary *leit-motives*, is Tom Keefer, the author's needed mouthpiece. It is he who serves as double and perhaps even evil genius for Maryk, who himself becomes the Cain of the piece when he relieves Queeg of his command. Keefer first explains why the story is a Cain story:

> "I've given up [putting in for transfer]. This ship is an outcast, manned by outcasts, and named for the greatest outcast of mankind. My destiny is the *Caine*. It's the purgatory for my sins. . . ." The captain regarded Keefer admiringly. "That's the literary mind for you. I never thought of *Caine* being a symbolic name—"
>
> "The extra *e* threw you off, Captain. God always likes to veil his symbols a bit, being, among his other attributes, the perfect literary mind." (p. 90)[14]

This is peculiar officers' mess banter. But the message of the cursed Cain is reinforced with greater ominousness when Maryk finds out that he is named executive officer of the *Caine*. On shore leave with Keefer in San Francisco, Maryk is in unaccountably low spirits. "Ever have one of those days, Tom, when you feel something bad is in the air—something bad's going to happen to you before the evening's out?" (p. 202). When they return to the boat Maryk learns of his new responsibilities, and Keefer learns that no order has come through for his transfer. "God damn the Caine," said Keefer, "and strike everyone aboard it, including me, with a curse." Maryk can only see his earlier premonitions confirmed. "'This is it,' he thought—but he could not have said what he meant by 'it'" (p. 206). Wouk utilizes the postromantic dimensions of the theme: in place of any insistence on human freedom, he endows his story with grim foreboding and with a sense of cursed destiny.

Obviously, in his reign of neurotic terror, Captain Queeg qualifies as a vindictive Cain, visiting all sorts of retaliatory punishments on the innocent seamen (in this regard, the repeated broadcast of the phrase, "condition Able," is eerie and ironic). But the point of the work, what makes it an extremely revealing document of the times, is the exchange of roles, the evident vindication of Queeg and the immolation of the cowardly intellectual, that is, the transformation—for which we are not unprepared—of the rebellious, malcontented Keefer into the malefactor Cain.

There are no brother murders in this work, but there is a brother death (significantly, the very early death of Willie Keith's father does seem to open the terrain of moral development, that is, leave it open for all the counterinfluences). Tom's brother, Roland (as his name indicates, he will hold heroically and fatally to his post), is an officer aboard the carrier *Montauk*. He sends a blinker message to his brother and their mutual friend, Willie, inviting them to visit him on the carrier. However, permission must first be gained from Captain Queeg. Keefer: "Guess I'll have to pay a visit to Grendel's cave. . . . Here's hoping he's not in a blood-drinking mood" (pp. 279–80). The request is of course denied. In a moving scene

Roland tries to shout his farewells to the two by means of a megaphone: "They could see Roland laugh and nod. He was far ahead of them in a moment. He called back once more but nothing was distinguishable except the word '. . . brother. . . .'"

In action at Leyte Gulf the carrier *Montauk*, under serious attack, is struck at its bridge by a Japanese suicide plane. Roland, engaged in heroic efforts to save the ship, is fatally burned. Anticipating his own later cowardice in a similar incident (for which he also provides the appropriate literary reference from *Lord Jim*), Tom is unsure how he would behave in similar circumstances, commenting, "Rollo had good instincts." The brothers had never been very close, Keefer confesses, "I'm afraid I thought he was too dumb." But then, in a nagging concession that is crucial for the purposes of the theme, Keefer admits that their father had always preferred Roland. "Maybe he knows something" (p. 286). Clearly preparations are being made for a turn against a complex consciousness on the basis of a defense of a simpler effectiveness.

Keefer is more important as the double—his name does suggest *Lucifer*, where the *c* would naturally have a hard sound. Typical of the double, he provides the guileless Maryk with arcane lore, now from the scientific field of psychology. Captain Queeg suffers from paranoia (of which Maryk admits he has never heard). Keefer further instructs his pupil in the fictionalized Articles 184, 185, and 186 of the Navy Regulations by which the captain may be relieved of his command. Not only does Keefer, as a kind of evil genius, provide the seeds of doubt, he even provides the literary text by which the captain's hatred of natural instincts may be understood. He specifically refers to *Billy Budd* and Claggart's envy of Billy (to which he adds his own sexual connotations):

> "Okay. He hates Stilwell for being handsome, healthy, young, competent and naturally popular and attractive—all the things that Queeg is not. Ever read *Billy Budd*, by Melville. Read it. That's the whole story. Stilwell is a symbol of all the captain's frustrations, all the things he would like to smash because he can't have them. . . . Infantilism is very strong in our captain." (p. 268)

But when the simpler and more forthright Maryk, finally convinced that Keefer is right, wishes to present his log of Queeg's bizarre and pathetic actions to the fleet commander, Admiral Halsey, Keefer backs off at the last moment. Keefer admits that he is scared, but wishes to be credited for his honesty (p. 316). This dishonest honesty causes Maryk to compare Keefer with Queeg, and indeed the exchange of roles is complete.

In the extraordinarily compelling "Typhoon" chapter, Queeg's pathetic incompetence and stubborn pride are fully revealed. In order to save the ship—and the hull of the sunken ship that they pass would seem to indicate the reality of the danger—Maryk relieves the captain of his command. He is the Sacred Executioner, who undertakes a desperate and extraordinary action at a crucial moment. The emotionally paralyzed and incompetent Queeg abdicates, and Maryk assumes the burden of responsibility. In this change of command, in the midst of the defection of authority, an abler leader, a new order of humanity, emerges. The significance of this change is not lost on Willie, who is the first of the young officers to support Maryk's decisive actions. It takes forty minutes for the *Caine* to restore itself, maneuvering by the lost ship and taking an enormous beating from the waves: "Willie was scared each time. But he now knew the difference between honest fright and animal terror. One was bearable, human, not incapacitating; the other was moral castration. He was no longer terrorized, and felt he no longer could be, even if the ship went down, provided Maryk were in the water with him" (p. 342). The passage is undeniably clear: a new order of humankind, not without its doubts and fears, is able to enter into the perils of critical, even revolutionary change and emerge with the restoration of order. Human resourcefulness reasserts itself. Queeg, already associated with Grendel, has, in his own psychic terror, reduced life to the level of the bestial. In the more significant and broader restoration of the human image, an apparent illegitimate act has been legitimized, and humankind has escaped from animalistic undifferentiation.

Given all this—the clear and evident support for Maryk's actions and the slow build-up of evidence that Queeg is an emotional basket case—the conclusion of the book amounts to a recantation. Wouk offers a palinode to the act of legitimate revolution that the novel itself seems to endorse. This surprise reversal is, however, not as strange as the reasons given for it. And here we approach the fault line of the novel. After all, we have already been given ample clues as to Keefer's character, and his failure to support Maryk in the court-martial was not unexpected. He is the Luciferean evil genius who switches places with Queeg and becomes the Cainite fall guy. This is prepared and anticipated. What is unexpected—and, what is more important, unprepared—are the reasons given, the strange argumentative displacement that occurs. Not content with sacrificing Keefer, his own surrogate and artistic mouthpiece, Wouk, in the words of his new moral and legal mouthpiece, Greenwald, must also vindicate Queeg. Authority that had defected must now, in the pact of postwar reconciliation that follows, be restored.

Greenwald's defense of Queeg is so displaced and skewed as to be practically incredible. Rather than the issue being Queeg's base incompetence—for which there is ample evidence—the terms of the argument are shifted to those of regular navy versus wartime enlistees and draftees. Greenwald argues that if it had not been for the regular navy types like

Queeg, Hitler would have triumphed and his Jewish mother would have been made into soap to wash Herman Goering's fat behind (pp. 447–48). Leaving aside the fact that Queeg was serving in the Pacific, the argument could more profitably go as follows: if the regular navy had been made up of any more Queegs what would there have been to prevent Goering from occupying Chicago? The argument has shifted from Queeg's evident manic incompetence to Keefer's guilt, and beyond Keefer's guilt to the general guilt of all those who "sat on the sidelines getting rich and pursuing their own careers, while the real grunts of the world were carrying out the necessary chores." The argument is actually that debased. Whenever the terms of the argument shift, or are displaced so radically, one must suspect a psychic fault line. The fault line is guilt (in this case, sadly, not transcended)—not Maryk's, not Keefer's, but Wouk's. Greenwald's argument is this: "See, while I was studying law 'n' old Keefer here was writing his play for the Theatre Guild, and Willie here was on the playing fields of Prinston, all that time these birds we call regulars—these stuffy, stupid Prussians, in the army and the navy—were manning the guns" (p. 446). The restoration of the regular army and navy—the people who hold the world together, Wouk might argue—could be valid but it certainly does not fit the book that Wouk has written up until this point. A different volition has overtaken the novel, an intrusive will that has a point to make against the would-be intellectual—and against himself. Like Keefer, Wouk wishes to have his cake and eat it too, to establish a literate *raisonneur* who will provide the mythic structure and literary resonances with which the work is somewhat encumbered, and then to disestablish him. It is like writing a book about the war in which the character who writes a book about the war is branded. The vindication of Cain in the works of Hesse and of Steinbeck requires some transcendence of guilt; this Wouk was unable to do. Unnaturally, given the circumstances of the work and its own inner coherence, Wouk could not overcome his sense of guilt, or those aspects of himself that he needed to condemn in the character of Keefer.

The importance of the intrusive retraction does not stop there. The hinge of the work, as Wouk describes it in his brief foreword, is the character of Willie Keith. In the absence of his father, Keith is open to the many influences present on the ship, and his developing character becomes something of a touchstone. Thus to Willie is left the final summing-up, a summation that he acknowledges is derived from Greenwald's own accusations in the bitter posttrial "victory" celebration, and that he sends in the form of a letter proposing marriage to May, the night-club singer with whom, he now recognizes, he is in love. In some ways the letter becomes the sad testament of a generation.

The Caine Mutiny is an important book, even a crucial book, and despite Wouk's obvious skills (the depiction of the V12 program at Columbia, the typhoon chapter, and the court-martial), it is more important for what it reveals unconsciously, almost against itself: the preparation of a generation for its descent into simple stagnation and moral sluggishness. Tired of war and trauma, suspicious of intellectuals, of ideology, and of animosities based upon ideas and issues, eager to get on with the business of living, this generation settled down, seeking out common interests, emotional cohesion, and community. In the projection of these idyllic qualities (they are Abelite), it is little wonder that any possibility of a regenerate Cain should be prohibited.

In the letter to May, Willie identifies Keefer as the troublemaker, but then goes on to declare, in the wake of Greenwald's denunciation, "But I don't think Maryk had to relieve the captain." He then reaches a further conclusion: "The idea is, once you get an incompetent ass of a skipper— and it's a chance of war—there's nothing to do but to serve him as though he were the wisest and the best, cover his mistakes, keep the ship going, and bear up" (p. 468). But here again we must demur: obviously Queeg is more than an "incompetent ass"—that phrasing itself is part of the go-along-with-it, nothing-really-is-all-that-important ingratiating message of the letter. Queeg is shown to be dementedly dangerous, an emotional disaster, but his true sickness is covered in the general need for reinstatement. The father, who had been absent in several ways in the regeneration of Cain, is now returned to his former commanding status when Cain is condemned. In this sense, we see how the letter compounds the book's general retreat into the undifferentiated sentiment from which Byron first tried to extricate the Cain-Abel theme.

If the figure of authority is restored, then the virtues of Abel are validated. Queeg, a Cain, is now justified by being an Abel, that is, part of a general mess of undifferentiated feeling and, actually, the victim of a hostile, divisive Cain (Keefer). By jettisoning Keefer-Cain, Wouk demonstrates his own credentials for admission into the common purposes of American life. For comparisons we can think back to our prior discussion of *The Secret Sharer* and anticipate the coming section on *Billy Budd*. (Both works being part of the background of *The Caine Mutiny*, in some ways we can see that Wouk's work is a literary response to and comment not only on them, but on the development of regenerate Cain himself.) Finally, the promotion of Queeg has the moral equivalence of the vindication of the captain of the *Sephora*, and to blame Maryk would be the same as delivering up Leggatt to the authorities. But, even more dangerous, this particular justification of Queeg for his being "regular navy" echoes strangely the sense of things rendered by the naval chronicle relating— from a great distance—the events of Claggart's death and of Billy's punishment in Melville's work. It should be remembered that it is this report, "News from the Mediterranean," that Melville's own "inside narrative" is designed to correct. In fact, what Wouk has done is to discredit the inside narrative that he himself has given us and to reaffirm the public evaluation. In the report, Billy is degraded to a knife-wielding foreigner, whose "crime" is all the more heinous because directed against "a middle-aged man respectable and discreet, belonging to that minor official grade, the petty officers, upon whom, as none know better than the commissioned gentlemen knew, the efficiency of His Majesty's navy so largely depends" (p. 1433). Wouk's vindication of Queeg resorts to the same defense of his general function, and indulges in the same consolatory practice: just as the "commissioned gentlemen" must give the "petty officer" his due, so the hotshot, successful, and college-educated draftees are made to appreciate the regular Navy as well as the regular values of American democratic life. The generalized process of undifferentiation seems demeaning for all concerned.[15]

In this becalmed world, all possibility of historical change is denied, and the Cain-Abel theme loses its modern meaning. An indication of this loss of the capacity for differentiation is the sloppiness of the letter. Lacking precise care and filled with disarming "I guesses," it suggests that all issues are really petty in nature and of no importance in the face of the larger vision of peace and the need for fusion. In the letter, eager intelligence and moral will are immobilized. When the only intellect conceivable is cowardly, then the modern Cain of consciousness is badly impaired. *The Caine Mutiny* remains one of the notable expressions of the regressive ethos of the 1950s, and of a generation that ratted on its diamond. In seeking to avoid the envy of the gods, in finding acceptance, it became the generation that the gods despised.

PART THREE

Dramas of Envy

Chapter Eight

BILLY BUDD

ALL OF THE works discussed within the pattern of regenerate Cain (and they do have their variations and individual qualities), from Byron's *Cain* to Wouk's *The Caine Mutiny*, provide illumination and insight into each other and into the larger issues that they contain. In some ways, in the postromantic world, this pattern, despite all of the surges and sags, countercurrents and evident devolutions, is still dominant. If we ask why this should be so, we can see that the pattern of regenerate Cain predominates because it involves a dramatic search for values and an attempt to reintegrate the forces represented by Cain and Abel—the fugitive and the conventional. Furthermore, in almost every instance, it seeks to renew the defective structures of authority.

The modern works of envy make an entirely different use of the Cain-Abel theme. If the program of the regenerate Cain may be enrolled in the pattern of the Sacred Executioner, that of envy revives many of the theological issues of the unregenerate Cain that were discussed in the chapter "Citizen Cain," but with crucial alterations. The dramas of envy promise no historical resolution; in exactly the opposite manner, their participants are trapped by history. Although appropriating the elements of Citizen Cain, they seem to have left behind the positive dimensions of Christian eschatology. These are godless dramas, exposed to the relentlessness of historical circumstances and the enmity of personal antagonisms.

In the stories of regenerate Cain, envy is dismissed totally or drastically reduced in practice. Byron in his Preface had already rejected it as a source of motivation for his metaphysical rebel. Because of its loathsomeness, it has traditionally been noted for its inadmissibility (Dante, Bacon, and Melville). The presence of envy in *Billy Budd*, in *Amadeus* (and, peripherally, the very recent, *Prick Up Your Ears*), and in Unamuno's *Abel Sánchez* (the works discussed in this chapter) should indicate that we are treating radically altered patterns of presentation. These are noteworthy examples that offer full details of the ghastliness of envy, as well as of its extraordinary moral and philosophical seriousness.

If envy is the determining emotion in the pattern of reprobate Cain, then the double is the critical addition to the situation of regenerate Cain. Whereas regenerate Cain experiences little of the feeling of envy (in fact, it must be banished from his repertoire), reprobate Cain hears no summons to encounter his double. Paradoxically, the presence of the double

indicates that regenerate Cain is committed to identity; the absence of the
double indicates that reprobate Cain shuns identity and is tied to the
being of another, and that his want is invaded by envy. Envy was theologically abhorrent because it rejected the conditions of existence; its quarrel
was an unholy one with God. In another age, envy is equally repugnant
because it denies the integrity of the self. Envy represents the great for-
feit—it means one has forfeited his being to another. In such situational
captivity there can be little hope for release or regeneration.

When trapped in the drama of envy, both Cain and Abel assume different characteristics and purposes. Cain is not confronted with a hopelessly
divided world but rather with difference and with the arbitrariness of preference (this is why, in the pattern of regenerate Cain, authority as king,
captain, or crowd is either defective, absent, or contested, as is God in
Byron's *Cain*; despite some complexities, clearly the invitation is to transcend such authorities). Reprobate Cain does not seek difference, rather
he is victimized by it. This Cain fits the traditional pattern of the older
brother who feels himself superseded. He adheres to community and to
continuity, or at least to a kind of historical succession and predictability.
By attempting to remove risk and the unpredictable, he tries to bargain
not only with God but also with history—and this defines the nature of his
poor offering. Because his first experience is actually a kind of naive historical expectation, division is not presented as a given (as it was to regenerate Cain), rather the fact of division comes later, as a rude shock that shatters his comfort. In the closest, most inescapable of circumstances he is
compelled to confront the tragedy of differentiation and the arbitrariness
of preference, and this latter, in its turn, provokes the mystery of iniquity.
In the moral quest of regenerate Cain, mystery adhered to the coming of
the double, the shaping agency of the self. In these stories, mystery adheres to the presence of evil. If, in the stories of regenerate Cain, evil is in
a way accidental or circumstantial—not actually integral to Cain's motivation or character—here, in the dramas of envy, evil is radical, not only
entwined in the closed situation, but essential to Cain's character.

Such a fundamental change in the intrinsic motivation must alter the
overall situation, as well as the roles of the two antagonists. In several of
the works, a person of not inconsiderable talents unaccountably and help-
lessly finds himself slipped behind a person of extraordinary genius, mag-
netic attractiveness, or simple personal brashness and perhaps vulgarity. In
these dramas, there is little opportunity or room for escape. The two characters are locked in every way, both morally and physically. There is no
double to create space, or liberate consciousness in any way, and there are
tight physical constraints—all suggested by the original fraternal nexus. As
Melville explains in *Billy Budd*, being shipboard provides little hope for
escape from animosities. Amadeus and Salieri are conjoined in the Aus-

trian court beset by intrigue. Joe Orton and Ken Halliwell share a bed-sitter for sixteen years, and Abel and Joaquín are enclosed by a claustro-phobic and fratricidal Spain. These works are not properly works of char-acter development, but rather works of situations, where we are brought to reflect on the monstrous design that traps and destroys both Cain and Abel.

In all of these works, Abel, rather than being demoted, is the figure who retains something of his earlier theological status and who continues to be the "preferred of God," *Ama-deus.* But, despite his traditional qual-ities, Abel also undergoes radical change. If Cain is demoted because of his attempts to halt change, to put history on hold, Abel is promoted be-cause of his absolute openness to change, the freedom with which he en-ters into experience. In this sense, the old innocence and simplicity con-tinue to serve the new Abel well. But they are changed. The old gargoyle Cain has become part of the new Abel. The scatological Cain of the medi-eval mystery has become the darling who dares, who confronts, who vio-lates, and who by violation itself succeeds. There is in fact a connection between scatology and his openness to God, to inspiration, to history. It might seem inappropriate to designate the scatological and even infantile Amadeus or the cruising homosexual Orton as the saintly Abel, but in their free responsiveness, their refusal of community, their acceptance of discontinuity, they move with the wind and are open to whatever occurs. Their free-moving genius is responsive to the divine afflatus that is indi-cated by Amadeus' flatulence or Orton's promiscuity. They live as free from historical constraints as from communal ones, while Cain, in the lan-guage of *Prick Up Your Ears,* is "tight-assed."

The same challenge of authenticity presents itself in these works as it did in *Demian.* Only here the Abel character of spirit seems instinctively adept. The word is of course, *instinctively.* He is not the character of con-sciousness who overcomes division, as was the regenerate Cain, but rather a figure of unitary force, and even unconscious ability and talent. In this sense, we begin to see why Abel becomes more of the artist, and also why Cain is rendered helpless—himself the victim, incapable of coping with the quality of the other precisely because it is a given, a gift. This Cain is reprobate, trapped not only by the past but also in his vindictive fury com-ing to represent history itself that refuses to permit escape and drags those who seek liberation back down.

If Abel is promoted, this does not mean that Cain is demoted. Or, if he is, he is only demoted in relation to the character duality in which he is an actor. The fact is that Cain, in these dramas of envy, is a "near-miss." Envy is of course more than the active realization that one is not good enough. It is most harbored by those who are not *quite* good enough. Claggart, for instance, is one of the two men on board who understands what Billy

Budd represents. Joaquín interprets Abel Sánchez's painting in a way that the latter never could. Salieri alone seems to appreciate Mozart's true genius, and Halliwell has been, as Orton privately acknowledges, a collaborator, providing titles, correcting lines, understanding significances.[1]

It is clear that even in these dramas Cain is not simply denounced. An extraordinary pathos invests his psychological situation. He must confront the tragedy of differentiation and the arbitrariness of preference in such a way that only his want is revealed. The horrible nature of the dualistic involvement insures the catastrophe. The Cain character almost literally senses that his being has been taken away from him. In a desperate struggle the lapsed Cain character then seeks to hold on to the very force of deprivation in order to regain his being. But this is the tragedy: fundamentally he has consigned his being to another. We see how significant then is the drama of the double with its summons to a fundamental confrontation with the self. The Cain of the dramas of envy is afforded no such possibility of release: he has no double and enjoys no self. In the need to repossess his own being, he lusts to possess that of another. It would appear that just as twinship would be the natural adjunct of the regenerate Cain and his double, so homoeroticism would be naturally implied in this relationship (indeed Beaver, in his excellent collection of Melville's shorter fiction, makes such a suggestion concerning Claggart's involvement with Billy).[2] But this does not necessarily imply sexual actions or desires. It indicates the relation where one's being requires the other; the other who is a constant reminder of one's own insufficiencies. Such impotence only has recourse to destruction, annihilating the other's personality in order to regain one's own—but also destroying the other in order to destroy simultaneously one's own. When comparison is invidious, the cycle is always vicious.

The character of Billy comes from the world of romance—he is the upright barbarian, the happy sailor of engaging innocence and simplicity; moreover, he is one who is unaware of his origins, a foundling. Billy is a character who, in his carefree innocence, seems to have escaped from history. Yet the direction of the story—as it does in the Cain-Abel accounts of whatever pattern—requires an involvement with history, and in *Billy Budd*, more particularly, the involvement of unsuspecting innocence with history and fatal destiny. *Billy Budd* is decidedly not a boy's adventure story, nor, as Melville himself reminds us, is it a romance. The character of no past, the new Adam—so dear to the American mythic imagination, innocent and guileless, yet loyal and unquestioning—becomes trapped in the gears of history. But this does not mean that Billy represents spiritual perfection; although innocent he is not a saint. His attractiveness does not depend upon his achievements (although he is known as a peacemaker), but rather upon his happy unself-consciousness, not upon what he does, but rather upon what he is. But his very guilelessness becomes an ingredient in the recipe for disaster. Thus it is that Melville, somewhat in the vein of Ambrose, indicates the significance of Billy's one physical defect, his tendency to stutter under stress: "Billy was a striking instance that the arch-interferer, the envious marplot of Eden, still has more or less to do with every human consignment to this planet of earth."[3] The escape to effortlessness, to innocence, can never fully elude the earth-bound pull. In this sense, the Cain-Abel story serves a quintessential American paradigm, where the move toward innocence is constrained by the complex of history.

As the words quoted would indicate, in *Billy Budd* the theological implications are persistent. Beyond romance, it also reaches beyond history. *Billy Budd* is a theological drama because in it evil is radical. We can see that this counters the idyllic pattern of the Enlightenment represented by Salomon Gessner's *Der Tod Abels*, where every attempt is made to "de-radicalize" events, to remove all dire possibilities, to forge a more common bond of human communion. But in *Billy Budd*, characters stand forth in radical delineation; that is, their traits are irreducible to further explanation.

As with many of the other Cain-Abel stories of the post-Byronic period, there exists in *Billy Budd* a strong discrepancy between the meaning of characters and events and the comprehension of the common understanding. For instance, Vere and Billy are described as representing in almost essential form rare qualities of human nature—"so rare indeed as to be all but incredible to average minds however cultivated . . ." (p. 1418). Like other Cain-Abel stories holding a mystery and thus appealing to initiates, *Billy Budd* is an "inside narrative." This is meant in the most obvious sense as an ironic counterpoint to the official naval chronicle, "News from the Mediterranean," which, like most "news," is ignorant of what really happens. So "inside" is the narrative that in the crucial episode, where Vere, alone with Billy, explains why Billy must hang, even the narrator adopts a pose of conjecture as to what is said. Here there is not even cryptophasic language—the curtain drops totally between our understanding and the mystery. Throughout the work, again and again, we as readers are asked to reflect upon the discrepancy between worldly knowledge and the kind of knowledge required to understand the nature of Billy, the antipathy of Claggart, and the mind of Vere. Invocation of this discrepancy might be the most prevalent aesthetic fact of *Billy Budd*. Yet, unlike what happens in our response to a work like *The Secret Sharer*, we are not left totally comfortable with the consequences of this special awareness. *Billy Budd* inclines us toward a vision of radical character differences, of fatal involvements, and of the mysteries surrounding these events. Yet equally, even naggingly present, is the question of whether a touch of humanity, an ingredient of common understanding, would not have been more useful than the tragic awareness so frequently invoked. And this perspective is not an external critical stance, but one actually promoted by the work itself.

Billy Budd is a story that deals little with normal social exchange. Rather than novelistic, its style and matter fit better into what we may call the morality play form of the Cain-Abel story. All emphasis rests upon a few dominant aspects of several characters who are brought together in a few crucial events—"with sky and sea for spectators and judge." We recall that in the spare account of Genesis 4 Cain and Abel go out into the field alone. This general scheme holds true for *Demian* and *The Secret Sharer*, as it does for *Abel Sánchez* and *Billy Budd*. These are all closed, internal stories, whose concern is the spirit in the duress of history, or some fatal action, or, more happily, following the nature of its own development. These have been the modern pressures of the Cain-Abel story, in which *Billy Budd* participates brilliantly and revealingly. Rather than a failed work, *Billy Budd* is a dense, complex masterpiece. Its cryptic elusiveness, its folds of mystery and sparseness of detail, do not show failures to create or define, but are, rather, the very heart of the matter.

The first character who sees more than meets the eye is the Dansker. Initially, he is enchanted by the happy light of Billy Budd. Upon subsequent encounters, a "quizzing sort of look" is aroused in the veteran's face, "sometimes replaced by an expression of speculative query as to what might eventually befall a nature like that, dropped into a world not without some mantraps and against whose subtleties simple courage lacking experience and address, and without any touch of defensive ugliness, is of little avail . . ." (p. 1378). Claggart and Billy are completely differentiated; in Billy, Claggart's malice is unreciprocated, but it is also unsuspected. It is the Dansker who explains to the disbelieving Billy that the series of minor incidents that have marred Billy's service on the *Bellipotent* have indeed originated with Claggart. And yet, in his "primitive" wisdom, he remains aloof from the events that must take their way undeterred. He provides the first instance, of which Vere is the most important, of acquiescence in fatality. Special knowledge unfortunately does not lead to any alteration of events, but rather to helplessness in front of their destined unfolding.

Claggart's antipathy to Billy is spontaneous and profound. In fact, such antipathy is mysterious because it is so radical, irreducible to further causal explanation. Melville, discoursing on the origins of such hatred, invokes its special mysteriousness when it seems to be provoked by good will and harmlessness (p. 1381). The passage recalls Augustine's discourse, referred to earlier, on Cain's hatred of Abel because of Abel's very goodness.

So special is Claggart's animosity that even Calvinism does not contribute to its comprehension. Calvinism extends a general taint to all mankind; everybody falls short of spiritual perfection. Claggart's however is a special case, in the sense that a few rare individuals are so possessed by an extraordinary malignity. To explain this phenomenon, Melville must have recourse to Plato and his concept of "natural depravity" (p. 1383). The Bible might have helped, but it was no longer "popular." By its very dismissal, the invocation of course establishes the Bible as primary evidentiary material. Stressing the indecipherability of Claggart to normal human sense, Melville refers to a worldly-wise man, who, although no adherent to any organized religion or systematic philosophy, nevertheless realizes that in some matters the "knowledge of the world" is not applicable. Again, we see that in a context that is determinedly secular, the Cain-Abel story seems to summon up more fundamental concerns. It seems to exist, as did Byron's catastrophist theories, in the land between the older religion (now denied or no longer popular) and the more benign modern secular thought. Since it contains such radical innocence and radical evil, it seems to serve as a mythic surrogate for what were once the concerns of "organized" religion. Common, even worldly understanding is helpless in these matters; one needs a special insight. "Coke and Blackstone hardly shed so much light into obscure spiritual places as the Hebrew prophets. And who were they? Mostly recluses" (p. 1382). In another passage, Melville acknowledges that suggestions of the "mystery of iniquity" have little to recommend them to a modern reader (p. 1384). The reference is arch because it is precisely the relevancy of such understanding that he wishes to introduce. The procedure seems to be one of introducing a level of reading that is retracted, but not so completely that the suggestion does not remain. A man out of favor is writing a story in an unpopular mode, and ironically invalidating an out-of-favor method of interpretation, while, at the same time, insinuating its singular appropriateness.

The mystery is Cainite in another sense. Although Billy's virtues, like those of Abel, predate "Cain's city and citified man" (p. 1362), Claggart's particular depravity derives from the combination of reasonable conduct with extraordinary malice. That is, it is abetted by civilization. "Civilization, especially of the austerer sort, is auspicious to it. It folds itself in the mantle of respectability" (p. 1383). Such external covering makes Claggart's innate depravity all the more pernicious. Melville could be describing Mengele at Auschwitz when he writes, "Toward the accomplishment of an aim which in wantonness of atrocity would seem to partake of the insane, he will direct a cool judgment, sagacious and sound" (p. 1383). In an earlier, now discarded reading of the manuscript, the phrase was transcribed as "wantonness of malignity," which in its recollection of Coleridge's apposite description of Iago's "motiveless malignity," seemed quite useful. But the currently accepted reading, "wantonness of atrocity," yields bleaker twentieth-century associations.

Like the other characters in the drama of envy, beginning perhaps with Lucifer himself, Claggart is not an ordinary person, nor is his envy quotidian. His own debility derives from the fact that he is one of the two people on board ship (the other being Vere) capable of comprehending what Billy represents. Billy, to whom all natural graces adhere, is precisely that—graced. Claggart, on the other hand, is a near-miss. And yet, it is the very connection, the relationship with Billy, that draws out Claggart's vice. A gifted creature bears heavily and yet unknowingly on another creature who has lost the gift, who lives in a fallen world, and who is inexplicably compelled to destroy the creature whom in his secret thoughts he loves—"To him the spirit lodged within Billy. . . ." What he knows bitterly is that Billy has never experienced a fallen world, that his spirit has "never willed malice nor experienced the reactionary bite of the serpent" (p. 1385). Billy seems autonomous, but not so much in his accomplishments, as in his nature. He is a naif, in the sense that Schiller used the word. No other matters of consciousness interfere with his apprehension of where and what he is.

Claggart, on the other hand, suffers from division. But, like Lucifer and Iago, this Cain possesses no positive energy or value that propells him to overcome division, to seek out some form of psychic reintegration, but instead he can only respond with a malignity that in truth masks despair, a self-surrender to the superior virtue of the other. With "cynic disdain" Claggart disparages Billy's innocence—"To be nothing more than innocent!" Yet, Melville continues, he appreciates the appeal of it, and would willingly have shared it, "but he despaired of it." In some way, the nature of their situation requires this, since it is the very presence of the happy Abel that calls into virtual being the defects of Cain. This is why the story summons the sense of mystery, of tragedy, of character determinism:

> With no power to annul the elemental evil in him, tho readily enough he could hide it; apprehending the good, but powerless to be it; a nature like Claggart's, surcharged with energy as such natures almost invariably are, what recourse is left to it but to recoil upon itself and, like the scorpion for which the Creator alone is responsible, act out to the end the part allotted to it. (p. 1385)

In the fatal nexus of their involvement, the two different natures—and the animal imagery reinforces the sense of determinism—are caught in a dance of death that must destroy each of them.

Over this fatal involvement, it is the responsibility of Vere to preside. He is the only character, other than Claggart, intellectually capable of appreciating what Billy represents. He is the only character who perceives the fatal mystery (unlike the Dansker who comprehends the vulnerability of Billy, Vere understands the knot of involvement in theological terms). He, for instance, rises to the level of the narrator, and in groping attempts to comprehend the malice of Claggart, refers to the " 'mystery of iniquity,' a matter for psychologic theologians to discuss" (p. 1412). After Billy has laid Claggart out with the punch, Vere whispers, "Fated boy" (p. 1405). Earlier he is not at all deceived by the lying Claggart, and over his dead body he recognizes "the divine judgment on Ananias." Stirred to his soul, he shortly thereafter exclaims, "Struck dead by an angel of God! Yet the angel must hang!" (p. 1406).

Remarkably enough, Vere perceives that Billy is a Sacred Executioner. However, many of the features that we had observed in the stories of a regenerate Cain and that partake of the general pattern of the Sacred Executioner are curiously reversed. Vere possesses the special knowledge of the mystery of the fatal involvement, even perhaps of its larger theological implications, and yet he must act as an officer of the law, as a judge within the regimen of naval justice. In a crucial paragraph, Melville explains: "In a legal view the apparent victim of the tragedy was he who had sought to victimize a man blameless; and the indisputable deed of the latter, navally regarded, constituted the most heinous of military crimes." Pointing out the complications of the case, the passage finally lays the burden in Captain Vere's hands: "The essential right and wrong involved in the matter, the clearer that might be, so much the worse for the responsibility of a loyal sea commander, inasmuch as he was not authorized to determine the matter on that primitive basis" (p. 1408).

Indeed Vere is trapped. And there is little wonder why in the decades of the 1950s and the 1960s this work should have inspired such opposed readings, presenting as it does the competing demands of essential moral integrity on one side and social responsibility on the other. On the one hand, *Billy Budd* is presented as an example of Melville's "political classicism," while on the other, it is regarded as a tragedy of moral principle, that is, Vere's.[4] Vere himself acknowledges a discrepancy between the two laws. "At the Last Assizes it shall acquit. But how here?" (p. 1415). The obvious tragedy lies in the separation, and so the question remains, bearing in mind Leggatt's role in *The Secret Sharer* and the regenerate pattern of the Sacred Executioner: If at the Last Assizes, why not here?

Despite the rare nobility and the philosophic quality of Vere's personality, a strange undertow of reservations persists in regard to his character and his actions.[5] For one, he is described as pedantic (pp. 1371, 1414). His action in establishing the drumhead court is questioned by the surgeon, and these doubts are shared by the lieutenants and the captain of the marines. Although in the actual trial he is technically a witness, he serves as prosecutor and judge. In short, he pulls rank on the members of the court, who are supposed to render judgment: "Loyal lieges, plain and practical, though at bottom they dissented from some points Captain Vere had put to them, they were without the faculty, hardly had the inclination, to gainsay one whom they felt to be an earnest man, one too not less their superior in mind than in naval rank" (p. 1417).

All the attempts of the practical seamen to create space around the event, to bring into consideration questions that were part of the pattern of the Sacred Executioner, are dismissed by the captain. The officer of the marines breaks in to plead that Billy "purposed neither mutiny nor homicide" (p. 1415). He looks to motive rather than event. The sailing master, speaking falteringly, asks, "Can we not convict and mitigate the penalty?" (p. 1416). Vere resists each suggestion. He takes the specific case and globalizes it, and in so doing returns the Cain-Abel story to the principled opposition that heralded its advent in history. But here the problem lies not directly in the religious scruples that moved Philo and Augustine, but rather in historical circumstances and an inability to break through the rules of war. The earlier mutinies and the entire wave of rebellion pushed on by the French Revolution inspire a rigidity of response. And yet, the rigidity seems strangely unnecessary. It does not appear that there would have been any kind of mutinous behavior had Billy been spared. The reaction of the men to his execution in fact seems to indicate the contrary to be true: grumbling occurred at his execution. Earlier, Melville reminds the reader that the very mutineers had performed bravely at Trafalgar. Would moral laxity and a kind of slippage in order have occurred had Billy been spared? There is no indication of that. The tendency to globalize an issue reveals the correlative incapacity to isolate a judgement, to see an event for what it is. (Here of course Vere's mental habits differ radically from the suppleness of judgment introduced by another political conservative, his intellectual model, Montaigne.) But why does he insist so much on the broader picture? I think it goes back not to his political conservatism but rather to his philosophical sense of things. Adhering to the higher sense of awareness, he bears witness to the theological drama that has unfolded. In this case, theology reinforces history, or, put another way, historical reasoning is only an excuse to invoke the prior theological perception: "Struck dead by an angel of God. Yet the angel must hang" (p. 1406). Such higher awareness in *The Secret Sharer* led to a sense of freedom and liberation in regard to Leggatt, but also in regard to the young captain. The same awareness works to different purpose in *Billy Budd*, forcing Billy and Vere into the constraints of historical necessity. Rather than serving to liberate humanity from history, which seems in a way to be the ultimate purpose of the regenerate Cain, Vere's higher theological awareness only serves to solidify the hold of history.

Billy Budd does not manifest a reintegration of spirit and authority. And here authority in the character of Captain Vere is itself the victim. Indeed, after the events described his career knows no confirmation. The fame that he had seeks, the secret ambition of his personality, eludes him. Mortally wounded, his unconscious thoughts, liberated by the morphine used to deaden his pain, return to the largest decision of his life, and he is heard to utter, "Billy Budd. Billy Budd." The attendant who reports his words declares that they were not said with any accent of remorse. But he is ignorant of the events that precede the utterance and of who Billy had been. He recounts this episode to the *Bellipotent*'s senior officer of the marines, "who, as the most reluctant to condemn of the members of the drumhead court, too well knew, though here he kept the knowledge to himself, who Billy Budd was" (p. 1432). In a work so dependent upon discrepant awarenesses, the report of no remorse in Vere's voice is brought by someone who does not know the story to someone who does, and who is the judge least inclined to condemn Billy. By what we have observed as a constant practice of the work, Melville manages to introduce a sentiment that he has apparently denied.

The Cain-Abel story habitually courts larger perspectives. If the setting of *Billy Budd* is an English man-of-war, the issues as well as the dimensions of the characters involved are American. In his Massey Lectures (1985) at Harvard University, Irving Howe places *Billy Budd* in the Emersonian context of "American newness," that bracing, heady time of the 1830s and the 1840s, when the democratic ideal led to true vision of openness and brotherhood. Twain and Melville continued to share in this moment, and admired characters like Captain Bixby or Jack Chase: "open, dignfied, proud yet egalitarian, these men breathe a spirit of friendliness." Even in the opening chapters of *Moby Dick*, "Melville honors the fraternity of workers, men of all nations, colors, beliefs, who come together on the *Pequod*." "For the early Melville the democratic ethos meant forging links with mariners, mutineers and cannibals; filling one's lungs with the world's air; and receiving the blessings rightly due the elect of staunch republicans."[6] Given the terms of this wide-striding openness—the emphasis on friendship and fraternity—it is appropriate that *Billy Budd*, with its properties and resources of the Cain-Abel theme, is the later Melville's answer to the hopefulness of his earlier self.

If the issues are American, the characters, too, have a stamp on them that is prophetically native: Billy Budd, the upright barbarian who cannot fathom duplicity, who is tongue-tied under emotional stress, and as a consequence can only respond to verbal abuse by means of violence; innocence makes its own inadvertent contribution by being so lacking in consciousness that it cannot fathom accusations. Captain Vere, who does not allow for any suppleness in civilization, but rather succumbs to the iron hand of history, is himself an epitome of a national problem. There is little room for liberation from history in this story when innocence is violent and philosophy is rigid. Understood on the national plane, the diagnostic seems distressingly pertinent particularly when leaders in messianic language persist in making "hard" decisions that turn out to be wrong, while deliberately eschewing easier, more sensible ways. As an American tragedy—and this accounts for its remarkable reverberations—*Billy Budd* shows a failure of civilization to make room for aberration, to create space around conventional thinking. *The Secret Sharer* is so stirring because one sees in the developed character of the young captain the possibility of law allowing for spirit, of order encompassing heterodoxy and energy. The twin is not destroyed but literally incorporated (the more hopeful meaning of the foundation sacrifice). And this is why severance is brave and forthright; neither character is left with a void in his being, with the sense of some possibility unrealized. Oddly enough, Vere, who despises Claggart the way a man of honor would despise debased lying, ends up like Claggart, an unfinished man. The unknowing attendant may not detect any remorse in Vere's voice, but we can be sure that Vere destroys himself when he fails to save the possibilities that Billy had represented.

Chapter Nine

AMADEUS AND *PRICK UP YOUR EARS*

WE INTRODUCE these very contemporary works here to show how and why the struggles of artists form a natural venue for the Cain-Abel story. Our concern here lies not with the expressive fury of the *poète maudit*, who welcomes the mark of Cain, nor with the fortunate accounts of regeneration, rather our interests are determined by the theological drama and the situation of envy established by the enclosed relationship of Billy and Claggart. These evoke the older Cain-Abel stories, where happy brightness is destroyed, where pages are ripped from the book of human history. Liberation is not in view here, where rivals and friends destroy one another, and where each is trapped in a situation that is determinedly inescapable.

This notion of conflict brings together artistic development and the Cain-Abel story in special ways. After all, nobody is born famous; nor is talent immediately recognized. (The exception to the first point actually proves the rule; the presence of an aristocracy is precisely to locate exceptionality in status and hence to remove it from the realm of achievement. Such removal seeks to dissolve envy as a social force. Out of one's orbit by reason of birth itself, and by means beyond one's control, the preeminence of inherited position does not enter into relationship with one's own and thus cannot be a basis for envy.) The story of artistic development requires early anonymity, lack of recognition, before one superior ability emerges from the pack. In this separation from what was at first a state of undifferentiation, some are obviously left behind. In Hesse's *Demian*, these are considered representatives of the herd mentality whom the superior Cain figure must abandon. In the dramas of envy, however, Cain is the superseded figure, one who is suddenly baffled by the arbitrariness of preference.

Art is itself an offering, deeply involved with personal talents and values; consequently, here much more of the self is at stake in acceptance, but even more in rejection. Saul Bellow has recently written, "A piece of writing is an offering. You bring it to the altar and hope it will be accepted. You pray at least that rejection will not throw you into a rage and turn you into a Cain."[1] The attractions of art are urged by the rewards, the acclaim, the glory, the fame. Milton called it the "sudden blaze"—and in so doing indicated its precariousness but also its astonishing quality. Young Salieri seems secure in his future promise amid the musical world of Vienna, when "suddenly, without warning . . ." the prodigy that was Mozart appeared.[2] Such arbitrariness of preference is a mystery that baffles the unsuspecting, who unaccountably find their own presentation diminished and unworthy. The collapse of the self into wantingness and vindictiveness is a perverse and yet understandable reaction. And this volatility of reaction is perhaps the most important relevancy of art for the Cain-Abel story. One's being is all the more wrapped up in an offering when the offering represents time, effort, talent, and values of the self. It is as if the interloper has taken what I was supposed to be. He has taken my "stuff"; he has taken myself. Thus abandoned, the self is left in a position of helplessness, and can only turn toward the favored one—the Amadeus—in order to recover by insidious, hostile, and, at times, physically violent means the being that was lost.

Despite the impressions of arbitrariness and the reactions of baffled astonishment, these works are not mute as to what constitutes worthy and unworthy offerings. In fact, their appeal is derived from their exploration of the opposed values. In clear ways, despite their apparent differences from the presentation of the regenerate Cain in works like *Demian*, these artistic versions of the drama of envy share the same historical basis—a need for authenticity, or put negatively, a rejection of the offering that is inauthentic. What we have witnessed, and what has been brought home most vividly by Hesse's work, is that the modernist bias is not toward the works that represent the traditions of Erasmus or of Arnold, not toward the sense of historical continuity, of gradual evolution, of unity, and finally of a more benign view of human experience, but rather toward the Germanic Lutheran past, the sense of radical discontinuity, of division, of "catastrophism." Whether regenerate or reprobate as far as Cain is concerned, this seems to be a controlling view of the theme. In this sense, Byron's link with twentieth-century literature is all the more evident.

We can see why Salieri and the character Halliwell presented in John Lahr's book and Alan Bennett's film script are demoted versions of the artist. Salieri wishes to make a bargain with God, while Halliwell is "programmed" to be the artist. The former can not elude conventionality, while the latter is an anachronism, witty, refined, and literate. "He behaved very much like a camp young man of the 30's," who had become, as he was cruelly informed, "a middle-aged nonentity."[3] Salieri does not seek literal authenticity, but rather historical security. "My one desire was to join all the composers who had celebrated [God's] glory through the long Italian past . . ." (p. 11). He adopts a labor theory of value when his own efforts are outshone by Mozart's, "You know how hard I've worked!" (p. 74). And he insists that God operate according to the dictates of human reason.

But the wind bloweth where it listeth. And nowhere is this truer than in the creatures (Mozart is called "the Creature" by Salieri) whom God favors. The combination of extraordinary talent with extraordinary vulgarity is appalling to reason and to respectability. In a great reversal, scatology is restored to the drama of envy, but it now belongs to the character of Abel and represents, to be sure, a backward view of the world, but one turned from true virtue rather than from would-be virtue. The forces of the monster Cain, of the scatological Cain, return to inhere in the character of Abel, who by his openness to history, to experience, to what comes, repudiates any conventional being. Abel continues to possess the qualities of simplicity, but in the new reaction to what "respectability" has come to connote, simplicity also implies freedom of all sorts, openness at both ends. This covers Joe Orton, as he is presented, who indeed does blow where he listeth.

If scatology has become an expression of openness to the divine afflatus, then Mozart is indeed God's own magic flute. His own creative fury brings him into opposition with the traditional and the conventional, and his response is obscene. "[Gluck] talked all his life about modernizing opera, but creates people so lofty they sound as though they shit marble" (p. 47). To preachments about the eternal in art, Mozart is similarly profane. "You're all up on perches, but it doesn't hide your arseholes. You don't give a shit about gods and heroes. If you are honest—each one of you—which of you isn't more at home with his hairdresser than with Hercules?" (p. 89). And yet out of this obscene, infantile personality came inspired music. Obviously, then, Salieri's war is not with Mozart but rather with God, the God who has betrayed him.

In *Prick Up Your Ears*, the situation is even more painful because Joe Orton is not immediately (or ever) a prodigy. He and his companion had lived in undifferentiated obscurity for many years before Orton's plays, with their brash antitraditional satire, found a receptive audience in the mid-sixties. Halliwell's plight goes beyond that of a common brotherhood; he is, in fact, the superseded older brother. It was he who had taken Orton under his wing, who had been something of a mentor, and then who is compelled to suffer as their relative careers alter perceptibly on that cruel seesaw of human comparison. From being mentor, Halliwell becomes collaborator, and then when Orton is the person in demand, he becomes a tagalong, a sidekick. More and more he senses not only his own unworthiness, but his extraordinary dependence upon the personality who has brought his unworthiness home to him.

Like Salieri, Halliwell is a constricted personality. He has never seemed young, in contrast to Orton, whose youthful upstart energy is a considerable part of his establishment-twitting charm. The effortlessness of the "gifted" partner, that of Billy, or of Shaffer's Amadeus, is never his. Where Orton is able to "generate easy affection," Halliwell's own sense of wantingness instills in him a sense that he is not wanted. "He could love literature but never life or himself." Orton's success activates Halliwell's nagging sense of his own worthlessness (p. 24). Halliwell is a nothing, and his only release is by annihilation, in this case, annihilation of the person who is somebody, and upon whom his being depends. The "inside narrative" by means of which this very dramatic story is unveiled is entitled by Joe Orton, "Diary of a Somebody." The suggestion could be, of course, and it is one that John Lahr makes, that only by killing a somebody could a nobody attain through violent death the notice that was denied him in life (unfortunately forming a pattern for many of the tragedies of the 1960s; p. 41).

In the more modern versions of the situation of envy, one is less inclined to blame. Although the contrast of virtues (that is, the qualities that determine worthiness and unworthiness on the merciless altar of art), is apparent, more and more attention is paid to the situation that made the disaster possible. In the terrible unmasking of Salieri, the climactic passage of the American version of the play, the maimed Italian rips Mozart's music in half, and in a black Mass parody of the Communion, the taking of the host, ingests a corner of the sheet music as a poison: "I eat what God gives me. Dose after dose. For all of life. His poison. We are both poisoned, Amadeus. I with you: you with me" (p. 139). This inverted pledge of brotherhood invokes the lethal communion of Iago and Othello: "I am your own forever," and indeed beyond brotherhood seems to celebrate an infernal marriage between the two men.

In this sense, the situation of envy contrasts radically with the stories of a regenerate Cain, where indeed the goal seems to be the reintegration of separate and divided qualities. In the works discussed in this chapter, the failure of reintegration is shown even more vengefully when the tables are turned on the audience itself. The very title of *Prick Up Your Ears* expresses the defiance with which the audience is addressed. In *Amadeus*, we are meant not only to follow the anguish of Salieri, but are described as his true devotees—Salieri consequently becomes our own patron saint, the patron saint of mediocrities—those who, although appreciating the play, would in their own lives commit Salieri's sin and would regard as boorish such radical incongruencies as are brought together by extraordinary genius and sheer vulgarity. This is part of the scatological *renversement du monde* that marks the medieval dramas of Cain. So perverse a trick as that of turning the tables on the audience itself was first earlier perpetrated by that most paradoxical of twentieth-century writers, Miguel de Unamuno, who entitled his novella, *Abel Sánchez*, and thereby seemed to corroborate the public evaluation of the leading character, a judgment that the "inside narrative" of the private journal most assuredly reverses. All of this seems to be part of the larger business of Cain, extending beyond the dramas of envy. Just as Leggatt, the noble Cain of *The Secret Sharer*, bears no mark that blazons his virtues to the world, so these Cains of equally doomed enterprise live in a tangle of contradictions that seem especially designed to baffle the small-minded.

In the situation of envy, the father figure, a crucial figure in the vindication of Abel and an absent one in the regeneration of Cain, is far from sustaining. In *What the Butler Saw*, one of Orton's characters declares, "I lived in a normal family. I had no love for my father." In fact, homosexuality can be regarded as an outright defiance of fatherhood, a way of preventing the processes of generation and continuity. When Vere counsels Billy as a father it is that very form of address that precipitates the violent reaction, and when he advises Billy in the mysterious scene from which we are all excluded, he is as Abraham to Isaac; but in this instance, no substitute dispatched by God intervenes to save the boy and justify the man of faith. The fatherly role that Vere adopts in this case helps effect the tragedy. In *Amadeus*, Mozart marries against his father's wishes. When news reaches Wolfgang of Leopold's death, Salieri is present. In a gesture that is less than paternal—an expression of a wish to take over Mozart's being, possess his skill—and, consequently, more than a gesture of male bonding, Salieri opens his arms to Mozart in a "wide gesture of paternal benevolence" (p. 109). Mozart at first inclines but then catches himself and returns to the memory of his true father. The consignment of his being to Salieri would have represented a falsification of his genius, a return to undifferentiated communion out of which the developing nature of his gifted genius had directed him.

The special appropriateness of the struggles and relationship of artists for the Cain-Abel theme must finally be ascribed to the position of art itself. Art is the stern mistress that brooks no competitor (hence Salieri's indulgence for sweets is seen as a substitute oral gratification, indicating a lack of true commitment). Art is, in the language of the play, an absolute. The unstinting pursuit of its rewards and its rejections must be viewed as the ultimate passion that takes possession of the characters. It is tempting to think that if the regeneration of Cain depends upon the transcendence of the patriarchy, then possibly the interruption of the circuit of enmity between rival talents would also depend upon demotion of art as an absolute. One could say that if this is not precisely what Shaffer intended in his play, it is much more obviously what Joe Orton set out to accomplish in his.

Yet it is in their art that Mozart (certainly) and Orton (possibly) have survived (in Orton's case, the success of the film has helped launch several revivals of his plays). The terrible discrepancies between art and life, the strange mixture of genius or talent and vulgarity, are forgotten as figures survive in their art, where they have emerged from the mixture of life into a strange and uncontaminated purity. There of course the accusing figure of the father in *Don Giovanni* is converted into the forgiving father of *The Magic Flute*: "Wolfgang feared Leopold no longer: a final legend has been made . . ." (p. 132). Salieri of course—in the play—knows no such transformations. In fact his punishment is equal to his political success: like Cain, in Ambrose's version of his story, he is condemned to outlive his fame and memory and hence his own life. Moreover, his fame will be guaranteed as the murderer of Mozart, a legend that his own "false confession" propagates. More than annihilation, he finds notoriety, but still within the bounds of his fatal attachment.[4]

Chapter Ten

ABEL SÁNCHEZ

IT BECOMES clearer that the pattern established by the regenerate Cain is the dominant one in the nineteenth and twentieth centuries, when we observe that it, or the forces that produced it, have been at work in transforming even the Cain-Abel stories that participate in the situation of envy. The envious Cain character, as we have seen, seems to be less an outright villain and more of a victim himself. There seems to be nobody really to blame in the dramas of envy. Even Melville alludes to this in his description of Claggart's deterministic helplessness.

But the dominance of the pattern of the regenerate Cain effects an even more stunning reversal. In *Abel Sánchez*, so thorough-going, so all-consuming is the envy of Joaquín, that Unamuno, by some perverse paradoxicality, is able to make it heroic. This revolution is remarkable because at no time has envy been admirable, particularly in the pattern of the regenerate Cain, where one of his major attributes is precisely the absence of envy. Unamuno blends the drama of envy with the patterns of the regenerate Cain.

Throughout his career, Unamuno was fascinated by Cain and Abel and the emotion of envy. The changes in his thought in relation to each are striking. His earliest approach was to cast the struggle of the biblical brothers in occupational terms, but occupational terms that indicate the beginning of class warfare. In so doing, he was partially able to address the intriguing anomaly of the Genesis text, wherein Cain, condemned to be a wanderer, could also be the founder of a city. According to Unamuno, the hard-pressed laborer in the field became the burdened urban proletariat (a transformation that Baudelaire already described, and one that will have strong but different vibrations in the thought of Michel Tournier). In these early essays (circa 1902), the appeal of the Cain-Abel theme is not merely this occupational opposition but the fact that this opposition marks the very beginning of history. ". . . The Hebrew legend of Cain and Abel presents one of the most profound intuitions on the beginning of history." History itself begins with division, in this case the warfare between the agrarian and the urban, between *homo rusticus* and *homo urbanus*: "¡Pueblos pastores que pasan sobre la tierra! ¡Pueblos laboradores que se agrupan en torno a las ciudades! Entera dualidad de la historia humana" ("Pastoral people who move over the earth. Workers who gather together in the cities. Here is the entire duality of human history").[2]

The potency of this myth lies in its historical persistence. When the Moriscos were expelled from Spain it was a case of the Spanish Abelites, in their hearts shepherds and peasants, rising up to get their revenge on the urbanized children of Cain, those who were skilled in the arts and crafts. (In Tournier's *Le Roi des aulnes*, the sedentary, citified Cains periodically expell the wandering Abels, gypsies, Jews, and other nomadic and migratory types.)

What was needed for his use of the theme to become truly universal was for Unamuno to transcend the occupational, and, although not ignoring this primitive yet persistent division of labor, to see in the theme more fundamental aspirations of the human soul and to see envy as the emotion typical of his nation (in fact, the Spanish disease); but to see in it also an heroic hunger, the expression of the need to return to God.

Quite early, Unamuno gained insight into envy as the Spanish disease (*la envidia hispanica*), envy as an emotion natural to a people without any energetic social life, people who have failed to progress and, as a consequence, have turned inward and against themselves.[3] This envy is a matter of self-poisoning. In this sense, Spain and *hispanidad* become as tight and enclosed a vessel as the ships in *Billy Budd*, *The Secret Sharer*, and *The Caine Mutiny*, they allow no space and grant no reprieve.

> ¡La envidia! Ésta, ésta es la terrible plaga de nuestras sociedades; ésta es la intima gangrena del alma española. ¿No fue a caso un español, Quevedo, el que escribió aquella terrible frase de que la envidia está flaca porque muerde y no come?

> (Envy. This is the terrible plague of our societies; this is the spiritual gangrene of the Spanish soul. It was not by chance that a Spaniard, Quevedo, wrote that terrifying sentence: Envy is thin because it bites but does not feed.) (p. 419)

This terrible inheritance from the blood of Cain—"la sangre de Cain, la envidia"—makes the Spanish peoples "descontentadizos, insurrectos y belicosos." In fact, envy is the infectious disease that Unamuno's ancestors transmitted to the Spanish Americas.

Envy is not only caused by social stagnation but also by mental idleness: "La envidia es hija de superficialidad mental y de falta de grandes preocupaciones intimas." ("Envy is the daughter of mental superficiality and of the lack of great spiritual concerns"; p. 423). But when we come to the great works, *The Tragic Sense of Life* and *Abel Sánchez*, envy, in the former cases perhaps more properly designated as resentment, now becomes the expression of extraordinarily powerful impulses and desires; it becomes the opposite of superficiality.

A tremendous passion is this longing that our memory may be rescued, if it is possible, from the oblivion which overtakes others. From it springs envy, the cause, according to the biblical narrative, of the crime with which human history opened: the murder of Abel by his brother Cain. It was not a struggle for bread—it was a struggle to survive in God, in the divine memory. Envy is a thousand times more terrible than hunger. If what we call the problem of life, the problem of bread, were once resolved, the earth would be turned into a hell by the emergence in more violent form of the struggle for survival.[4]

As in Dante's *Commedia*, envy is an expression of a frustrated or indeed a rebuffed need for immortality, a need to return to God, "to survive in the divine memory." Hence the great importance of fame in these works, and the close association of the sense of the self with an offering. By means of the offering we are presenting ourselves; when this is rejected we are denied in our beings. In the search for fame we are seeking to extend ourselves, to procure survival of the self through continuity. This is an expression of a need to return to God. Far from being petty, envy then is a divine hunger, and for this reason finds its natural habitat in theological dramas. When its natural victim and troubled exponent is Cain, then, correspondingly, Abel becomes a figure representing indifference and an absence of concern. This is the basis of the major revolution that Unamuno has brought about—the envious character for the first time in the history of the theme is given justification—and this paradoxical transvaluation provides the key to *Abel Sánchez*.

The general, relative, dialectical demotion of Abel in conjunction with this broader anthropology—or better, theology—of desire explains why it is that the very presence of this most loathsome of emotions converts Joaquín into a hero. In 1928, writing a prologue for the forthcoming second edition of *Abel Sánchez*, Unamuno has cause to remark: "Y al fin la envidia que yo traté de mostrar en el alma de mi Joaquín Monegro es una envidia tragica, una envidia que se defiende, una envidia que podría llamarse angélica"[5] ("In the end, the envy that I was concerned to reveal in the soul of my Joaquín Monegro is a tragic envy, an envy that is capable, an envy that could be called angelic").

Two things need to be said in regard to this point of view. First, it is possible that in writing the novella Unamuno was not quite as clear about the heroic dimensions of "his" Joaquín Monegro. The fuller realization may have come later, as he tells us, on his first rereading of the work since it had been printed. Second, as he goes on to explain, he has made a distinction between common envy, which we have called resentment, a reactionary emotion possessed of no positive desire, and envy proper, which is derived from that frustrated desire to establish the continuity of the self. "... he sentido la grandeza de la pasión de mi Joaquín Monegro y cuán superior es, a todos los Abeles. No es Caín, lo malo; lo malo es los cainitas. Y los abelitos" ("I have felt the grandeur of Joaquín Monegro's passion, and how superior he is to all the Abels. It is not Cain who is evil, but rather the Cainites and the Abelites"; p. 13).

Unamuno has given personal expression to many of the primary qualities of the Cain-Abel theme. Little attention is paid to the day-to-day activities, or even to the social beings of the characters, but much is devoted to the important crises of the spirit. As in a morality play, with all external influences excluded, attention is devoted to the agonists in each other's grasp. If, as Joaquín explains to Abel's son, Abelín, envy requires a relationship, it is precisely this relationship that is established from the outset of the work. As a drama of envy, *Abel Sánchez* opens with a sense of communion. Again we see that what is important is not necessarily the relationship of brothers, but something like a brotherly relationship that is then shattered, in these cases by the sense of differentiation and the arbitrariness of preference. What this means is that consciousness itself is a product of a sensed division. When Joaquín sets about to preserve the secret and intimate record of his personal struggles, he calls it his *Confession*, "the intimate account of his struggle with the passion which consumed his life, the struggle against the demon which had possessed him from the first stirrings of his conscious life [desde el albor de su mente dueña de sí]."[6]

The opening paragraph of Unamuno's narrative invokes the theme's sense of original unity: "Neither Abel Sánchez nor Joaquín Monegro could remember a time when they had not known each other. They had known each other since before childhood.... They each had learned about each other as they learned about themselves. Thus had they grown up, friends from birth, and treated almost as brothers in their upbringing" (p. 255/15).

But mysteriously, suprisingly, this harmony is disrupted when their schoolmates respond to their character differences. Abel is naturally winning, easy in his temperament; their friends incline toward him rather than toward the more difficult, even antipathetic Joaquín. The victimized Joaquín can do little in his helplessness, except to react and reflect. Consciousness itself then is the product of this invidious relationship.

If Abel is largely unaware of this difficulty, and thus is true to his prototype, Joaquín is launched into consciousness and into exacerbated self-consciousness. His Confession is the natural product of this division. Like other Cain-Abel stories—be they as interpreted by the first great allegorist, Philo, or from the divided modern strains of Byron's, Conrad's, or Hesse's regenerate Cain, or of the doomed and envious Cain—*Abel Sánchez* proceeds at two levels: the narrative of events appealing to the common understanding and the secret record of the events' ulterior meaning. As was already remarked, the title *Abel Sánchez* is intentionally misleading, serving to make the reader an accomplice to the common understanding, which prefers Abel, the immensely popular painter. In this sense, popular perception is as much a part of the arbitrariness of favor as is God's grace. As we shall see, Abel is a representation of the new type of "technical man," while Joaquín seems to harken back to a more theological age. Waylaying the common assessment and insistently, even perversely, bringing to the front not only his own reason for being but his need for being is Joaquín's own "inside narrative."

It is no accident that this effort is called his confession. In *The Tragic Sense of Life*, several pages before a crucial reference to the Cain-Abel story, Unamuno concludes a lengthy, searching quotation from Rousseau's *Émile* with the thought, "How much substantial truth there is in these gloomy confessions of this man of painful sincerity!"[7] How much of the truth would be left unrecorded in *Abel Sánchez* were it not for the terrible Confession that Joaquín keeps. It is of significance that in this work there are no secret sharers, no doubles. Joaquín stands alone burdened with terrible truths. In his prologue to *La tía Tula*, which followed *Abel Sánchez*, Unamuno wrote,

En mi novela Abel Sánchez intenté escarbar en ciertos sótanos y escondrijos del corazón, en ciertas catacumbas del alma, adonde no gustan descender los más de los mortales. Creen que en esas catacumbas hay muertos, a los que mejor es no visitar, y esos muertos, sin embargo, nos gobiernan. Es la herencia de Caín.

(In my novella *Abel Sánchez* I tried to probe certain underground and hidden places of the heart, the catacombs of the soul, places to which most mortals do not much care to descend. They believe that in these catacombs are the dead it is better not to visit; nevertheless these dead continue to control us. This is the heritage of Cain.)[8]

The normal situation of envy is disturbed by the fact of Joaquín's subterranean revelations. His perverse envy is the source of speculation and inquiry, and hence of an expressive search for identity, a motive that is normally lacking in the victimized Cains of the dramas of envy. The relative weights of the character duality also subvert the situation of envy. In *Abel Sánchez*, Cain's malice is unreciprocated; the "brothers" are to that extent differentiated. Not only is the envy apparently unreciprocated, it is unacknowledged and ignored. But this ignorance does not derive from an innocence similar to Billy Budd's; it comes rather from self-involvement and lack of concern. Just as Joaquín's envy is so perverse that it becomes heroic, so Abel's unawareness—a kind of blithe indifference—becomes reprehensible. His unawareness indicates worse than superficiality; it indicates indifference to the very existence of other people. If Cain's guilt in Byron's play at least acknowledges the value of existence (in distinction to the cosmic insignificance taught by Lucifer), Joaquín's horrible perversity at least requires the existence of others; it is, in fact, fatally dependent upon others. As that of a new technical man, Abel's nature dismisses the very problems that Unamuno would insist are necessary for existence, such as the state of being itself.[9] At one point, Abel's son admits that his father paints "like a machine," that he is made of cork (p. 313/164). What this new kind of character does is dismiss the validity of existence. He does so by failing to acknowledge a want in being. Joaquín's envy is heroically based upon such an acknowledgment of personal want, of a need to be acknowledged. He bursts out in an address to God, " 'Oh, if only he envied me . . . if only he envied me.' And this idea, which flashed lividly across the black clouds of his bitter spirit, brought him a relaxing joy, a joy which caused him to tremble in the marrow of his shivering soul, 'To be envied . . . Only to be envied!' " (p. 304/141).

In this sense, Joaquín is the greater figure. He moves from envy to an understanding of the greater severance in which he is involved; but Abel is unaware of the drama in which he is involved. The Cain figure, albeit a figure of envy, is most aware of his origins, even his literary and philosophical origins. He habitually provides the texture of literary reference, intertextuality. This is more than literary allusiveness, however; it seems to be an integral part of his own search for an understanding of his nature, the penalty that he incurred when he first fell into the division of consciousness. Joaquín can only look in astonishment at Abel's painting of the Cain-Abel story; he realizes that there is nothing of himself or of the painter Abel in the work (p. 296/119).

In their discussion of the Genesis text prior to the painting, it is clear that Abel adheres to surface readings, while Joaquín, from the anguish of his own personal experience, interrogates the text. Why, Joaquín asks (as have great orthodox and unorthodox thinkers), did God reject Cain's offering and favor that of his brother. Abel responds, " 'It isn't explained here' " (p. 282/83). Lacking personal experience or even curiosity, he is textually submissive. To Abel's faltering response that Cain's sacrifice was repulsed because God foresaw the invidious nature of Cain, Joaquín's retort is sharp, " 'If he was envious it was because God had made him envious and had given him a philter . . .' " (pp. 282/83–84). The simple straightforward argument of moral responsibility is turned around. Joaquín pushes the argument back, anteriorizes it into its preconditions: God did not reject Cain because of his sin, rather Cain sinned because he felt rejected. He did not wish to be envious; without defenses, he offered himself to the world and was rejected, while Abel, with equal innocence, offered himself to the world and was favored. The sense of being abandoned created the envious feelings, and this locates the mystery of iniquity (which is invoked by Joaquín) in the tragedy of differentiation.

Joaquín then turns to the contributions that the favored make to the situations of envy. Are they not culpable for not attempting to conceal the benefits of grace? Joaquín proceeds to attack the very "respectability" of the Abelites, showing Unamuno's indebtedness to Schopenhauer, and adding his pages to the modern demotion of Abel, whereby Abel becomes the titular figure for the nineteenth-century bourgeoisie: "'Those who believe themselves to be of the company of the just tend to be supremely arrogant people bent on crushing others under the ostentation of their "justice." As someone once said there is no worse canaille than "honorable" people . . .'" (pp. 283/85–86). Justification of Cain becomes related to this example of the conventionalization of the ethical, to its becoming priggish and, in a way (as the captain of the *Sephora* would evidence) actually creating the Cain figure, pushing him to the extreme, for the sake of self-gratification or exculpation. "'Abel's successors, the Abelites, have invented Hell as a place for the Cainites, because, if there were no such place, the Abelites would find their glory insipid. Their pleasure is to see others suffer while they themselves stay free of suffering'" (pp. 283–84/86). Although misapplied to any dominant culture that is confident in its positive strengths and values, here the arguments are neither perverse nor outlandish, but strong keys to a major direction of nineteenth-century thought, the rehabilitation of Cain and the corresponding demotion of Abel.

This more personal interrogation of the text applies to the question of women. Joaquín is convinced that Helena, whom he had loved prior to her becoming Abel's wife, has conspired with Abel. Their romance did not originate, it seems, in any positive attraction but rather from the possibility of spiting Joaquín. A common opposition, he is convinced, not a common attraction brought them together. Not unaccountably, he asks Abel if his wife had provided him with any inspiration for the painting. And once again Abel, who rarely relies on any self-reference, is non-plussed: "'My wife? . . . There was no woman in this tragedy.'" To which Joaquín can only utter the grim truth of his own experience: "'There is in every tragedy'" (p. 284/87).

In the stories of regenerate Cain, the woman is always an active and loyal companion. But when Cain does not represent a new order of being, but is instead fatalistically constrained, then women are forces in the tragedy (like Helena), or are not true partners (like Antonia, Joaquín's wife).

Antonia's underbearing piety is masochistic and elicits the worst rage and the most devastating truthfulness from her husband, when on his death bed he informs her, "'I have never loved you.'" But this is also an admission of his own incapacity, "'I could have loved you, I should have loved you, it would have been my salvation, but I did not'" (p. 344/241). By reversion, his failure explains the role of the woman in the stories of regenerate Cain. Had he been able to love Antonia, the void in his own being would have been filled and he would have thus been liberated from his terrible fixation on Abel and Helena. That the regenerate Cain is thus able to do so indicates the more active and positive energies and directions of his being.

Unamuno brings about yet another transformation of the theme. Throughout the nineteenth century, there was a close association between the first malefactor and the *poète maudit*. But in Unamuno, it is the plastic artist who is the superficial personality, and the medical doctor who is the true clinician of the soul. Being a man of science, he incorporates into his professional calling the lessons of determinism. He confesses his hatred to a priest, but also admits that there is nothing to be done about it: "'I do not believe in free will, Father. I am a doctor'" (p. 294/113). The priest counters that the envy is derived from Joaquín's religious doubts. But again Joaquín goes back behind the argument and replies that he doubts God because God has made him so, "'Just as he made Cain evil, God made me doubt. . . .'" Joaquín figures himself, we must not forget, among "the great predestined ones" (p. 294/194).

But this very determinism when encountered via Byron's *Cain* transports Joaquín beyond science and into religion. "And I began to believe in Hell, and in Death as a being, as the Devil, as hatred made flesh, as God of the soul. Everything that science did not explain, the terrible poem of the great hater Lord Byron made clear to me" (p. 285/92).

The relationship with Byron's text is intense and complex.[10] In fact, throughout Unamuno's career Byron has been an active presence, mainly by virtue of the sternness of his character. He is called "monstrous," and as a consequence contrasted with Wordsworth ("the sweet, the intimate, the religious and Christian"—a letter of 1897).[11] But it is fitting that in the rehabilitation that Cain undergoes in Unamuno's thought, Byron himself—still called a "great hater"—should be more influential.

Abel Sánchez enters into discourse with Byron's *Cain*. (This has already been noted by the Spanish scholar, Casares.)[12] If hatred is immortal, even transmissable, what is to become of the hope for some reconciliation of the antagonistic principles, that genetically the blood of Abel might somehow have intermixed with and tempered the sternness of Cain's personality? Indeed, the marriage of Joaquín's daughter to Abel's son does provide a form of revenge, as Joaquín is able to take Abelín under his wing. But

Joaquinito, the offspring of that marriage, is turned into a counterinstrument of torture when he obviously favors the paternal grandfather. In the final confrontation, Abel and Joaquín dispute over the affection of the child, Abel insisting that the boy is repulsed by Joaquín's "bad blood," and Joaquín turning on his eternal brother-in-enmity, hissing that Abel is a thief. In that grip, but not by that grip, Abel succumbs to the pressure and dies of a heart attack. Again there is ambiguity around the event, but not for the self-conscious Joaquín, who recognizes in what pattern they have been acting: "Yes, he's dead. And I killed him. Abel has been killed again by Cain, by your grandfather who is Cain" (p. 341/235).

Joaquín is repulsive and heroic. In these dramas of envy, characters are frequently so. In this case, however, it is the envious Cain who understands the greater void he is suffering in the midst of the petty distress. It is for this reason that the changes of this Cain are among the most remarkable, even miraculous, where Unamuno succeeds in admitting what had been inadmissible—and that is envy itself.

Unamuno's own character thrived on paradoxes. In perhaps his greatest moment—when as rector of the University of Salamanca he defied and answered General Millan Astray—he described himself as one "who has spent [my] life shaping paradoxes which have aroused uncomprehending anger in others."[13] But of course there is nothing too difficult to understand in *Abel Sánchez* once Abel is seen as the new technical man, who not only denies the need for being but does not even understand the question. In this particular demotion, Joaquín's renewed quest for being, for his own continuity, and his real horror at being robbed of his being, make his envy admirable. But the entire story is even more comprehensible when in the bitter struggle of the "brothers" Unamuno describes the soul of Spain. It is not a story about the power of history, of the past, to bring down the energy of liberation, but rather one of deadly antagonism, where each provokes and defeats the other. Unamuno's childhood knew the vivid excesses of the Carlist civil war in the region of his native Bilbao; he knew exile, voluntary or not, under the dictatorship; and his old age knew the beginnings of the terrible civil war of recent memory. His Cain story is the story of his nation, where precisely no new order of being is introduced. This is the last lament of Joaquín: "Why must I have been born into a country of hatreds? Into a land where the precept seems to be: 'Hate thy neighbor as thyself.' For I have lived hating myself; and here we all live hating ourselves" (p. 343/239).

PART FOUR

Tomorrow's Cain

Chapter Eleven

CAIN OF FUTURE HISTORY

THE FIRST chapter of Part Two enumerates the distinct contributions made by Salomon Gessner's *Der Tod Abels* to the Cain story, showing how it entered into and became part of a new line of regenerate Cains. But there is another discernible line of development in the Cain-Abel story that takes its inception from Gessner's work, particularly the crucial yet false dream that sets Cain in his course of violent action. These works, assembled here, may or may not be theological, but they are decidedly historical and social. They use the past in order to recreate a future history, intermixing, in a highly speculative and visionary way, remembrance and prophecy, extending the drama of the first two men down the corridors of time to a revolutionary act that will establish a reign of brotherhood, or conversely, in skeptical reaction, of cannibalism. These works are less concerned with the tragedy of differentiation than they are with inequities of economic and social division. After Gessner's, these works include Vittorio Alfieri's *Abele,* Baudelaire's "Abel et Cain," Leconte de Lisle's "Qaïn," Dostoevsky's *The Brothers Karamazov,* H. G. Wells's *The Time Machine,* and, last, Alexander Trocchi's *Cain's Book.*

The story of the first division between brothers is a suitable myth by which to retell future social divisions among humankind, particularly those divisions that resulted from the economic and class struggles of the nineteenth century. Benjamin Disraeli's categorization of England as now being "two nations" is revealing, since it applies the biblical associations of Esau and Jacob to social differences, and it indicates how dire and unbridgeable the distinctions then appeared. Wells goes even further in his *The Time Machine,* which shows the revolutionary potential in the early act of fraternal supersession; "Ages ago . . . man had thrust his brother man out of the ease and sunshine. And now that brother was coming back—changed."[1]

Traditionally, the Cain-Abel story seems to invite historical speculation. This is derived in part from its prominent position in Genesis, but also from the archetypal significance given the theme by Augustine. Even within the dimensions of the regenerate Cain, in the very need to create space around the tight nexus of involvement, we see a push to liberate the theme by expanding its horizons, by invoking a larger frame of time. Thus the vision of "future history" is a necessary component of the modern versions of the Cain-Abel story.

This enlarged arena of consideration—encouraged by any discussion of the first two men—also explains the suitability of the theme for scientific speculation. This suitability is derived from science's willingness to envision what Wells has called "the great scheme of space and time."[2] Science may have replaced theology or eschatology, in the sense of having repudiated its tenets about time and the nature of the universe, but it also replaced it in the sense of carrying on the same dimensions of speculation. Rather than an opposite, Thomas Huxley's remarkable essay, *Evolution and Ethics*, is a modern correlative to the vast considerations of Augustine's *City of God*.[3]

But there are other reasons why Baron Cuvier's work on geology fits so well into Byron's play—in fact, helps to make it the masterpiece that it is—and also why Huxley's essay figures so prominently in Wells's work. This is because, like the Cain-Abel story, a significant part of large nineteenth-century scientific speculations embraced a vision of the world that was violent and dire. A violent commencement should have an answerable sequestration. Long-term prospects, whether in the distant past or in the dim and far-off future, were not particularly edifying. Indeed, far from being monistic, science encouraged a view of the world that was itself dualistic, where moral man was set off against the certainly indifferent and perhaps inimical forces of an incomprehensible universe or universes. Cosmically, scientific speculators were pessimists. Like Byron, Huxley and Wells were looking for a "sanction for morality in the ways of the cosmos" (*Evolution and Ethics*, p. 53), and failed to find it. Unlike Byron, they were able to accept the Victorian resolution, "as if" (that is, behaving like moral men as if the universe were responsive to such ethical conduct, although fully understanding that it was not). Outer appearances conceal these inner and horrid truths—another "inside narrative"—of which the scientist is the supreme articulator.

THE FUTURE AS NIGHTMARE

The first of the great future visions out of the Cain-Abel material is provided by Salomon Gessner. To be sure, this may be a specific case showing the derivation of the future history from the large conceptions of Christian eschatology, since it is clear that Gessner's "false" picture of the future was inspired by the last two books of *Paradise Lost*. Although Milton fervently believed that in summarizing biblical history he was presenting the actual dynamics of history, even including the reasons for the defeats of the revolutionary struggles of his own time, Gessner renders a nightmare, one born of diabolical insinuation, from passion and imagination *(Leidenschaft* and *Einbildungskraft)*, the constant foes of the kindly reasonableness that is more typical of human nature.[4]

If illusionary, the view into the future is still prophetic and premonitory of the violent consequences of social injustice. In Gessner's vision of the *inégalité qui est parmi nous*, human greed and class laziness combine to subvert even the last semblance of social peace. In Anamalech's vision of the future, fraternal unity has long been broken: the children of Cain have been forced out of the better areas and into the *Wildnisse*, where their lot is one of hard and unremitting poverty. "Wie elend ist dieses Leben," complains Eliel, the first-born son of Cain. But his next concern is more to the point. He asks if God's curse extends to all of Cain's progeny, generation after generation, or only to the first-born. The question has to do with the importance of social hopefulness: will conditions continue as they are or even worsen, or will some form of social amelioration lessen the already sharp division between the separate families? Will lineage become class? Abel's children find pleasant relief in the shade; in fact, all of nature seems to bless the effeminate laziness (*weiblichen Trägheit*) of Abel's children. The picture then shifts to the pleasureable life of Abel's children, depicted as a kind of love-elite. So attractive is their scene that no traditional classic sites of pleasure might compare, not Tempe, not Gnidus, where amid "glanzanden Saülen der Venustempel stund . . ." Sharing the qualities of their place, Abel's children are "wie Liebesgötter schön," "schön wie die Grazien . . ." (pp. 150–53).

But this love-elite of art and culture is not content with its evident advantages. In time they come to resent that the hands that touch the harp should also tend the sheep. Consequently, they devise a scheme to fall upon the unsuspecting children of Cain (who, in this instance, are the innocent ones), and to enslave them, having them perform the odious manual chores. Worse than the separate and unequal conditions that had prevailed, this is the first act of exploitation, where one class of society actually enjoys the benefits of art and elegance, but does no labor, while another class, a subclass, does all the work.

Cain looks into the *Hölle der Zukunft* (p. 153), which, like other nightmares, was to be all-too-terribly realized. The vision may have been falsely inspired, but its social reality was patent. The terror that it inspires lies in the revolutionary and violent fervor of Cain's reaction: the idyll of familial unity is broken by Cain's response to the evident injustice of the conditions imposed upon his children. We are well on the way to an honorable Cain, one whose reaction is not prompted by self-regard but rather by a concern for his progeny, obliged to labor without any sense of future hope. Social resentment is derived from a sense of justice, one that predictably enough leads to violence. In this potent scene, one that sends shock waves throughout the entire program of cultural unity based upon affectionate sensibility, Gessner sounded a warning in the mid-eighteenth century that was not to be heeded.

Tragically, this dire division was harmful to both classes, and introduced to the historical process itself a kind of nemesis, one to be fully exploited by H. G. Wells, in whose thought the non-laboring classes would become effete and highly vulnerable, while the laboring classes would become monstrous. But the pattern, whatever transformations it would undergo, was established by Gessner, and it is clear, showing another fruitful dimension of the Cain-Abel story in the modern world. Its concern will be primarily with social justice and not theology, with history and not metaphysics, with divisions in the way people live and not with the conditions of being. As such, we can see how its arguments may be clearly separated from those of its modern-day counterparts—regenerate Cain and the dramas of envy.

Vittorio Alfieri derives the key element of his posthumously published *Abele*—a diabolically inspired and misleading dream and an apparition of an earthly paradise—from Gessner's *Der Tod Abels*.[5] The theological residue is even more apparent in *Abele* than in its predecessor, and this takes its effect in a remarkable vision of Christ, the Christ who breaks the bonds of destiny, and its correlative, a Cain who is not redeemed. Nevertheless, Cain in his character does show some of the traits that would continue in the modern presentations: a certain roughness, if not sternness of temperament; emotional anguish; and moreover a higher vision, if not of justice, at least of a better order of being.

More than any work perhaps as far back as Dante's, Alfieri's emphasizes the remarkable emotional and physical unity prevailing among the first family, the integrity of whose existence has somehow been reclaimed after the first fall. The play, in its start, is centered around family feeling, togetherness, and pious religious observation. In *terza rima* the brothers are pictured as little cubs, physically entwined:

> Caino e Abele in dolci nodi stanno
> Abbracciati giacendo in quieto sonno,
> Che li restora del diurno affanno.

(Cain and Abel, sweetly knotted arm in arm, lie in quiet sleep, which restores them from their daily toil.)

But already within the unity powerful differences exist, as always they must. With all of his surges of emotional conflict, Cain is a robust figure (in fact, of all the Cains, he is the one most similar physically and spiritually to Byron's Cain—despite the English poet's disavowal of ever having read Alfieri's play). It is *Peccato* (Sin) who describes the differences in temperament that exist between the brothers. As in Gessner's work, here the brothers are fundamentally different biological types. Abel is a youngster—"il giovinetto"—who leads his sheep, sheep that are so white that he mirrors himself in them ("candide sí ch' egli si specchia in elle"), which is of course an early prefiguration of Abel's identity with Christ. Cain, on the other hand, is more adult, more masculine, and to him falls the sturdier tasks of tilling the fields. In fact, Cain is the more thoughtful, helpful custodian of his more vulnerable brother (p. 354).

These differences obviously provoke differing parental reactions. Abel is Eve's latest born, but even without this still lingering maternal care, there is something in Abel that is "piú innocente e docile" than in the qualities of Cain. Where Abel attracts by a semblance of vulnerability, Cain puts off with his rugged, masculine brow, in fact, the presence of some lurking and threatening shadow. She asks Adam if he, too, does not detect some such "sign,"

> un certo
> non so qual tetro inesplicabil segno,
> come se fosse una nube di sangue,
> non ti sembr' egli pur tra ciglio e ciglio
> veder scolpito da Caino in fronte?

(Does there not appear to be carved out on Cain's forehead some kind of dark inexplicable sign, almost like a cloud of blood?)

(p. 363)

This ominous potentiality is realized when Cain is thrown into turmoil by a chorus of diabolical figures (including personifications of envy and of death). At first they trouble his sleep. Unlike the false dreams in Gessner's work, however, the turbulent apparitions bring to his consciousness inequalities that already exist. What has been happily accepted in the innocent and cooperative harmony of early family life now comes to seem grossly unfair. In a remarkable dramatic monologue, Cain now mocks his role: "It's Cain do this, Cain do that. It's Cain do everything. and yet the doting parents only have eyes for Abel" (p. 370). In the shifting drama of his thoughts, the various currents and countercurrents that overtake him, he wonders why he remains among such "hostile folk." He determines, therefore, to leave his family, to make his own way. In an extraordinary exemplification of Philo's Cain, the spirit of individualism consumes him. With his trusty pickax (*mara*), the eventual murder weapon, he need fear no one. In fact, modern political language works its way into his thoughts: the "pact" between him and his family was too unequal; now he will seek out his own liberty. Yet, as he rages he too senses himself to be moved along by an "invisible hand," one that pushes him to play his destined role in an inevitable drama (pp. 370–71).

The final incentive to murder is itself an apparition, as if one needs to be "possessed" in order to bring about so radical a change in attitude.

Envy and Death assume the appearances of superior people (in fact, somewhat resembling Eve and Abel). Into Cain's disturbed imagination they insinuate the existence of an earthly paradise, one that Adam has reserved for Abel, and of which he has kept Cain ignorant. The fact that Adam had previously kept secret from Cain his and Eve's banishment from a genuine earthly paradise lends corroboration to Cain's suspicions.

In aspirations that are actually quite close to those of Byron's Cain, Alfieri's creation finds presented to him his own idealizations of life. In this garden everyone lives in communion, everyone is happy, everything is possible. To prove his point, Envy directs a masque of male and female dancers and singers who demonstrate for Cain and Abel the happiness present in the land beyond the river. A female voice sings alluringly to Cain:

> Vieni, o figliuol d'Adamo,
> La, dove in fest'eterna
> Uguale alla superna
> Vita noi pur viviamo.

(Come, o son of Adam, to where we live in feast eternal the life that is fitting supernal being.)

(p. 386)

They urge him to rush to the place before Abel. Paradoxically, and yet intrinsically to the Cain-Abel theme, this very vision of a better life (to be sure, inspired by Envy and Death) leads to murder. Both Gessner and Alfieri, in their related productions, have established the dire relevancy of the Cain-Abel story for the modern world. In these situations, the character of Cain becomes the battlefield of moral conflict, of the burdens and consequences of action, and of action that is in some way inspired by justice and by the dreams of social harmony. The garden life behind has inspired the earthly paradise ahead. But the action to which such vision leads is murderous, in fact, it is disruptive of the very fraternal communion represented in the higher vision.

Depite assertions that Cain "was not himself," not his normally reasonable and kindly self, this play, unlike Gessner's, allows for no reconciliation after the rupture. The divisions under the surface unity are deep-running fault lines. A conclusion, in fact coming from God himself, reinforces the sense that the play had already communicated of theological dependence: "Uom, lasciato a te stesso, ecco qual sei" ("Left to yourself, man, this is what you are"). It is curious that, although its format is social and historical, the play's conclusion is traditional, abiding within the essential arguments laid down by Philo: Cain is a character who seeks his own order, and is, as a consequence, condemned to violence and eventual self-destruction, since he is obliged to kill off the better part of himself, represented by the innocent Abel. Unlike the other characters of Cain initiated by the Enlightenment, this is not a Cain to whom future reconciliation is possible. Somewhat in the manner of the Cain presented in Dante's *Purgatorio*, this Cain remains a terrible example: "feroce esemplo spaventoso ai rei" (p. 397). History cannot be overcome by false dreams and violence. Only the sacrifice of Christ, which Abel's death anticipates, will liberate humankind from the chains of historical destiny.

Rebellion and Brotherhood

Reckoning ahead O Soul
As fill'd with friendship, love complete,
The elder brother found,
The younger melts in fondness in his arms.
—Walt Whitman, "Passage to India" (1871)

These two future visions, although falsely inspired, reveal the revolutionary paradox: Cain's actions, although violent, are inspired by a vision of justice and even true communal life. With two eminent French poets of the nineteenth century, Charles Baudelaire and Leconte de Lisle, the vision of the future is equally violent and revolutionary, but there is no indication in "Abel et Cain" and in "Qain" that the vision is false. Rather, it is based upon the realities of social division, for which Cain and Abel continue to stand, and in major ways the ideals of the predominant event for the nineteenth century, the French Revolution.[6] Brotherhood, *fraternité*, the last term of the triadic slogan of the revolution, has become the new ideal now that the oppressive figure of authority, the king, is dethroned. This emergence of brotherhood as a great ideal helps to explain the renewed importance of Cain and Abel. If the theme of Cain-Abel can be used to serve as a master metaphor for division in existence, then by altering some of its features the same theme can also be used to suggest the restoration of unity in the ideal of brotherhood, particularly when this ideal arises out of a context of violent revolution.

The very title of Baudelaire's poem is significant.[7] This is one of the few works, if not the only work, where Abel's name precedes Cain's. That this is so would seem then to indicate that Cain is ordinarily seen as dramatically stronger. But despite this formal preeminence, Abel continues along the lines of pejoration that will become prevalent in later works, particularly *Finnegans Wake*. Abel is not discounted because of excessive simplicity, or an unseemly innocence, but rather because he is too successful. He sits on top of the heap. His acceptance of and abidance by the limits of social order have accrued extraordinary benefits and satisfactions. A kind of simplicity adheres to this transformation: Abel is still unaware but smugly unaware. The terms with which his unconsciousness is described move less generously from the pastoral to the bovine.

Although we write *Cain* or *Abel* Baudelaire more accurately specifies the theme's dimensions when he addresses, "race d'Abel" and "race de Cain." The issue is not between personnages but between lineages, groups of peoples and their inheritances. Receiving impetus from the vision of "future history" brought into the theme by Gessner's *Der Tod Abels*, the poem addresses the continuation of social division and its inevitable violent consequence. The race of Abel will multiply even as its goods and money increase, while the race of Cain bleakly faces an unending curse ("Ton supplice / Aura-t-il jamais une fin"). Condemned to vagabondage, the Cainite will drag his family in hunger along the roads. Such hopelessness only worsens severe social division, and finally provokes the violent response.

The poem is thus based upon sixteen terse distichs that present radically contrasting lots in life. In his new and radically transformed position, Abelites enjoy the physical satisfaction of existence (Hamlet would have called them "bestial"): "Race d' Abel, dors, bois et mange . . ." Within this bovine contentedness, a strong complicity exists between the unoffending Abel and the authorities of the world structure. Abel's kin warm their stomachs at the "foyer patriarcal" and even God smiles complacently upon this satisfied life. Abel's respectability, his self-satisfaction, stinks to high heaven.

Traditional elements of the "monstrous Cain" infiltrate Baudelaire's poem. While Abelites watch their goods prosper, outcast Cainites shiver in a cave. Like gypsies, they are obliged to wander. It may be true (although probably unprovable) that, as Walter Benjamin informs us, the race of Cain "can be none other than the proletariat . . . the race of those who possess no commodity but their labor-power."[8] But throughout the poem there is no reference to Cain as having any labor power at all. Original division has led to such dismal future consequences. But the true turning point of the poem takes place in the final four distichs (set off as a second part). These will be shown in the undoing of Abel—and Baudelaire's curiously "noble" reasons for this pejoration—and Cain's violent act of rebellion.

Despite their evident prosperity, the rewards of the Abelites will not be any different from those of the Cainites: ("your carcasses / will fatten the reeking earth!"). Although Cain is monstrous, there is no reason to suspect that the countervailing Abelites are in any way capable of forming a civilization. In *Beowulf*, a material but worthy civilization is threatened by the monstrous consequences of the feud, but Abel's culture is built upon no such positive bases. In fact, it lacks both grandeur and nobility, and its shame is that it has not earned its preeminence. No qualities of personal risk or daring helped them gain their position; in fact, exactly the opposite seems to be true: in the crucial lines of the poem, they are reprimanded for having exchanged the sword for the spear. The ruling bourgeoisie has traded nobility for the appearances of commonness (as well as distance and insulation from the blood-acts of existence). It is curious that Baudelaire's quarrel is not with the new preeminence per se, but rather with a class that does not understand the merits of its position and is consequently badly placed to justify its very bases.

This debasement of Abelite culture has another consequence. In his very commonness, Abel becomes more of a pawn. He is no longer the suitable antagonist for his enraged brother, who is now exhorted to rise up against the keystone of the system that supports Abel, and that is God himself.

> Race de Cain, au ciel monte
> Et sur la terre jette Dieu!

(Rise up, Race of Cain and cast God down upon the earth.)

Baudelaire adds to a major shift in the theme itself. Traditionally, Cain has suffered from anger displacement: the rage he feels against the father he takes out upon his brother. In Baudelaire's poem, Cain rises to the source of the conflict, the apparent world system that would prefer the observances and offerings of Abel. Violence is directed against the father figure and not against the brother. In this sense, Baudelaire's poem, despite the underlying unworthiness of Abel, actually implies the greater ideal of brotherhood that will inspire the "Qain" of Leconte de Lisle.[9]

Like Baudelaire's, Leconte de Lisle's poem depends upon a future vision that has already occurred. Unlike Gessner's vision, it is not a false dream but rather a "sommeil prophétique," in short, one recounting an inspired future history. Like Byron's Cain, de Lisle's is an upstanding figure of clear and noble sentiment. He is moved both by the dream of Eden and by the thirst for social justice. Refusing to renounce his human dignity, he declines to pray or to supplicate. To the cherub who preaches submission before the power of God, who declares that man is an "earthworm" who would be better off accepting his nature, Qain refuses to bow, "je resterai debout." And if to accept God's world means that he must resign himself to his destiny—to the enchainments of history—this also he refuses to do. His final quarrel is with the conditions of existence themselves: "Que m' importait la vie au prix où tu la vends?"[10]

In this poem, as Qain is just, so Abel is innocent (as well as unsuspecting):

> O jeune homme, tes yeux, tels qu' un ciel sans nuage,
> Étaient calmes et doux, ton coeur était leger
> Comme l'agneau qui sort de l'enclos du berger . . .

(O young man, your eyes, like the sky without clouds, were calm and gentle, your heart was as innocent as that of a lamb who has just left its sheepfold . . .)

(p. 16)

The question remains, as it did in Gessner's prose poem, whence cometh evil? Qain is activated by a vision of Eden, an Eden lost. "Eden! o Vision éblouissante et breve . . . Eden, O le plus cher et le plus doux des songes . . ." ("Eden, O vision dazzling and brief . . . Eden, the dearest and sweetest of dreams . . ."; p. 12). He cannot tolerate this exclusion, which accounts for his bitterness and his sense of division. Instead of diabolical inspiration, the source of evil is located in the historical past, a kind of destiny. Qain is the "misérable héritier de l'angoisse premiere" ("miserable inheritor of the primal anguish"; p. 13). Even his murder of Abel is regarded as an historical condition, an inescapable trap, and an ambush set by God and the very conditions of existence ("J'ai heurté d'Iahveh l'inévitable embûche; Il m'a précipite dans le crime tendu"; p. 16).

If the situation is historical, so is the solution; Eden lost has its correspondent Eden recaptured. The prophetic spirit of Qain raised up before the Flood looks down the centuries to the dawn of a new era. In effect, his future vision is an account of human liberation from religious control since the Renaissance. In response to the Reformation, the forces of reaction will vainly introduce the Inquisition, but despite brutal suppression, the rebellious spirit of Qain will continue to revive (here, although the forces are reversed, the legacy of Qain will continue to import, as it did for Philo, never-ending conflict). At long last, new people will come forward who do not know God's name and who will not have drunk in sin, guilt and terror with their mother's milk: "Et les petits enfants de nations vengées, / Ne sachant plus ton nom, riront dans leur berceaux" ("And the little children of liberated nations, not knowing your name will smile in their cradles"; p. 18). A happy people born into the sun and not into darkness will finally bring about the death of God: "Qui t'y cherchera ne t'y trouvera pas." This will be the day of universal brotherhood:

> Et d'étoile en étoile,
> Le bienheureux Eden longuement regretté
> Verra renaitre Abel sur mon coeur abrité . . .

("From star to star, a new and happy Eden, so long desired, will finally see Abel reborn and sheltered on my breast.")

(p. 19)

This extraordinary final vision seems to have brought the theme full circle. History has itself reversed the processes of history. The brother sacrificed is now the brother restored in a world where the father and all that he came to represent have been removed.

Quite specifically, we can see here how the dramas of future history contained within the Cain-Abel story are still controlled by that story and hence differ from those with distinctly Utopian bases. To be sure, the Utopian impulse places its sights on a city with strong coordinates and elaborate systems of governance, and Cain himself has been associated from the very beginning with a city. But his is a fallen, not an ideal city; in fact, it is one that must be restored after its long period of condemnation. Moreover, in the restoration of brotherhood, fatherhood must absent itself—this disappearance of the father could be called the providential inverse of the virgin birth. In Utopian literature, the founding lawmaker is an essential factor—if only to account for the existence of a new order of history that seems itself to have transcended history. Finally, we must say that the newer vision of Cain and Abel harkens back to their original, primary unity; consequently, its final commitment must be to the restoration of brotherhood, and this is represented by a simple, emotional communion, without reference to elaborate codes of social restructuring such as we are likely to find in Utopia.

Several questions remain. It is quite possible that Leconte de Lisle would not have admired very much this new innocent race of children born into the sun and the light. He might have been quite disturbed by their illiteracy, by their lack of interest in his poems; he may well have anticipated California surfers. Further, it is troublesome that brotherhood is obtained at the cost of fatherhood. Clearly such a resolution does not remove the price of sacrifice from existence: it only alters the figure casting the shadow. Moreover, one can wonder if such a requirement is not indeed based upon an extremely fragile ego, a liability that does not bode well for the future of the goals expressed. In another sense, one can also see in the Whitmanesque image of brotherhood a new aspect of the theme, one that will only become more prominent in later versions of the story, and that is the growing relevancy of the Cain-Abel theme for questions of androgyny and homosexuality.

It should be borne in mind that this impetus toward the regeneration of a revolutionary Cain did not go unchallenged, particularly when two of the challengers happened to be among the greatest novelists of the century, Dickens and Dostoevsky. Because Dickens was a reformer and not a revolutionary, his primary purpose was to endow capitalism with a heart, to overcome militant class division in a reintegrated view of the family. He could not tolerate a truncated family, with an absent authority, a demoted Abel and a promoted Cain.[11] Dickens's counterpart was Dostoevsky, who similarly resisted the tendencies to radicalize division. But in some ways, in *The Brothers Karamazov*, he goes beyond Dickens in facing up to the consequences of the French Revolution. The king is dead and so is the father—the novel's name is after all *The Brothers Karamazov*, and its theme is not only that of parricide but also the meaning of this event in the life of the brothers. That gigantic but incomplete visionary work encounters the great ideal of the revolution, *fraternité*. In fact, one could say that Dostoevsky specifically confronts the contradictions involved with that ideal, particularly the ways required for its achievement, but also the fundamental data upon which it is based.

In its largest debates and even in specific details, *The Brothers Karamazov* uses the Cain-Abel theme to formulate the crucial issues deriving from the consequences of the French Revolution. That the father figure of authority is dead or deposed seems to be the indisputable fact; brotherhood is the necessary new ideal. The question is, in what ways will brotherhood be achieved? One view of brotherhood is that of a future project at which we arrive when unjust division is overcome by a violent act; another view, harkening back to the Abel figure who emerged in contrast with the Citizen Cain of Augustine's two cities, and which comes to be endorsed by Father Zosima and Alyosha in Dostoevsky's novel, regards the human world as a true unity, where we are bound together by a spiritualized Christianity.

In his attitudes toward division and the double, one can already see Dostoevsky's dissidence, not only in regard to the presentation of Cain in Baudelaire and in Leconte de Lisle, but also to the pattern of regenerate Cain. Division for Dostoevsky is not a *given* of experience, the recognition of which would be an indication of superior consciousness and a necessary precondition to future growth. Rather, division is described as *nadryv*, that important word indicating the tearing apart of what was unified, the way one might tear a muscle or a tendon. It impedes the ability to function.[12] The coming of the double then, far from representing the recuperation of larger dimensions of experience, an expansion that includes the "other," is actually a kind of mental rupture, the consequence of intellectual irritation that is schismatic and disordered. Moreover, rather than representing freedom and possibility, the double suggests extraordinary limitation. Whether in his encounters with Smerdyakov or with the devil, Ivan finds his own possibilities enormously reduced by the apparition of his double. Far from bringing reintegration, these encounters are disintegrative and move him toward the mental illness that the double can also induce. In these two instances, we get a brief foretaste of the way that Dostoevsky wrote against a dominant intellectual trend.

Books 5 and 6 in Part Two ("Pro and Contra" and "The Russian Monk") form the foundation of the novel, not only of the completed first volume but of the totality of Dostoevsky's larger, unrealized conception. The central contrast is between the view of the world as represented by Ivan and presented in the "Grand Inquisitor" section (which is frequently and unfortunately excerpted), and the view of the world as represented and presented by Father Zosima. This central contest of values is rooted in the larger dimensions of the Cain-Abel story, where fundamental issues of society and its foundation are invoked.

Striking, specific details call to mind the Cain-Abel theme and, of course, the crucial fraternal context. Early in Book 5, Alyosha anxiously inquires if his brother Dmitri will return. "Quietly, distinctly and superciliously," Smerdyakov replies, "How am I to know about Dmitri Fyodorovitch? It's not as if I were his keeper."[13] In the very next section, Alyosha asks a more serious question of Ivan, "What of Dmitri and father? How will it end?" To which Ivan responds, "You are always harping on it! What have I to do with it? Am I my brother's keeper?" More conscious than Smerdyakov, he immediately recognizes what he has said. "Cain's answer to God, about his murdered brother, wasn't it? Perhaps that's what you are thinking at this moment. Well, damn it all, I can't stay here to be their keeper, can I?" (p. 213).

The key itself is small but the issues it opens up are extensive. Ivan, like Byron's Cain, is a metaphysical rebel, and his quarrel is with the nature of God's world. "In the final result, I don't accept it at all. It's not that I don't accept God, you must understand, it's the world created by Him I don't and cannot accept" (p. 216). What Ivan specifically rejects is the "mystery" of salvation history, where presumably in the final unfolding of Christian eschatology the rank injustices of human suffering will be clarified and resolved. As a vision of world harmony—however postponed—Christian mystery is a way of preserving the monistic view of the world in the midst of its evident contradictions. Ivan revolts at this proposition; the purchase of final harmony at the price of the death of an innocent child he finds obscene. It is incumbent upon the mother of a murdered child not to forgive its murderer. As it has moved other Cains, an implacable sense of justice motivates Ivan. Final harmony is not worth the asking price. As de Lisle's Qain has protested, "Que m'importait la vie au prix où tu la vends?" Like Byron's Cain, Ivan is not an atheist; he is dedicated to justice, holding God to what he believes is a superior moral rule.

This section of protest is followed by social compliance, Ivan's narration of the encounter between Christ and the Grand Inquisitor, where spiritualized Christianity yields to theocratic Caesarism. Because Christ's message, as construed by the Grand Inquisitor, calls people to a terrible freedom, his return after long silence is regarded as unsettling to social peace. In fact, the Grand Inquisitor draws an explicit connection between the Christian message of individual freedom and scientific rationalism: each is harmful. Because humankind is by nature weak and vile, it cannot tolerate any form of strenuous freedom. People want what the Church offers, mystery, miracle, and authority—another triad that starkly contrasts with the mottoes of the French Revolution. For this reason, after tasting the freedom of the future, they will return to the material comforts and spiritual satisfactions offered by the Church. Given the circumstances of the Cain-Abel theme, the Grand Inquisitor's vision of the future and its consequences are revealing. The temple will fall, but it will be replaced by the "terrible tower of Babel," and finally by what will cause people to return to religion, cannibalism. "Oh, ages are yet to come of the confusion of free thought, of their science and cannibalism. For having begun to build their tower of Babel without us, they will end, of course, with cannibalism" (p. 238).

Within the fraternal confines of the Cain-Abel story, cannibalism seems to be the ultimate revocation of the vision of communion. But here, the perspective of the Grand Inquisitor is far from that endorsed by the heroic culture of *Beowulf* or the spiritual community of Dante. The social program of the Grand Inquisitor represents the lowest form of degradation that the conventionalization of the ethical has produced. It rests upon a special division between the masses and the elite. The masses shall exchange their freedom in order to enjoy the "quite humble happiness of weak creatures," while the elite, like the Grand Inquisitor, will wrestle with the problems of existence. In some sense, the Grand Inquisitor episode is another "inside narrative": this secret dialogue between Christ and the Grand Inquisitor is an unwritten poem paraphrased in prose by Ivan for Alyosha's sake. Its protagonist is an aged priest who shoulders the burden of the mystery. He assumes the sins of the world and by this assumption absolves his people: he is in this sense a neo-Christ and consequently has no need of an authentic Christ.

But his vision is profoundly un-Christian, and whatever sense of radical schism it conveys is immediately contradicted by Alyosha's kiss of his brother. Beneath the differences generated by intellectual turmoil, the kiss seems to indicate a common relatedness, and abiding brotherhood, particularly because of the trauma that Ivan is undergoing. Alyosha embraces his brother in his desperation. Nor does this inside narrative contain the highest awareness. It seems to be involved in broader patterns of connectedness than those presented. Not only is it followed by Alyosha's embrace, but also by Ivan's passive complicity in Smerdyakov's plot, a complicity that is unexpressed but nevertheless understood. Ivan's vulnerability to Smerdyakov is the negative corollary to Alyosha's embrace.

In practice and in preachment the arguments of the Grand Inquisitor are confronted by Father Zosima. These two face each other across Dostoevsky's pages and present the overarching and contending arguments and arrangements of life under which the brothers shall act. Zosima epitomizes the Christian ideal of true brotherhood; in fact, he carries with him the image of his own dead brother, whom he is not willing to discard but rather has incorporated into his own experience. By his own experience with his servant Afanasy, and with the desperate case of Markel, he was educated to the reality that all—not only the elect—are capable of undergoing (are indeed called to undergo) extraordinary agonies. In pointed contrast to the earlier retorts of Smerdyakov and of Ivan, Zosima is startled himself by the way Markel has absorbed his own understanding of the fraternal compact: "And that we are all responsible to all for all . . ." (p. 282).

Like Dante, Dostoevsky regards a spiritualized Christianity as a requirement for social peace. (Dante also saw as crucial an independent and powerful emperor.) At some point, Zosima declares, restraint must be placed upon desire. If this does not occur, the rich move toward "isolation and spiritual suicide" and the poor toward "envy and murder" (p. 292). The problem of envy in society explains the extraordinary relevancy of the Cain-Abel theme for discussions of social order. How does one insure social peace in the midst of such evident material inequality? Zosima does not accept the notion of regeneration through violence: "In Europe the people are already rising up against the rich with violence, and the leaders of the people are everywhere leading them into bloodshed, and teaching them that their wrath is righteous but their 'wrath is cursed, for it is cruel'" [Gen. 49.7] (p. 294). Similar to the arguments of the Grand Inquisitor, Zosima does not believe that society can be founded upon the rational principles of science. "Of a truth, they have more fantastic dreams than we. They aim at justice, but denying Christ, they will end up by flooding the earth with blood, for blood cries out for blood, and he that taketh up the sword shall perish by the sword" (p. 297). At its heart, this argument, like Dante's (of which it is a major modern version), rejects the notion of foundation sacrifice, even of the symbolic sort.[14] Such a gospel of original violence does not stop bloodshed but only leads to further violence. In an inspired vision of unity—unity with the past as well as with the future—the sacrificed brother is always borne with one. At last, we see, the rejection of the foundation sacrifice as a social code is prompted by a denial of death itself. Dostoevsky would side with those who argue that modern social resentment and hence revolution may be attributed to a loss of the faith in immortality. Without that enormous belief, one is left to confront social inequity as a final accounting of things, and this balance is inevitably found to be unacceptable. Immortality has always been the most significant antidote to the social consequences of envy. It holds that those things that we have known can never be gone, and that finally true judgment will be rendered. How crucial then that the vision of brotherhood, the redemption of Abel, comes from *Father* Zosima.

Dostoevsky denies that any ideal or even realistic social organization can emerge from acts of blood. He does not as a consequence accept the qualified political notion of a reestablished peace after a necessary act of rebellion (or the regenerate city after a long period of oppression). He does not have to deal with the New Prince of Machiavelli, nor with the qualified and strongly conditioned arguments of Shakespeare's political ethics. His arguments are directed against the fervent utopianism of the French Revolution, a unitary, totalizing conception of society that is rendered even more extreme in its adoption by the Russian *intelligentsia*. Therefore, his arguments seem to run into the same totalistic error, and miss the possibilities of conditioned, qualified, half-way revolutions, where the demands of conscience, of the ethical world, and of order are met within the complex actions of historical change. He can envision the Cain-Abel theme used to scrutinize the invalidity of violent change, but he cannot countenance the Cain-Abel theme used as a program for scrutiny in which change, even violent change, may be validated.

But the very totality of his vision results in some inspired hits. There can be no stable society, Dostoevsky, like Dante, argues, that is not based upon a sense of responsibility and of brotherhood. For this reason, the Cain-Abel theme looms so strongly in each. The actions that begin with Smerdyakov and Ivan each denying that he is his brother's keeper; that engage so strongly the most profound speculations aroused by the Cain-Abel theme; that deal in so bold and imposing an outline with the paradoxes and dilemma of the joint revolutionary ideals of violence and brotherhood; that suggest in counter-outline the necessary restoration of the lost brother; end with the most terrifying future vision, the perfect counterpoise to the struggle of the first two men, and that is the hostility of the last two men: "And if it were not for Christ's covenant, they would slaughter one another down to the last two men on earth. And these last two men would not be able to rest in each other in their pride, and the one would slay the other and then himself" (p. 297).

The nineteenth century's future history of Cain meets its palinode in Dostoevsky's stark correspondence between the first two men and the last two. Cain and Abel are still active in future history. But in Dostoevsky's moral imagination, the problem is not an act of injustice that enslaves and turns iniquity into inequity, rather, in the absence of broader principles of conduct (those deriving, like Dante's, from a spiritualized Christianity), the original act of violence is condemned to replication, even down to the bleak parallelism of the last two man. And if the motives revealed in the first two persist in the last two, the result will be the same, only worse. The last two men will fall upon each other (we note that these are *frères ennemis*, and not the differentiated Cain and Abel), one will kill the other and then will meet the isolation that is the true meaning of his individualism. For the last man to kill his brother gives more terrible meaning to Philo's argument that by killing Abel Cain in effect slew himself. It is altogether fitting that the basic myth treating the origins of history should have enormous presence and play in the final projections of future history.

HISTORY AS NEMESIS: H. G. WELLS'S
THE TIME MACHINE

In Byron's *Cain* we have already witnessed the unexpected suitability of large, scientific speculation for the Cain-Abel theme. In Baron Cuvier's geology, Byron found a view of the world that was violent, historically bleak and deeply dualistic. In Thomas Huxley's Victorian credo, *Evolution and Ethics*, H. G. Wells found similarly discomforting truths. His own work, *The Time Machine*, takes speculation out of the biblical past and projects it into the incomprehensibly far future (the year 802,701, to be exact).[15] *The Time Machine* fits well into the material we have been discussing, particularly with its future projection, which reveals a fundamental division based upon the exclusion of one brother by another. Its scope moves from the first division to the final darkness, from primitive differentiation to the ultimate undifferentiation. Its scientific vision of the world, like that of Byron's *Cain*, is terribly dualistic, violent, and historically dire. The difference is that a new hero emerges, the scientist-adventurer whose own moral being is not agitated by cosmic grimness, and who, in the narration of Wells's work, is quite willing to accept the great Victorian "as if." Not only is the world divided between human ethics and the facts of evolution, it is also divided between those who are aware of the grim facts—those who participate in the inside narrative—and those who exist at the level of common understanding. The scientist is the new high priest who holds the key to the *mysterium* and who also bears the burden of the mystery.

Wells's speculations are cosmically historical. Unlike Byron's *Cain*, Wells's *The Time Machine* entertains no personal experience of a cursed family line, a line of descent that does not share in the happy contentedness of existence. For him, the historical process itself breeds its own nemesis. The basis of historical devolution is the fact that each generation encounters conditions that are different from those of the preceding generation, because they meet those that the preceding generation itself created. This means that the competency of subsequent generations will require different qualities from those of preceding generations; in fact, their conditions will no longer require the qualities that helped create the conditions of their own life. This means of course that civilization can be undone by its own development. Mechanical invention can render unnecessary the very intellectual qualities that created the devices, and invention itself can result in a falling away of the powers of invention. In the long run—hence the extraordinary extent of time in *The Time Machine*—an enfeeblement of human powers is the necessary product of the development of civilization.

This is where the Cain-Abel story enters, and where *The Time Machine* benefits from being aligned with Gessner's *Der Tod Abels*, and the other visions of future history. Indeed, the races of man are two, the Eloi—suggesting the God-like—and the Morlocks, sounding like Warlocks. The Eloi, the favored ones, had at some historical moment thrust their brothers out, but rather than living to enjoy the fruits of their ascendancy, they are undone by some variant of the process I describe above. The Eloi have fallen victim, not to revolution—the abrupt and violent uprising of the dispossessed—but rather to the historical processes that have rendered the people of the overworld defenseless, and the people of the underworld predatory. If the Morlocks have become cannibals, the Eloi have become as helpless as the herds that Abel tended. "Very pleasant was their day, as pleasant as the day of the cattle in the field. Like the cattle, they knew of no enemies and provided against no needs and their end was the same" (p. 107). Far from being a Utopia, Wells's *The Time Machine* is something of a *Thebaid*, or an *Inferno* of dark imaginings, where grasping and malevolent underground powers take the blood from the already pallid overlords. Cannibalism summarizes the ultimate reversal in all three.

The dimensions of the Cain-Abel theme have been vastly expanded by their adaptation to the scientific scheme. Where Byron raised the temporal vistas to the distant past, in fact to preexistent worlds, Wells shifts them to the greatly distant future. *The Time Machine* still concerns groups of people, two fundamental races, and their development from an earlier, unjust division. But from science itself comes another element very germane to the Cain-Abel story: whether in the past or in the future, the perspective necessarily inclines toward that which is catastrophic. In the large and powerful nineteenth-century imaginings, the roles of the first two men inevitably call up the struggle of the last two men, and actually beyond— the imagination of horrors, the triumph of gigantic crab-like creatures, or, the eventual triumph of darkness, the death of the sun.

This propensity of science for "cosmic pessimism" introduces other divisions into the theme. Where Christian eschatology found an image for man, a deliverance from the chains of destiny in the person of Christ, science, although assuming the same sense of cosmic drama, in essence, has separated mankind from the universe. This separation was a drastic one and led eventually in Byron's *Cain* to the sort of malaise that prompted murder. Cain's depression at his experience of *le mal cosmique* induces him to duplicate its own violent proceedings. Science also inspires its own inside narrative—the world we see before us is not what it seems (the language of "Dover Beach," so prototypically Victorian, comes readily to mind)—and we must be of a mind to understand this other reality.

The scientist is the instructor, revealing special truths that the future will all too painfully make clear. In fact, the hypothesis is the preferred mode of procedure, and *The Time Machine* is structured around three such hypotheses. They all lead to the final horrible truth. The first two, although dismissed, are not contradicted—they are simply incomplete. They do, however contribute valuable speculations about the progress of the races.

The first explanation—discarded, but only after having been registered—is that finally the human race has achieved its "social paradise," a kind of golden age where all needs are finally and fully satisfied. But this Utopia carries with it extreme disappointment: the race is infantile and moronic, a tribe of unisexual flower children. The Eloi are indolent, easily fatigued, with extraordinarily short attention spans. They all have the signs of being "laid back." Moreover, they have allowed their constructed world to go to ruin. A kind of Golden Age, of the sort anticipated by Gonzalo in *The Tempest*, has been achieved, one dominated by negation; the people seem to have no need, there is no illness, no labor, no social or economic struggle. But if all needs are satisfied, so too are left undeveloped the necessary responses to need: intelligence and resourcefulness.

> I thought of the physical slightness of the people, their lack of intelligence, and those big abundant ruins, and it strengthened my belief in the perfect conquest of Nature. For after the battle comes Quiet. Humanity had been strong, energetic, and intelligent and had used its abundant vitality to alter the conditions under which it lived. And now came the reaction of the altered conditions. (p. 47)

Although somewhat taken aback by their imbecility—there are other disquieting features—the Time Traveller is quite willing to understand their qualities as the product of the race's triumph over nature. "This has ever been the fate of energy in security; it takes to art and to eroticism, and then come languor and decay" (p. 48). Androgyny is a perfectly understandable adjustment to the new conditions—without any struggle in existence, gender differentiation is no longer required. The historical process itself has yielded undifferentiation.

But this hypothesis proves to be inadequate in the face of the evidence of a terrible division. The Time Traveller discovers a second species of subterranean people, and for their existence he adduces an economic explanation. The division between capitalist and laborer was already pronounced in Wells's time (witness Disraeli's warning). As with the tendency toward androgyny, Wells cites contemporary evidence. In the London of his own day, he notes the greater confinement of the laboring classes to the underground, and their exclusion from the "prettier country" about London. The increased costs of education seem to compound this division by precluding the remediation made possible by intermarriage. A kind of social wall has been erected between the classes, and this division has been exacerbated. "So, in the end, above ground you must have the Haves, pursuing pleasure and comfort and beauty, and below ground the Have-nots, getting continually adapted to the conditions of their labour" (p. 69). This division, a clear extension from the social division frightfully imagined in Gessner's *Der Tod Abels*, results in the Eloi and the Morlocks, a decayed aristocracy requiring an oppressed, literally subservient class. "The great triumph of Humanity" had not resulted in genuine cooperation but rather in extreme exploitation (p. 70).

Even this hypothesis is not adequate to the full horror of the situation. Nineteenth-century imagining was particularly sensitive to the rebellion of the slaves. *Benito Cereno* would be an example, and, continuing along the lines of psychic rebellion, so would *The Strange Case of Dr. Jekyll and Mr. Hyde*, and more crucially, at the end of the century, merely a few years after *The Time Machine*, Conrad's *Heart of Darkness*. The powers of darkness now reclaim their own. *The Time Machine* is an historically extended, sociological heart of darkness, with the exception that the anguish is not internalized but remains external. The Morlocks remain the "abhorred other," bestial, cannibalistic "inhuman sons of men." The oppressed lower classes, with no dream of brotherhood, with no motive of rebellion but rather dire necessity, have become part of the monstrous progeny of Cain. The process that Gessner had surmised and warned against has been carried to an ultimate and damaging turnabout. Out of a need for survival, the abhorred other has returned to feed upon the race of the brother that had historically excluded his ancestor from the sunshine. Division between brothers continues to be the simple explanation for widespread class and racial distinctions. But this is not a noble Cain who rises up, a metaphysical rebel on the side of individual consciousness, but rather an abominable one, representing the downward slide of the race toward invertebrateness, to indistinguishability. One witnesses again the terrible dynamic by which cannibalism is the inevitable inverse of brotherhood.

This dismal prospect has its cosmic corollary. As the Time Traveller, in desperate flight from the groping appetite of the Morlocks, guns his machine farther into the future, he discovers even bleaker prospects. Millions of years into the future, he finds the world overrun by giant crab-like creatures and then less complicated lichens and green rock slime as the only evidence of life. The coming darkness is more dismal than that of Byron's famous poem; it represents the pure triumph of the underground, undifferentiation: "the sky was absolutely black" (p. 116).[16]

It should not be surprising that the Cain-Abel story, so essentially human, in fact, so expressive of what it means to be human, should yield itself so readily to such vast imaginings, that its insistence on a fundamental division in existence should work its way into the thought of nineteenth-century speculative science, conditioned as it was by the "imagination of terror." Bearing the burden of discrepant awareness that exists between the ethical nature of humankind and the dismal prospects of the universe, the Time Traveller is a kind of Beowulf in the midst of a scientific saga; he too beats down the monsters, themselves descended from Cain. Yet, it appears, he himself is unable to sustain the profound difference that his time travels have revealed, and in some kind of desperation seems compelled to return to the most flagrant and violent expressions of upheaval.

The narrator himself does not succumb to the vision of despair. It remains for him (and his response is typical of other early modernist works; think only of *Heart of Darkness*) to pick up the thread of the discourse and to continue the story's apparently dual need to express a vision of violence in a language of mystery. He wonders if the Time Traveller will ever return:

> It may be that he swept back into the past, and fell among the blooddrinking, hairy savages of the Age of Unpolished Stone; into the abysses of the Cretaceous Sea; or among the grotesque saurians, the huge reptilian brutes of the Jurassic times. He may even now—if I may use the phrase—be wandering on some plesiosaurus-haunted Oolitic coral reef, or beside the lonely saline lakes of the Triassic period. (p. 125)

It is curious that the language of science—intending "objectivity"—should be so horrific. This might be the further sense by which science assumed some of the larger offices of religious speculation. However, the heavy impedimenta of scientific jargon—not without its unintentional humor—are unlikely to communicate any sense of human belonging. In this vision, humankind have become wanderers once again, but without a City of God, or even a City of Man—the latter rendered insignificant under the cosmic prospect of belittlement. The scientist has become the real Grand Inquisitor of the nineteenth century with his own brand of mystery, miracle, and authority. Nevertheless, the burden he assumes—the great "as if"—can be heroic. The narrator, who lives to reflect upon the more desperate projections of the Time Traveller, thus can conclude, "It remains for us to live as if it were not so."

THE DEATH OF THE FUTURE

Oddly enough, the possibilities of "future history" closed very quickly. This may or may not have had something to do with the demise of the Utopian spirit. After all, the Cain-Abel story, far from Utopian even in its beneficent projections, was still involved with future events. What closed was not so much the sense of optimism in regard to the future but the sense of the future itself, the sense of a time that was to come and that would be in some way significantly different. Literature in the nineteenth century was alive with the future, with the sense of imminence, the sense that some things of extraordinary significance were about to be born.

Wells's *The Time Machine* may have shown the long-run destructiveness of the processes of history; nevertheless, its author's imagination, like Dostoevsky's, moving from the first two men to the last scene, is still pregnant with the scope of great things, with great imaginings and great significances. However dire it might be, the future still exists in an enormous, eventful, and significant continuum with the present and the past. The message is dire but the means are still coherent and stirring.

One of the distinguishing features of post–World War II thought and spirit is the sense that history has already occurred. Expectancy has been flattened out and the sense of imminence depleted. Indeed, the future was already past, the future was dead. No great prospects, not even the fears of annihilation, seemed worth the trouble. There are many reasons for this new depiction of the human condition. If humanity is something that counts for nothing, eventually the message will be received at home, and people will be less willing to engage in the great "as if," to rise to the standards of humane ethical conduct when the terms of existence seem to indicate the futility of such action. Following several world wars of horrible and massive slaughter, the worst fears of the future may have been realized. So Virgil quietly nudges Dante that it is time to leave the Inferno: "ché tutto avem veduto" ("We have seen it all").

There are two other explanations that may be useful. In the intriguing way of thoughts that exist on the same axis, it may have been that the death of the sense of the past contributed, in corresponding fashion, to the death of the future. In killing the past, in embracing so fully the dimension of the future, we may have paradoxically killed the future as well, because we cut off our thought from one of the bases of understanding. Thus maimed, it too was destined to collapse. Equally significant could be the extraordinary growth in the role of consciousness, even self-consciousness and self-reflexivity, as a realm of endeavor that is in some way separate and distinct from actions and event. In its later manifestation, this essential bequest of modernism brings us most fully to the uses of Cain and Abel in the late 1950s and early 1960s. If words and thought have little relationship to events, if words, *les mots*, are thought to perpetrate violence against things, *les chôses*, then out of this distinctly postmodernist situation a new breed of hyperconscious yet violent monster will be born for which Cain will once again serve as cover.

Alexander Trocchi's *Cain's Book*, as its title would indicate, is dominated by the configurations (and strikingly many of the appurtenances) of the Cain-Abel story.[17] Here Cain makes his inevitable, one might say last-ditch appearance and final incarnation as a played-out post–World War II existential hero, homosexual, and druggie artist. Aligned against him are the massive powers of state authority ("the Man"), against which he directs his rage in the surprisingly soapbox rhetoric of a pathetic anarchic libertarianism. In any event, this is a Cain to whom the city is alien. Like Grendel or his dam, this is a monstrous Cain who keeps to the fens and moors. In fact, he is a scowman on the Hudson—that is, outside the city, yet close enough to make periodic forays into the confines of civilization (the Village) for the much-needed bloody score.

He has in his retinue, if not progeny (although he himself is part of a writing clan that derives from DeSade by way of Burroughs) then at least confederates who assume many of the elements of the monstrous progeny of Cain: lepers, werewolves, the Wandering Jew, placeless wanderers detested and distrusted by all and for whom the scowman, living on the ambiguous and threatening water, is a fitting emblem.[18] These are stealthy intruders, big-city troglodytes haunting their cave-like pads. They speak a special language, one that closes in as much as it keeps out: boost, push, shit, dime—as in, "the count we got for the dime wasn't much" (p. 164). They share an intricate street knowledge, the ways of the junkie, ever in need of their greater possession for which they would be willing to say or do anything (sex, as a matter of subordinate interest, becomes androgynous, not even promiscuous but rather indifferent), and when they have it they partake of their fix with the eager and awe-filled expectation of a sacred ritual. They are Cainites, outlaws for whom no code, not even that of the underworld, prevails. Fay is described as an underground Florence Nightingale, but by the Marquis de Sade: "She'd suck the fix out of your ass" (p. 102). No wergild is honored in this possessed and fixated society.

Throughout these "experiences" the main consciousness of the novel, Joe Necchi, is a cooler participant and witness. Writing his notes (which are the novel we read), he is the Proustian recording secretary of a group far past disintegration, the one who brings into awareness the reasons for his own assault upon stylistic tradition and commitment to the experience of the moment. The reasons for his highs, and ultimately his own distress, are located as much in the larger politics and economics of the twentieth century as they are in its metaphysics.

"—Cain at his orisons, Narcissus at his mirror." This fragment cited from *Cain's Book* serves to point up what happens to the Cain-Abel story in the modernist and postmodernist period. In some ways a grim and fundamental theme, the Cain-Abel story comes bound in issues of destiny and identity, and above all of consequences. Involved with history, it also implies story. Aesthetically, the Cain of Trocchi's devising must be part of this in that he intends to assault narrative, he plans to rape history, the entire literary pattern of consecutiveness. But his Cain is to be better associated with the second half of the fragment, with Narcissus at his mirror. As early as Byron, where Abel was simple, even simple-minded, Cain was associated with complexity, with divided consciousness, with self-awareness. As we have seen, the growth of Cain toward greater consciousness is in accord with modernism's interest in a complex central consciousness, even the self-reflexivity of aesthetic form itself.

Cain's Book is the title of the published book we read as well as the title of the work in progress that appears occasionally in fragmentary form throughout the novel. So far has the consciousness of Cain developed that the book is his, and the problems and anxieties of an author confronting his text are Cainite. As with other Cain-Abel stories, *Cain's Book* has an "inside narrative," but this inside narrative contains no higher forms of understanding, as does *Billy Budd*, nor does it communicate essential, if secretive information, as does Joaquín's Confession. Rather, it is an inside narrative intended to be superseded by the larger consciousness of the author himself; the entries are like characters with subordinate and controlled roles to play.

> Reading what I have written, now, then, I have a familiar feeling that everything I say is somehow beside the point. I am of course incapable of sustaining a simple narrative . . . with no fixed valid categories . . . not so much a line of thought as an area of experience . . . the immediate broth; I am left with a coherence of posture(s). . . . Moreover, what's not beside the point is false. (pp. 230–31)

Later he adds, "It's a dead cert the frontal attack is obsolete." Caught in the mirror of reflection, the integrity of any posture is immediately discomfited. The centrality of any posture immediately jerks one's head aside to fix on what is not within the particular frame; merely by being within the frame it becomes fragile and fugitive as the object of perception. The present point of view cannot be true, and is in fact unsustainable for such extreme self-reflexiveness. One is engaged in a never-ending search for what is elusively and necessarily "beside the point."

This extreme self-consciousness enters into the Cain-Abel story in yet another way, for not only is novelistic naïveté, that is, simple unreflective storytelling, obsolete, it is also strangely inauthentic. From the thought of Philo to that of Hesse, we have observed the association of Cain with authenticity—and with contrasting evaluations. Cain, from Byron onward, has variously been associated with consciousness, that is, not pastoral unity but a sense of division. In regard to history itself, we have seen how those who chose to remain within the comforting idyll of historical evolution, whether Pistorius in *Demian*, or such characters in the drama of envy as Salieri or Halliwell, have been shocked out of their existence by a strong emergence of an authentic character capable of encountering historical change more fully. It is not a far stretch to include artistic style itself as part of the same dilemma, and to regard that style that depends upon consecutiveness—narrative—as itself belonging to the Abelite confines of the unventuresome. Conversely, this means that the style of Cain is most authentic when fragmentary—itself part of the disruption of its time—elusive, and self-conscious.

Necchi, the narrator, draws out the philosophical importance of style. "For a long time I have felt that writing which is not ostensibly self-conscious is in a vital way inauthentic for our time" (p. 59). He then adds, "I think every statement should be dated." The supreme role of the novelist is as diarist, for whom statements are true or accurate only for the very restricted frame in which they are given and not necessarily connected with what has preceded or what follows. Finding some scrap of notes, he writes, "The notes are not consecutive; they go on and on like tapeworm; Cain's testament, the product of those moments when I feel impelled to outflank my deep desire to be silent, to say nothing, expose nothing" (p. 238). Writing is an "outflanking" maneuver, where one must surprise oneself, as it were, even fall upon oneself in fleeting conscious immediacy: "To fall on myself from above, like the owl on the wee gray mouse" (p. 233).

If Hesse was able to justify the violence of Cain as part of a developing quest for reintegrated being, Trocchi, for his part—and here we can begin to discern the sensibility of postmodernism—equates the quest for truth with the denial of being. If the consecutiveness of history and of story has been attacked as the Abelite need for order (expressions of a kind of benignity in regard to time), so too the consciously "meaningful" statement is open to assault. The statements of Cain now become provisional and play-like. Authenticity is registered by an assault on the deadly serious, which seems ponderous and hence false to the changing moment. At this moment in his reflections, and the moment is as specific as in Hesse's *Demian*, the narrator feels the mark of Cain. "To be a hermit, even in company. To wish for the thousandth-making time for the strength to be alone and play. Immediately there was a flower on my brow. Cain's flower." The mark of Cain is not the mark of sin and guilt, but rather the flower of play. "To mean everything and for everything to be a confidence trick . . ." (pp. 71–72). That is, Cain in his self-consciousness is actually a confidence man, enticing the reader into a story that is not a story, asserting fictions and acknowledging delusions, but while so doing, also registering changes in the historical coherences of consciousness, that is, adopting the violent language of replacement to suggest the inappropriateness of that which is outmoded, and using Cain to suggest a new order of personal and stylistic being.

But, of course, given the reflexiveness of the work, even Cain cannot be totally sustained as a figure. The guns must be turned against him. The narrator quotes a passage from Edward Dahlberg's *The Sorrows of Priapus*, where Philo is described as calling Cain a profligate. Cain is then described, in the manner of *Finnegans Wake*, as fulfilling his role as profligate, wanderer. "Third profligate, first poet-adventurer, he creased her massive centrale, moved his carcassone through her paiorkneees into her soft spain before Moses engraved his tablets." But even this allowable, if silly, playfulness ends with an inverted lament: "Not enough to lament, Jeremiah, even the decay of symbols" (p. 231). The lament is for the impossibility of lament, even at the nonusability of such potent symbols as Cain himself. Perhaps this is yet another meaning to Philo's long-lasting thought that when Cain kills Abel he in reality kills himself.

Two features from the apparatus of Cain that may be invoked in regard to *Cain's Book* are the monster and the double, the first by its overwhelming presence, the second by its absence. In fact, one of the early working titles for the book was "Notes toward the Making of the monster." One reason for this obviously is that the drug addict willingly assumes the role of monster. Unlike the alcoholic who pretends to abide by the standards of social living, the drug addict long ago abandoned such pretenses. Like Grendel, he lurks as a desperate and, above all, needy predator. Against this need, all other matters of life and living are reduced to undifferentiated mess. In this sense, of course, the monster and the undifferentiated once again coalesce, as they do in *Beowulf*.

Yet, with all his acceptance of violence, even his outright exhortation of violence, this is not the picture of a Cain who accepts division in the heart of existence, the foundation sacrifice at the basis of life. This is a Cain who seems to recoil from that reality and who requires, even insists on, unity and completion. Oddly enough, given this circumstance, in this work there is no double who comes with the promise of such completion, as in the other works I have discussed in which the double appeared in response to some need for freedom, for lack of constriction or containment. In *Cain's Book*, there is no double, no twin. Drugs have taken their places. Drugs have replaced the double and have brought with their temporary onset two experiences that along with authenticity loom large in the book—that of "abeyance" and that of being "inviolable." If history is a nightmare, then one escapes to a world that is "inviolable," and drugs rush one to that access. Heroin, for instance, provides the organism with "a sense of being intact and unbrittle, and, above all, inviolable. . . . One is no longer grotesquely involved in becoming. One simply is . . ." (p. 11). But such a quest is outmoded in Great Britain and in the America to which Necchi had transplanted himself. "It's a fact that in America nothing was ever in abeyance. Things moved or they were subversive" (p. 13).

Oddly enough, by seeking inviolability or abeyance, Trocchi's creation has become a monster. We can begin to understand this paradox by observing how Trocchi's Cain differs from the patterns of regenerate Cain. By seeking abeyance, Trocchi seeks an avoidance of history, although the

Cain theme has always called for an encounter with history. Whatever he may be, Cain is never inviolate, and this is especially true of regenerate Cain. It is curious that, while attacking the unsuspecting Abel (banal in his need for story and meaning), Trocchi also shows himself to be at odds with the most serious expressions of a modern Cain. We have noted the strange absence of the double. But this has further interesting implications. In the absence of the father, the coming of the double directs action toward the regeneration of the self. But this would indicate some division in the self and in its conditions. The absence of the double would indicate that Trocchi's character regards himself as undivided, hence in no need of reintegration. Indeed, he is pictured as a "singular" character, with no sense of guilt, let alone reponsibility, and consequently in no need of recuperation. In fact, Trocchi's work conveys no sense of a self to be brought together. As the future is dead, so the self is absent, and with the self any sense of responsibility or guilt. Cain may thus be a monster.

This argument attached to the absence of the double also shows the great relevancy of the foundation sacrifice in earlier versions of regenerate Cain and the meaning of its absence here. Although part of a larger and in some ways mysterious process, the character who comes into being and who responds to the coming of the double, is still a responsible agent. This might be the ulterior and farthest-reaching meaning of the foundation sacrifice. It suggests that in committing the second slaying, one has finally acknowledged responsibility for one's life and actions—one is ready to stand alone without a double as a prop. One is now a fully functioning moral agent with an identity and a separate destiny. This is the fuller meaning of the young captain's reluctant agreement to Leggatt's departure. He is reluctant because such consent would mean an assumption of responsibility, and indeed Leggatt's departure is followed by strongly directed actions in his captaincy and command. The foundation sacrifice and its complicity with the double are crucial components in the emergence of a regenerate Cain as a character of guilt and responsibility, where guilt itself implies responsibility.

The absence of the double and of the foundation sacrifice in Trocchi's *Cain's Book* are thus revealing omissions that lead to yet another extraordinary conclusion. Two works of the 1950s, *The Caine Mutiny* from the earlier part of the decade and *Cain's Book* from the later part, speak to one another across that complex time. Although apparently opposites, each represents a repudiation of the double and the foundation sacrifice as crucial to the regeneration of existence. Whether by revocation (Wouk) or by devolution (Trocchi), each seems to go against the arguments of a regenerate Cain, and each suffers from consequent undifferentiation.

Trocchi's Cain is a Cain of the future because his quarrel is not with the conditions of existence—with divisions from birth—but with social and historical conditions, with historical causes. Trocchi's characters are un-committed but not apolitical. The differentiation he experiences is not theological—not radical as in Byron's *Cain*, in *Billy Budd*, or even in Unamuno's *Abel Sánchez*—but social differentiation, a schism in the heart of society. This is the difference that is derived from Salomon Gessner's *Der Tod Abels*, by way of Baudelaire, where it has been translated to the experience of class. Such difference is again told in terms of Cain and Abel, where the ingredient of violence is ever-present. As with other major Cainite texts, Trocchi's retells the story of Genesis 4. Incorporated into the adaptation are strong echoes of Byron as well as of Baudelaire. "Abel waxed fat and rich breeding sheep for the slaughter while Cain tilled. Cain made an offering to the Lord. Abel followed suit with his quaking fat calves. Who'd have gruel rather than a T-bone" (p. 179). The occupa-tional distinction reeks with social injustice. "And soon Abel had vast herds and air-conditioned slaughterhouses and meat storehouses and meat package-plants, and there was a blight on Cain's crop" (p. 179). That Cain should be understandably disturbed by this inequity in fortune was called *sin*. When Abel saw his haggard brother he offered him a job. It was at this point that Cain slew Abel (pp. 179–80). Joe Necchi is not so much distressed by the social inequities he has experiencd but rather by the fact "that others had the impertinence to assume that I would forbear to react violently against them" (p. 186).

It is of course possible to say that the description of the Cain-Abel theme in purely occupational terms is inferior to the grander philosophical uses to which the theme has been put by Philo or Augustine, whose reso-nances are still with us. And in our own time, even the thought of Una-muno does seem to rise to better heights when he shows the discordant brothers to be expressions of different religious principles rather than rep-resenting different vocations. But we must also concede that, as Dante recognized centuries ago, and as Dostoevsky did closer to our time, Cain and Abel are intimately involved with issues of social justice. And Troc-chi's interpretation, although economic and historical, is not occupa-tional. He is describing a much larger change in Western existence, one to which modernists responded with great force. The vision of one class of people, the descendants of Abel, strolling in sunlit pleasure, and the de-scendants of Cain struggling and dying young, imprisoned themselves by doctrines of labor, is a vision of the tragedy of social differentiation that Gessner first described. This tragedy of differentiation is no less painful for being social. Its result is to produce a storm-tossed turbulent Cain: "Whenever I contemplated our poverty and how it situated me, appar-ently at the edge of an uncrossable gulf at whose far side strolled those fortunate few who lived their lives in well-mannered leisure, I felt like a tent pegged down in a high wind" (p. 248).

While Gessner's Cain is made rabid by the vision of his children's enslavement, Trocchi's Cain is weighted down by his father's nullification and the early death of his mother. The future is past. His father has returned home from World War I to quasi-permanent unemployment. Although the father is somewhat embarrassed by the fact—which he never acknowledges—that he has been unemployed (but proudly not on the dole) for thirty years, the son, for his part, regards it as a masterful legacy, one which he will maintain with honor. It is because he is aware where his father is unaware that he adopts the role of Cain. Like *A Portrait of the Artist as a Young Man* or Lawrence's *Sons and Lovers*, Trocchi's work—and it does follow many of the patterns of those quintessential early modernist works—tells of distintegration, and the primary forces of disintegration are the relegation of the father to the sidelines and the death of the mother. Yet, unlike these works, the narrator's energies are more directed to passivity and impotent expressions of outrage bordering on shrill hysteria. Where Stephen will emulate Icarus, and Paul Morel with closed fist moves toward the challenging and inviting lights of the city—those alternatives to death—Joe Necchi is more like a "tent pegged down in a high wind." The image is accurate.

Cain's Book figures directly in the modernist line of descent, not only for its aesthetic stance and some of its familial and emotional patterns, but also by reason of its larger sense of history and its willingness to offer antidotes. The son of an Italian immigrant in Scotland, Necchi is well-placed to discern the actualities of class oppression. In the larger sense, he feels his own interests and those of his family were better served by a world that predated the Industrial Revolution, and he himself feels handicapped that this industrial culture has such little interest in play, in abeyance, in simply being. Yet, in his responses, Trocchi, by way of his character, does seem to engage in answers that, as José Guilherme Merquior regrets, tend to make some modernists more a part of the problem than of any possible solution.[19]

Perhaps the Cain-Abel material we have built up here can help us understand why. These episodes, which began with a certain amount of hopefulness about the future ideal of brotherhood, terminate in violence and horror. In *The Time Machine*, the horror lies in the historical process itself, whereby with a grim inevitability happy security becomes effete vulnerability, and the downtrodden themselves are turned into monsters. In Trocchi's work, the historical process itself collapses and one is left with no prospects—not even those of horror.

Trocchi's own vision is impaired by his failure to engage the forces of Abel in a sustainable polarity, by what could be called monovocality. This quite apt and ready term can have specific content. Cain and Abel never engage in any discourse across the pages of Trocchi's work (somewhat like the sexual encounters that are grim and silent). In fact, there exists in the work no Abelite personality at all; there is a system, a doctrine, an historical process, and an ethnic and socially superior class, but never a person. This is a story about Cain without an antagonist, one where there is no other, even where there is an unwillingness to construe or confront another. Perhaps we should return to Philo to bring some complications to the notion of monovocality. This absence of Abel means that Cain should be absent as well. The absence of the double, the absence of the foundation sacrifice, all indicate the absence of a self willing to incur both guilt and responsibility. In fact, what we are presented with is a Cain of violence and passivity. Sexuality requires the glittering knife. Yet, despite the book's regular tendency to resort to images of violence, these are images of impotence that tend to result in verbal lashing and then at length self-questioning and ironic self-reflexiveness, where the social Cain is undone by the aesthetic Cain. This combination of violence and passivity helps explain why, despite his book's broad understanding of his characters and their historical placement, Trocchi's solutions dissolve so easily into self-projections and imaginings, homosexuality and drugs.

The pattern of regenerate Cain brought standards of validation to the processes of becoming. One does not leap to being, as does Trocchi's character Joe Necchi, as abruptly on the wings of drugs—again we are reminded that Cain and Abel are not sky-children—but rather through historical actions that themselves come under extraordinary scrutiny. Drugs suggest an at-onement without the sacrifice, without the self that is both guilty and responsible. From within the pattern of regenerate Cain we have been able to evolve concepts that bring detailed content and specific meaning to the charge of monovocality. In regard to classic examples of regenerate Cain, Trocchi's *Cain's Book* is something of a deformation. Nevertheless, the pattern of dualistic thinking that has been so bound up with the emergence and extended life of the Cain-Abel theme is not the end of the line. We turn to greater modernists, specifically Joyce, to elaborate more significant ways of transcending duality itself.

Chapter Twelve

TWINNING THE TWAIN

ROMANTICISM, while transforming basic character evaluations of the Cain-Abel theme, did not challenge its essential dualistic structure. This was left for twentieth-century modernists who tried to alter the primary seesaw psychology of the theme. Whether in the stories of the regenerate Cain or in those of a Cain rooted in theological envy, when one side was up, the other side was down. What the modernists did was alleviate this cruel dynamic and expand on the terribly invidious and dualistic bases for judgment. They set about to establish points of interchange, of reflection, what we have come to call "complementarities."[1] Modernists began to see that in many cases opposites are not contradictory but rather comprise the horizon of a situation; they are mutually defining terms, the opposite sides of a coin that share a common metal, the opposing banks that do indeed form the river. They are terms that not only call to one another but actually call forth one another. We speak of the fascination of opposites, and of the magnetism generated by opposing poles. Rivals must at least speak a common language in order for there to be any basis to a difference. So-called opposites are frequently nothing more than related principles of organization built along the same structural axis. This is why opposites frequently emerge together historically, and, curiously enough, suffer parallel declines. The appropriate metaphor for opposites is not the seesaw but rather the raft. When one side slips under the other is not long in following.[2] We observe this historically in the quarrel between the universal Church and Empire in the thirteenth century, or that between Erasmus and Luther in the sixteenth. These are the recognitions that led major modernists to look for relationships where there had been enmity, to look for "family resemblances." Their project was to twin the twain.

It is surprising that the Cain-Abel theme has not had an extensive association with twinship. "Two lay down and seven rose up," is one humorous Talmudic version of the prolific powers of Adam and Eve.[3] The grim struggle between Esau and Jacob was used retrospectively to insert a bar of exclusivity between Cain and Abel—as two nations striving for superiority or later as rival principles, only one of the two should be deserving of allegiance. But if Cain and Abel can stand forth as forming a master metaphor of fundamental division—the twain that never shall meet—they can with increased effectiveness come to be used as the means by which the twain can be brought together. If in the earlier, classical Christian era, the character of Cain was especially useful to indicate some intractability in existence, then in later epochs, of a different mind, the rival brothers could be conjoined as twins to suggest the interests of mutuality. This can be put another way. The Introduction argues an essential distinction between Cain and Abel and Castor and Pollux, and the simple impossibility of the former pair ever arriving at the elevated status of the latter pair. The Cain-Abel story has given expression to dire exclusion, to the grim consequences of history, in fact, to the very origins of history itself, while the heavenly twins, in the wonderful metamorphic genius of the Hellenic imagination, look on events from a position of history transformed and transcended. Yet, again, summary illustration may be gained from Dante's *Commedia*: when Dante triumphs over exile and his earth-bound and necessarily divided native city, *la città partita*, he realizes his victory while circling with the *eterni gemelli* (*Paradiso*, 22). But when we come to twentieth-century literature, where the idea of twinship has had a special affinity for the Cain-Abel theme we will witness the prominent commingling of Cain-Abel and the Gemini.

If surprise is warranted it should be registered at the fact that the notions of twinship and Cain-Abel had not emerged more fully prior to the twentieth century; not that this time should have been the epoch of their emergence. This is particularly the case when one considers the ways that twinship places in clear focus and even magnifies the true energies and hidden resources for which the Cain-Abel theme is, as we have said, a cover letter. How much more seriously aggravated are the tensions between brothers if, in fact, their unity had been even more intimate, if more than simply brothers, the rivals had been twins. More than being brothers and having emerged from the same womb, twins actually berth together, sharing as much as human beings can near total sensual communion. This fact brings into much sharper tension the issues over which the theme presides—the tragedy of differentiation and the hazards of undifferentiation, the need for communion but also the sad facts of the necessary disruption of that unity and the need for individuation. With twinship, unity is more complete than with any other pairs of beings, extending as we have seen in *The Secret Sharer*, even to customized methods of communication. All the more painful and grievous then is the recognition of the different callings of personal destiny and individuation. At the same time, although it aggravates the tension, twinship also provides more grounds for integration. Family resemblances can emerge more resolutely in the midst of difference, emphasizing indeed the common metal shared by both sides of the coin. These and other such linkages suggest the similarities that transcend difference, and encourage the perception of complementariness.

There is yet another and perhaps more interesting reason why twinship should comply with the greater purposes of the Cain-Abel theme in twentieth-century literature. If modernist literature and thought seem committed to "strategies of inwardness," to finding interchangeability and similitude, where indeed all things resemble or come to stand for potentially all other things, this sense of doubleness and of twinship becomes more prominent.[4] The mind is indeed that ocean where each kind does straight its own resemblance find. But if Cain-Abel has always contained a strong element of reality therapy—where the will and consciousness are not absolute masters but are indeed subject to the consequences of actions, to moral judgment, and to other such intrusions and impediments of history and external event—then we can see that the fusion of twinship with the Cain-Abel story represents the fuller dynamic of the age's greatest literature. That literature is committed to the elaboration not only of strategies of inwardness but also of its dread opposite, the intervention of some imminent external agent or event, or even better, the literal realization of some objective shaping of a personal destiny. In this sense, the Cain-Abel theme, which always bore with it a social and an ethical component—the Hellenic play of consciousness and liberation along with the Hebraic sense of responsibility and guilt—has come to fit with the increased internalization of twentieth-century literature, but even more fully it shows that literature's broader and more dramatic capacity to challenge its very assumptions, to show the real significance of events of history intruding upon the claims of consciousness. This is the real theme of twentieth-century literature, and will be present throughout my discussions in this chapter of *Finnegans Wake*, Unamuno's *El Otro*, and Michel Tournier's *Les météores*.

FINNEGANS WAKE: A STORY OF "CRIME AND LIBEL"

Childs will be wilds . . .
Them boys is so contrairy . . .
News of the great big world. Sonnies had a scrap . . .

Despite the clear and specific differences that twentieth-century modernism introduced to the romantic versions of the Cain-Abel theme (and these shall be more fully brought out in *Finnegans Wake*), the theme itself carries a remarkable charge of both continuity and transcendence between the two highly distinctive and formative cultural epochs. In its emphasis on division and disunity, the painful experiences of social and even cosmic separateness, the Cain-Abel story turns out to be a vital connecting link.

Showing this continuity, *Finnegans Wake* brings to comic completion the changes in the theme that Byron had initiated. Cain is the outcast, the original malefactor, even the *poète maudit*, who nevertheless struggles through to some sense of regeneration, while Abel is cast further down the slopes of deterioration.

For James Joyce, Cain supremely expresses the dilemma of self-definition on the part of an artist, particularly an artist who is struggling to establish himself and his vision in the midst of sagging familial fortunes. Beyond the bondage created by Ireland's subservience to Rome and London, there is a home-felt meaning to Stephen Dedalus's determination to escape from the nightmare of history. Joyce deliberately chose to open *Ulysses* at the moment in 1904 when his own aspirations and fortunes were at their lowest. A promising young star who had gone both to London and to Paris armed with letters from the brightest lights of the Irish literary galaxy, he returned from France having suffered something of a defeat.[5] Furthermore, his family was in grave decline. His younger brother George had died (something not mentioned in *Ulysses*), and he suffered through his mother's protracted agony. On top of that, his loquacious but ne'er-do-well father neglected his sisters, who took on (as *Ulysses* indicates) the appearances of street urchins. This was not the program of the young man who, as Icarus, was determined to fly above the nets. Moreover, through his own heavy drinking, whoring, and bad company, he himself began to acquire a rake's reputation. But despite these setbacks to his purpose, his own agonizing doubts, and his self-questionings, his spirit and mind still seemed remarkably intact and determined. Countervailing forces were moving toward self-realization and identity, as surely as the silent ship moves upstream. Given this context, separation is inevitable, but this bestows even greater appropriateness on the assimilation of Cain. In his single-minded determination to follow his ambitions, needs, and aspirations, the young artist must finally shed and abandon those closest to him; symbolic slayings on the part of the Cainite personality are required in the processes of artistic self-determination; the mythic pattern of escaping from the Inferno requires such acts of supersession.

Just as the struggle of the young modernist artist merges with the pattern of regenerate Cain, so too Abel fulfills a familiar role. His innocence moves to outermost simplicity, until his purity, becomes "puerity," or puerile. The brother pairs in *Finnegans Wake* exist on an axis of meaning and value. Where one of the pairs, Shem (James-Cain) is dispossessed, Shaun (Abel) beomes more and more the man of the world. But more fundamentally, where Shaun represents an untainted innocence, the embodiment of the unconscious need for unity in the world, Shem stands for division, the complexity of mind that registers discrepancy. This means of course that Shaun can only become a sentimentalized figure, while Shem will embody a complex consciousness. Despite the cultural origins of such division in the Byronic aspect of romanticism, Shaun will come to represent a romanticized consciousness, while Shem will stand for a more modernist awareness. We have already seen this duality in Caleb and Aron.

This line of connection from Byron to the modernists, one that stresses division in consciousness and character, is a dominant line of development. Based upon the consciousness of a breach in existence as well as in the personality, this sense of division might itself be a requirement for creativity. The representative character of unity seems to proceed along set lines, unwilling to risk any separation or isolation. At the same time, Shem will be the character willing to make a break, the one struggling to install new values. From within the fallen world, he seems to represent a fecundity, however woeful it might appear, that has been for some time absent from the commanding world of Shaun. Despite his ignominious conditions, the Cain character embodies qualities that the public world can ill afford to dismiss.

"Felixed is who culpas does." The *felix culpa*, the world of the Fall—of many falls before the Fall, of repeated falls—informs the world of *Finnegans Wake*, that great creative masterpiece that most fully summarizes the continuities between romanticism and modernism. At the same time, it transcends the romantic dualisms, in that the presentations are comic and distanced, and are preparations for another order of things and of awareness—that of complementarities.

.   .   .

The brother motif in Joyce's work moves out of the closet in *Portrait* (Cranly) and *Ulysses* (Mulligan), where it was disguised as cohort-rivalry, to the full display of its power in *Finnegans Wake*.[6] But when Stanislaus Joyce (at one point referred to as "Stainusless") appears as the Shaun-Abel prototype, we must realize that he shares few of the "false friend" attributes of Cranly and Mulligan. Stanislaus was not a hostile brother. Indeed, he was a consistent defender of his brother's life, reputation, and works. His record of Joyce's early development, *My Brother's Keeper*, is a minor classic, not only for what it reveals but for what it is: a calm, judicious, and sympathetic account of the early development of a man of genius written by the only person to have intimate knowledge and intelligence enough to render competent judgment. The title of the work, ironically intended, is of course the record of a brother who actually did provide for his most improvident brother. Unlike false friends, Stanislaus was not waiting to serve the poisoned bowl. His work is still the best guide (except for Joyce's own works) to the nature of his brother's temperament. Brothers in *Finnegans Wake* are not so much enemy brothers as they are brothers doing what the Cain-Abel story has done best, and that is to stand for rival principles, representing a division that is so fundamental that only the differences existing between brothers can adequately suggest them.[7]

In *Finnegans Wake*, brother rivalry becomes a master metaphor for oppositions of all kinds, extending from the microcosm of the family (Shem-Shaun, Glugg-Chuff, Kev-Dolph, Butt-Tav), to the larger figures and issues of history (Brutus and Cassius, the Roman Church and the Irish Church, Mensheviks and Bolsheviks), to great dualistic principles (Space and Time, Mercy and Justice, and finally realism and idealism). Such an abundance of dualistic opposition must bear its own force of disintegration; indeed, the dualities are tenuous and unstable for a variety of reasons.[8] First, of course, is their sheer number: to be part of such an ongoing and apparently never-ending series of pairs might expand the meaning of any pair, but it most certainly reduces the significance and seriousness of all of them. The linguistic punning also means that each phrase carries within itself the means of its own undoing—frequently, as we shall see, its opposite. Eventually, each term of the many pairs will shade into its supposed opposite but actually complementary partner. *Finnegans Wake* is the fullest expression of Joyce's extraordinarily aloof personality and frankly comic genius.

The shifting world of *Finnegans Wake* is difficult to fix because fixation is its main purpose to avoid. Its fantail of cross-references starts out with the family, the brothers, and then spreads to historical personnages, great (and not-so-great) political issues and cosmic and philosophical principles. Everything is almost literally involved with everything else. This means then that the Shem and Shaun controversy is both as real and as foolishly one-sided as that of any dispute between Space and Time, Justice and Mercy, philosophical realism and idealism. Historically, even the division between Brutus and Cassius is reduced (or comically enhanced) to the argument of Butter versus Cheese.

Typically, we only know of the characteristics of Shem-Cain (James) through the denunciations of his accusers; also historically we only know of the Gnostics through the attacks of the early Church heresiologists. Shem is denounced as a malcontent, as one who refuses to accept the plentifulness of life's offerings, so committed is he to griping about its deficiencies. So Justius (or Justice) makes his charge: "and now, forsooth, a bogger among the blankards of this dastard century, you have become of twosome twiminds forenenst gods, hidden and discovered, nay condemned fool, anarch, egoarch, hiresiarch, you have reared your disunited kingdom on the vacuum of your most intensely doubtful soul" (p. 188).[9] Later, Mercius (Mercy) will open his defense by echoing lines that call to mind the possibilities of regeneration, "My fault, his fault, a kingship through a fault!" As we have seen in the chapter, "Cain as Sacred Executioner," new kingships could be established only through a fault. Furthermore, Shem resembles Stephen, particularly Stephen of the Joyce's "Scylla and Charybdis" chapter, who is of "twosome twiminds" as he attempts to elude the dangers of critical idealism and positivism, the Saxon smile and the Yankee yawp.

Where Shem is vilified as a "seeker of the nest of evil in the bosom of a good word" (p. 189), Shaun upholds the honor of the family, of the maternal bosom, of the original word. He is "that other, immaculatus, from head to foot, sir, that pure one, Altrues of other times, he who was well known to celestine circles before he sped aloft, our handsome young spiritual physician that was to be, seducing every sense to selfwilling celebesty. . . ." But this "chum of the angelets" Shem, like Cain, "laid low with one hand one fine May morning in the Meddle of your Might, your bosom foe. . . ." Accurately enough, this first murder is then followed by a description of Cain as Nimrod, the master builder of Babel (Ibsen's play is also present), as well as Marcion, the heresiarch accused of "deploring unity" (pp. 191–92).

Abundant and detailed (and probably accurate) as are Justius's accusations, they are discounted not because they are unfounded but because the speaker in his prosecutorial intensity is too rigid. Consequently, he misses out on the necessary and even beneficial qualities in Shem-Cain. Like his own favorite, Shaun-Abel, the voice of Justius ends in sterility. "He points the deathbone and the quick are still. *Insomnia, somnia somniorum. Awmawm.*" The reign of Shaun-Abel will deteriorate to the status of Yawn. But also represented is the maternal matrix view of the world in which Shaun resides: he is a mamma's boy. In contrast, Mercius, concluding his defense, "lifts the lifewand and the dumb speak." The famous Washers at the Ford episode follows.

Shaun-Abel is the female favorite because he confirms the desire for innocence. This is seen in the final sililoquy of Anna Livia Plurabelle (ALP) as she takes leave of the world she has known. Her world has been disenchanted. HCE himself has lost powerful charms and has become detumescent: "I thought you were great in all things, in guilt and in glory. You're but a puny" (p. 627). The conditions of existence seem to lead to betrayal. She loves to be spoken to "in the languo of flows"—the language and the languor of flowing and flowers. But these sensations are dependent upon a distinct bodily reality. "Reach down. A lil mo. So. Draw back your glave. Hot and hairy, hugon, is your hand! Here's where the falskin begins." The falsing begins with a recollection of the duplicity of Jacob, but it inheres in the conditions of existence. "Smoos as an infams." An infant's skin is smooth, but it already contains the "infans," the unspeakable, and is breeding ground for the infamous. The whole design is fell ("of fell design"), leading to a fall. That is the basis of H. C. Ear-

wicker's (HCE's) collapse; his scar is more fundamental and not only because at one time, like Cain, he took a life. Given these realities, she would
prefer not to see. "I'll close me eyes. So not to see. Or see only a youth in
his florizel, a boy in innocence, peeling a twig, a child beside a weenywhite
steed. The child we all love to place our hope in forever. All men has done
something. Be the time they've come to the weight of old fletch" (p.
621). The devil, the itch, is in the flesh, and in this discrepancy of existence we are all guilty. She would rather retain the image of childhood,
and it is this image that Abel vindicates and Cain contradicts.

Although ALP's lyrical language is sublime, and in many ways justifies
the colossal linguistic daring of *Finnegans Wake*, its sentimental sources
are duplicated in the early preferences of the young girls, who compound
the sensed divergence between Shem and Shaun, now in their early child-
hoods known as Glugg and Chuff. Joyce confirms Unamuno's testimony
by way of Joaquín that women are present in every Cain-Abel tragedy.
The arbitrariness of preference aggravates the tragedy of differentiation,
and furthers its deleterious effects, forcing difference into division. Chuff
is the "fine frank fairhaired fellow of the fairytales, who wrestles for the
tophole with the bold bad bleak boy Glugg geminally. . . ." The young
girls prefer "enchainted, dear sweet Stainusless," whose non-threatening
powers are represented in his name. "You are pure. You are in your puerity." As I have indicated, his purity is puerile, but more significantly he
represents no significant otherness to them, no male challenge. "Sweet-
staker, Abel lord of all our haloease . . ." (p. 237). He confirms their own
halo ease, their own denial of a difference in the male-female polarity, and
for this is "princesome handsome angeline chiuff" (p. 239). In all of this
he is contrasted with the foul offending Cain, who in his characteristics
summarizes many of the features of Cain as "abhorrent other," including
that of werewolf (p. 244).

As always in Joyce, the contest inevitably yet humorously reaches out to
a world of correspondences. "Childs will be wilds. 'Twastold. And vamp,
vamp, vamp, the girls are merchand."

> For these are not on terms, they twain, bartrossers, since their baffle of What-
> alose when Adam Leftus and the devil took our hindmost, gegifting her with
> his painapple, nor will be atoned at all in fight to no finish, that dark deed
> doer, this wellwilled wooer, Jerkoff and Eatsoup, Yem or Yan, while felixed
> is who culpas does and harm's worth healing and Brune is bad French for
> Jour d'Anno. Tiggers and Tuggers they're all for tenzones. Bettlimbraves.
> (p. 246)

Differences are indeed radical, originating with the conditions of the first
fall, when Eve was poisoned with the devil's "pain apple." The brothers
will always be twain, never "at-oned" in a struggle that is unending. In

this particular instance, though, as with the sentimental persistence both of ALP's and of the girls' requirements, the source of division reverts to the psychological needs of the chooser: "For she must walk out. And it must be with who. Teaseforhim. Toesforhim. Tossforhim. Two. Else there is danger of. Solitude" (p. 246). The selection of a mate requires a twosome, and coincidentally requires exclusion of the other, thus preventing the twain from ever becoming as one. Female nesting needs themselves present obstacles to inclusiveness.

Whatever the aggravating reasons, divergence is part of the physical conditions of existence. "Them boys is so contrairy," is ALP's conclusion. "The Head does be worrying himself. Heel trouble and heal travel. Galliver and Gellover. Unless they changes by mistake. I seen the likes in the twinngling of an aye. Som. So oft. Sim. Time after time. The sehm asnuh. Two bredder as doffered as nors in soun. When one of them sighs or one of him cries 'tis you all over. No peace at all" (p. 620). The difference between brothers is as physical and as inevitable as that between north and south (or a Norseman in the South). "O, foetal sleep! Ah, fatal slip! the one loved, the other left. . . ." The foetal sleep was the fatal slip, as basic as Esau and Jacob. But the very inevitability leads to a larger philosophical picturing and understanding. "But they are two very blizky little portereens after their bredscrums, Jerkoff and Eatsup. . . ." Indeed, Joyce's insistence on the universality of this brotherly division leads him back to the broader mystery of Christian eschatology: "weeping shouldst not thou be when man falls but that divine scheming ever adoring be." ALP bids adieu to the quarreling sons, "Still tosorrow," till tomorrow will continue the sorrow (p. 563).

The father, HCE, seems to participate in the same dream of preference as does the mother, ALP. Where the mother requires innocence (as do the young girls with "stainusless"), the father endorses the virtues of the publicly recognized leader of men. These happen to be the qualities of Shaun, which are also, unlike those of the more searching Shem, supportive and non-threatening to the guilt-ridden father. The father, like the mother, has an active personal purpose in the drama of preference. This also explains how "innocent" Abel could become the social conqueror—from "charming" he becomes "chairmanly."

In Dante's *Commedia*, the principles of reconciliation are finally lodged in the vision of the father. Antagonists, the universal Church and Empire, Franciscan and Dominican, become reconciled because each accepts with justice the functions assigned it in the overriding divine purpose. Only this larger vision of higher purpose is capable of overcoming division. Perhaps from the French Revolution onward, clearly in aspects of the Cain-Abel story and certainly in literary modernism, it is rather the very absence of the father that seems to promote the quest for *fraternité*. It is precisely because the Godhead has been shattered that the many pieces are held to be constitutive of reality. Einsteinian relativity coincides with modernist perspectivism, each denying the notion of any "master" print of reality. "For if sciencium (what's what) can mute uns nought, 'a thought, about the Great Sommbody within the Omniboss, perhops an artsaccord (hoot's hoot) might sing ums tumtim abutt the Little Newbuddies that ring his panch." Science, accustomed to telling us what's what, that is, being descriptive, has no capacity to account for the assumptions of its own procedures, its own metaphysic. The artist (hoot!) might however tell us something about the manifestations of the Godhead. ". . . for O'Cronione lags acrumbling in his sands but his sunsunsuns still tumble on" (p. 415). The sands of Chronos, of any Father Time, are spilled, and we have only the day-to-day and generation-after-generation sons (suns). It is their composite that makes up the picture.

Consequently, Shem and Shaun and the other dualities require one another. This comes out in many ways. Guilty though they might be, they are "fellows culpows." The "felix culpa" makes fellows of them. At the division of Glugg and Chuff, "each was wrought with his other. And his continence fell" (p. 252). The singular anger of Cain is transformed into one that is mutual and that was wrought by means of the other. This same line occurs with the older versions of the twins, "And kev was wreathed with his pother" (p. 303). And not only wrought, but wreathed in with his brother. And the phrase reminds us of Hesiod's dictum that only a potter can envy a potter. The very relationship creates the antagonism.

This recognition of complementarities receives its fullest expression in the fable of the Mookse and the Gripes, and even more importantly in the well-known song attributed to the Gracehoper-Grasshopper (Shem) in the fable actually told by Shaun, the Ondt-Ant of the piece. Each of these tellings is based upon another prevalent but also impossible duality of Time and Space. It was Joyce's quite sensible way of responding to Wyndham Lewis's accusation in *Time and Western Man*, that the literature of the twentieth century, following Einstein, was dominated by a time-mentality.[10] In this depiction, the world lost its substantiality, its localized reality, and became an assortment of merely ephemeral mental impressions. Joyce is recorded as allowing Lewis a measure of truth (about ten percent), but he saved his greatest response, the fullest register of his thinking, for *Finnegans Wake*. The quarrel between mutually defining (and necessary) opposites is as foolish as a quarrel between Space and Time: "The Mookse had a sound eyes right but he could not all hear. The Gripes had light ears left yet he could but ill see" (p. 158).

The interdependence of such various human faculties is made even more apparent (and possiblly more humorous) in Shaun's tale of the Ant and the Grasshopper, and it shows the intermixture, the wreathing together, that Shem's song contained within the retold fable. "I apologuise, Shaun began, but I would rather spinooze you one from the grimm gests of Jacko and Esaup, fable one, feeble two" (pp. 414–19). These jests from the brothers Grimm, are also grim jests about essential divisions, where one is able and the other is feeble. The Grasshopper, or gracehoper, embodying the modern philosophical tradition of Kant and Schopenhauer, has squandered all of his time. The Ondt (a spatialist, hence his name from the Italian *onde*, or "where") was, on the other hand, "a weltall fellow, raumybult and abelboobied. . . . He was sair sair sullemn and chairmanlooking when he was not making spaces in his psyche, but laus! when he wore making spaces on his ikey, he ware mouche mothst secred and muravyingly wisechairmanlooking." The Ant as a creature of space is committed to the world and capable in it—"raumybult." Indeed, he is the leading person of his time, charming and chairmanly, but this able-bodied man is also an Abel booby.[11]

Finally, it is the Grasshopper's song as repeated by the Ant that exposes the true nature of their mutually involved relationship. The error of the Ant (and it is an error that was exposed earlier in the rigid exclusivity of Justius) is to ignore how much he is involved with his opposite. Here the Shem and Shaun duality actually becomes transformed into that of Castor and Pollux. The frugal Ant actually requires the spendthrift Grasshopper. "For the prize of your save is the price of my spend." The song proceeds to indicate intricacies of other intimate relationshsips;

> Can castwhores pulladeftkiss if oldpollocks forsake 'em
> Or Culex feel etchy if Pulex don't wake him?
> A locus to love, a term it t'embarass,
> These twain are the twins that tick Homo Vulgaris.
>
> (p. 418)

Castwhores (Castors) cannot ply their try without ballocks (Pollux). A place might be to love, but one requires a time in which to do it. Together the twain as twins make up human nature.

"We are Wastenot with Want, precondamned, two and true." Like Dante's Avaricious and Prodigal sinners in canto 7 of the *Inferno*, polar opposites meet together; indeed, forming a nexus of involvement, they are "precondamned," historically joined together by the conditions of their existence, as all great dualities are. They are sentenced together, each the predicate of the other. "An extense must impull, an elapse must elopes" (p. 418). To separate Shem and Shaun, the Grasshopper and the Ant, Br'er Rabbit and Br'er Fox, would be to deprive each of the other defining force of his existence. It would be as difficult as separating time and space, whose two representatives Shem and Shaun become in Joyce's great puzzle of existence.

The song ends with great ironic praise of the Ondt: "Your genius is worldwide, your spaces sublime." But then, as does the discourse of Justius, it ends with an indication of his weakness, "But Holy Saltmartin, why can't you beat time?" (p. 419). The wastrel Grashopper invokes the god of drunkenness, of unpredictability and even spontaneity. These conclusions give an inevitable historical and dialectical placement to Joyce's vision. He seems quite willing to concede, even to advertise, the notable defects of the Cainite character, Shem, as in many ways his own caricature. He is also willing to allow that the dominant personage of the time is doubtlessly the chairmanly Abel. But he has a further purpose, and that is to show the insecure tenure of the dominant personality when his victory is so one-sided, so dependent upon the total exclusion of the qualities that Cain represents. In this sense, he indicates the nemesis attending the absolute predominance of the controlling rational intellect. He sees its termination in sterility as predestined, and in fact a product of the oppositional thinking that is so exclusive. Not only is Joyce's thought, then, of historical moment—he is describing a specific moment in Western intellectual development—it is also dialectical, bringing back into focus and association valuable and fertile aspects of the human personality, in many ways associated with the artistic temperament (which, although given to foolishness and extremes, represents an apprehension of reality that the public world can ill afford to dismiss). If this is modernism's message to modernity, it is a message well worth making, and it is made by bringing into a nexus of necessary involvement—or complementariness—Cain and Abel, who had been theretofore drastically sundered.

· · ·

> VLADIMIR: I tell you his name is Pozzo.
> ESTRAGON: We'll soon see. Abel! Abel!
> POZZO: Help!
> ESTRAGON: Got it in one!
> VLADIMIR: I begin to weary of this motif.
> ESTRAGON: Perhaps the other is called Cain. Cain! Cain!
> POZZO: Help!
> ESTRAGON: He's all humanity.
> —Samuel Beckett, *Waiting for Godot*

Despite its sometime hysterical, always high-pitched rhetorical questioning and the striking absence of anything approaching comic imagination, *El Otro* rightly fits under the shadow of *Finnegans Wake*, a work with which it shares many concerns.[12] To be sure, it lacks the unusual mythic scope and grandeur of that work, but as a surrealistic psychodrama it does oddly enough compare with Beckett's *Waiting for Godot*. Cosme and

Damián are twin brothers. They are in love with the same woman; in the absence of the one, the other marries her. The brothers confront each other, and one is killed. But no one, not even the wife, knows which one has survived, that is to say, which one is the killer. He is simply called "el Otro." A second woman claims she is also wife of one of the brothers, in fact, that she is pregnant, also with twins. This work was written in 1926 (although not performed until 1932) at Hendaye, when Unamuno also composed the much more fully conscious and understanding defense of his character Joaquín in *Abel Sánchez*.

At the end of Unamuno's novella, Abel and Joaquín had come to resemble each other. The apparently indifferent Abel is shown to have a driving compulsion for fame and a need to guard his own accomplishments, even to the extent of preventing his son from following a career as a painter. So intense has the relationship been that a resemblance is bound to emerge: "each was wrought with his other." Their common history has forged a kind of identity.

Not only thoughts, but actual lines from *Abel Sánchez* are carried over into *El Otro* and the Cain-Abel theme continues to provide the mythic patterns for this intense dynamic. El Otro feels that he is Cain and Abel, executioner and victim. If Cain had not killed Abel, then Abel would have killed Cain. The schoolboy question is again repeated, "Who killed Cain?" Complicity is so compelling that the punishment of Cain is to feel that he is Abel, and that of Abel to feel himself to be Cain.

Where in *Abel Sánchez* one senses that Unamuno only came later to understand the fuller implications of his remarkable story, in *El Otro* the larger philosophical perspective and even contemporary understanding are much more explicit. *El Otro* brings into conscious realization the fuller dimensions of the Cain-Abel story, the tragedy of differentiation, the hazards of undifferentiation. However far apart they may seem, the issues with which Unamuno is grappling, those bound up with the Cain-Abel story, are the same that Conrad confronts in *The Secret Sharer*. Identity is required, yet identity insists on its cruel exactions; community is desired, yet indistinguishability may lead to madness. Similar to the young captain, the surviving brother in *El Otro* bears no name. In fact, retrospectively we can see that the young captain is nameless not only because he is in the process of formation, but also because his character has the capacity to incorporate "the other," that is, he is himself not yet an identity but rather a duality.

At the same time, this doubleness is seen as a curse. The interchangeability of the supposed opposites reaches an extreme, even dangerous position, in Unamuno's and in the modern consciousness. Indistinguishability, made manifest by twinship and also by a vagrant consciousness, seems intolerable. El Otro exclaims, "Ah, terrible tortura la de nacer doble. De no ser siempre uno y el mismo" ("O what a terrible torture to be born double. Never to be one and the same"; p. 686). The same phrase is repeated later (p. 700). The duality itself is pernicious. "Cuando uno no es siempre uno se hace malo. Para volverse malo no hay como tener de continuo un espejo delante, y más un espejo vivo, que respira . . ." ("When one is not always one he becomes evil. To become evil there is nothing like looking into a mirror continuously, especially a living, breathing mirror"; p. 679). The demands of the mirror, representing not only doubleness but indistinguishability, and the key, representing singleness and identity, can never be reconciled. "Un espejo y una llave no pueden estar juntos . . ." ("A mirror and a key can not be joined"; p. 661).

Much more consciously than *Abel Sánchez*, *El Otro* is addressed as a "mystery"; in fact, it is so subtitled, as is Byron's *Cain*. Within the context of the Cain-Abel theme this means that one reaches a level so fundamental that further discourse is impossible, and this, as we have seen, was one of the major resources of the theme. Over such basic divisions not only is God silent, but God himself—as in Byron's work—is double. "Todos doble. . . . Dios también doble!"

Not one to avoid repetition, Unamuno replicates the brothers in contending spouses, Laura and Damiana. The latter is pregnant with twins. Carrying on his contention with Byron, Unamuno does not believe that the continuity of the race is likely to provide any reconciliation but only further complications. These twins, like Esau and Jacob, struggle within the womb, "con odio fraternal." So essential is this conflict that it actually exists before birth. This is why the same hatred is called here, as in the new prologue to *Abel Sánchez*, "amor demoníaco." The animosity is so essential that it is part of the conditions of existence, part of its very doubleness. It is the cost of being born. If "la vida es un crimen," the "el haber nacido" requires forgiveness. Birth itself requires individuation, and is thus an indication of a genuine foundation sacrifice as essential to existence. Thus it is a crime.

Few authors explore the inner resources and energies of the Cain-Abel story as intensely as does Unamuno. More than carrying on the theological traditions of the past, he brings the theme into the heart of contemporary understanding. In his "Autocrítica," Unamuno describes *El Otro* as the natural offshoot of his obsession with the "mystery of personality," "del sentimiento congojoso de nuestra identidad y continuidad individual y personal" ("The anguished sense of our identity and individual and personal continuity"). Every Cain is an Abel because every murder is a suicide. In destroying the other, one is destroying that which helps create the self, that which marks the line where the self is not, the other side of the defining boundary. In this sense, the other is required, as are Cain and Abel. But the conditions of existence lodge us in singleness, in individual responsibility and identity, while our consciousness inclines us toward reflective otherness. The other name for God is destiny, and the wife of destiny is fatality. The acceptance of destiny pushes us into the embrace of fatality, and this is what the mirror of consciousness seeks to avoid most, in fact, desperately strives to avoid. To choose identity is to risk fatality, but to seek out similitude is to risk sterility. It would seem then that the conditions of existence call us to choices of death or dying. In this sense, and this is Unamuno's argument, we are Cain and Abel, and where each murder is a suicide, so also each self-definition requires excision.

It is of course no accident that at the end of this play Unamuno should have recourse to the classic of the Spanish stage, one that gives final expression to the conditions treated at so fundamental a level: Calderón's *La vida es sueño*. It is curious that the matter of his play, which began with the realities of division, ends by contemplating their final unreality. But if we think of Spain in 1926, when the play was written, and again in 1932, when it was first staged, we can conclude that its anguished concerns were of the greatest social relevancy and reality. The national perspective must involve universal forgiveness, for all are guilty: "¡Perdonémonos los unos a los otros para que Dios nos perdone a todos!" ("Let us forgive one another so that God will forgive us all"; p. 709).

. . .

As did Joyce's and Unamuno's, Michel Tournier's fascination with Cain and Abel extends throughout his works, beginning with brief but arresting mention in *Vendredi* (1967; English translation, *Friday*, 1969). The theme receives full conceptual amplification in *Le roi des aulnes* (1970; English translation, *The Ogre*, 1972), and then enters remarkably into, even taking possession of, the articulation of *Les météores* (1975; English translation, *Gemini*, 1981).[13]

In *The Ogre* (like *Gemini*, not at all mistitled in translation), Tournier begins by reversing many of the more modern versions of the theme, those that have prevailed since romanticism. First, he restores Abel to centrality, a role he had not occupied since the eighteenth century. But he does this by bestowing upon Abel many of the traits both traditional and modern that have usually been conferred upon Cain. Abel Tiffauges is giant-like, a wanderer and something of a cannibal, since his preferred diet is raw meat. His abiding interests are decidedly scatological, but rather like those of a Rabelaisian giant, innocent as he expatiates on the pleasure of defecation and the germinating powers of excrement. This proclivity is added to later in life when in the German wood he develops expert knowledge about animal droppings. To scatology is added phallology when he discourses on the physical potencies of the great stags from their testicles to their antlers.

As Tournier describes his work, however, it is a story of "malign inversion," where all of the things that Abel Tiffauges loves become perverted, the opposite of themselves, by reason of historical circumstances. He is a child lover who is accused of being a child abuser and is only saved by the outbreak of World War II; a connoisseur of the meanings of signs, he finds himself, after being taken prisoner, unintentionally abetting Nazi programs because of his fascination with the meaning of their symbolism. In all of these instances, although feared by the neighboring villagers and regarded as the Ogre of Kaltenborn, he is not the perpetrator of violence. Although uprooted, he is not Cainite. Caught up in the violent upheavals and dislocations of the war, his own thoughts are clearly inoffensive and even pacific.

These thoughts become clear by means of his own secret journal. These "écrits sinistres" accord with an essential element of Cainite literature, and thus provide another inside narrative by means of which the genuine information, that is, the products of speculative understanding, are communicated. The Ogre himself abides within the essential carriage of the theme, imparting secret, even conspiratorial knowledge not for the uninitiated.

Abel Tiffauges believes his name is fortuitous until he reads the relevant passage in Genesis 4. Through this reading, Tournier devises yet another interpretation of that most adaptable of biblical texts, again casting the brothers as rival principles but principles that are active throughout history. As Augustine was the first to do, and as Unamuno in his earlier writings also did, Tournier sees the brothers as standing for groups of people—nomads and sedentaries—who are historically opposed (pp. 31–32/ 39–41). His interpretation is valuable since it attempts to reconcile the apparent anomaly between verses 12 and 14 and verse 17. When God sentences Cain to be a wanderer, he fixes on the man of the soil the most heinous form of punishment, deracination. In outright defiance of God's judgment, Cain founds a city; by necessity then the city is infernal, a place designed by revenge for purposes of retaliation. Throughout history, then, the Cainites, now citified and sedentary, will carry on a vindictive war against the truly nomadic Abelites. In romantic literature, it is Cain who is the wanderer, and who thus enjoys an association with the Wandering Jew. But in Tournier's late twentieth-century imagination, the innocent and Christ-bearing Abel shares the fates of the other wandering victims, Jews and gypsies. (In one of his sinister writings, Abel wonders about his origins: "I inherited my swarthy complexion and straight black hair from my mother, who looked like a gypsy. I never had the curiosity to look into her background . . . but it wouldn't surprise me if there were horses and caravans there somewhere"; p. 31). In the nineteenth century,

the dispossessed peasantry came to form the proletariat of the great industrial cities. Rather than the force of rebellion, these neophyte citizens of
Cain's city will harbor resentment against the nomadic types. Tiffauges,
himself nomadic—he repairs automobiles and lives under the Mobil gas
sign, ready to take wing—waits for the day when God will tire of the
crimes of the Cainite city dwellers. "Then, like Cain, they will be flung in
disorder on the roads, fleeing madly from their accursed cities and the
earth that refuses to nourish them. And I Abel, the only one who will be
smiling and satisfied, will spread the great wings I keep under my garage
owner's disguise and, with a kick at their shadowy skulls, fly up among
the stars."

To move to the stars from the disorders of history is, apparently, not
only the fervent desire of Dante but of Tournier as well, and *Gemini* will
more than confirm that instinct. But in *The Ogre*, the visitation he desires
is soon to be unleashed (the entry just quoted was from February 18,
1938). But it is a Cainite onslaught that brings judgment against the descendants of Cain. The conservative mythology of Hitlerism was essentially sedentary. In one of Abel's private entries, he writes of the cyclical
nature of the conservative time world (and we are cast back almost immediately to Thomas Mann's *Der Zauberberg*, as Tournier's closest spiritual
ancestor): "Hitlerism is resistant to any idea of progress, discovery or
imagination of an unknown future. Its virtue is not rupture but restoration: hence the cult of race, ancestors, the dead, the soil . . ." (p. 266/
281). Later, one of the philosophers of the movement explains the
Hitlerian emphasis on race as opposed to the "Bolshevik-Jewish" emphasis on social factors: "Hitlerism is a doctrine of farmers and sedentaries
strongly rooted in the ancient world of Germany. . . . For us, everything
is in the hereditary equipment handed down from generation to generation according to known and inflexible laws" (p. 276). "Blood and Soil"
mark the fundament of the Hitlerian appeal. As Abel listens to the "mad
speech," he recalls the lines from Genesis 4, "The voice of thy brother's
blood calleth to me from the ground. . . ." The Cainite appeal of Hitlerism is then patent and diabolical and will be met with appropriate divine
vengeance (pp. 276–77/293–94).

Despite his urge for transcendence, his desire to take flight on his
winged horse, to escape from history falsified by a "malign inversion,"
Abel Tiffauges is inescapably trapped in time and history. And it is as a
representative of these forces—as opposed to the completion and fulfillment of twinship, the eternal avoidance of chance and history—that he
makes his appearance in *Gemini*.

Twinship acquires interest in *The Ogre*, but it used in a manner far different from the fuller involvement of twins in the great issues of Cain and

Abel seen in *Finnegans Wake*, in *El Otro*, and in *Gemini*. Rather than representing spiritual completion—the possibility of freedom, even of immortality—twinship, in the concluding sections of *The Ogre*, is seen as the triumph of the body over the spirit. In the training of the Hitler youth, individuality is subdued to the larger body. Twinship—partnership, or subjugation to the other, that is, undifferentiation—is then a natural manifestation of this larger public purpose.

But in *Gemini*, the purposes are altogether different, and it is as a threat to these principles of communion that Abel reappears somewhat mysteriously and unnamed, representing time, change, and history. As a force of personal destiny, he interrupts the communal twinship of Jean and Paul, representing a centrifugal force working against the essential centripetal pressures of twinship. Paul, who is the brother most committed and in need of the cellular contentments of twinship, recognizes the dangers that Abel Tiffauges represents both in his great size and in the appeal of his force to his brother Jean. For his part, Jean is unhappy with the security of undifferentiation, with the confinement of twinship; he wishes to break out and achieve his own individual identity. Long before his affairs with women, Jean is ready, Paul recognizes, for a break in the compact of twinship.

The first defection, in this sense, the first fall (the fall before the Fall), was not the experience with women, but rather his encounter with Abel: "That man, little brother, carried solitude, individualism, total ruthless dedication to a particular destiny, everything, in short, that is the very opposite of ourselves, everything that goes against the very essence of twinship, to its ultimate conclusion" (p. 142/169). Not only do Paul's complaints constitute a marvelous contemporary retelling of the Cain-Abel story, but they go on to uncover some of its essential motives. Twinship, for Paul, seems to resist the essential fratricidal struggle for existence. To be born is itself a struggle. In fact, all children were essentially two, but one of them, the more aggressive of the two devoured the other in the womb. The Cain-Abel story is used to express the very cannibalism of existence. That Abel is large is proof enough of his monstrous cannibalism, and that the twins are small ("jockey-size") is indication of their inviolate nature. The extralarge size of the twinless comes from his having devoured his other self in the womb:

> Every pregnant woman carries *two* children in her womb. But the stronger will not tolerate the presence of a brother with whom he will have to share everything. He strangles him in his mother's belly and, having strangled him, he eats him, then comes into the world alone, stained with that original crime, doomed to solitariness and betrayed by the stigma of his monstrous size. Mankind is made up of ogres, strong men, yes, with stranglers' hands

and cannibal teeth. And these ogres roam the world, in desperate loneliness and remorse, having by their original fratricide unleashed the torrent of crime and violence which we call history. (p. 142/170)

This understanding of the inner reserves and dimensions, as well as the public historical processes of the Cain-Abel story, is remarkable. Although the murderous act is at the source of history, true brotherly aggression takes place far back in the process, even before birth, when singleness rather than twinship is established. Singleness at birth and individuation in life are the real abnormalities because twinship represents the original intention of existence. Only twins—here the Dioskouri are opposites of Cain and Abel—seem to be innocent: "We alone came into this world hand in hand, a smile of brotherhood on our lips" (p. 142/170). Cain and Abel come to stand for the divisions of existence in contrast to which twinship offers true brotherhood, shared existence. In fact, harkening backward, one can hear the original spiritual motives of the religious Abel, refusing to accept the conditions of existence (as, paradoxically enough, the romantic Cain will do), and instead adopting toward life an attitude of dispossession based on true spiritual brotherhood. In this modern retelling, one feels one is probing the radiating nuclear strength and powerful appeal of this theme.

It pains Paul that Jean feels within him, and without, powerful pressures to relinquish their innocent and complete world. For Paul, twinship does not mean an openness to that which is new or a readiness to incorporate the other—that which is different—as it does in *The Secret Sharer* and to a certain extent in *El Otro*, but instead a given completion and sensed totality of being. Rather than sharing such innocent contentment of twinship, Jean only knows its suffocating constriction, what one might call the repetitive sameness of the double. In his reflections, his temperament inclines toward the challenges of existence:

The geminate cell is the opposite of being, it is the negation of time, of history, of everything that happens, all the vicissitudes, quarrels, weariness, betrayals, old age—which those who set out on the great river whose troubled waters roll on toward death accept as the entry fee and, as it were, the price of living. Between unchanging stillness and living impurity, I choose life. (p. 196/237)

Doubleness and twinship are expressions of the need for unity, to go back beyond, to reverse the conditions of existence; they finally give expression to the human need for philosophies of completion and of immortality itself. The acceptance of the price of living, the cost of existence, casts one as Cain into the divisions of existence, and into the earthly city itself committed to time and to change and to history, but which is also built upon the sacrifice of the brother. In times of historical change and innovation (the Renaissance might be described as one), this second version of the story emerges, as it does with some complications in the postromantic era. The greatness of Tournier lies in such stirring "re-tellings" as well as in the breadth of his capacity to entertain both "voices."[14]

There is another form of doubleness, and this not by the way of twinship, not the way of the Dioskouri, but rather that of Narcissus. The homosexual in his quest for similitude makes of the double a sexual likeness. Where the twins have a created likeness, the homosexual is committed to doubleness but in fact condemned to singleness. The homosexual of Alexander Trocchi is an active predator, a member of the hunting clan of the "monstrous Cain." The homosexual of Tournier becomes more of a victim and prey, himself undone by his own need for twinship.

The great character, in fact, the most prodigious creation in *Gemini* is the uncle Alexandre, a character who in stature can rightly be compared with Proust's Baron de Charlus. In his conscious need to create similitude he is in need of twinship, in the quest for which he constantly courts danger. Audacious, he is scornful of the "hetero riffraff." They are tied to obligatory processes and acts of nature, while for the homosexual "all things are possible, none obligatory. Your [heterosexual] loves are clamped within the reproductive processes, ours are open to all innovations, all discoveries. . . ." The homosexual partner is then the double who serves to deny the limitations of natural identity. Not only is he a double, he is a twin. "Fraternal. The big word slipped from my pen. For if the bed is the mother's womb, the man who comes, becoming unborn, to join me there, can only be my brother. My twin brother, of course . . ." (p. 178/215).

In such conditions, we have come to expect a variation of the Esau and Jacob story. Alexandre does offer his own version, one which denies the sundering of the pair.

> The Bible tells us that Jacob and Esau, the rival twins, struggled together even in the mother's womb. It goes on to say that Esau coming first into the world, his brother took hold of his heel. What does this mean but that he wanted to prevent him from leaving the maternal limbo where they dwelt entwined together. Those moments of the double fetus . . . why interpret them as a struggle? Ought they not rather to be seen as the soft, caressing life of the geminate pair? (p. 178/215)

But Alexandre lives in quest of physical similitude, he was not born to it. When he is undone, in the chapter entitled "Death of a Hunter," he is undone not so much by the prey-turned-predators whom he has been stalking amid the sordid and deadly docks of Casablanca, but rather by the naturally twinned relationship of his own nephews, Jean and Paul, a relationship he recognizes as out of his reach.

Mysteriously, not knowing of their presence in Casablanca, he is astounded to cross the path of this young person (he had not seen them for years), who seemed to be everywhere. He soon realizes that this apparent ubiquity is really twinship; he senses himself excluded by the twins' natural condition of doubleness. His own ideal is shown to be elusive, in fact, artifical, and he is crushed by this intervention of a genuine limitation. "Geminateness . . . rejected me because it is completeness, absolute sufficiency, a cell enclosed upon itself. I am outside. I do not belong [Je suis dehors. Je suis à la porte.]. These children have no need of me. They have no need of anyone" (p. 276/333). Then, in a gesture of desperate bravery, he scours the docks for conquest, defying all prudent counsel. Moving into the position of Trocchi's predator, this vulnerable hunter becomes prey to the thugs who were hunting him.

The epitaph of this extraordinary character is provided by Paul—as habitually in the development of the novel we follow his words and changes. The ovoid fetal position of the twins expresses their "determination not to become involved in the dialectic of life and time" (p. 278/335). Heterosexual loving is committed to an encounter with otherness, and through this form of procreative completion to overcome time and death (typically Tournier assigns only a procreative function to heterosexuals, rarely allowing them either affection or lust, caring or carnality). The homosexual is caught between these two possibilities; he rejects the dialectic of time and change, and yet he cannot actually be privy to twinned communion—as Alexandre belatedly realizes:

> He rejects procreation, growth, fertility, time and weather and their vicissitudes. He goes wailing in search of the twin brother with whom to enclose himself in an endless embrace. He is usurping a condition that does not belong to him. The homosexual is like the Bourgeois Gentilhomme. Intended by his plebeian birth for useful work and a family, he clamors wildly for the free and uninhibited life of a gentleman. (pp. 278/335–36)

Heterosexuals are committed to the instinctual role of propagation of the species. The homosexual is an actor but also an improviser, an artist; his part seems most fluid, characteristically opposed to fixity and identity. Oddly enough, according to Tournier's interpretation, the homosexual would figure as the opposite of the young captain in *The Secret Sharer*. Where the young captain makes room for the other, conspiratorial though he may be and linked by doubleness, Alexandre seeks the unchanging qualities of similitude; where the young captain comes into the assurance of identity, Alexandre seems ever determined to resist that ultimate commitment to time and to change.

Gemini shows the twentieth-century interest in the twinship presiding over difference and division; the Dioskouri, Castor and Pollux, emerge, where Cain and Abel had reigned. Yet we must remember that even the Gemini cannot escape so easily their own basis in violent division. Although the containment of twinship seems to offer a reprieve from the forces of destiny and time, these forces must inevitably reassert themselves and reclaim their lost powers. Twins are welded together and cannot be separated unless, Paul adds ominously, "by the stroke of an axe."[15] The story of the twins is not only caught up in the events of World War II, but more significantly in the divided postwar world, whose epitome is the partitioned city of Berlin.

Tournier seems to have a predilection for the passive character, the one to whom things happen. So it is that in *Gemini* we do not focus on Jean's active pursuit of change but rather on the dependent Paul. Like Abel Tiffauges, Paul is the more Abelite character, clinging to unity yet cast into the historical drama of his time. He arrives in Berlin the same week that the Berlin Wall is erected. Attempting to escape to the Western sector of the city, Paul is literally devoured by the jagged teeth of a collapsed tunnel wall, the hard reality of history itself eating into his flesh and amputating his left arm and leg. But this physical maiming restores, we are led to believe, a larger wholeness than the one he had been seeking with his physical twin.

A prototype of this later transformation, which might be considered a translation from the physical to the universal, is given earlier in the novel, when Alexandre meets up with one of his schooltime chums, now a priest. He had been celebrated among his classmates for having devised the "dry come" method of masturbation, that is, orgasm without emission, an evident boon for young boys suffering in a boring geometry class. Father Thomas and Alexandre engage in remarkable speculations about twinship. Thomas tells Alexandre that, while in the monastery, he had identified himself with Thomas Didumos, whom he regarded as actually having been twin to Christ. So taken with the nature of this identity, he had begun to imitate Christ, but Theodore, an elder of his monastery, disabused him of this Western incarnationist fallacy. The Western presentations of Christ are quite different from those of the Eastern Christ, Christ the divine, the majestic. This thought could not abide violence being done to the godhead, the circumcision, the crucifixion, the violent humiliations of the flesh, the essential facts of division that indeed made Abel come to prefigure Christ. For Theodore, the Western insistence on physical verisimilitude (what Dante discovered to be "nostra effige" in the divine) prevents the true reign of the Spirit, the Paraclete superseding Christ.

Thomas transmits this lesson to Alexandre, who is too physical to appropriate it, but it is a lesson that Paul would learn:

> I had transformed my unpaired state, from which I was suffering as from an amputation, onto Jesus—and that was right. . . . But it was a mistake to remain a prisoner of the body Crucified. It was for Father Theodore to unfold the whirlwind of the spirit to me. The flaming wind of the Paraclete devastated and illumined my heart. The common factor which I had found only in Jesus revealed itself to me in every living man. My didumy become universal. The unpaired twin died and a brother to all men was born in his place. (p. 116/138)[16]

It is interesting that, as in Hesse's *Demian*, the double dies in order for the single to become universal. The more accurate interpretation that Tournier's work casts retrospectively on *Demian* is that it is not only his own *daimon* of which Emil Sinclair comes into possession, but a broader one, that of all humankind.

Despite its flowering into the Dioskouri, the story of Paul and Jean is that of Cain and Abel, one requiring a severance, even an amputation. The spiritual journey of Paul is made against the tableaux of the Cain-Abel story and stories hung on the walls of our inner museums from Philo and Augustine to Joyce and Unamuno. The actual maiming of Paul is intriguing since its terms recapitulate the earlier description of the surviving brother ingesting in the womb the never-to-be-born brother: "He braced himself, gathering a pathetic assortment of material around him, and as the soft, slithering jaws closed slowly over his crucified body he felt the hard edges grinding into it like teeth of steel" (p. 435/523). The Cain-Abel story has violent severance at its core. In twentieth-century literature, physical severance seems to be the requirement for mental transcendence. In Tournier's *Gemini*, the violent act of severance does not lead to individuation, as is the case in *The Secret Sharer*, but rather to universalism, the universalism of the speculative mind and the questing spirit. In their way, the twins, the Gemini, have overcome Cain and Abel, however rooted they may be in the latter pair's earthbound and violent patterns.

EPILOGUE

THIS STUDY of Cain and Abel has revealed four major areas or patterns of the theme in the literature since romanticism. These patterns—regenerate Cain, envious Cain, Cain of future history, and Cain and Abel as complementary figures (incidentally, the first three do seem to continue the three ancient traditions of the theme)—indicate that there is no single paradigm of romantic and postromantic Cain, and that the view expressed by an older generation (itself formed critically by romanticism) of Cain as a tormented, doomed, but heroic rebel, the archsymbol of the "rebel against God" is not tenable. Although it would have been quite possible for this study to limit its contribution to the valid confines of such significant scholarly revision, in some ways the story this book has had to tell in its long extent and its many twists and turns is both simpler and more startling.

To begin with the more palpable, other than Cain there is no large mythical figure who for almost a millenium and a half has represented the essence of utter reprobation, and who now for almost two centuries has come to represent the serious possibilities—complex though they may be—of moral regeneration and some hopefulness. To take into consideration only the largest and longest-enduring figures, one sees that such a claim could not legitimately be made for Adam and Eve, nor for Lucifer, and certainly not for Ulysses. Adam and Eve, in the ample and generous Christian program of salvation, bear a direct connection as first parents with ultimate redemption; Lucifer, in whatever forms and guises—from Satan to Mephistopheles—his several metamorphoses have taken, has never been able to shed the role of instigator, that is, of a subordinate temptor, and even in modern culture he runs the risk of being a shabby, if not frivolous character.[1] Just as Cain and Abel could not be called sky-children, so, conversely, Cain has never been depicted as frivolous (although the comic Cain of the medieval mysteries does come close). And Ulysses, for his part, has never been able to elude the suspicion with which people ordinarily treat resourceful intelligence: this means that even his triumphs (one could say, *especially* his triumphs) are greeted with some moral ambiguity. In this sense, Cain as the first fall guy stands alone, and the extraordinary changes of Cain, and what they reveal about basic alterations in our cultural history, constitute the remarkable fact of this story.

Recognition of this crucial turnabout in the character of this erstwhile malefactor brings to the surface once again the primary importance of the Cain-Abel theme for the modern world, and this seems to have been the direction that has overtaken this study. The general Introduction has already alluded to this importance—in the absence of a commanding moral standard, which is reflected in the demotion of Abel, Cain emerges as a true searcher for values, but one whose quest is as problematic as the nature of revolutionary violence itself.

There are arguments of even greater appropriateness, some deriving from the deeper recesses of the theme. These reach forward and backward into the true significance of Cain and Abel for Christian as well as pagan thought, with the nature and the needs of the religious mind and the quest of the secular mind. Although differing in their directions, each category begins by addressing the fundamental proposition over which the theme presides, that is, the reality of a fracture at the basis of existence, a breach in its heart, and the correlative need for finding and promoting means of reconstitution. This address to a breach in existence is the constant factor that places the modern versions of the Cain-Abel story in touch with the most significant thought of our cultural past.

Cain-Abel, in the course of its history, has entered into two major alliances, one with the foundation sacrifice and the other with the double. These are the kinds of alliances that are made from special affinities, and accordingly have yielded bountiful harvests. Although it was Philo who provided the essential arguments for Christian approaches to Cain and Abel, it was Augustine who associated the biblical brothers with the foundation sacrifice at the origins of Rome. And this meant that the brothers were implicated with and came to represent not only all foundation sacrifices but foundation sacrifice at the heart of existence, indeed, foundation sacrifice as a parable for existence. The reason for the creative florescence of the Cain-Abel story in conjunction with the foundation sacrifice is that, unlike Romulus and Remus, it came to stand for two opposed responses to the common event. If existence is purchased at the price of another, then for Abel of the older, religious dispensation the cost is too dear. Abel declines the citizenship that is built over this crack in existence. He declines both political identification and self for the sake of a fuller identity and a better self—those that do not require sacrifice and loss. The more realistic Cain is quite willing to cope with the divisions of life, to forge an identity and a self—even if such identity means one must live with the broken mirror.

This difference explains why it is that Cain and Abel have procured for themselves such productive afterlives, have indeed superseded the *frères ennemis*, of which motif, in principle, they as a theme are a subordinate part. It is the very fact that each represents a divergent manner of confronting the foundation sacrifice that accounts for the extraordinary appeal of the theme. The importance of the conjunction of the Romulus and Remus story with Cain-Abel is that it brings together the religious with the political. Of course, this dualism was suggested first by Philo without reference to foundation sacrifice. What the conjunction suggests is that the religious and the political are both obliged to confront the same central event. At the origin of each is the brother's death, itself serving as a lesson from which not only different but radically divergent morals may be derived. The future of the theme is enhanced when we see that out of this fundamental conflict two divergent views may emerge, one lending itself to a religious interpretation of existence, and the other to a political, and that in a later period when the political acquires ascendancy a new respect will be granted to Cain and the burden that he endures.

In the Renaissance, that cultural period so crucial and formative for the burgeoning modern consciousness, Cain, by assuming the function of the Sacred Executioner, provides a pattern for all future regenerate Cains. Cain assumes responsibility for entering into historical change and for bringing out of change a new unity—and in the representativeness of the New Prince a new identity as well. He is thus engaged in the two modern issues of revolution and legitimation, issues with which regenerate Cain must most certainly grapple. In *L'Homme révolté* (1951), Albert Camus recognizes this dilemma:

> The present interest in the problem of rebellion only springs from the fact that nowadays whole societies have wanted to discard the sacred. We live in an unsacrosanct moment in history. Insurrection is certainly not the sum total of human experience, but history today, with all its storm and strife, compels us to say that rebellion is one of the essential dimensions of man. It is our historical reality. Unless we choose to ignore reality, we must find our values in it. Is it possible to find a rule of conduct outside the realm of religion and absolute values? That is the question reaised by rebellion.[2]

If rebellion and revolution are part of the foundation sacrifice itself, then we can see that the issue of legitimation that Camus so rightly signals is not solely a contemporary problem (although certainly one that has been made more pressing since the French Revolution) but rather a perennial one, one born of the fact of sacrifice and loss at the basis of existence. In this sense, religion, far from being "absolute" in its values, has the same starting point as politics.

The political mind of Max Weber in that address of special acuity, "Politik als Beruf" ("Politics as a Vocation"), recognizes the common origin of the two. Rejecting the politics of the unarmed prophet in its modern variation, Weber finds it "astonishing that such a thesis could come to light two thousand five hundred years after the Upanishads. . . ." We come closer to the moment of this study when Weber notes, ". . . it is by no means a modern disbelief born from the hero worship of the Renaissance which poses the problem of political ethics. *All religions have wrestled with it. . . ."*[3]

For Weber, the Renaissance was a period committed to working out means and tests for legitimation (his notion of an ethic of responsibility complies nicely with the pattern of regenerate Cain), but this applies to the Reformation as well. In this sense, however much they may have differed, Machiavelli and Luther were about the same task. The religious, reformist corollary to the Sacred Executioner would be the "calling." Curiously enough, each turns out to be vital for this study, since each enters into modern arguments of legitimation. The New Prince accepts responsibility for the consequences of his actions—in fact, he is willing to encounter "ethical paradoxes" for the sake of political order. For his part, Luther provides the supreme instance of the calling: Here I stand; I can do no other. After the most intense travail and scrutiny, one is brought to a position that seems necessary according to the requirements of understanding, morality, and conscience. These two forces, the pattern of the Sacred Executioner and the sense of a calling—formidable expressions of the Renaissance and Reformation—become crucial in the development of a regenerate Cain.

Obviously the sense of a calling becomes part of the Cain-Abel story by means of the double, that other grand alliance into which the theme enters. The double comes both issuing and in response to a summons; this meeting is fraught with mystery, as if a fundamental and unavoidable encounter with the self is taking place. If the political order looks to legitimation, the personal order looks to authenticity (as we most fully saw in the discussion of Hesse's *Demian*). Again showing his connection with the continental and the modern, Byron was the first to introduce the double to the theme. To be sure, both Gessner and Alfieri exploited the devil as an insinuator of illusory fears and distempered projections, but it was Byron who established the personal dynamics and interactions of the double with his corespondent Cain. The double certifies the validity of the divisions within Cain as part of a larger search for identity—the double and selfhood are thus the ultimate partners of the story. In fact, those who fail to respond to the double—like those who fail to see the ghost in *Hamlet*—are necessarily diminished. They are oblivious to the starting conditions and final goals, but more important, to the race in between. For this reason, Abel is disregarded; his refusal to acknowledge the mystery of the double ranks him among the stalwart defenders—the new citizen—of the accepted conditions of existence.

Cain is the new secular hero because in some way he is reespousing the old religious quest—different as his conditions and final goal are acknowledged to be. Byron was the first to highlight an extraordinary change and that is the possibility that in the modern world the secular mind had become the more serious mind. This obviously controversial point rests, on the one side, on the conventionalization of the ethical, as represented by Abel and by his resigned commitment to assumptions of unity, and, on the other, on Cain's determined confrontation with division, the seriousness of his search, his need for reintegration, and, finally, with his saddened and reluctant acknowledgment of the sacrifice required by identity itself. In this sense, with his double, he is responsive to mystery, and this must be the final value of the Cain-Abel story in the modern world: the seriousness and the scope of the drama that the issues of heaven and hell once provided in the classical Christian epoch are part of the contest within the person of Cain in the modern epoch.

Foundation sacrifice, mystery, and the double do not operate only on the level of the religious quest; they are indicative of the historical level as well. The Sacred Executioner contributed valuable meaning to the foundation sacrifice by locating it at the level of history, that is, the level of change. This shows that division is not simply a product of dissidence and malcontentedness, but rather it is part of a larger shift in values, of change itself. Hence the role of the Sacred Executioner, in whose pattern the modern Cain fits, is not only to mark change but also to introduce change. Dissonance itself comes from the historical nature of humankind, and a response to these changing conditions of existence seems to call for a new representative hero. From Machiavelli's New Prince, to Shakespeare's Henrys—so unnecessarily demoted by postromantic criticism—to the modern regenerate Cains, a slaying, symbolic or real, is required to suggest the very loss that is needed in order for a new being to emerge. As a program of scrutiny, the Cain-Abel story has been used to address these perilous matters of historical change. In this larger historical view, we can see how and why these formations of the Cain-Abel story contribute to a defense of the modern world: they grapple with the foundation sacrifice that is at the basis of change in order to provide means for justifying both change and identity. It is hard to see how, in the issues they address and in the full complex of arguments they introduce to adjudicate such matters, the new versions of Cain-Abel are without value for the larger community, or how they could avoid bringing needed assistance to the sagging structures of authority, themselves in need of infusion.

But there is perhaps an even more important way by which the Cain-Abel story engages and justifies the large movements of the modern world. Although the world has been enriched by stories that speak of unity, harmony, peaceful growth, and communion, it has also found it necessary to confront the facts of difference, discord, and dislocation. Yet the Cain-Abel story does more than show such unpromising beginnings;

it shows them as having been overcome. Although thought to be an unlovely theme, it is here that the story acquires beauty from an involvement
with historical change itself and the ways that individuals and groups can
eventually find some redemption. We have already witnessed in Steinbeck's *East of Eden* this extraordinary appropriateness of the regeneration
of Cain for the modern world. Memorable for the powerful presentation
of the effects of the arbitrariness of preference in regard to the offerings,
this work, in its genuine faith and understanding, captures the appropriateness of Cain for a singular group of people—the uprooted, those who
are confronted with no recourse, and who are obliged to bridge the distance between the old worlds they have left behind and the new worlds
they have come to settle. In their very persons they embody the psychic
dimensions of the Sacred Executioner—killers of the old and bearers of
the new—as they come to a place where they themselves are strangers and
only offered scant enjoyment of the new order they have established.

This large relevancy of Cain-Abel for what it means to be part of a new
world, for the New World itself, is amply brought home in that magnifi-
cent study of Octavio Paz, *Sor Juana*. With power and poignancy Paz describes the *mestizo* as bearing "Cain and Abel in a single soul." "A true
pariah" with a "spectacular career: bandit to policeman to soldier to gue-
rilla to local boss to political leader or university professor to chief of state.
The ascent of the *mestizo* was a result not solely of demographic trends . . .
but equally of his capacity to live and survive under the most adverse conditions, of his daring, strength, skill, fortitude, ingenuity, adaptability, in-
dustry, and resourcefulness." Not only did the *mestizos* establish themselves and their own, they also defined the nature of the new world: "They
were New Spain's true novelty. More important, they made New Spain
not only new but *other*."[4] These pages may serve as part of the mounting
pressure of this volume; they rise up and carry the argument to the level
toward which it was tending, where the larger significance of Cain in the
history of the modern world is revealed, indeed, where the appropriateness of Cain for the modern world—for the new world, for historical
change itself—stands clearly revealed.

· · ·

The danger in this study has been to overemphasize the interplay of romanticism and the Cain-Abel theme and to slight the contributions of the
Enlightenment. This is partly because the consequences of the addition of
the double to the theme have been simply prodigious, involving as they
do the decline of the father, the regeneration of the self in an atmosphere
of momentousness and mystery, the eclipse of Abel, and the reintroduc-
tion of the crucial alliance with the foundation sacrifice, thus necessitating

the second slaying, not of the inferior brother but of the better brother, who has brought with himself reorientations toward being, change, and difference.

In this persistence of the foundation sacrifice, we can see why it is easy to neglect the theme's critical and crucial engagement with the Enlightenment and even to argue that Cain-Abel is an anti-Enlightenment theme. If we consider the commitment of thinkers of the Enlightenment to the unity of the human family, to the avoidance of drastic solutions or radical conceptions of evil, to dispelling any sense of tragedy and mystery, we can see how the resources of the theme ran counter to the spirit and to the intellectual pronouncements of that age. Nevertheless, the Enlightenment may have exercised the most pervasive and longest-lasting influence on the modern versions of the theme. The generalized view of the Enlightenment was ameliorative; eschewing radical extremes, it offered an inclusive view of the human family, with no dire exclusions, no extremes of heaven or of hell. Moreover, the pastoralism of the heart found its idyllic location within the conjugal family. Such domestication was an essential ingredient to civilization, just as male bonding, the perilous blood-brotherhood, was dissolved by the softening touch of the woman.[5] Every one of these features—the ameliorative, the domesticated, the feminine—became part of the makeup of a regenerate Cain. The role of the female principle is particularly important because it interrupts the closed circuit of male isolation, but even more crucially the woman brings a completeness that was sensed as lost by the sundered brother. In fact, she becomes a substitute for the brother, one where no violent sacrifice is required, not even that at the source of the discipleship of the blood. If, in the past, Cain-Abel replaced the story of Adam and Eve as a better parable (in conjunction with the foundation sacrifice) for existence, then in the Enlightenment, we can say, the process of domestication, of civilization, reunited the original family, Adam and Eve and Cain and Abel.

But the encounter of the theme with the culture of the Enlightenment is even more significant because of the way it engages the problem of modernism. We have of late come to realize that the real contest of modernism is not with romanticism, not with postmodernism, but rather with the Enlightenment. The genuine issue at the heart of modernism is its relationship with the Enlightenment. The question asked again and again is if modernism, in its essential arguments, is anti-Enlightenment, even countermodernity, and antinomian—in short, does it avoid the simple ethical concerns of the society at large.

Cain-Abel is well placed to address this question, and, in fact, to expand its formulations. For one, the theme involves questionable acts of violence, acts that are cordoned off, as it were, perhaps even sanctioned by a somewhat generous distinction between special knowledge and the common understanding. In this sense, it would seem to be not only indifferent to community ethics, but downright hostile. In the grips of his own divided consciousness, an individual of special designation engages in a psychodrama of enormous significance, a significance that is lost however on an oblivious general population. In this sense, Cain-Abel in its postromantic dress is nothing else than revived Gnosticism, whereby a transcendent consciousness seeks to go beyond the "authorities of matter," the archons of the world.

There can be no question that Cain-Abel has provided one extremely strong connecting link between the Byronic version of romanticism and modernism, that is, it is perfectly placed to provide evidence and to bear witness. The authors included here form a highly representative group, illustrious and illustrative of major tendencies of the literature of our time. They have the capacity to enter into the argument and to show forth major tendencies of the thought and culture. In this sense, then, they are useful in revealing not only dimensions of the Cain-Abel theme, its resources and dimensions, but more extensively what those dimensions themselves indicate about modern culture.

We have already seen that Cain-Abel has stood in defense of modernity, that is, of a culture seeking means to validate change. What such addresses to the principle of the foundation sacrifice implicit in the Cain-Abel story have done is to set up a program of scrutiny and even discernment whereby judgment may be rendered. In effect, the very prevalence of the Cain-Abel story in the literature of romanticism and modernism would indicate an essential concern with matters of justice, and this cuts across the board from regenerate Cain, to the dramas of envy, to Cain of future history. Utilization of Cain-Abel is in most instances *prima facie* evidence that one is addressing community ethics in the most serious sense, that one is addressing principles of validation for acts of innovative change.

The problem derives from the fact that change itself implies challenge to what has come to be accepted; it itself removes discussion to a newly formed gray area, a no-man's-land 'twixt land and sea, where matters are in abeyance, and difficult moments of choice and decision are being experienced. For this reason of course Cain-Abel enlists the shadowy, the mysterious, those things that seem to represent the other, the fugitive, the vagrant, the different. These become part of that tenuous moment of suspended judgment, where crucial steps will be made, where a critical calling will be undertaken. This accounts for the quite literal momentousness of the theme. Far from being adverse to questions of community ethics, the theme addresses them in the most fundamental and serious way, and the literature that respond to the fuller dimensions of Cain-Abel engages these issues as well.

The Cain-Abel theme shows that history cannot be divided simply between ages of being and ages of becoming. There does seem to be a third
area, that always elusive *tertium quid*, where standards of evaluation, principles of validation are evoked and scrutinized as means of allowing or
disallowing change itself. Historically, we can see this in arguments of
antinomianism. As an eminent Miltonist, Barbara Lewalski, has shown,
the great English epic poet invoked principles that enabled him "in prose
tracts and poems to read the scriptures as a thoroughly radical, utopian
text. . . . Yet as his *Christian Doctrine* makes clear none of this sanctions
antinomian licentiousness, because the works of faith which flow from the
internal law of God inscribed on the heart comprise a higher moral standard: 'It is not a less perfect life that is required from Christians, but, in
fact, a more perfect life than was required from those who were under the
law.'"[6] And instantly the mind leaps to Leggatt and other Cains who hold
themselves to a stricter, even harsher sentence of the moral law.

Milton's two overarching hermeneutic principles, Lewalski argues, are
a radical concept of Christian liberty and "the primacy of the indwelling
Spirit of God." But each of these is qualified, in fact, rendered public and
open to argumentation by other broader principles of conduct and interpretation. If the final appeal of interpreting a scriptural text is the individual Christian's experience of the law in the heart, "the standard of measure
is a life that freely but yet manifestly conforms to widely recognized moral
principles." And even in regard to the "internal Prophetic spirit," Milton
"appeals constantly to reasoned argument, textual evidence and common
human experience as normative guides to interpret the Divine revelation
conveyed by scripture and the Spirit." Milton's appeal finally in matters of
hermeneutics is to evidence and reason as confirmed by the human spirit
and experience. We are returned to our own theme, with its own blend of
Hebraism and Hellenism, of conscience and consciousness, when Professor Lewalski concludes that, "from one perspective, Milton's stance toward divine revelation can be seen as a remarkable personal amalgam of
Renaissance and Reformation concepts."

The Cain-Abel theme may provide not only a program for scrutiny but
also some principles of discernment. Applied to both *The Caine Mutiny*
and *Cain's Book*, these principles reveal notable defects in each, each tending toward undifferentiation. The one, anticipating the abused attitudes
of the 1950s, seems to revoke the installation of a new regime that its own
revolutionary act and foundation sacrifice had installed, and the other, by
eschewing both the double and the foundation sacrifice, shows its own
reluctance to assume guilt and responsibility, individual conscience as well
as consciousness. While one succumbs to guilt, and the other denies it,
neither seems to promote what it means to be human. In exculpating
Queeg, Wouk seems to reinstate the monster, and Trocchi exhorts the

monstrous in that curious blend of outraged passivity and rhetorical, as well as sexual, violence. What this means is that there are modernist works that do indeed fall short of the so-called project of the Enlightenment, but there are also others that address the ethical nature of humankind and that even move beyond the Enlightenment in redefining that nature in the midst of changed historical circumstances.

．　．　．

Obviously one cannot finish a study like this. Rather, one brings it to a discreet and reasonable close. Even as I write, numerous works of fiction—novels, films, plays—have appeared, and reviewers have been alert in signaling the Cain and Abelite dimensions of such efforts. Moreover, this study has chosen to eliminate much that could have been included—for instance, the depictions of Cain and Abel in the plastic and visual arts, and their various generic presentations, such as the drama.[7] But I would be remiss were I not to return in these concluding comments to the American experience, which I have addressed periodically, either centrally or aslant, throughout this study. From *Billy Budd* to *East of Eden*, and that conglomeration of novels and films in the 1950s, America has provided a hospitable home for Cain and Abel. Its own receptivity to the ideals of fraternity ran into conflict with its rooted and homegrown individualism; its own commitment to freedom seemed strangely to succumb to the demands of a restrictive history, and its marriage to the machine from the very earliest days meant its own ideals of community were subjected to the severest tests of disruption, just as its nostalgic attachment to the homeplace endured incessant dislocation.

In some ways, America has been the testing ground, even the laboratory of Cain and Abel in the modern world. Its own preeminence as an emergent nation means that it has been brought face to face with the casualties of its own choices, the liabilities of its own history—and that is the myth of the foundation sacrifice, always present to remind us of the need for change and yet of its undeniable costs. America has seemed itself more than dedicated to doctrines of change, innovation, newness; it has come to epitomize all of their manifestations in the twentieth century, and it has responded to and benefited from all that they have brought. And this means the peoples, too, who have chosen to find in America a refuge from their former lives. Such changes—where the dispossessed can find a home, where the *mestizos* have come into their own, making America their own and, consequently, defining the essence of the new—are some of the lasting contributions of America to the modern world.

Yet American writers have also invoked Cain and Abel in order to illustrate the sad consequences of this doctrine of change, this advance toward the new. They have reflected on the expense of dislocation and the pain of division. It is no accident that *Citizen Kane*, that film of genius that was in its earlier phases called "The American," should be rooted in *The Great Gatsby*, each work depicting yet another schism in the nature of the new American citizen, a schism in the soul such as the earlier Cain of the Roman Empire was obliged to confront. But this new schism is not based upon a realistic contentment with the cracked mirror of history, as the ancient Citizen Cain may have manifested, but rather a break with the normal confines of experience in pursuit of some wild and even grandiose dream. This division does not lead to a restrained social order but rather to social disorder and, in fact, a wrenching split in the self, what Dostoevsky called *nadryv*, a tear in the muscle of being. Such dislocation motivates one to fabricate another self, to fabulate, to reinvent a past, and to behave so grotesquely as to transplant a castle from Europe to the California coast. These are modern Cains but not regenerate ones; monstrous Cains but not outcasts. Rather, they frequently come to occupy places of great power, where they fancy themselves populists but are in fact demagogues. Far from producing a citizen, it seems that the American message has bred exactly its opposite, a monster of great and voracious appetite, spawned by instability and nourished by dreams. If a major purpose of the changes of Cain in the romantic and postromantic epochs has been the exploration of means by which imbalance may finally be righted and even justified, of ways that persons who are out of step may actually be readying themselves to play the new tune, then we can say that here the theme of Cain and Abel, in its manifold capacities for alternative and antithetical adjustments, shows its ability to breed its own antimyth, one revealing no final rectification but instead only another page torn from the bright book of life.

NOTES

INTRODUCTION

1. There has been a strange lack of any comprehensive study of the Cain and Abel theme. However, valuable studies within a more limited range are those of Viktor Aptowitzer, *Kain und Abel in der Agada, den Apokryphen, der hellenistischen, cristlichen und muhammedanischen Literatur* (Vienna and Leipzig: R. Lowit Verlag, 1922); Auguste Brieger, *Kain und Abel in der deutschen Dichtung* (Berlin and Leipzig: Walter de Gruyter, 1934); Ruth Mellinkoff, *The Mark of Cain* (Berkeley and Los Angeles: University of California Press, 1981). Mellinkoff's attention to Cain and Abel in religious iconography has yielded abundant material and argument. David Williams, *Cain and Beowulf: A Study in Secular Allegory* (Toronto: University of Toronto Press, 1982) covers much material up through the time of his subject. Interesting essay-surveys include Enrique José Varona, "El personaje biblico Cain en las literaturas modernas," (1873) in *Obras*, vol. 2 *Estudias y conferencias* (Havana, 1936), pp. 13ff.; Arturo Graf, "La Poesia di Caino," a two-part essay that appeared in *Nuova Antologia* 134 (March–April 1908): 193 and 425; and Philippe Sellier, "Le mythe de Cain," *Canadian Review of Comparative Literature* 13 (1986): 17–28. On individual topics (particularly *Beowulf*, the medieval mystery plays, Byron, Unamuno, and Conrad) the secondary literature is quite ample and will be presented appropriately in the course of this study.

2. For the material that follows I am indebted to Marcel David, *Fraternité et Revolution Française* (Paris: Aubier, 1987). For the material from Chamfort, see the excellent biography, *Chamfort* by Claude Arnaud (Paris: Robert Laffont, 1988), p. 278. See also Gerald Antoine, *Liberté, Egalité, Fraternité, ou les Fluctuations d'une Devise* (UNESCO, 1981), pp. 133–79. Wyn Kelly pertinently concludes, "The Cain and Abel story thus forcefully demonstrates the close and hidden relationship between fraternity as a personal and social ideal, and fratricide as a fact of human history" ("Melville's Cain," *American Literature* 55 [1983]: 27).

3. Some of the more ironic connotations of brotherhood are captured by George Orwell in his Big Brother of *1984.*

4. For this material, see my essay, "Ulysses' Brother: The Cain and Abel Theme in Dante's *Commedia*," *Renaissance Studies in Honor of Craig Hugh Smyth* (Florence: Giunti Barbera, 1985). Auerbach's essay appeared in *Mimesis*, trans. Willard Trask (Princeton, N.J.: Princeton University Press, 1953).

5. *The Ulysses Theme*, 2d ed. (Ann Arbor, Mich.: University of Michigan Press, 1968).

6. By acknowledging a "moule généalogique" to Cain and Abel, Philippe Sellier then is able to conclude that the theme seems disposed to the epic style (p. 26). Nothing could be further from the truth. Sellier confuses the propensities of the Wandering Jew with the dualistic properties of Cain and Abel. Martin Buber better understands the true properties of the original account in Genesis and the theme's

later exfoliation when he writes that, with the story of Cain and Abel and, more particularly, God's exhortation to prevail over sin at the door, "we have arrived at the circumscribed area peculiar to man, in which only good and evil still confront each other. It is peculiar to man . . . because it can only be perceived introspectively, can only be recognised in the conduct of the soul towards itself: . . . self-perception and self-relation are the peculiarly human, the irruption of a strange element into nature, the inner lot of man" (*Good and Evil: Two Interpretations* [New York: Charles Scribner's Sons, 1953], pp. 81–89). Buber brings together genuine aspects of the theme: its inner struggle as a moral contest between good and evil, the presence of the demoniac, and the struggle of the self as a decision toward the good, which itself means a confirmation of the divine.

7. For some discussions of what may be called "thematics," see Raymond Trousson, *Un problème de littérature comparée: les études de themes* (Paris: M. J. Minard, 1965). It should also be noted that Cain-Abel even differs from those myths and legends that provide a fraternal context (later in Part One, chapters 1 and 3, I shall indicate the differences between Cain-Abel and even the overarching motif of *frères ennemis*). For instance, Cain and Abel are not Dioskouri, of which J. Rendell Harris has written in *The Cult of the Heavenly Twins* (Cambridge: Cambridge University Press, 1906), see n. 12 below.

8. Eli Weisel, "Cain and Abel: The First Genocide," in *Messengers of God: Biblical Portraits and Legends*, trans. Marion Weisel (New York: Random House, 1976), pp. 37–64.

9. Graf, "La poesia di Caino" (see n. 1 above), p. 440.

10. Brieger, *Kain und Abel in der deutschen Dichtung* (see n. 1 above), locates "two centers" to the theme—sacrifice and fratricide—and these two centers turn out to be determinants of a dualism that Brieger calls variously "das religiose Moment" and "das menschliche Moment." The religious moment, or structure, revolves around the sacrifice, and the humanistic around the fratricide. But each of these moments can have further historical spin-offs, with the humanistic, for instance, revealing a struggle between Man and God or between Man and Man that results in an "erotic" moment, which may involve incest or a brother-conflict for possession of the Mother (pp. 1–2). Brieger's discussions are quite valid, but perhaps he may go wrong in not allowing for other component parts and not seeing more of these parts as active within the various moments.

11. *Les Jumeaux, le couple et la personne*, 2 vols. (Paris: Presses Universitaires de France, 1960), chapter 8, "Les asymétries du couple," pp. 614ff. and "Dernières remarques": "La différenciation de deux partenaires par l'influence de l'un sur l'autre s'opere meme dans le cas défavorable à l'extrême où les deux partenaires sont identiques, génétiquement" ("This differentiation of two partners by the influence of one on the other is active even in the most unfavorable of cases where the two are genetically identical"; p. 707).

12. (Paris: Gallimard, 1975, pp. 514–16, and *Gemini*, trans. Anne Carter (Garden City, N.Y.: Doubleday and Company, 1981), pp. 429–30. See Part Four, chapter 12 below.

13. London: Thames and Hudson, 1983, pp. 7–40.

14. Sellier, "Le mythe de Cain," comments, "l'histoire de Cain, souvent mise en rapport avec celle de la Tour de Babel, symbolise infiniment mieux le désastre

de la transgression que ne fait l'anodin vol d'une pomme" ("The story of Cain, often related to that of the Tower of Babel, is an infinitely better symbol of the disaster of the Fall than any harmless theft of an apple"; p. 17). Martin Buber also writes, "It [Cain-Abel] and not the former [Adam and Eve] is the story of the first 'iniquity.'" *Good and Evil*, p. 81. Buber does however stress the "perspective founded on the combination of the two tales" (p. 82).

15. See Helmut Schoeck, *Envy: A Theory of Social Behavior*, trans. Michael Glenny and Betty Ross (New York: Harcourt, Brace and World, 1969), p. 4 and throughout for a comprehensive study of envy. Rather than sociological, Schoeck's volume is a work of moral philosophy with a special thesis: envy is at the basis of democratic egalitarianism and is thus either sanitized (a work may be *enviable*) or unacknowledged (he notes its absence in the language of modern social scientists and even in the works of literary critics who discuss *Billy Budd*!). From our perspective, we can note the curious bibliographical lack of Cain and Abel studies in relation to *Billy Budd* and *East of Eden*. See also Peter Walcot, *Envy and the Greeks* (Warminster: Aris and Phillips, 1978), and Leslie H. Farber, "Faces of Envy" in *The Ways of the Will: Essays toward a Psychology and Psychopathology of Will* (New York: Basic Books, 1966) and "On Jealousy," *Commentary* 56 (1973): 50–56.

16. *Envy and Gratitude and Other Works, 1946–1963* (New York: Dell Publishing Co., 1975), pp. 176–235.

17. Francis Bacon, "Of Envy," included in the *Essays* of 1625 and *Billy Budd, Sailor (An Inside Narrative)* by Herman Melville (New York: The Library of America, 1984), p. 1384. In light of future associations of Cain and monstrousness, it is revealing that Melville's address to Envy is preceded by the rhetorical question, "Is Envy then such a monster?"

18. Envy derives from the Latin *in-videre*, indicating a looking inward; it is thus a primitive emotion associated with the eyes and vision (it knows nothing of *respicere*, the looking again that results in respect, nor the *ad-mirare*, the looking up and outward that results in admiration).

19. Interestingly enough, Dante's conception of envy is more like *Schadenfreude*, that is, more of a delight in another's misfortune than fear of another's success. This might reflect the powerful direction of his own personality. If, as Schoeck argues, envy is appropriate to democratic societies, then Dante's weakness of pride is more appropriate to his own concern with *gentilezza*, or nobility. In this sense, Dante's society, like Shakespeare's, is not threatened by a leveling resentment but rather by emulation, the energetic activity that aspires to be like the great. It is "ascencionist."

20. For discussions of envy and jealousy, see Schoeck, pp. 95–97. Such distinctions are of course sliding and slippery. We might try another tack: if envy is the corelational opposite of admiration ("admiration is happy self-abandon, envy, unhappy self-assertion" Kierkegaard, as quoted by Schoeck, p. 172), then envy might be dissolved by admiration, but the problems of jealousy would not be solved by admiration. Othello's problems would not be less severe if he admired Cassio—as in weakened moments he is brought to do. Iago's envy would be resolved if he brought himself frankly to admire Othello.

21. This quarrel with God the Father explains the later role of Cain as revolu-

tionary figure. The easy transformation is understood by Albert Camus, in his *L'Homme révolté*, when he writes, "The history of rebellion, as we are experiencing it today, has far more to do with the children of Cain than with the disciples of Prometheus. In this sense it is the God of the Old Testament who is primarily responsible for mobilizing the force of rebellion." *The Rebel*, trans. Anthony Bower (New York: Vintage Books, 1956), p. 32.

22. This passage occurs in the *Works and Days* immediately after Hesiod distinguishes between two kinds of strife (Eris)—the bad Eris that leads to destruction and the good Eris that leads to competition and improvement.

> This strife is good for mortals.
> Then potters eye one another's success and craftsmen, too;
> The beggar's envy is a beggar, the singer's a singer.

From *Hesiod*, trans. Apostolos N. Athanassakis (Baltimore and London: Johns Hopkins University Press, 1983), p. 67. This incentive to work should not surprise us, given the title, as well as the fact that the exhortation is addressed to his brother!

CHAPTER ONE
CITIZEN CAIN

1. This, as well as subsequent quotations from the four commentaries, comes from *Philo*, trans. F. H. Colson and G. H. Whitaker, The Loeb Classical Library (Cambridge, Mass.: Harvard University Press, 1929), 2:95–97.

2. As Neil Forsyth has recently shown in *The Old Enemy: Satan and the Combat Myth* (Princeton, N.J.: Princeton University Press, 1987), the encounter with what would become Satan was itself molded out of the combat myth, the forces of light versus the forces of darkness. A valuable essay by Michael Lieb, "'Hate in Heav'n': Milton and the *Odium Dei*," *ELH* 53 (1986): 519ff. traces the idea of a God capable of wrath and hatred back to the passage where Esau and Jacob are characterized as being of two nations. For the early continuation of the battle motif among the apostolic fathers see Jeffrey Burton Russell, *Satan: The Early Christian Tradition* (Ithaca, N.Y.: Cornell University Press, 1981), pp. 35–47.

3. *Philo*, The Loeb Classical Library, trans. Ralph Marcus, supp. 1, p. 441.

4. For the presence of a division between the brothers based upon principle prior to Philo, see John Bowker, *The Targums and Rabbinic Literature: An Introduction to Jewish Interpretations of Scripture* (Cambridge: Cambridge University Press, 1969), pp. 14–15, 19, 25, 26, 57, 59. Although denying that a *direct* (his emphasis) connection can be established between "the written Targums and the targum as it might have been rendered in the synagogues in the earliest days," Bowker does allow that "the written Targums contain interpretative material which is known from other sources to go back to an early date . . ." (p. 14). In the Pseudo-Jonathon, the brothers quarrel over a theological point: if, in fact, justice rules the world. Cain, hurt by the rejection of his offering, bitterly denounces the injustice of God's judgment. In heated response to Abel's defense of God's impartiality, Cain goes even further: "There is no judgment and no judge and no world

hereafter; there is no good reward to be given to the righteous, nor any account to be taken of the wicked." In this Targum, there is clear presentation of the kind of principled division between the brothers, representing different worldviews, similar to that we find in Philo. In the Great Midrashic commentary on Genesis, the brothers are more like *frères ennemis*: their quarrels originate in the physical differences that exist between one brother, whose goods are movable (the shepherd), and the other, whose goods are of the earth. According to another rabbi, the brothers quarreled over location of the temple, each wanting it in his district. In interpreting the actual killing, the Midrash shows one brother to be virtuous. That Cain "rose up" means that Abel had had at first the upper hand in the struggle but then relented out of pity, only to have Cain turn around and kill him. From this, the commentator draws the chilling conclusion, "Do not do good to an evil man, then evil will not befall you." But these are divisions of character, not those of rival principle such that we find in Philo or in the Targum of Pseudo-Jonathon. See *Midrash Rabbah*, ed. and trans. Rabbi H. Freedman and Maurice Simon, 10 vols. (London: Soncino Press, 1939), *Genesis*, ed. Freedman, 1 and 2:187. For other causes of the brothers' quarrel, see Bowker, pp. 136–41, and Aptowitzer, *Kain und Abel in der Agada*, pp. 11–23. In the Genesis Rabbah, the commentator employs Cain and Abel to explicate Psalm 37.14. "The wicked have drawn out their sword"—this refers to Cain; "To cut down the poor and needy"—this refers to Abel. But "This sword shall enter into their own heart" (p. 188 and see also p. 193). For valuable summaries, see Louis Ginzberg, *The Legends of the Jews* (Philadelphia: The Jewish Publication Society of America, 1925), 5:133–48 and Index, vol. 8.

5. *Philo*, Colson and Whitaker (1932), 4:77–79.

6. See Helmut Koester, *Introduction to the New Testament, History and Literature of Early Christianity* (Philadelphia: Fortress Press, 1982), 2:193–95, 246–48, and 272–76 for the fuller discussion of the anti-Gnosticism of these texts.

7. See Hans Jonas, *The Gnostic Religion: The Message of the Alien God*, 2d ed. (Boston: Beacon Press, enlarged, 1963). See the excellent Introduction, pp. 3–27. With some good reason, Gnosticism has enchanted the contemporary imagination. See Elaine Pagels, *The Gnostic Gospels* (New York: Random House, 1979). The involvements of Gnosticism and Cain will engage the arguments of this study from beginning to end, particularly when it emerges in the postromantic consciousness. In the midst of the enchantment, Arthur D. Nock's commonsensical words are refreshing: "Gnosticism was to have a long history, and for centuries it appealed to a great many individuals and produced a luxuriant abundance of likenesses that I find incomprehensible in detail. Early Valentinianism has its complexities, but has also a certain charm and freshness. Some of the late developments convey a certain impression of auto-intoxication." *Essays on Religion and the Ancient World*, ed. Zeph Stewart (Cambridge, Mass.: Harvard University Press, 1972), p. 958.

8. See Jonas, pp. 23–25.

9. See Introduction, Werner Foerster, *Gnosis: A Selection of Gnostic Texts*, ed. and trans. R. McLachlan Wilson et al., *The Patristic Evidence* (Oxford: Clarendon Press, 1972), 1:1–23.

10. In *On the Origin of the World*, the linkage is succinct and systematic:

> The man followed the earth
> The woman followed the man,
> And marriage followed the woman,
> And reproduction followed marriage,
> And death followed reproduction.

See *The Nag Hammadi Library in English*, ed. James T. Robinson (Leiden: J. Brill, 1977), p. 168. This presentation of the "authorities of matter" does seem to bear a resemblance to the systematic world of religion and reproduction that young Stephen Dedalus is trying to elude in *A Portrait of the Artist as a Young Man*.

11. See *Kain und Abel in der Agada*, p. 24.

12. See Carl Siegfried, *Philo von Alexandria als Ausleger des Alten Testament* (Jena: Dufft, 1875), pp. 371–91.

13. All quotations from *Saint Ambrose: Hexameron, Paradise, and Cain and Abel*, trans. John J. Savage (New York: Fathers of the Church, Inc., 1961), p. 360.

14. See Ruth Mellinkoff, *The Mark of Cain*, pp. 16–17, for differences of opinion relating to the mark's purpose. This opinion is not as grotesque as it appears, and is part of the presentation of Cain in Dante, Agrippa d'Aubigné and Victor Hugo. Substantiating this affiliation is A. Mehat, "Sur le châtiment de Cain, de Philon d'Alexandre aux *Tragiques* d'Agrippa d'Aubigné," *Bibliothèque d'Humanisme et Renaissance* (1970), 32:119ff. This belief that extended age means added punishment is part of common lore. According to a recent newspaper account (1989), a woman who died at the age of 114 in Philadelphia, when asked to what she attributed her longevity, responded that she must have been bad and this was God's way of punishing her.

15. *"Paradise Lost" and the Genesis Tradition* (Oxford: Clarendon, 1968), p. 93.

16. See the "Reply to Faustus the Manichean," *Writings in Connection with the Manichean Heresy*, trans. Richard Stothert (Edinburgh: T. and T. Clark, 1872), pp. 209–14.

17. *De Civitate Dei, Corpus Scriptorum Ecclesiasticorum Latinorum* (*CSEL*) 40:2 Sancti Aurelii Augustini, ed. Emanuel Hoffmann (1900; reprint, 1962), and *The City of God*, trans. Marcus Dods (New York: The Modern Library, 1950), to which all textual citations refer.

18. *Augustine of Hippo* (Berkeley and Los Angeles: University of California Press, 1967), p. 321.

19. François Lenormant's "The First Murder and the Founding of the First City," *The Contemporary Review* 37 (1880): 263–74 is an imaginative essay that makes valuable contributions. He understands the larger issues contained in the commingling of the brothers and foundation sacrifice. The third month (Sivan in the Chaldean and Babylonian Calender) is the month when bricks are made from the receding rivers, and its sign is the twins (Gemini). "How can these facts fail to remind us of the Bible narrative, which connects the building of the first city with the first murder, committed by a brother upon his brother?" (p. 264). Moreover, some interesting extrapolations may be gained when he observes that the founda-

tion of the city requires the sprinkling of "pure blood," and that Remus (originally named Romus) "surpasses his brother who murdered him." This is clearly the case with Christian Abel, and even in later thought, when the double is sacrificed, we see that this "twin" has a tutelary nature. Lenormant argues a "continuous parallelism"—"one might even almost say the identity"—of the Biblical and the Chaldean, that is, of the religious and the pagan (p. 272). He also notes the differences, "There are certain reasons for suspecting that the Chaldeans took the part of the murderer, of Cain against Abel, as the Romans did that of Romulus against Remus" (p. 273). See also Armin Ehrenzweig, "Kain und Lamech," *Zeitschrift für die alttestamentliche Wissenschaft* 35 (1915): 1ff. "Biblische und Klassische Urgeschicte," idem, 38 (1919–1920): 65ff.; his response in idem, 39 (1921): 82–83.

20. Harry Levin has made this important distinction in "Thematics and Criticism," reprinted in *The Disciplines of Criticism: Essays in Literary Theory, Interpretation and History Honoring René Wellek on the Occasion of his Sixty-fifth Birthday,* ed. Peter Demetz, Thomas Greene, and Lowry Nelson, Jr. (New Haven and London: Yale University Press, 1968).

21. On this important distinction—actually it is tripartite—see Hans Leisegang, "Der Ursprung der Lehre Augustins von der *Civitas Dei,*" *Archiv für Kulturgeschichte* 16 (1926): 127–58. Leisegang makes Ambrose the mediator between these distinctions and their source in Philo, whom Augustine had not read (pp. 152, 156). Following Leisegang, see also R. H. Barrow, *Introduction to St. Augustine, "The City of God"* (London: Faber and Faber, 1950), pp. 136, 140–44 and Appendix 1, pp. 267–73. Barrow nicely points out that "in the passages in the Epistles which use the idea of 'sojourning,' the Greek word frequently used is the word denoting the status of 'resident aliens' (*paroikoi*) officially recognized in the Greek city state; it is also combined with 'strangers' (*xenoi*) that is, utter 'foreigners.' Yet another word 'pilgrim' (*parepedimos*) is combined with 'foreigner,' or with 'sojourner'; it simply denoted a foreigner residing in a place but possessing no rights at all. The Vulgate translation (*peregrini, peregrinor*) maintains the technical idea of foreigner, for the *peregrini* were aliens resident in Rome but not possessing civic rights" (p. 141).

Chapter Two
Monstrous Cain

1. See *The Works of Flavius Josephus,* trans. William Whiston, 4 vols. (London, 1822), 1:11–14.

2. Cain and the city is one of the longer-lasting and sturdier associations of the theme. It is almost superfluous to litanize the great names that have elaborated the implications of this conjunction. Beyond Philo, Josephus, and Augustine, the association persists, perhaps summarized by Abraham Cowley in his "The Garden": "God the first Garden made, and / The first city Cain." This contrast persists in Melville's *Billy Budd,* where Billy represents the garden innocence, "a sort of upright barbarian, just such perhaps as Adam presumably might have been ere the *urbane* (my emphasis) Serpent wriggled himself into his company." Then Melville adds that should any "pristine and unadulterate" virtues appear in a person they should not be considered as a product of civilization, "but rather to be out of

keeping with these, as if exceptionally transmitted from a period prior to Cain's city and citified man." (See below, Part 3, chapter 8 and Wyn Kelly, "Melville's Cain" *American Literature* 55 (1983): 26–27. So familiar had this association become that Charles Dickens, quite willing to accept the presence of Cain amid the squalors of industrialized city life, is shocked to report, in a journalistic piece, "Cain Among the Fields" (*Uncollected Writings from "Household Words,"* 1850– 1859, ed. Harry Stone (Bloomington: University of Indiana Press, 1977), 1:275ff. See Alexander Welsh, *The City of Dickens* for other manifold examples. In fact, the association is too abundant even to summarize here, and requires the entire length of this book to explore its full growth and ramifications. In a counterexample from the nineteenth century, one more in tune with the dynamics of rebellion and regeneration, a descendant of the Titans, and cohort of Cain (whose implacable fury he shares) while damned, is busy resowing the seeds of Cadmus ("Je ressème à ses pieds les dents du vieux dragon"), from which will spring the revived city of Thebes, a kind of reconciliation born out of discord. See "Anteros" in *Oeuvres de Gerard de Nerval*, ed. Albert Beguin and Jean Richer (Paris: Pléiade, 1960), 1:4– 5. For the complex symbolism and mythographic content of Nerval's poem, see Jean Richer, *Nerval: Expérience et Création* (Paris: Hachette, 1963), pp. 150–67. See also John W. Kneller, "Anteros, Son of Cain," *Writing in a Modern Temper: Essays on French Literature and Thought in Memos of Henri Peyre*, ed. Mary Ann Caws, Stanford French and Italian Studies, 33 (Saratoga, Calif.: Anima Libri, 1984), pp. 91ff. For an interesting discussion of the city as derived from Genesis, see Jacques Ellul, *Sans feu ni lieu: Signification biblique de la Grande Ville* (Paris: Gallimard, 1975). In comments most pertinent for Tournier, Ellul describes Cain as a sedentary who builds his city in defiance of God: "La ville est la consequence directe du meurtre de Cain et du refus par Cain de recevoir sa protection de Dieu" ("The city is the direct consequence of the murder by Cain and of his refusal to accept God's protection"), p. 29.

3. For a full discussion of the theme's spread to the North, see Robert E. Kaske, "*Beowulf* and the Book of Enoch," *Speculum* 46 (1971): 421–31 and Ruth Mellinkoff, "Cain's Monstrous Progeny in *Beowulf*," *Anglo-Saxon England*, 8 (1979): 143–62; and 9 (1981): 183–97. Mellinkoff writes, ". . . there is nothing inherently unlikely in the general supposition that Jewish lore, both the ancient pre-rabbinic kind contained in the pseudepigrapha such as the Noah story, and the later classical ideas in Talmud and Midrash . . . was known in Anglo-Saxon England at the time of the composition of *Beowulf*. The possibility of the transmission of a large repertoire of ideas, stories and themes that have previously seemed too exotic, too oriental, too proscribed by official church lists to have survived the journey, has recently come more and more to be regarded as credible" (p. 157). For a recent, very full, and intricate discussion of the convergence of the Watcher Angels with Satan, and the eventual replacement as the cause of the first fall of the Watcher Angels by the rebellious angels see Neil Forsyth, *The Old Enemy: Satan and the Combat Myth*. The Watcher Angels were not totally replaced, but were relegated to responsibility for the earthly demons—the giant offspring (p. 385). David Williams in his *Cain and "Beowulf"* discusses the "Cain Tradition", pp. 19–39.

4. *PMLA* 21 (1906): 831–929.

5. For discussions of the actual weapon of death see Meyer Schapiro, "Cain's Jaw-bone that Did the First Murder," *Art Bulletin* 24 (1942): 205ff.; George Henderson, "Cain's Jaw Bone," *Journal of Warburg and Courtauld Institutes* 24 (1961): 108–14; A. A. Barb, "Cain's Murder Weapon and Samson's Jawbone of an Ass," *Journal of Warburg and Courtauld Institutes* 35 (1972): 386ff.

6. See lines 1261–65 for these phrases. I have used *Beowulf, with the Finnesburg Fragment*, 3d ed., ed. C. L. Wrenn, revised by W. F. Bolton (New York: St. Martin's Press, 1973). For translations, see that of E. Talbot Donaldson in *Beowulf*, ed. Joseph F. Tuso (New York: W. W. Norton, 1975) and especially that of William Alfred in *Medieval Epics* (New York: The Modern Library, 1963). For a recent scholarly study with many valuable things to say, see John D. Niles, *Beowulf: The Poem and Its Tradition* (Cambridge, Mass.: Harvard University Press, 1983). For an indication of the significance of such exile referred to in the text see Bennett A. Brockman, "'Heroic' and 'Christian' in *Genesis A:* The Evidence of the Cain and Abel Episode" *Modern Language Quarterly* 35 (1974): 122–23, and n. 18.

7. In *"To Double Business Bound": Essays in Literature, Mimesis and Anthropology* (Baltimore: Johns Hopkins University Press, 1978), pp. 163–65.

8. In the development of Christian apologetics, and in response to the Gnostic and other heretical preachments of a cosmic dualism, Christianity had recourse to a Fall incited by the rebellious and envious Satan. With the development of the larger program of salvation history, and its own system of correspondences, Adam and Eve are aligned with Christ and Mary. This leaves Cain alone, as the true progenitor of recurrent evil, as sire of the "damaging remnant." As a product (according to some sources) of the coupling of one of the demonic Watcher Angels and Eve, he is naturally placed to sire breeds of giants and monsters. See Forsyth, p. 312.

9. For a representation of this thought see Hayden White, "The Forms of Wildness: Archeology of an Idea," in *The Wild Man Within*, ed. Edward Dudley and Maximillian E. Novak (Pittsburgh, Pa.: University of Pittsburgh Press, 1972), pp. 6–7.

10. For a summary of the arguments see Nye, pp. 235–47 and for the more positive values of the poem, see chapters "Reciprocity" and "The Controlling Theme" pp. 213ff. and 224ff.

11. On the history of the Church and the Jews (with documents), see Solomon Grayzel, *The Church and the Jews in the XIIIth Century* (New York: Hermon Press, 1966); Guido Kisch, "The Yellow Badge in History," *Historia Judaica* 4 (1941): 81–144; Ruth Mellinkoff (1), "Cain and the Jews," *Journal of Jewish Art* 6 (1979): 16–38; *ibid., The Mark of Cain* (Berkeley and Los Angeles: University of California Press, 1981); for some iconographic manifestation of anti-Semitism in superior art, see *ibid., The Devil at Isenheim: Reflections of Popular Belief in Grunewald's Altarpiece*, California studies in the History of Art, Discovery Series 1 (Berkeley and Los Angeles: University of California Press, 1988), pp. 60–67; Wolfgang S. Seiferth, *Synagogue and Church in the Middle Ages, Two Symbols in Art and Literature* (New York: Ungar, 1970); Rosemary Radford Ruether, *Faith and Fratricide: The Theological Roots of Anti-Semitism* (New York: The Seabury Press, 1974); Yosef Hayim Yerushalmi, "Medieval Jewry: From Within and From

Without," in *Aspects of Jewish Culture in the Middle Ages*, ed. Paul E. Szarmarch (Albany: State University of New York Press, 1979), pp. 1–26; Jeremy Cohen, *The Friars and the Jews: The Evolution of Medieval Anti-Judaism* (Ithaca, N.Y.: Cornell University Press, 1982). On the relationship of the Western Church to blacks, see the monumental study, *The Image of the Black in Western Art*, ed. Ladislas Bugner, vol. 2, part 1, Jean Devisse, *From the Demonic Threat to the Incarnation of Sainthood* (New York: William Morrow, 1979); part 2, *Africans in the Christian Ordinance of the World (Fourteenth to the Sixteenth Century)*, by Jean Devisse and Michel Mollat (1979); for Cain and Ham, John Block Friedman, *The Monstrous Races in Medieval Thought and Art* (Cambridge, Mass.: Harvard University Press, 1981). Brilliant essays by Leslie Fiedler, 2 vols. (New York: Stein and Day, 1971), 1:451–70, 2:164–74.

12. The connection between Cain and the Jews does not stop here but does in fact know a somewhat happier association in the time of romanticism. Both in origins and afterlife Cain and the Wandering Jew may be joined. As George K. Anderson has suggested in his definitive study, *The Legend of the Wandering Jew* (Providence, R.I.: Brown University Press, 1965), "the example of Cain in the Scriptures may have suggested the creation of Ahasuerus outside the scriptures" (p. 182). Each has committed some offense to religious principle (Ahasuerus through his denial of rest to Christ, Cain through the murder of Abel—the prefigurement of Christ); each is marked with a curse and sentenced to eternal wandering; each is touched by the sacred, and hence has something literally awful and amazing in demeanor. Although the Wandering Jew is more a character of legend and folklore, very early Cain received formidable intellectual definition. Where Cain was always involved with issues, the tendency was for the Wandering Jew to be merely a device, in some cases, an instrument for the travelogue (See Anderson, pp. 171ff., where he accurately describes the incapacity of the theme of the Wandering Jew to sustain a long dramatic narrative). Despite these inherent differences, the two themes were intertwined particularly after Byron's masterpiece in postromantic literature: ". . . the long line of German writers in the nineteenth century who felt compelled to write about Ahasuerus and to make him symbolic of the trials and sorrows of mankind, of the resolution to defy the universe, of the sinister and the sinful, of the arrogant world-shaker and blasphemous striker against God—all wrote as they did largely because Byron had created his Cain, his Child Harold, and his Manfred" (p. 183). As a description of Byron's Cain, this is more legendary than real.

13. See Jean Marie Courtes, "The Theme of 'Ethiopia' and 'Ethiopians' in Patristic Literature," Devisse, p. 9, for blackness as just a darker shade of skin, and Jeffrey Burton Russell, *Satan: The Early Christian Tradition*, p. 40 for counterexamples.

14. We must not forget the black Saint Maurice (Devisse, pp. 149ff.), nor that at times white and black were equally enslaved—to sin—and in need of liberation (Devisse, p. 113).

15. Major book-length studies of the medieval English mystery cycles are Eleanor Prosser, *Drama and Religion in the English Mystery Plays* (Stanford, Calif.: Stanford University Press, 1961); V. A. Kolve, *The Play Called Corpus*

Christi (Stanford, Calif.: Stanford University Press, 1966); Rosemary Woolf, *The English Mystery Plays* (London: Routledge and Kegan Paul, 1972) and Martin Stevens, *Four Medieval English Mystery Cycles* (Princeton, N. J.: Princeton University Press, 1987). Of specific relevancy for the Cain-Abel theme see John E. Bernbrock, "Notes on the Townley Cycle slaying of Abel," *Journal of English and Germanic Philology* 62 (1963): 317ff.; Blair W. Boone, "The Skill of Cain in the English Mystery Cycles," *Comparative Drama* 16 (1982): 112–29; Bennett A. Brockman, "Comic and Tragic Counterpoint in the Medieval Drama; The Wakefield *Mactatio Abel*," *Medieval Studies* 39 (1977): 331–40; "Cain and Abel in the Chester *Creation*: Narrative Tradition and Dramatic Potential," *Medievalia et Humanistica* n.s. 5 (1974): 169–82; "The Law of Man and the Peace of God: Judicial Process as Satiric Theme in the Wakefield *Mactatio Abel*," *Speculum* 49 (1974): 19–24: David L. Jeffrey, "Stewardship in the Wakefield *Mactatio Abel* and Noe Plays," *American Benedictine Review* 22 (1971): 64–76; Clifford Davidson, *From Creation to Doom: The York Cycle of Mystery Plays* (New York: AMS Press, 1984), pp. 43–48.

16. Under the demonic Watcher angel theme, Cain enlists a large coterie of rejects and malefactors, including Jews (Forsyth, pp. 236, 328–29), giants and monsters, Gnostics and other heretics. This demonic provenance accounts for the monstrous progeny of Cain.

17. "'Cokkel in our Clene Corne': Some Implications of Cain's Sacrifice," *Gesta* 7 (1968): 15–28.

18. See *The Construction of the Wakefield Cycle* (Carbondale and Edwardsville, Ill.: Southern Illinois University Press, 1974), p. 25.

19. *The Chester Plays*, ed. Hermann Deimling (1892; reprint, London: Early English Text Society, 1926), pp. 37–47. The crucial arguments of Cain are in lines 529–52.

20. *The York Cycle of Mystery Plays*, ed. J. S. Purvis (London: The Society for Promoting Christian Knowledge, 1957), pp. 41–44.

21. *The Wakefield Pageants*, ed. A. C. Cawley (Manchester: Manchester University Press, 1958). I have benefited from seeing *The Plaie Called Corpus Christi*, staged by the Focused Research Program in Medieval Theater Studies, University of California at Irvine, September, 1985.

22. "The Symbolic Significance of *Figurae Scatologicae* in Gothic Manuscripts," in *Word, Picture, and Spectacle*, ed. Clifford Davidson (Kalamazoo, Mich.: Medieval Institute Publications, 1984), p. 12.

23. This view is specifically contested by T. W. Craik, "Violence in the English Mystery Play," *Medieval Drama Stratford-upon-Avon Studies*, 16, ed. Neville Denny (London: Edward Arnold, 1973) 16:12. ". . . it can hardly be doubted that the playwright wanted to amuse the spectators, not to edify them."

24. "On the Essence of Laughter," trans. Jonathon Mayne, reprinted in *Comedy: Meaning and Form*, ed. Robert W. Corrigan (San Francisco: Chandler Publishing Co., 1965), pp. 451, 453.

25. *The Byronic Hero: Types and Prototypes* (Minneapolis: University of Minnesota Press, 1962), p. 107.

26. "Funeral Customs," *Generally Speaking* (New York: Dodd and Mead,

1949), p. 120. To be sure, Chesterton's intention is not to demote brotherhood, but instead to make it more inclusive.

27. All quotations from *The Riverside Shakespeare*, ed. G. Blakemore Evans et al. (Boston: Houghton Mifflin, 1974).

CHAPTER THREE
CAIN AS SACRED EXECUTIONER

1. In August, 1985, Professor Harold Fisch, himself profiting from Maccoby's suggestive arguments, delivered a paper, "Cain as Sacred Executioner," to be reprinted in *Byron, the Bible, and Religion: Essays from 12th International Byron Seminar* (Newark: University of Delaware Press, 1990). Judging from his *précis*, wherein Byron's Cain is described as a rebel, and a Promethean seeker after knowledge, and Cain's crime, like Adam's, as "an event in salvation history, a kind of *felix culpa*," there might be some divergences in our uses of the phrase, "sacred executioner."

Sections from the material on Dante below (but also including other aspects of Cain) have already appeared in "Ulysses' Brother: The Cain and Abel Theme in Dante's *Commedia*," in *Renaissance Studies in Honour of Craig Hugh Smyth* and in a related piece, "Foundation Sacrifice and Florentine History in Dante's *Commedia*," *Lectura Dantis* 4 (1989): 10ff.

2. Nathan Rosenberg and L. E. Birdzell, Jr., *How the West Grew Rich: The Economic Transformation of the Industrial World* (New York: Basic Books, 1986), pp. 20–34. See also my *Renaissance Discovery of Time* (Cambridge, Mass.: Harvard University Press, 1972), and for a general summary of the main lines of that book, "The New Dynamic of Time in Renaissance Literature and Society," in *Time: The Greatest Innovator*, ed. Rachel Doggett (Washington, D.C.: The Folger Shakespeare Library, 1987), pp. 25–37. Although in such a work as this—one that seeks to show significant changes—it is proper to emphasize the innovative elements that will in time become dominant, it should be remarked that in large part Renaissance treatments of Cain and Abel were traditional. Francis Bacon allied Abel as shepherd with the contemplative life and Cain as tiller of the soil with the active life. Judy Z. Kronenfeld, in a paper delivered at an MLA session in 1977, "Abel, the Contemplative Shepherd, and Renaissance Pastoral," described the ways by which the traditional association of Abel with religious trust and contentment entered into the presentations of the life of the shepherd. In the July eclogue of *The Shepheardes Calender*, Edmund Spenser likens the ideal shepherd to Abel. John Donne, in "The Progresse of the Soule," describes Abel "as white, and milde as his sheepe were, / (Who, in that trade, of Church, and kingdomes, there / Was the first type) . . ." (stanza 41). It is surprising that in Chaucer's work there is only one reference, none in Philip Sidney, and none in Ben Jonson. In the same epoch, special attention should be directed to Agrippa d'Aubigné's *Les Tragiques*, the long Protestant epic poem anticipatory of *Paradise Lost*, but without Milton's classical conceptual power, where Cain is the haunted malefactor unable to find any rest and thus punished by a fate worse than death. See Part One, Chapter 1, n. 14. Apparently in the same epoch of religious wars, Thomas Lecoq wrote his "Tragédie representant l'odieus et sanglant meurtre commis par le maudit Cain a

l'encontre de son frère Abel." See the highly intelligent defense of this play by Enea Balmas, "*La Tragédie de Cain* de Thomas Lecoq," in *Mélanges à la memoire de V. L. Saulnier* (Geneva: Droz, 1984), pp. 651ff. In an admittedly waggish mood—as designated poet he felt obliged to introduce a merrier note to a solemn theological discussion—Erasmus concocted another fable, one whereby Cain, ever the con man, managed to persuade an angel guarding the gates of the earthly Paradise to allow him to pilfer a few seeds. This "Promethean" Cain was thus punished even more terribly and the gullible angel was sacked. See *Opus Epistolarum Desiderii Erasmi Rotterdami*, ed. P. S. Allen (Oxford: Clarendon Press, 1906), 1:268–71.

3. I am thinking particularly of *Richard II* and *Hamlet* where two significant references in each call to mind the issues of Cain and Abel. *Richard II*, 1.1.104 and 5.1.43; *Hamlet*, 3.3.37 and 5.1.85.

4. See *The Myth of the State* (New Haven, Conn.: Yale University Press, 1946), pp. 156–62.

5. The Italian text from *La Divina Commedia*, 2d ed. rev. ed. Natalino Sapegno, 3 vols., (Florence: La Nuova Italia, 1968), and the English from *The Divine Comedy of Dante Alighieri*, rev. ed. trans. John D. Sinclair, (New York: Oxford University Press, 1958).

6. *Homo Necans*, 1972, trans. Peter Bing (Berkeley and Los Angeles: University of California Press, 1983); Burkert's contributions to *Violent Origins*, below, are also invaluable.

7. Helpful discussions of the "dark event," as well as a general summary of Girard's arguments and those of Burkert, occur in the volume, *Violent Origins*, ed. Robert G. Hammerton-Kelly (Stanford, Calif.: Stanford University Press, 1987), esp. pp. 118–29.

8. See also Girard, *Des Choses cachées depuis la fondation du monde*, with J. Oughourlian and G. Lefort (Paris: Grasset, 1978), where the specific notion of the antimyth is developed with the purpose of countering the foundation sacrifice, and *Le Bouc émissaire* (Paris: Grasset, 1982), *The Scapegoat*, trans. Yvonne Freccero (Baltimore, Md.: Johns Hopkins University Press, 1986) esp. pp. 89–94.

9. See his essential commentary *The Divine Comedy*, Bollingen Series 80, 3 vols. trans. Charles S. Singleton (Princeton, N.J.: Princeton University Press, 1970). In addition to the larger logic, numerous anthropophagal references support the argument of cannibalism.

10. *The City of God*, trans. Marcus Dods, p. 482.

11. *The Interpersonal Theory of Psychology* (New York: Norton, 1953), p. 347.

12. See the *Enciclopedia Dantesca* (Rome: Istituto dell' Enciclopedia Italiana, 1970). The word *frate*, a term of address indicating a spiritual brotherhood and fraternal equality in the ways of pilgrimage, is employed thirteen times in the *Purgatorio*. Ulysses calls his comrades "O frati," but this is an appeal to the brotherhood of warfaring and adventure. It should be obvious that although brotherhood calls forth issues of fatherhood, this in no way is intended to slight the roles of Beatrice, or Mary, or the feminine principle itself.

13. See Livy, *The History of Rome*, Loeb Classical Library (Cambridge, Mass.: Harvard University Press, 1935), 1:16, as well as Horace's regret that this founda-

tion myth constitutes something of a curse, which itself leads to civil war. *Epode VII*:

> Sic est: acerba fata Romanos agunt
> scelusque fraternae necis,
> ut immerentis fluxit interram Remi
> Sacer nepotibus cruor.

(So this is how it is: harsh Fate drives Romans on To kill their brothers,— and so has It always done since sinless Remus' blood became A curse on all his lineage.)

The Complete Works of Horace, trans. Charles E. Passage (New York: Frederick Ungar, 1983), pp. 107–8.

14. "Dell'ambizione," *Tutte le opere*, 2:714 (see n. 15 below). See Sebastian de Grazia, *Machiavelli in Hell* (Princeton, N.J.: Princeton University Press, 1989), pp. 67, 74, 77, 80.

15. See the fundamental Book One, chapter 9 in *Discorsi sopra la Prima Deca di Titi Livi* in *Tutte le Opere di Niccolo Machiavelli*, 2d ed., ed. Francesco Flora and Carlo Cordie (Florence: Mondadori, 1968), 1:119–21; *The Discourses* in *The Portable Machiavelli*, ed. and trans. Peter Bondanella and Mark Musa (New York: Penguin Books, 1979), pp. 200–203. In the same edition, the editors remind us that the crucial phrase from *The Prince*, "si guarda al fine" ("one must consider the final result")—preeminently sound advice—should not be translated into the phrase, "the end justifies the means," which, they add, is "something Machiavelli never wrote" (p. 135).

16. All quotations conform to *The Riverside Shakespeare*, ed. G. Blakemore Evans et al. (Boston: Houghton Mifflin, 1974).

17. See my *The Renaissance Discovery of Time*, p. 334.

18. *La Crainte et l'angoisse dans le théâtre d'Eschyle* (Paris: Les belles Lettres, 1958).

CHAPTER FOUR
BYRON'S *CAIN* AND ITS ANTECEDENTS

1. I borrow the term "metaphysical rebel" from Camus' *The Rebel*. Encompassing more than Byron's character, Camus is correct when he declares that "the rebel defies more than he denies. Originally, at least, he does not suppress God; he merely talks to him as an equal." But for Camus, the rebel soon becomes totalitarian. This dialogue is not polite. "It is a polemic animated by the desire to conquer. The slave begins by demanding justice and ends by wanting to wear a crown" (p. 25). This later twist is not one to which regenerate Cain consents.

2. This phrase is derived from the now-classical essay of the late Helen Gardner, "Milton's Satan and the Theme of Damnation in Elizabethan Tragedy," *English Studies* n.s. 1 (1948): 46–66.

3. For an excellent discussion of Gessner, as well as of some of his predecessors and contemporaries who also treated the Cain-Abel theme, see Brieger, *Kain und*

Abel in der deutschen Dichtung, pp. 46–64. Of worthy interest are Christian Weise's *Kain und Abel*, Meta Klopstock's *Der Tod Abels*, and Friedrich Gottlieb Klopstock's *Der Tod Adams*. For a full study of Gessner, see John Hibberd, *Salomon Gessner: His Creative Achievement and Influence* (Cambridge: Cambridge University Press, 1976). References are to *Der Tod Abels* in *Gessners Werke*, selected by A. Frey (Berlin and Stuttgart: W. Spemann, n.d.).

4. Meta Klopstock also introduces a sister, beloved of Abel, but only one, while Gessner squares the triangle and thus increases the possibility of more fortunate resolutions. The Targum literature raises the possibilities of sisters, even twin sisters. See Bowker, p. 137. In the *Book of Jubilee*, Cain takes Aqan to be his wife *after* the death of Abel. The medieval *Le Mystère du Vieil Testament* provides sister-wives for Abel and Cain in Delbora and Calmana, respectively. These are the same pairs that Thomas Lecoq employs in his *Tragédie de Cain*. John Donne, in "The Progresse of the Soule," has Themesh as sister and wife (ll. 510–11). The point about Gessner (and to a lesser extent Klopstock) is that the domestication he presents is crucial to the sensibility of the work.

5. See Daniel Pickering Taylor, *The Decline of Hell: Seventeenth-Century Discussions of Eternal Torment* (Chicago: University of Chicago Press, 1964). In *The Prince of Darkness*, Jeffrey Russell discusses the "disintegration of Hell," pp. 206–20. Of course Hell, like the Devil, existed within a system of relations. "No Devil, no God," was Wesley's comment (see Forsyth, pp. 7–8). But the idea of Heaven, for instance, did not disappear or disintegrate. Rather it underwent a startling transformation complicit with romantic love and nineteenth-century domestication. See Colleen MacDannell and Benhard Lang, *Heaven: A History* (New Haven, Conn.: Yale University Press, 1988), chapters 7 and 8.

6. Weber's own "ethic of responsibility" as a principle of legitimation in the calling of the political leader is pertinent here, particularly since it returns us to Machiavelli and the Renaissance and, for instance, Bolingbroke-Henry IV's overburdened sense of responsibility.

7. *Naive and Sentimental Poetry* in *Two Essays by Friedrich von Schiller*, trans. Julius A. Elias, Milestones of Thought (New York: Frederick Ungar, 1966), p. 176; *Schiller: Werke*, vol. 4, *Schriften* (Frankfurt am Main: Insel Verlag, 1966), to which all citations in the text refer respectively.

8. See Camus, *The Rebel*: "But the fact remains that, by its consequences, the condemnation of the King is at the crux of our contemporary history. It symbolized the secularization of our history and the disincarnation of the Christian God" (p. 120). Discussing the thought of Alexandre Kojève, Michael Roth writes, "The equality of brotherhood offered by Christianity, Kojeve emphasizes, presupposes subservience to the Father." *Knowing and History: Appropriations of Hegel in Twentieth-Century France* (Ithaca, N.Y.: Cornell University Press, 1988). See also *The Fictional Father: Lacanian Readings of the Text*, ed. Robert Con Davis (Amherst: University of Massachussetts Press, 1981). The "symbolic father" is the "agency of the law" (p. 2).

9. The first gathering place for criticism of Byron's *Cain* must be Truman Guy Steffan, *Lord Byron's "Cain": Twelve Essays and a Text with Variants and Annotations* (Austin, Tex.: University of Texas Press, 1968). For more recent criticism,

see Stephen L. Goldstein, "Byron's *Cain* and the Painites," *Studies in Romanticism* 14 (1975): 391ff.; William P. Fitzpatrick, "Byron's Mysteries: The Paradoxical Drive toward Eden," *Studies in English Literature, 1500–1900* 15 (1975): 615ff.; Paul A. Cantor, "Byron's *Cain*: A Romantic Version of the Fall," *The Kenyon Review* n.s. 2 (1980): 50ff. (reprinted in *Creature and Creator: Mythmaking in English Romanticism*, 1984); Wolf Z. Hirst, "Byron's Lapse into Orthodoxy: An Unorthodox Reading of Cain," *Keats Shelley Journal* 29 (1980): 151ff.; Daniel M. McVeigh, " 'In Caines Cynne': Byron and the Mark of Cain," *Modern Language Quarterly* 43 (1982): 337ff.; and of related interest, Daniel P. Watkins, "Politics and Religion in Byron's *Heaven and Earth*," *The Byron Journal* 11 (1983): 30ff.; and Charles E. Robinson, "The Devil as Doppelganger in *The Deformed Transformed*: The Sources and Meaning of Byron's Unfinished Drama," *Bulletin of the New York Public Library* 24 (1970): 177. Some of the material of this section will appear in my "Byron's *Cain*: Between Theology and History," in *Byron, the Bible, and Religion: Essays from the Twelfth International Byron Seminar* (Newark, Del.: University of Delaware Press, forthcoming).

10. (Cambridge: Bowes and Bowes, 1949), p. 15; see also Otto Rank, *The Double: A Psychoanalytic Study*, ed. and trans. Harry Tucker, Jr. (Chapel Hill, N.C.: The University of North Carolina Press, 1971); and Clement Rosset, *Le Réel et son double*, 2d ed. rev. (Paris: Gallimard, 1986). See also Claire Rosenfield, "The Shadow Within: The Conscious and Unconscious Use of the Double," in *Stories of the Double*, ed. Albert J. Guerard (Philadelphia and New York: J. B. Lippincott, 1967), where the double is presented as a "shadow self," with "antisocial tendencies" (p. 311). The double is antisocial, perhaps, but also with the possibilities for regeneration, and thus distinguishable as *daimon* from the diabolic.

11. Citations in the text refer to *Cain* in the most convenient *Selected Works of George Gordon, Lord Byron*, ed. Edward E. Bostetter (New York: Holt, Rinehart and Winston, revised and enlarged, 1972).

12. (Baltimore, Md.: Johns Hopkins University Press, 1972), p. 42. See my *Mapping Literary Modernism* (Princeton, N.J.: Princeton University Press, 1985), pp. 31 and 46, for a placement of this evolutionary historicism within the intellectual context of modernism.

13. See Baron Georges Cuvier, *Essay on the Theory of the Earth*, 5th ed., trans. Robert Jameson (Edinburgh: Blackwood, 1827), p. 15. Here is recent testimony from the editorial pages of the Los Angeles *Times*, " . . . the Earth is in constant turmoil just beneath the surface. Plates of the Earth's crust, floating on molten rock, drift and plunge, scrape against each other and collide. The result is the thrusting up of mountain ranges and the opening of oceans—and the origination of earthquakes and volcanoes. Italy was once part of an Adriatic plate, driven into Europe by Africa. The West Coast was in Wyoming. California will someday be an island. As residents of the Pacific Rim, we all live literally on the edge" (November 15, 1985). Contrary to the charges of his antagonists, it should be clear that Byron most certainly read Cuvier (as he himself tells us in his 1821 Preface). Although he may have had recourse to Bayle's *Dictionary* for other matters, there was no such need in speculations about prior worlds. Indeed, Bayle's own conjectures are far from radical, writing little of Cain or his family with which Augustine would not have concurred.

14. The account of this "quarrel" is taken from Stephen Jay Gould, *Time's Arrow, Time's Cycle: Myth and Metaphor in the Discovery of Geological Time* (Cambridge, Mass.: Harvard University Press, 1987), pp. 115–75, to which all citations in the text refer.

15. *Romantic Contraries: Freedom versus Destiny* (New Haven, Conn.: Yale University Press, 1984), p. 7.

16. "'If I had only got her with me—if only I had' he said. 'Hard work would be nothing to me then. But that was not to be. I—Cain—go alone as I deserve—an outcast and a vagabond. But my punishment is *not* greater than I can bear.'" *The Mayor of Casterbridge* (New York: Holt, Rinehart and Winston, 1960), p. 316.

17. Byron of course defined *mystery* as a "tragedy on a sacred subject." See Bostetter, p. 229.

18. Modern interpretive criticism seems to have settled on this position. Cantor: "In writing the tragedy of Cain, Byron was in many ways writing his own tragedy, and perhaps the tragedy of romanticism itself. And in exploring the phenomenon of metaphysical rebellion, and uncovering the link between nihilism in thought and violence in action, Byron provided a profound clue for understanding, not just the spiritual history of the nineteenth and twentieth centuries, but the political history as well" (p. 71); McVeigh: "Byron is a poet, not of despair, but of existential uncertainty" (p. 348). In his own time, both Goethe and Shelley recognized the greatness of *Cain* (for Goethe, see Steffan, pp. 324–29; for Shelley, see Steffan, p. 314). Blake's response was evidently "The Ghost of Abel." See Steffan, pp. 320–24. Blake's "playlet" is indeed a response, that is, a thoughtful alternative based upon a genuine, if partial understanding of Byron's work. It is addressed to "Lord Byron in the wilderness," as if understanding that Byron himself, in an adopted posture of Cain, could not come to resolution. Blake's poem adheres to the "vision of Jehovah," which is an endorsement of imagination ("Imagination is Eternity"). Abel returns seeking blood revenge. Jehovah's vision transcends the blood sacrifice, anticipating the disappearance of Satan: "Such is my will . . . that Thou thyself go to Eternal Death / In self Annihilation even till Satan Self-subdued put off Satan." In contrast to the Elohim of the Heathens who swear vengeance, Jehovah promises forgiveness. Eventually, even the Elohim will be "each in his station fixt in the Firmament by peace Brotherhood and Love." See also Leslie Tannenbaum, "Lord Byron in the Wilderness: Biblical Tradition in Byron's *Cain* and Blake's *The Ghost of Abel*," *Modern Philology* 72 (1975): 350–64; "Blake and the Iconography of Cain," in *Blake in His Time*, ed. Robert N. Essick and Donald Pearce (Bloomington, Ind.: Indiana University Press, 1978), pp. 23ff.; Martin Bidney, "*Cain* and *The Ghost of Abel*: Contexts for Understanding Blake's Response to Byron," *Blake Studies* 8 (1979): 145–65. Blake believed that in accepting a tragic view of things dependent upon a foundation sacrifice, Byron at last succumbed to the authorities of matter. If the "dispute" seems familiar, it is, summarizing as it does the division between the Gnostics and the Christian apologists. See Stuart Curran, "Blake and the Gnostic Hyle: A Double Negative," *Blake Studies* 4 (1972): 117–33. Coleridge mustered his own ghost of Abel in the aborted "Wanderings of Cain," the joint venture with Wordsworth of which only Coleridge's contribution has survived. There we learn that Abel's condition

after death is far from blissful, and the question to be answered is, "who is the God of the dead?" As it stands, it is a negligible piece, and one wonders why Philippe Sellier, in his recent survey, *Le Mythe de Cain*, would even refer to it (probably for the same reason he identifies the sister-wife of Byron's Cain as Alcinia).

CHAPTER FIVE
THE SECRET SHARER

1. For discussions of Cain in relation to *The Secret Sharer*, see Daniel Curley, "Legate of the Ideal" in *Conrad: A Collection of Critical Essays*, ed. Marvin Mudrick (Englewood Cliffs, N.J.: Prentice-Hall, 1966), pp. 75ff.; Porter Williams, Jr., "The Brand of Cain in *The Secret Sharer*," *Modern Fiction Studies* 10 (1964): 26ff.; and "The Matter of Conscience in Conrad's *The Secret Sharer*," *PMLA* 79 (1964): 626–30; J. L. Simmons, "The Dual Morality of Conrad's *The Secret Sharer*," *Studies in Short Fiction* vol. 2, 3 (1965): 209–20; Marjorie Garber and Barbara Johnson, "Secret Sharing: Reading Conrad Psychoanalytically," *College English* 49 (1987): 628ff.; Mark A. R. Facknitz, "Cryptic Allusion and the Moral of the Story: The Case of Conrad's *The Secret Sharer*," *The Journal of Narrative Technique* 17 (1987): 115ff.

2. All quotations from Joseph Conrad, *'Twixt Land and Sea* (Garden City, N.Y.: Doubleday, 1926), to which citations in the text refer.

3. See Frederick R. Karl, *A Reader's Guide to Joseph Conrad*, rev. ed. (New York: Farrar, Straus and Giroux, 1969), pp. 230–36. For his part, Karl consistently demotes *The Secret Sharer*—partially in response to psychologizing critics.

4. For Schopenhauer's influence see Ian Watt *Conrad in the Nineteenth Century* (Berkeley and Los Angeles: University of California Press, 1979), p. 237.

5. *Complete Essays of Schopenhauer*, trans. T. Bailey Saunders (New York: Willey Book Co., 1942), pp. 97–103. See Ian Watt, ibid., p. 237.

6. Rosset, *Le réel et son double*, 2d ed. (Paris: Gallimard, 1984), p. 119.

7. Melanie Klein in *Envy and Gratitude* summarizes the concerns of a developing age, when she writes, "As we all know, the ultimate aim of psycho-analysis is the integration of the patient's personality" (p. 231). By placing his *The Secret Sharer* in the context of Cain and Abel, Conrad succeeds in enlarging his concerns beyond the "patient," to those of society and ethics.

CHAPTER SIX
DEMIAN

1. *Demian: The Story of Emil Sinclair's Youth*, trans. Michael Roloff and Michael Lebeck (New York and Evanston: Harper and Row, 1965), p. 145; *Hermann Hesse: Gesammelte Schriften*, 7 vols. (Frankfurt am Main: Suhrkamp Verlag, 1968), 3:232, to which all future citations in the text refer, respectively separated by a slash.

2. See my *Mapping Literary Modernism*, p. 22.

3. Ibid., pp. 54–55, for a discussion of the displacement of the father in early modernist texts.

4. *My Belief: Essays on Life and Art*, ed. Theodore Ziolkowski and trans. Denver Lindley (New York: Farrar, Straus and Giroux, 1974), p. 191; *Gesammelte Schriften*, 7:391.

5. See *Mapping Literary Modernism*, pp. 150–52.

6. *My Belief*, pp. 72–73; *Gesammelte Schriften*, 7:162–63.

7. Mellinkoff (*The Mark of Cain*, pp. 87–91) calls them "puerile" and "superficial."

8. See Part One, Chapter 1, above.

9. See *Mapping Literary Modernism*, p. 26.

10. It is astonishing and noteworthy that the presentation of Cain and Abel among the major modernists should have little to say about the fratricidal dimension of war itself. It is certainly revealing that their major interest should be the psychic implications of the war. For important countertestimony, see Dick Ringler, "Cain and Abel and The Origins of War," from a session, "Peace, Literature and Pedagogy," Midwest MLA, November, 1987. He looks back to Henry Vaughan's brilliant "Abel's Blood," as well as to Siegfried Sassoon's "Ancient History," where Adam, "the gaunt wild man" must contemplate the loss of his "lovely sons." He makes final mention of Demetrias Capetanakis's "Abel," *The Shores of Darkness: Poems and Essays* (1949; reprint, Freeport, N.Y.: Books for Libraries Press, 1969), p. 24. He could well have referred in addition to A. D. Hope's "Imperial Adam" where Cain, "the first murderer," is the natural issue of the violent lust of Adam and, particularly in this poem, of Eve.

CHAPTER SEVEN
THE NEW AMERICAN CAIN: *EAST OF EDEN* AND OTHER
WORKS OF POST–WORLD WAR II AMERICA

1. In general, the presentation of Cain-Abel after World War II differed substantially from the uses of the theme after the American Civil War. Professor Ely Stock discoursed effectively on this latter experience during an MLA session (1977), "The Cain and Abel Theme in Literature," which I co-chaired with my colleague Professor Edith Potter of Scripps College. Professor Stock addressed the subject, "Chaos, the Self and the Cain Myth: John Hay and Henry Adams," and showed how the Cain myth had replaced the Adamic myth to underscore the new pessimism after America's own fratricidal conflict. "The Cain myth must have seemed to a non-theological age to be more closely related to history than the Adamic myth." More is implied here than the sense of fratricidal strife. Cain-Abel is appropriate for conjuring up another foundation sacrifice wherein bloody strife is required in order for there to be rebirth. After World War II, Cain underwent another transformation, one where violence is more ambiguous, and somehow regarded as necessary to the preservation of civilization. A regenerate Cain thus is mythic confirmation of America's role in World War II. *The Gunfighter*, where Jimmy Ringo is hounded throughout his later life, does not quite fit; and finally in *High Noon*, Will Kane—who importantly *does not exist* in the original story—is not a willing server of the community's safety. But it just as stoutly insists upon the necessity of violence in regard to hostile, if not monstrous forces. *High Noon* is

from John M. Cunningham's *The Tin Star*, reprinted in *Bad Men and Good*, Western Writers of America Series (New York: Dodd, Mead, 1953).

2. (New York: Viking Press, 1952), to which all citations in the text refer. It is an understatement to note that the secondary literature on the Cain-Abel theme in the course of Steinbeck's work is not as abundant as it might be; in fact, the lack of such attention, particularly in contrast to the secondary literature devoted to Unamuno, is startling, if not scandalous. See William Goldhurst, "*Of Mice and Men*: John Steinbeck's Parable of the Curse of Cain," *Western American Literature* 6 (1971): 123–35.

3. See *Journal of a Novel: The "East of Eden" Letters* (New York: Viking Press, 1969).

4. There might indeed be a stronger parallel between the stories of Cain and Ham than we had suspected. After all, it was the latter who exposed his father's weakness, that is, his mortality.

5. Steinbeck thus dramatizes the earlier significance of Cain-Abel for a post–Civil War generation that Professor Stock has summarized.

6. *The True Adventures of John Steinbeck, Writer* (New York: Viking, 1984), p. 668.

7. See *Mapping Literary Modernism*, pp. 91–114.

8. Cain had already become the mythic figure for the African American. See Charles W. Scruggs, "The Mark of Cain and the Redemption of Art: A Study in Theme and Structure of Jean Toomer's *Cane*," *American Literature* 44 (1972): 276ff. Scruggs suggests the broader possibilities of significance in the theme of Cain, with the Cain of Melville replacing that of the new American Adam: ". . . if the dominant culture can make sense out of its experience through the myth of Adam, I would suggest that Negroes have used the myth of Cain to explain their own uprootedness, an experience antithetical to the outer culture." Cain had not in black culture become Citizen Cain, because there the native remained uprooted. Yet, the sadness remains that he would like to become part of the enterprise. "Langston Hughes reminds America that he too sings—'The darker brother'" (p. 290).

9. All citations refer to *Shane, The Critical Edition*, ed. James C. Work (Lincoln, Nebraska: The University of Nebraska Press, 1984).

10. See the similar pun, as Charles W. Scruggs remarks, in Toomer's *Cane*.

11. This very fact might cause us to revise the generalization made by M. E. Grenander in "The Heritage of Cain: Crime in American Fiction", *Annals of The American Academy of Political and Social Science* 423 (1976): "The western story reflects a frontier society's desire for an uncomplicated system of law and order" (p. 48). The great danger is to confuse myth, or even mythology, with lack of complication. I owe this reference to my late colleague, John Snortum.

12. I borrow this phrase from William Kittredge's discussion of Louis L'Amour, Los Angeles *Times*, June 23, 1988: "There's a darker problem with the Western. It's a story inhabited by a mythology about power and the social utility of violence, an American version of an ancient dream of warrior righteousness. And because of that, it's a story many of us find threatening. We don't want to live in a society fascinated by fantasies of killer wish-fulfillment. We keep hoping the Western will just go away. But it won't." This last desire has certainly been realized

insofar as the cinematic Western is concerned. If the Civil War invoked the myth of Cain-Abel as a pessimistic revocation of the dream of an agricultural paradise, and World War II reinstated Cain in a drama of national and individual regeneration, the Vietnam War (perhaps under the barrage of realistic television depiction) put an end to any mythology of regenerative violence.

13. We must remember that this story appeared in 1949, when the myth it presented could very well be construed as a defense of the recently achieved victory of American armed forces. It is hard to conceive *East of Eden* or *Shane* without bringing into the formula this national emergence. Some thirty-five years later, in the midst of rampant development in the West and from the perspective of a naturalist, Jack Schaefer would alter this perspective somewhat. He does not recant on the roles of exceptional individuals, but he comes to believe it is a skewed view to judge the species by its heroes and not by its mass (as we judge other species):

> What replaced that assumption [judgment on the basis of peak performances of selected individuals] was a deepening conviction that my species, taken as a whole as in any objective view it should be, is more ignoble than noble, more contemptible than admirable, is a dangerous evolutionary experiment, a menace to all important forms of life including itself on this spaceship earth. (p. 423)

Schaefer's revision is all the more interesting in regard to *Shane*. Shane does more than show the power of the six-gun mystique. As a hero of the American West, he is also technological man: in his spare, deadly efficiency he exhibits the perfect marriage of America and the machine This is the strong recollection Bob retains: "I would see the man and the weapon welded in the one indivisible deadliness. I would see the man and the tool, a good man and a good tool, doing what had to be done" (p. 273).

14. All page references in the text are to *The Caine Mutiny* (Garden City, N.Y.: Doubleday, 1951).

15. For a recent description of this overall process, see Loren Baritz, *The Good Life: The Meaning of Success for the American Middle Class* (New York; Alfred A. Knopf, 1989): "The compulsion to adjust to community norms filled familyroom bookcases with self-help, junk psychology, and mindless educational literature, all focused on the joys of belonging. . . . Senator McCarthy exploited this desire to become 'indistinguishable from others.' David Riesman called it 'other-directedness'" (p. 200). For the sake of contrast, we can refer here to Melville's "Timoleon"—a poem that deserves much fuller treatment. The title character, Timoleon, performs the transcendent deed—slaying his tyrant brother—and then is overwhelmed by the Furies of guilt. As Melville asks, "Shall the good heart whose patriot fire / leaps to a good deed of startling note / Do it, then flinch? Shall good in weak expire?" Where envy is a secret act of hostility against the gods, legitimation appeals to principles of justice. Timoleon affirms that "This quarrel is with gods." In succumbing to guilt, Wouk flinches, and in his faltering he drowns the gods themselves—principles of justice—in undifferentiation. Incidentally, like Will Kane, Timoleon rejects the honors the city bestowed upon him after having abandoned him to his solitary agony.

CHAPTER EIGHT
BILLY BUDD

1. See John Lahr, *Prick Up Your Ears: The Biography of Joe Orton* (New York: Vintage, 1987), p. 27, for specific praise.

2. *Herman Melville, Billy Budd and Other Stories*, ed. Harold Beaver (Harmondsworth: Penquin, 1967), p. 43–44.

3. Herman Melville, *Pierre, Israel Potter . . . Billy Budd* (New York: The Library of America, 1984), pp. 1362–63. All future citations in the text refer to this edition. Wyn Kelly, in "Melville's Cain," provides a remarkably clear and cogent account of Melville's fascination throughout his works with the character of Cain. Kelly would place *Pierre* in the tradition of the romantic Cain derived from Byron, and *Billy Budd* in the tradition of the Augustinian Citizen Cain (although throughout Kelly shows Melville's aversion to the city as the place of Cain). He indicates how *Redburn*, in the antipathy of Jackson against Redburn, dramatizes an earlier version of the Claggart-Billy character duality. He also shows the relevancy of that remarkable poem "Timoleon" for the theme. Although my own categories differ from those of Kelly—mainly in my use of "regenerate Cain" as showing qualities that are different from the "heroic, intellectual, criminal" Cain—nevertheless, I find his essay to be a welcomed and valuable contribution to the literature on the theme. It should be remarked that the presence and opinions of such characters as Mortmain and particularly Ungar in *Clarel* are powerful attacks not only on the myth of the New World and the New Adam, but also on future prospects of larger social and democratic regeneration. The despair of Melville in his use of Cain-like figures is a despair in regard to democracy itself.

4. See Milton R. Stern, *The Fine Hammered Steel of Herman Melville* (Urbana: University of Illinois Press, 1957), pp. 206ff., for a discussion of the political classicism of *Billy Budd*. *Billy Budd* has continued to engage the ongoing currents of contemporary criticism. See Edward H. Rosenberry, "The Problem of *Billy Budd*," *PMLA* 80 (1965): 489–98, for an intelligent discussion of earlier critical positions. For later critical methods drawn to *Billy Budd*, see (from among many) Ann Douglas, *The Feminization of American Culture* (1977; reprint, New York: Avon, 1978), pp. 388–95; Barbara Johnson, "Meville's Fist: The Execution of "*Billy Budd*," *Studies in Romanticism* 18 (1979): 567ff.; Robert K. Martin, *Hero, Captain and Stranger: Male Friendship, Social Critique, and Literary Form in the Sea Novels of Herman Melville* (Chapel Hill, N.C.: University of North Carolina Press, 1986), pp. 107–24; and Eve Kosofksy Sedgwick, *Billy Budd: After the Homosexual*," paper delivered at a conference sponsored by the Scripps College Humanities Institute, December, 1988. While Martin in his interpretation distances himself from deconstruction (see p. 123, where he specifically responds to Professor Johnson's piece), Sedgwick attempts a reconciliation of the two critical modes. Johnson's essay, in particular, draws into some of the special properties of the Cain-Abel story: division and violence. The essay is valuable because of its superior quality, but also for what it reveals. *Billy Budd*, like *The Secret Sharer*, is particularly responsive to modern criticism because of the issues that emanate from the resources of Cain-Abel. In fact, *Billy Budd* and *The Secret Sharer* speak to one another (interestingly enough, Professor Johnson in collaboration with Marjorie

Garber has also written well about Conrad's story), because they represent different solutions to the problems of division and violence. As a more modernist work, *The Secret Sharer* does seem to indicate the possibility—but also the desirability—of working to eliminate replication. In any event, Professor Johnson's essay is of great value for the repercussions that it sets off, indications that it is grappling with the most powerful dimensions of great literature.

5. See *Billy Budd*, ed. Harrison Hayford and Merton M. Sealts, Jr. (Chicago: University of Chicago Press, 1970), pp. 32, 87.

6. *The American Newness: Culture and Politics in the Age of Emerson* (Cambridge, Mass.: Harvard University Press, 1986), pp. 81–82, 66, 69.

CHAPTER NINE

AMADEUS AND *PRICK UP YOUR EARS*

1. See Introduction to Alan Bloom, *The Closing of the American Mind* (New York: Simon and Schuster, 1987), p. 15.

2. See Peter Shaffer, *Amadeus* (New York: New American Library/Signet, 1984), p. 17. All citations in the text refer to this edition.

3. John Lahr, *Prick Up Your Ears*, pp. 26–27. All future citations refer to this text.

4. The use of Cain-Abel patterns for *Amadeus* receives some impetus when we realize that Peter Shaffer is a fraternal twin to Anthony Shaffer. See Jules Glenn, "Twins in the Theater: A Study of Plays by Peter and Anthony Shaffer," *Blood Brothers, Siblings as Writers*, ed. Norman Kiell (New York: International Universities Press, 1983), see esp. pp. 295–96. But see also the earlier dramatic piece by Evgenii Pushkin, *Mozart and Salieri*, trans. A.F.B. Clark in *The Works of Alexander Pushkin*, ed. Avrahm Yarmolinsky (New York: Random House, 1936), p. 432. Salieri's quarrel is with God's justice, which would so rebuff his ardor by rewarding the frivolousness of a young upstart. Eaten away by envy, Salieri must acknowledge that Mozart has genius ("You, Mozart, are a god and know it not! / I know it . . .") but still persists in serving the "poisoned bowl."

CHAPTER TEN

ABEL SÁNCHEZ

1. The secondary literature concerning Unamuno and Cain-Abel is copious. Basic, in part because of its familiarity with earlier writers such as Arturo Graf, is Carlos Clavería, "Sobre el tema de Caín en la obra de Unamuno," *Temas de Unamuno* (Madrid: Gredos, 1953), pp. 97ff. See also Paul Ilie, "Unamuno, Gorky, and the Cain Myth: Toward a Theory of Personality," *Hispanic Review* 29 (1961): 310ff.; Michael D. McGaha, "*Abel Sánchez* y la envidia de Unamuno," *Cuadernos de la Cátedra de Unamuno* 21 (1971): 91ff.; Arthur F. Kinney, "The Multiple Heroes of *Abel Sánchez*," *Studies in Short Fiction* 1 (1964): 251ff.; Christopher H. Cobb, "Sobre la elaboración de *Abel Sánchez*," *Cuadernos de la Cátedra de Unamuno* 22 (1972): 127ff.; A. Dobson, "Unamuno's *Abel Sánchez*: An Interpretation," *Modern Languages: Journal of the Modern Language Association* 54 (1973): 62ff.; Salvador Jiménez-Fajardo, "Unamuno's *Abel Sánchez*: Envy

as a Work of Art," *Journal of Spanish Studies* 4 (1976): 89ff.; Linda C. Fox, "The Vision of Cain in Spain's 'Generation of '98," *College Language Association Journal* 21 (1978): 499ff. (first delivered at MLA session, chaired by Potter and Quinones, 1977); Dorothy H. Lee, "Joaquín Monegro in Unamuno's *Abel Sánchez* Thrice Exiled: Cain / Esau / Satan," *Journal of Spanish Studies* 7 (1979): 63–71ff.; Mariano Lopez, "Individuo, personalidad y destino en Unamuno; *Niebla*, *Abel Sánchez y El Otro*," *Arbor: Ciencia, Pensamiento y Cultura* 399 (1979): 71ff.; Nelson R. Orringer, "Civil War Within: The Clash between Sources of Unamuno's *Abel Sánchez*," *Anales de la Literatura Española Contemporanea* 11 (1986): 295ff. As to the cause of the attention to envy and fraternal conflict in Unamuno's work, Clavería reports that a younger brother who intensely disliked the fame of Unamuno wore a button, advising "Don't speak to me of my brother." Of particular interest is the literary dualism, now passed into the vernacular, between Unamuno and Ortega y Gasset. Emilio Salcedo, "Unamuno y Ortega y Gasset, diálogo entre dos españoles," *Cuadernos de la Cátedra de Unamuno* 7 (1956): 97ff., Hugo Rodriguez-Alcala, "Un aspecto del antagonismo de Unamuno y Ortega," *Revista de la Universidad de Buenos Aires* 2 (1957): 267ff. See also Manuel Garcia Blanco, "Unamuno y Ortega," *En Torno a Unamuno* (Madrid: Taurus, 1965), pp. 351–60, and pp. 253–60 for Antonio Machado's letter to Unamuno concerning Cain and *Abel Sánchez*.

2. "Paisajes," *Obras completas* (Madrid: Escelicer, 1966), 1:66–67; see also "Ciudad y campo," *Ensayos* (Madrid: Publicaciones de la residencia de estudiantes, 1916), p. 180.

3. "La envidia hispanica," *Obras completas*, vol. 4, ensayo 2 (Madrid: Aguado, 1958), pp. 411–25. See Arthur Wills, *España y Unamuno* (New York: Instituto de las Españas, 1938), p. 197.

4. *The Tragic Sense of Life*, trans. J. E. Crawford Flitch (New York: Dover, 1954), p. 55. See Michael's Roth's understanding of Alexandre Kojève, ". . . the struggle for recognition is not only at the origin of the human community but at the very foundation of the self . . ." and ". . . the being that cannot risk its life in a Struggle for *Recognition*, in a fight for pure *prestige*—is not a true human being.'" These are, to be sure, Kojève's views of Hegel. Michael S. Roth, *Knowing and History*, pp. 103, 107.

5. *Abel Sánchez: Una Historia de Pasión*, 2d ed. (Madrid: Renacimiento, 1928), p. 12.

6. *Abel Sánchez*, trans. Anthony Kerrigan, in *Eleven Modern Short Novels*, 2d ed., ed. Leo Hamalian and Edmond L. Volpe (New York: Putnam, 1970), p. 255. This text, here slightly modified in translation, will be referred to by all citations in the text preceding the slash. Following the slash, the page reference is to the second edition indicated in n. 5 above.

7. New York: Dover, 1954, p. 53.

8. *La tía Tula* (Madrid: Renacimiento, 1921), p. 15.

9. See *The Tragic Sense of Life*, where Unamuno expresses a preference for the inquisitor over the merchant: ". . . the merchant . . . regards me merely as a customer, as a means to an end, and his indulgence and tolerance are at bottom nothing but a supreme indifference to my destiny" (p. 279).

10. See Peter G. Earle, *Unamuno and English Literature* (New York: Hispanic Institute in the United States, 1960), pp. 85–94, as well as the essential essay by Clavería.

11. Letter to Juan Arzadun, October 30, 1987, *Sur* 14 (1944): 57.

12. See Earle, *Unamuno and English Literature*, p. 87.

13. I note the use of this episode in Erich Fromm's *The Heart of Man: Its Genius for Good and Evil* (New York: Harper and Row), pp. 37–38. The apparent "irrationalism" of Unamuno is set in proper perspective, when in answer to those who cried out "Down with intelligence," Unamuno, speaking as Rector denounced the Falangists and their reliance on force: They might win, but they will not convince or persuade. ". . . in order to persuade you need what you lack: Reason and Right in the struggle" (p. 38).

CHAPTER ELEVEN
CAIN OF FUTURE HISTORY

1. Disraeli's phrase comes from *Sybil*. For Wells's quotation, see *The Time Machine* (New York: Airmont Books, 1964), p. 81.

2. Quoted by Mark R. Hillegas, *The Future as Nightmare: H. G. Wells and the Anti-Utopians* (New York: Oxford University Press, 1967), p. 19.

3. *Evolution and Ethics and Other Essays* (1896; reprint, New York: AMS Press, 1970).

4. For Gessner, see Part Two, chapter 4 above. Page citations refer to that text.

5. See *Tragedie di Vittorio Alfieri* (Florence: Monnier, 1855), vol. 2, to which all page citations in the text refer.

6. In the early part of this century, Cain was predominantly associated with this tradition of revolt. Perhaps the fullest expression of postromantic critical opinion may be found in the words of the Cuban writer Enrique José Varona. His description of Cain at the end of the play could call to mind DeSanctis describing Francesca: ". . . condenado mas no sometido, sombrío y desesperado, pero siempre soberbio" ("condemned but not subdued, sombre and desperate but always proud"). Varona concludes with this judgment: "Jamás, después de los tiempos del sublime Lucrecio, la poesía se ha identificado de ese modo con la filosofía," ("Never since the time of the sublime Lucretius has poetry been identical in this manner with philosophy"; p. 34). See Graf: Byron's *Cain* is a philosophical drama of "spiritual rebellion and Titanic over-weeningness" ("un dramma di ribellione spirituale e di tracotanza titanica"; p. 425). Paul van Tieghem established Cain for a generation of comparatists as "le symbole du révolté contre Dieu" ("the symbol of the rebel against God"). *La Littérature comparée* (Paris: Armand Colin, 1946), p. 95. I have already referred to Gerard de Nerval's poem, "Anteros," whose title figure is from among the Titans a rebellious cohort of Cain. "Je retourne les dards contre le dieu vainqueur" ("I hurl back spears against the conquering God"). Anteros is among those marked by Satan ("le Vengeur"). With his own ancestors he is an indomitable opponent to "tyranny," and although having taken refuge in the Cainite City of Fire, he continues to sow the seeds from which will be found the new earthly city, Thebes. (We can think back to the coherence of Dante's Cocytus,

inspired by Statius's *Thebaid*—the horrors of Pisa in regard to Ugolino call to mind a "novella Tebe"—which is introduced by the armed guard of Titans and whose first place is the *Caina*.) See Nerval, *Oeuvres* (Paris: Garnier, 1958), 1:699. Incidentally, Hugo in his "La Conscience" has Cain and his family in titanic manner also firing their spears at the heavens. In this poem, the construction of an unholy city—also a City of Fire—is a mere defense against the all-searching eye of conscience. His Cain, like Dante's, is more terrified than terrible. In each poem, the contest is over the nature of the city. M. Rudwin, in his *The Devil in Legend and Literature* (Chicago, Ill.: University of Chicago Press, 1931), has remarked, "It is significant that the story of Cain has inspired three of the greatest poets of the past century, Byron, Hugo and Leconte de Lisle" (p. 305). Peter Thorslev, Jr., in his *The Byronic Hero* (Minneapolis: University of Minnesota Press, 1962), argues that Cain is a lesser romantic figure: "Byron is the only major Romantic poet to have used him as a protagonist in a major work" (p. 93). This judgment may or may not be accurate—it would be more accurate had he written "major *English* Romantic poet"—but it does neglect the imaginative importance that Cain would acquire because of the work of Byron.

7. See *Les Fleurs du Mal*, with a new translation by Richard Howard (Boston: David R. Godine, 1982), pp. 142, 320.

8. *Charles Baudelaire: A Lyric Poet in the Era of High Capitalism*, trans. Harry Zohn (London: New Left Books 1973), p. 22.

9. See Henri Bernes, "Le *Qain* de Leconte de Lisle et ses origines litteraires," *Revue d'histoire littéraire de la France* 18 (1911): 485ff. Regis Messac, "Cain et le problème du mal dans Voltaire, Byron et Leconte de Lisle," *Revue de la Littérature comparée* 4 (1924): 620ff.; Daniel Mornet, "Une source negligée du *Qain* de Leconte de Lisle," *Mélanges d'histoire littéraire generale et comparée offerts à Fernand Baldensperger*, 2 vols. (Paris: 1930), 2:110–15; Alison Fairlie, *Leconte de Lisle's Poems on the Barbarian Races* (Cambridge: Cambridge University Press, 1947), pp. 213–85.

10. All citations from *Oeuvres de Leconte de Lisle: Poèmes barbares* (Paris: Lemerre, n.d.).

11. In his *The City of Dickens* (Oxford: Clarendon Press, 1971), Alexander Welsh has useful and suggestive pages about Cain and Abel in Dickens's novels. He compiles a substantial list: Bill Sikes and Monks, Ralph Nickleby and Squeers, Rudge (Barnaby's father) and Sir John Chester, James Carker, Uriah Heep, Tulkinghorn, Rigaud (alias Blandois), Madame Defarge, Orlick, Drummle and Compeyson, Rogue Riderhood. Welsh ascribes reprobation to these characters. "The Cain-like villains may be human enough, but are originally and irrevocably committed to evil, as if from spite" (p. 125). Moreover, Welsh is correct in asserting that "the descendants of Abel in the novels of Dickens triumph over the descendants of Cain" (p. 135). Not only do they triumph, but it is morally right that they should triumph (unlike some modern instances, for example, Joyce, where Abel is the social master but regrettably so). Along with this radical distinction between Cain and Abel, Welsh also sees in Dickens's character delineations of "a romantic idea of the personality in which evil is threatening from within," and hence adduces some interesting pages in which Rigaud is described as a double to Arthur Clennam (pp. 134–35). The radical distinction of character Welsh attrib-

utes with some historical accuracy to Calvinism. (However, it is not essential. Prior to Calvinism Philo and Augustine had such oppositions in mind, and in *Beowulf* Cain is a monster, and that later Melville in *Billy Budd* will specifically rule out Calvinism in interpreting the enmity of Claggart toward Billy.)

12. For *nadryv*, generally translated as "laceration," see Victor Terras, *A Karamazov Companion: Commentary on the Genesis, Language, and Style of Dostoevsky's Novel* (Madison, Wis.: University of Wisconsin Press, 1981), pp. 82–83, 191, 196 and 198, where the phrase is developed as a leitmotif.

13. All citations refer to *The Brothers Karamazov*, ed. Ralph E. Matlaw (New York: Norton, 1976), p. 208.

14. One can see in some ways that Dostoevsky is a modern Dante, who, although fully understanding the coherence of the issues radiating from the Genesis tale of Cain and Abel and its alliance with the foundation sacrifice, rejects this notion. As in the first and fourth centuries, a unified Christian vision takes issue with the very heart and nature of the city, as represented by Citizen Cain. It is quite revealing then to compare the associations of Cain and the city in the above-mentioned poems of Nerval and Leconte de Lisle and even, in a forbidding way, in Hugo's "La Conscience."

15. See n. 1 above for the text of *The Time Machine*, to which all citations refer.

16. See Byron's "Darkness" (Bostetter, p. 30), where a dog is still faithful, and two enemies die without knowing the identity of each other.

17. (New York: Grove Press Outrider, 1979).

18. Thinking back to *Beowulf* and other aspects of monstrous Cain, we see that Trocchi is instinctively correct in placing his Cain on the amorphous waters.

19. See *From Prague to Paris: A Critique of Structuralist and Poststructuralist Thought* (London: Verso, 1987), and *In Quest of Modern Culture: Hysterical or Historical Humanism*, monograph series 2 (Claremont, Calif. Gould Center for Humanistic Studies, 1988), p. 12.

CHAPTER TWELVE
TWINNING THE TWAIN

1. See my *Mapping Literary Modernism*, pp. 200, 220, and 292 for some sense of the meaning of this concept in twentieth-century thought.

2. I have used this metaphor in my *Dante Alighieri*, Twayne World Authors Series (Boston: G. K. Hall, 1979), pp. 13–17.

3. See Bowker, *The Targums and Rabbinic Literature*, p. 137.

4. Fredric Jameson invokes the notion of "strategies of inwardness" to characterize modernism. See *Mapping Literary Modernism*, p. 249.

5. See Stanlislaus Joyce, *My Brother's Keeper: James Joyce's Early Years* (New York: Viking Press, 1958); "So, possibly, his stay in Paris must be written off as a failure" (p. 231).

6. See Margot Norris, *The Decentered Universe of* Finnegans Wake (Baltimore: Johns Hopkins University Press, 1976); Morris Beja, "Dividual Chaoses: Case Histories of Multiple Personality and *Finnegans Wake*," *James Joyce Quarterly* 14 (1977): 241ff.; Jean Kimball, "James and Stanislaus Joyce: A Jungian Speculation," in *Blood Brothers: Siblings as Writers*, pp. 73ff.; and "Lui, c'est moi: The

Brother Relationship in *Ulysses*," *James Joyce Quarterly* 25 (1988): 227ff.; and Mary T. Reynolds, "Joyce and His Brothers: The Process of Fictional Transformation," *James Joyce Quarterly* 25 (1988): 217ff.

7. At last count, there were more than one hundred references to Cain and Abel in *Finnegans Wake*, Adaline Glasheen, *A Third Census of* Finnegans Wake (Evanston, Ill.: Northwestern University Press, 1977).

8. See Margot Norris, *Decentered Universe*, p. 120.

9. All references in text are to *Finnegans Wake* (New York: Viking Press, 1971).

10. For a summary of this quarrel and Joyce's response see *Mapping Literary Modernism*, pp. 216–18.

11. There is also an historical antagonism present in the description, and that is between the Roman Church (raumybult–Roman Bull) and the Irish Church, more mystical and vulnerable.

12. For *El Otro*, see Frances Wyers, *Unamuno: The Contrary Self* (London: Tamesis, 1976), esp. pp. 82ff.; Roberta Johnson, "Archetypes, Structures and Myth in Unamuno's *El Otro*" in *The Analysis of Hispanic Texts: Current Trends in Methodology*, ed. Lisa E. Davis and Isabel C. Taran (New York: Bilingual Press, 1976), pp. 32ff. All citations in the text refer to *Unamuno: Obras Completas* (Madrid: Escelicer, 1968), vol. 5, *Teatro*. For an acting text see, *El Otro: misterio en tres jornadas y un epilogio*, colección voz imagen (Barcelona: Ayma, 1964).

13. All citations in the text refer to *The Ogre*, trans. Barbara Bray (Garden City, N.Y.: Doubleday, 1972) and, following slash, to *Le Roi des aulnes* (Paris: Gallimard, 1970); and to *Gemini*, trans. Anne Carter (New York: Doubleday, 1980) and, following slash, to *Les météores* (Paris: Gallimard, 1975).

14. See the interview with Tournier in the *Partisan Review* 53 (1986), pp. 407ff., and most importantly *The Wind Spirit: An Autobiography*, trans. Arthur Goldhammer (Boston: The Beacon Press, 1988), pp. 198ff.

15. The ever-present threat of violence, in fact, the requirement of a violent sundering, if a separation is to take place, shows the appropriateness of the Cain-Abel theme for the interests of twinship. René Zazzo, like Tournier, introduces the note of ominousness when he writes that twins are bound together in their particular mutually defining relationship: "à moins qu'un jour ils n'essaient violemment de s'en delivrer comme de la tunique de Nessus" ("until one day when they will try to free themselves violently as from the shirt of Nessus"), p. 707. Many practical suggestions about the lives of twins, given full elaboration in Tournier's novel, have their origins in Zazzo's study.

16. Tournier's autobiographical piece is called *Le Vent paraclet*.

EPILOGUE

1. This point is in obvious need of some elaboration. See Jeffrey Burton Russell, *The Prince of Darkness: Radical Evil and the Power of Good in History* (Ithaca, N.Y.: Cornell University Press, 1988), a convenient condensation of his four-volume study. Following the Enlightenment, according to Russell, and under the influence of Goethe's *Faust*, "most of the literary Devils of the following two centuries took the suave, ironic and ambiguous shape of Goethe's Mephistophe-

les. . . . writers wishing their Devils to be taken seriously as traditional personifications of Evil had since *Faust* to overcome powerful resistance" (p. 216). Apart from the solemnity of Hugo ("La fin de Satan"), "irony parody and whimsy were the dominant modes in nineteenth-century treatments of Satan" (p. 233). As a creature whose main task is to bring evil to others (and thus he is without true heroic potential), the Devil is susceptible to grand irony (he who "ever seeks evil and ever does good"), and even his apparently successful efforts are greeted with jeers. Thus ironized, Satan is also amorphous and ambiguous; not actually an entity or a person in his own right, he is necessarily deficient. In fact, once again Arturo Graf finds some precedence in these studies when, in his major study, *Il Diavolo* (1889), he can report the devil as dying, if not dead. See *The Story of the Devil*, trans. Edward Noble Stine (New York: Macmillan, 1931), p. 251

2. *The Rebel*, p. 21.

3. "Politics as a Vocation" is included in *From Max Weber: Essays in Sociology*, ed. and trans. with an introduction by H. H. Gerth and C. Wright Mills (New York: Oxford university Press, 1946), pp. 122–27.

4. *Sor Juana, or The Traps of Faith*, trans. Margaret Sayers Peden (Cambridge, Mass.: Harvard University Press, 1988) pp. 32–33.

5. For a recent, excellent summary see John McManners, *Death and the Enlightenment: Changing Attitudes to Death among Christians and Unbelievers in Eighteenth-century France* (Oxford: Clarendon Press, 1981).

6. From a paper, "Milton: Divine Revelation and the Poetics of Experience," delivered at the Renaissance Conference of Southern California, April 8, 1989, reprinted in the volume forthcoming from that conference. Subsequent quotations in the text attributed to Lewalski are from this edition.

7. See Honor Matthews, *The Primal Curse: The Myth of Cain and Abel in the Theatre* (New York: Schocken Books, 1967), including such important dramas as Christopher Fry's *A Sleep of Prisoners* (1951), but ignoring Thornton Wilder's *The Skin of Our Teeth* (1942), another play of civilization, where Henry (Cain) stands forth "as a representation of strong unreconciled evil." Christopher Morley's one-act play *East of Eden* is unique (and frankly welcomed) in its light-hearted approach, as is D. H. Lawrence's short story "Love Among the Haystacks."

INDEX